Cross-Linguistic Aspects of Processability Theory

Studies in Bilingualism (SiBil)

Volume 30

Cross-Linguistic Aspects of Processability Theory
Edited by Manfred Pienemann

Cross-Linguistic Aspects
of Processability Theory

Edited by

Manfred Pienemann

University of Paderborn & University of Newcastle upon Tyne

John Benjamins Publishing Company

Amsterdam / Philadelphia

TM The paper used in this publication meets the minimum requirements
of American National Standard for Information Sciences – Permanence
of Paper for Printed Library Materials, ANSI z39.48-1984.

Library of Congress Cataloging-in-Publication Data

Cross-Linguistic Aspects of Processability Theory / edited by Manfred
  Pienemann.
       p. cm. (Studies in Bilingualism, ISSN 0928–1533 ; v. 30)
    Includes bibliographical references and indexes.
         1. Interlanguage (Language learning) 2. Second language acquisition.
    3. Psycholinguistics. I. Pienemann, Manfred, 1951- II. Series.

    P118.23.C76 2005
    401'.93--dc22   20050543674
    ISBN 90 272 4141 4 (Hb; alk. paper)

John Benjamins Publishing Co. · P.O. Box 36224 · 1020 ME Amsterdam · The Netherlands
John Benjamins North America · P.O. Box 27519 · Philadelphia PA 19118-0519 · USA

Table of contents

Abbreviations

Some abbreviations used by the authors in this book.

ACC	Accusative
ADJ	Adjunct
Aff	Affix
ASP	Aspect
BENE	Benefactive
CAUSE	Causative
COMP	Complementiser
Cop	Copula
DAT	Dative
DF	Discourse function
FOC	Focus
GEN	Genitive
GF	Grammatical function
Ll	First language
L2	Second language
LFG	Lexical Functional Grammar
LOC	Locative
MLU	Mean Length of Utterance
NOM	Nominative
ø	Ellipsis
O/OBJ	Object
OBLag	Oblique agent
P	Particle
PASS	Passive
POL	Polite
PROG	Progressive
PT	Processability Theory
Q	Question
SUBJ	Subject
SLA	Second Language Acquisition
SLI	Specific Language Impairment
TL	Target language
TOP	Topic
UG	Universal Grammar

Preface

The focus of this book

Processability Theory (Pienemann 1998) delineates the way in which language processing mechanisms shape the course of language development by spelling out which second language forms are processable at which developmental stage and which variants of grammatical forms may occur at any given stage, thus delineating interlanguage variation (including task variation) and age-related differences in language acquisition. The theory is based on research into language processing and is formalised within Lexical-Functional Grammar.

In the 1998 volume, the predictions of the theory were applied to the second language development of English, German, Japanese and Swedish, and the theory was also tested in on-line experiments. The key innovation of PT is the addition of a psychological component to the search for a theory of second language acquisition. In the 1998 volume (Pienemann 1998:1) I argue as follows:

> Learnability is defined as a purely logico-mathematical problem .... Such a perspective ignores the fact that this problem has to be solved, not by an unconstrained computational device, but by a mind that operates within human psychological constraints.
> In this book I propose a theory which adds to learnability theory the perspective of processability.... In my view, the logico-mathematical hypothesis space in which the learner operates is further constrained by the architecture of human language processing.

The focus of this new volume is on the cross-linguistic applicability of PT. Although the database used for the 98 volume is rather extensive, including a substantial number of empirical studies covering the full range of grammatical structures within the scope of PT, the majority of these studies was based on three closely related Germanic languages which have a substantial number of grammatical features in common. Given the universal claim inherent in PT, a study of the cross-linguistic applicability of the theory is therefore inevitable.

Applying a theoretical framework such as PT to a range of typologically diverse languages, including Arabic (Mansouri's chapter), Chinese (Zhang's chapter) and Japanese (Kawaguchi's chapter) is not a simple matter of matching constituent structures across languages. Instead, the universal processability hierarchy that forms the core of PT has to be applied to the specific grammars of these L2s using a formalism that is compatible with the psycholinguistic assumptions underlying PT.

Given the typological diversity of these additional 'test languages' and their typological distances from the more configurational Germanic languages for which PT is 'tried and tested', it is not at all surprising that the development of constraints on constituent structure which are central for Germanic languages is far less important for the test languages included in this volume. The authors of these chapters therefore had to apply the notion of 'transfer of grammatical information' to grammatical areas other than constituent structure in order to implement the PT hierarchy into these grammatical systems.

In this context the need arose to extend the scope of PT. The 98 version of PT focused on the transfer of grammatical information within constituent structure (with the inclusion of functional structure). In their chapter Pienemann, Di Biase and Kawaguchi extend the architecture of PT by adding a second set of principles that contributes to the formal modelling of levels of processability, namely the mapping of argument-structure onto functional structure and the mapping of constituent structure onto functional structure. This step yields the inclusion of a range of additional phenomena in the processability hierarchy thus widening the scope of PT. In her chapter Kawaguchi applies this extended framework to the acquisition of Japanese.

In other words, this volume brings together co-ordinated research on the acquisition of Arabic (Mansouri), Chinese (Zhang) and Japanese (Kawaguchi) and demonstrates the capacity of PT to make detailed and falsifiable predictions about the developmental schedule for each of these typologically different target languages.

This cross-linguistic perspective is also applied to the study of L1 transfer (Pienemann, Di Biase, Kawaguchi and Håkansson) by comparing the impact of processability and typological proximity. The typological perspective is extended beyond the comparison of developmental trajectories in different target languages by including a comparison of different types of language acquisition (i.e. L1, L2 and SLI) (Håkansson).

How to read this book

The ideas presented in this book build upon the 1998 PT volume. Readers not familiar with that publication will find it useful to start with Chapter 1 which contains an extensive introduction to PT covering all major aspects of the theory.

Chapter 2 gives an overview of research within the PT framework and examines points of critique that have been raised.

Chapters 2 to 7 assume a basic familiarity with PT – either based on the 1998 volume or on Chapter 1.

Chapter 8 is based on aspects of the extension of PT presented in Chapter 7. Therefore it would be useful to read Chapter 8 after Chapter 7. Otherwise, Chapters 2 to 7 were not written with a specific sequence for the reading schedule in mind.

Acknowledgements

Considering the task of applying PT to typologically different languages and to the notion of L1 transfer in typologically diverse scenarios and considering the added task of substantially extending PT, it may be obvious that this is not a job for one single author.

It was a very fortunate coincidence that the authors of the chapters of this book are unified by their use of PT as a theoretical framework for the study of second language acquisition, and each of the authors invested a considerable amount of time and mental energy into attending a long sequence of workshops and symposia in the years from 2000 until 2005 to discuss a wide range of issues that needed to be resolved for this publication.

The need for this volume with its typological focus derives quite logically from the state of affairs as described in the 1998 volume. It was clear that the 98 framework called for a typological validation. At EUROSLA 2000 (Paderborn) the authors of the various chapters contained in this volume set out to undertake this task which turned out to be a five-year expedition with camps in a whole range of far-away places, including the following:

- The 1st Symposium on Second Language Acquisition and Processability, University of Western Sydney, School of Languages and Linguistics, December 2000 (chair: Bruno Di Biase).

- The 2nd Symposium on Second Language Acquisition and Processability, Australian National University, School of Languages and Linguistics, July 2001 (chair: Louise Jansen).
- Symposium on Processability, Paderborn University, English Department, June 2002 (chair: Manfred Pienemann).
- The 3rd Symposium on Second Language Acquisition and Processability, MARCS Auditory Laboratories, University of Western Sydney, February 2003 (chair: Bruno Di Biase).
- PhD Seminar on Processability, SLA and bilingual first language acquisition, MARCS Auditory Laboratories, University of Western Sydney, December 2003 (chair: Bruno Di Biase).
- The 4th International Symposium on Processability, Second Language Acquisition and Bilingualism, University of Sassari, Italy, April 2004 (chair: Gabriele Pallotti).
- The 5th International Symposium on Processability, Second Language Acquisition and Bilingualism, Deakin University, Victoria, Australia, September 2005 (chair: Fethi Mansouri).

These symposia provided an excellent platform for the development of new ideas. Over the years they attracted numbers of young scholars, thus creating an intellectual biotope of its own that has generated a respectable number of high-quality papers. This is due to the great team spirit of the group of authors of this volume and above all to the enormous integrative power of one person, Bruno Di Biase, who was instrumental in setting up the symposia and in keeping them going. With his excellent knowledge of LFG, PT and related issues Bruno provided great academic leadership for everyone involved in this enterprise. I would like to thank the whole group of authors, Bruno Di Biase, Gisela Håkansson, Satomi Kawaguchi, Fethi Mansouri, and Yanyin Zhang, for their enthusiasm and their endurance in solving a set of problems that is anything but trivial. This endeavour was greatly facilitated by the advice on matters relating to Lexical-Functional Grammar that was provided in a generous manner by Peter Sells (Stanford).

I would also like to thank the following people for their input into discussions relating to psycholinguistic, typological and empirical issues in the extension of the PT framework: Camilla Bettoni (Verona), Jörg Keßler (Paderborn), Judi Kroll (Penn State), Gabriele Pallotti (Sassari) and Helmut Zobl (Carlton).

My thanks also go to Bridgid O'Connor and Annabelle David (both Newcastle) for their support in the style editing of this manuscript and above all to Kees Vaes from Benjamins for his patient and manifold support of this project.

Manfred Pienemann
Paderborn, July 2005

CHAPTER 1

An introduction to Processability Theory*

Manfred Pienemann

University of Paderborn and University of Newcastle upon Tyne

In this chapter Processability Theory (PT) is summarised in the way it was conceptualised in Pienemann (1998). To exemplify the application of the psycholinguistic core of the theory, it is applied to the development of key grammatical aspects of German and English as second languages. The developmental dynamics found in German SLA are then compared with those found in the acquisition of German as the first language. One key factor that constrains the differential developmental dynamics found in L1 and L2 acquisition is the Generative Entrenchment (Wimsatt 1986, 1991) of the initial hypotheses and their propagation in the developmental processes.

This chapter also contains a summary of the relationship between development and variation in PT. In a nutshell, variation is constrained by PT. In this chapter the theoretical basis for this claim will be summarised together with supporting empirical evidence. PT constraints also apply to L1 transfer (cf. Chapter 2 of this volume). A brief summary of the notion "developmentally moderated L1 transfer" will be given in this chapter together with empirical evidence. A further application of PT includes an explanation of fossilisation/ stabilisation. This chapter contains an outline of how PT constraints on variation and Generative Entrenchment jointly constrain L2 developmental dynamics to result in fossilisation/ stabilisation given a certain succession of developmental choices made by the learner.

1. The interplay between language processing and language acquisition

1.1 The wider context

Learnability is defined as a purely logico-mathematical problem (e.g. Berwick & Weinberg 1984). Such a perspective ignores the fact that this problem has to be solved, not by an unconstrained computational device, but by a mind that operates within human psychological constraints.

In this section I will sketch out a theory which adds to learnability theory the perspective of processability, i.e. Processability Theory (Pienemann 1998). In my view, the logico-mathematical hypothesis space in which the learner operates is further constrained by the architecture of human language processing. Structural options that may be formally possible will be produced by the language learner only if the necessary processing resources are available that are needed to carry out, within the given minimal time frame, those computations required for the processing of the structure in question. Once we can spell out the sequence in which language processing routines develop in the learner, we can delineate those grammars that are processable at different points of development.

The architecture of human language processing therefore forms the basis of Processability Theory. In this perspective the language processor is seen with Kaplan and Bresnan (1982) as the computational routines that operate on (but are separate from) the native speaker's linguistic knowledge. Processability Theory primarily deals with the nature of those computational routines and the sequence in which they become available to the learner. From this perspective, I argue that language acquisition incorporates as one essential component the gradual acquisition of those very computational routines. In other words, the task of acquiring a language includes the acquisition of the *procedural skills* needed for the processing of the language. It follows from this that the sequence in which the target language[1] (TL) unfolds in the learner is determined by the sequence in which processing routines develop which are needed to handle the TL's components.

In the rationalist tradition, learnability analyses have in the past been based on four components that must be specified in any learnability theory (e.g. Wexler & Culicover 1980; Pinker 1979):

i.   the target grammar,
ii. the data input to the learner,
iii. the learning device that must acquire that grammar, and
iv. the initial state.

The idea behind this is that a learnability theory must specify how a learner develops from an initial state to the target grammar with the available input and the given learning device.[2]

The rationale for assuming these components is rooted in the way in which learnability theory has been formulated in response to the 'logical problem' in language acquisition (cf. Wexler 1982). The logical problem basically describes the following paradox: children acquire in a relatively short period of time and on the basis of limited linguistic input the basic principles of their native language, although many of these principles are seen to be impossible to be inferred from the observations made by the learner.

It has been noted by several rationalist researchers (e.g. Felix 1984, 1991; Clahsen 1992; Gregg 1996) that besides linguistic knowledge, a theory of language acquisition must also explain what causes the development of the TL to follow a describable route. This explanatory issue has been referred to as the "developmental problem" (Felix 1984).

My fundamental point is that recourse needs to be made to key psychological aspects of human language processing in order to account for the developmental problem, because describable developmental routes are, at least in part, caused by the architecture of the human language processor. For linguistic hypotheses to transform into executable procedural knowledge (i.e. a certain processing skill), the processor needs to have the capacity of processing those hypotheses.

1.2 Key psychological factors in language processing

It is the aim of Processability Theory to hypothesise, on the basis of the general architecture of the language processor, a universal hierarchy of processing resources which can be related to the requirements of the specific procedural skills needed for the TL. In this way, predictions can be made for language development which can be tested empirically. Before I describe the architecture of the hypothesised hierarchy of processability and the model of language production on which it is based, it will be useful to sketch out briefly a number of key psychological factors in language processing to characterise the processing environment within which the learning of language takes place. The framework that follows from this will then be used to establish a hierarchy of processing prerequisites. The formal system adopted for the description of the processing hierarchy will be shown to reflect key properties of language processing.

The view on language production followed in Processability Theory is largely that described by Levelt (1989), which overlaps to some extent with the computational model of Kempen and Hoenkamp (1987) which in turn emulates much of Merrill Garrett's work (e.g. Garrett 1976, 1980, 1982) and on which the corresponding section of Levelt's model is based. The basic premises of that view are the following:

i.   Processing components are relatively autonomous specialists which operate largely automatically;

ii. Processing is incremental;

iii. The output of the processor is linear, while it may not be mapped onto the underlying meaning in a linear way;

iv. Grammatical processing has access to a grammatical memory store.

Below I will briefly describe each of these premises and highlight some of the empirical research supporting them.

1. *Processing components are relatively autonomous specialists which operate largely automatically.*

The appeal of this proposition is that it can account for the *speed* with which language is processed. Levelt shows that the opposite assumption to autonomous and automatic components leads to serious problems. If the processing components were not autonomous, exchange of information between all processing components (or levels of processing) would have to be co-ordinated by a central control and processing would have to be executed in a serial manner, which would lead to extremely slow lock-step style processing. However, it has been shown that language processing is not only much faster than would be predicted by such a model, but empirical evidence also shows that different processing components exchange information in a parallel (i.e. non-serial) manner (Levelt 1989; Engelkamp & Zimmer 1983; Sridhar 1988).

In addition, a central control would imply that the operation of the processing components is consciously attended to, while empirical studies have shown that grammatical information is normally not attended to and can only be memorised if attention is focused on it (Bock 1978; Kintsch 1974; Garman 1990).

Autonomous specialist processing components can further be characterised as processing devices which are able to accept and pass on only information of a highly specific nature, for instance, only information concerning NPs. The advantage of such task-specificity is a gain in processing speed, since non-attended processes can be executed in parallel. Thus the notion of task-specificity is in line with the observation that grammatical information can only be memorised if it is attended to. Below it will become clear that the notion of automatic unattended processing is closely related to the nature of processing resources.

2. *Processing is incremental.*

This premise basically says that "…the next processor can start working on the still-incomplete output of the current processor…" (Levelt 1989: 24). The idea is that the surface lexico-grammatical form is gradually being constructed while conceptualisation is still ongoing. This feature was highlighted for the comprehension system by Marslen-Wilson and Tyler's (1980) study which demonstrated that in on-line processing semantic representations are being constructed by the comprehension system before grammatical structures have been "worked off".

Incremental processing is a feature of human language processing. One important implication of this feature for the structure of processing algorithms is that in order to be in line with human processing they must be able to cope with non-linear linguistic form without much "lookahead" (Levelt 1989). In other words every processing component can "see" only a small section of the current processing event rather than having the complete event displayed.

Incremental processing therefore necessitates the use of storage facilities to allow for non-linearity in the matching of underlying meaning onto surface form. This has important implications for the concepts which will be developed below in relation to the acquisition of language. We will therefore briefly look at the interrelation between non-linearity and memory.

3. *The output of the processor is linear, while it may not be mapped onto the underlying meaning in a linear way.*

One case of non-linearity is the relationship between the natural sequence of events and the order of clauses. As Levelt (1983) points out, propositions do not necessarily have to be produced in language in the natural order of events. Consider the following example:

(1)   Before the man rode off, he mounted his horse.

In this example the event described in the second clause happens before the one described in the first clause. In order to produce such sentences then, the speaker has to store one proposition in memory.

There are similar *linearisation problems* (Levelt 1983) which operate at the morpho-syntactic level. Such cases involve the storage of grammatical information. One such example is subject-verb agreement. Consider the following example:

(2)   She gives him a book.

The insertion of the verbal agreement marker crucially hinges on the storage of grammatical information which is created before the verb is produced, namely person and number marking of the subject. Note that the nature of the information held in memory is not the same in this example as it was in the above example. In the previous example it was propositional content which had to be stored, while in this example storage for grammatical information is needed.

4.   *Grammatical processing has access to a grammatical memory store*

Both types of information need to be held only temporarily until incorporated into the generation of the message. However, the difference between the two types of information is this: grammatical information is highly specific, and (conscious or unconscious) attention to it is not necessary; one does not need to be aware of or control the fact that the information concerning "person" and "number" matches between the lexical entries of the verb and the grammatical subject. In fact, it is possible to attend to only a small number of such processes. With the normal speed of language generation Working Memory would otherwise get "clogged up." On the other hand, attention must be focused on the propositional content, because it reflects the intended conceptualisation the speaker wants to express.

Working Memory is the resource for temporary attentive processes which include conceptualising and monitoring (Baddeley 1990; Broadbent 1975). It has a highly limited capacity and is therefore not suitable to process great amounts of grammatical information at high speed. Levelt (1989) and other authors (e.g. Engelkamp 1974) assume that grammatical information is held temporarily in the grammatical memory store which is highly task-specific and in which specialised grammatical processors can deposit information of a specific nature. In Kempen and Hoenkamp's (1987) Incremental Procedural Grammar, the locus of the grammatical buffer is the specialised procedures which process NPs, VPs etc.

One can see that the grammatical memory store is a requirement that arises from the automatic (i.e. inattentive) nature of grammatical processing: grammatical processors handle highly specific information which the grammatical memory store can hold temporarily. Empirical evidence for the different nature of the processing of propositional content and grammatical information comes, amongst other things, from the study of aphasia. Cooper and Zurif (1983), for instance, showed that in Broca's and, to a lesser extent, in Wernicke's aphasia lexical retrieval and semantic representation are functional while grammatical information cannot be processed. This is true for production as well as for comprehension.

As with other motor and cognitive skills, automatic processes in language production utilise what is known as "procedural knowledge" or "procedural memory", which is contrasted with "declarative knowledge/ memory." The latter "...concerns everything that can be represented at a conscious level, and which groups together what Tulving (1990) called 'episodic' memory, and Penfield termed 'experiential' memory" (Penfield & Roberts 1959; Paradis 1994: 395). There is ample empirical evidence for the dissociation of procedural and declarative memory (Paradis 1994) from studies of amnesia and aphasia, based on the patients' loss of ability to perform or to learn to perform certain tasks which can be defined according to the procedural-declarative distinction.

1.3 Incremental language generation

The process of incremental language generation as envisaged by Levelt (1989) and Kempen and Hoenkamp (1987) is exemplified in Figure 1, which illustrates some of the key processes involved in the generation of the example sentence "a child gives a cat to the mother." First of all, the concepts underlying this sentence are produced in the Conceptualiser. I will ignore the internal structure of this component of language generation for the purpose of this paper except for several features of the output produced by the Conceptualiser.

In the example chosen in Figure 1, the conceptual material produced first activates the lemma CHILD in the lexicon. The lemma contains the category information N which calls the categorial procedure NP. This procedure can build the phrasal category in which N is head, i.e. NP. The categorial procedure inspects the conceptual material of the current iteration (the material currently being processed) for possible complements and specifiers and provides values for diacritic features, including those from the head of phrase. I will assume that the first referent is marked "– accessible". This ensures that the branch Det is attached to NP, the lemma for 'A' is activated, and that the lexeme 'a' is inserted. Functorisation Rules instigate the activation of free grammatical morphemes and the insertion of bound grammatical morphemes.

The above attachment of Det to the NP node illustrates a key feature of the language production process, which is crucial in the context of language acquisition. The selection of the lemma for 'A' partly depends on the value of a diacritic feature ('singular') of the head being checked against that of the targeted lemma. The value of the diacritic feature is 'stored' by the categorial procedure until it is checked against that of the modifier.

Our production process has proceeded to the point where the structure of a phrase has been created and the associated lemmata are activated. What is missing to make this the beginning of a continuous and fluent utterance is establishing a relation between the phrase and the rest of the intended message. This is accomplished by assigning a grammatical function to the newly created

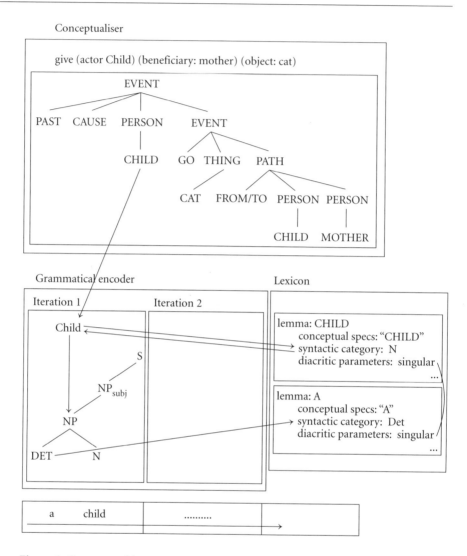

Figure 1. Incremental language generation

phrase. In fact, it is the categorial procedure itself that chooses its functional destination. This highlights the active nature of syntactic procedures.

Possible functional destinations are defined in a set of so-called Appointment Rules which are also language-specific. The default for NP procedures is 'subject of S'. However, this does not quite solve the problem of allowing the tree created so far to grow into a sentence and to make the production of the sentence continuous. What is missing is the attachment of the NP to a higher node. In the above example NP$_{subj}$ calls the procedure S which accepts the calling NP as its subject and stores the diacritic features deposited in the NP, namely the values for 'person' and 'number'.

The outcome of all of this is depicted by a tree structure in Figure 1. While this structure is produced and the associated lemmata are activated, the next conceptual fragment would have been processed in parallel and the output of the Formulator would have been delivered to the Articulator. This means that new conceptualisation occurs while the conceptual structure of the previous iteration is being produced. The whole process then moves on from itineration to iteration. This is what Kempen and Hoenkamp (1987) and Levelt (1989) mean by incremental production.

In the above summary of the process of grammatical encoding one aspect was left aside, namely word order. The definition of the acceptable set of word order constellations for configurational languages is carried out by Word Order Rules, which co-ordinate the assembly of phrasal subprocedures. I assume that for non-configurational languages grammatical roles can be specified directly from the semantic roles specified in the conceptual structure. And different procedures are assumed in the above model for the processing of matrix and subordinate clauses.

To recoup, in the incremental process of language generation, the following processing prerequisites are activated – amongst other things – in the following sequence:

i.   the lemma,
ii. the category procedure (lexical category of the lemma),
iii. the phrasal procedure (instigated by the category of the head),
iv. the S-procedure and the target language word order rules,
v.   the subordinate clause procedure – if applicable.

1.4 A hierarchy of processing resources

It is important to note that this account of grammatical processing and memory applies only to mature users of language, not to language learners. While even beginning second language learners can make recourse to the same *general* cognitive resources as mature native language users, they have to create language-specific processing routines. For L1 learners there are obviously no pre-existing procedures which can be transferred. L1 learners therefore have to develop all specific L1 procedures. Below I will generate hypotheses as to how language-specific processing routines develop, given the general architecture of the language processor.

In this context it is important to ensure that Levelt's model can, in principle, account for language processing in bilinguals, since second language acquisition will lead to a bilingual language processor. De Bot (1992) adapted Levelt's model to language production in bilinguals. Based on work by Paradis (1987), he shows that information about the specific language to be used is present in each part of the preverbal message and this subsequently informs the selection of language-specific lexical items and of the language-specific routines in the Formulator. Drawing from Paradis's (1987) research, de Bot concludes that "...the speaker who speaks two closely related languages will for most part use the same procedural and lexical knowledge when speaking either of the two languages, while in the case of languages which are not related an appeal is made to much more language-specific knowledge." (de Bot 1992:9). De Bot further shows that Paradis' (1987) 'Subset hypothesis' about the bilingual lexicon is in line with the overall design of Levelt's model. According to the subset hypothesis, the bilingual lexicon is a single storage system in which links between elements are enforced through continued use. This has the effect that links will be stronger between elements from one language. However, in the case of bilingual communities with a tendency for code-switching, links between elements from different languages may be similar to those in a monolingual lexicon.

De Bot (1992) demonstrates that the extended version of Levelt's model accounts for the majority of the additional requirements a language production model has to meet in a bilingual context. These include the following requirements. The two language systems concerned may be used quite separately from each other or in varying degrees of mixes (code-switching). The two systems may influence each other. Neither system will necessarily slow down in speech rate in comparison with a monolingual speaker, and the bilingual speaker may master the two (or more) systems to differing degrees.

Given the focus of Processability Theory on the Formulator, the key assumption from de Bot's work for the present context is that in all cases where the L2 is not closely related to the L1, different (language-specific) procedures have to be assumed. Based on our previous discussion, the following language-specific processing devices are the least L2 learners have to construct to acquire the L2 grammar:

- Word order rules,
- Syntactic procedures and their specific stores,

- Diacritic features in the lexicon,
- The lexical category of lemmata,
- Functorisation rules.

Obviously, word order rules are language-specific and there is no *a priori* way of knowing for the language learner how closely related L1 and L2 are. Learners therefore have to be equipped to bridge maximal typological gaps in their L2 acquisition. Diacritic features of lemmata contain items such as 'tense', 'number', 'gender', 'case', etc. Again it is obvious that the list of diacritic features varies from language to language.

Similarly, syntactic procedures that build constituent structures and store temporarily specific grammatical information such as diacritic features are not the same across languages. Given that diacritic features are language-specific and that these are stored in syntactic procedures, L1 procedures are not equipped to handle the specific storage task required by the L2.

The lexical category of lemmata may also vary from language to language. Again, the language learner is only fit to acquire any of the world's languages if he or she tests the lexical category for every new lexical item.

The reader will recall that Functorisation Rules instigate the activation of free and bound grammatical morphemes. And the same is true for grammatical morphemes as what was said about word order rules: these are language-specific and therefore have to be acquired with the L2.

1.5 Exchange of grammatical information

In other words, the L2 learner is initially unable to deposit information into syntactic procedures, because (1) the lexicon is not fully annotated, and more importantly (2) because even if the L1 annotation was transferred, the syntactic procedures have not specialised to hold the specific L2 syntactic information. For this reason one can predict that the beginning learner is unable to produce any structures which rely on the exchange of specific L2 grammatical information using syntactic procedures, or in LFG terms the 'unification' of lexical features.

One can expand on the principle of grammatical information exchange in line with the architecture of the Formulator. In Figure 1 above I illustrated the flow of grammatical information in the production process and the different temporary stores used in that process. One type of process is the use of grammatical information that proceeds without reliance on temporary storage. An example is the morphological marking of reference to time. The information about tense is contained in the verb lemma with the value 'past' for the dia-critic feature 'tense'. This means that the diacritic feature in question is available in the same location where the morpheme for the marking of past (i.e. '-ed') has to occur and no information has to be deposited into any syntactic pro-cedure to achieve this process. I call the resulting class of morphemes 'lexical'. Since lexical morphemes can be produced without phrasal procedures, they can develop before phrasal procedures.

A second type of process is one in which the grammatical information is stored in a phrasal procedure. An example was given in Figure 1, namely the NP 'a child'. The lemma CHILD is marked 'singular', and the value of this diacritic feature has to match that of the determiner. To achieve this, the lemma infor-mation for CHILD has to be deposited in the NP-procedure and kept there for the activation of the lemma 'A'.[3] In other words, this second type of morpheme is linguistically characterised by agreement between the head of phrase and another phrasal constituent. Its processing characteristic is that of the storage of diacritic features in phrasal procedures. We can infer that this type of pro-cess will become available to the language learner once phrasal procedures have been developed for the L2. I call this class of morphemes 'phrasal'.

There is one further type of process which involves the exchange of gram-matical information, namely agreement between heads of different phrases as in subject-verb agreement. For SV agreement to occur the diacritic fea-tures 'third person' and 'singular' have to be deposited in the S-procedure until utilised for the activation for the verb lemma. I call this class of mor-phemes 'inter-phrasal'. This process obviously requires the S-procedure to have developed, and it involves the exchange of grammatical information between phrases.

One can now see that the three classes of morphemes are based on different processes. Lexical morphemes do not require phrasal procedures while phrasal morphemes do. On the other hand, phrasal agreement will mostly occur in one and the same iteration. This is unlikely to apply to inter-phrasal agree-ment due to the incremental nature of language production. In other words, while the one phrase is being produced, the head of the agreeing phrase has not been conceptualised. This means that the relevant diacritic information cannot be stored in the phrasal procedure. Instead, it has to be stored in the S-procedure. However, in order to arrive there the functional destination of the phrase from which it originates has to be determined. This is carried out by a set of language-specific Appointment Rules as discussed above.

1.6 Principles of processability

The above brief exposition of the processability of different classes of morphemes may serve as an illustration of the fundamental principle of processability. Language-specific processing resources have to be acquired to make the processing of the TL possible. These processing resources are interrelated in two ways. (1) They feed into each other in the temporal event of language generation, i.e. one is utilised before the other. (2) The information processed and generated in one is required in the other. In this way these resources from a hierarchy. If one building block of the hierarchy is missing, the top cannot be reached. The following processing resources were discussed above as part of the incremental language generation process:[4]

- – word/ lemma
- – category procedure (lexical category)
- – Phrasal procedures (head)
- – S-procedure and Word Order Rules
- – matrix/subordinate clause

These processing resources form a hierarchy which arises from the fact that the resource of each lower level is a prerequisite for the functioning of the higher level. A word needs to be added to the L2 lexicon before its grammatical category can be assigned. The grammatical category of a lemma is needed before a category procedure can be called. Only if the grammatical category of the head of phrase is assigned can the phrasal procedure be called. Only if a phrasal procedure has been completed and its value is returned can Appointment Rules determine the function of the phrase. And only if the function of the phrase has been determined can it be attached to the S-node and sentential information be stored in the S-procedure. And only if the latter has occurred can the target language word order be arranged. In other words, it is hypothesised that processing devices will be acquired in their sequence of activation in the production process. The reason for this assumption is that they constitute an implicational hierarchy in the production process. The implicational nature of the hierarchy would make it impossible for processing devices to develop before all other requisite devices have developed.

What happens when an element is missing in this implicational hierarchy? My hypothesis is that for the learner grammar the hierarchy will be cut off at the point of the missing processing device and the rest of the hierarchy will be replaced by a direct mapping of conceptual structures onto surface form as long as there are lemmata that match the conceptually instigated searches of

Table 1. Hypothetical hierarchy of processing procedures

	t_1	t_2	t_3	t_4	t_5
S'-procedure (EmbeddedS)	–	–	–	–	+
S-procedure	–	simplified	simplified	inter-phrasal information exchange	inter-phrasal information exchange
Phrasal procedure (head)	–	–	phrasal information exchange	phrasal information exchange	phrasal information exchange
category procedure (lex. categ.)	–	lexical morphemes	lexical morphemes	lexical morphemes	lexical morphemes
word/lemma	+	+	+	+	+

the lexicon.[5] A case in point is the development of target language word or-der. Below I will demonstrate that the production of subject-verb inversion in German requires certain bits of grammatical information to be exchanged be-tween the grammatical subject and the verb. I will show that for such exchange of grammatical information to be possible it has to be held in the S-procedure. I will show that as long as this information exchange is not enabled by the available processing prerequisites the learner is limited to the use of canonical sentence schemata.

In other words, it is hypothesised that processing procedures and the ca-pacity for the exchange of grammatical information will be acquired in their implicational sequence as depicted in Table 1.

One point in Table 1 needs to be borne in mind when this hierarchy is ex-pressed in LFG terms. The underlying assumption is that in the first three stages of the hierarchy, phrases are assembled using simplified procedures, and not the S-procedure. Strictly speaking, structures appearing at levels 1–3 cannot be represented by constituent structure rules of the type S → X, Y, Z because the S-procedure has not developed. Indeed, we assume that at these stages sen-tences are formed using simplified procedures based on a direct mapping of argument structure onto functional structure. However, to keep this presenta-tion readable, we will nevertheless use consistent constituent structure rules, albeit with the informal assumption that the underlying process is simplified at levels 1–3.

1.7 LFG and processability

If the above hierarchy is to be universally applicable to language acquisition, then it needs to be interpretable in relation to grammatical structures in individual languages. This is achieved by interpreting the processability hierarchy through a theory of grammar which is typologically and psychologically plausible. The theory of grammar I chose for this purpose is LFG which shares three key features with Kempen and Hoenkamp's (1987) procedural account of language generation, namely (i) the assumption that grammars are lexically driven and (ii) the assumption that functional annotations of phrases (e.g. 'subject of') assume the status of primitives and (iii) the mechanism of feature matching.

The key aspect of operationalising the above hierarchy of processing resources with LFG is the fact that the aspect of procedural memory inherent in Kempen and Hoenkamp's procedural approach can be captured by the process of feature unification in LFG. Above I illustrated the aspect of procedural memory with SV agreement marking and I noted that for SV agreement to occur the diacritic features 'third person' and 'singular' have to be deposited in the S-procedure until they are matched with that of the verb entry. In LFG, this process is modelled by feature unification.[6] I will therefore use feature unification as a comparative metric to evaluate the developmental level of IL forms.

Similarly with Pinker (1984) and Levelt (1989), I use LFG as a convenient reference point which has been formalised and tested sufficiently to be practical for this purpose. The architecture of LFG coincides with the key points made above in relation to language processing.

1.8 A brief sketch of LFG

Before I demonstrate how the processability hierarchy is implemented into an LFG-based description of a target language (and the developing interlanguage), I will give a brief outline of Lexical-Functional Grammar. LFG is a unification grammar, the most prominent characteristic of which is that of the unification of features. Put simply, the process of feature unification ensures that the different parts that constitute a sentence do actually fit together.

In the original version (Bresnan 1982; Kaplan & Bresnan 1982), LFG consisted of three parts: (i) a constituent structure (= c-structure) component that generates "surface structure" constituents and c-structure relationships, (ii) a lexicon, whose entries contain syntactic and other information relevant to the generation of sentences, and (iii) a functional component which compiles for every sentence all the grammatical information needed to interpret the sentence semantically.

In her 2001 monograph, Bresnan presents LFG with the additonal features that emerged since the original theory was published. The new architecture does not deviate in principle from its original design. Instead it contains a number of revisions and additions that were necessitated to some extent by requirements of typological plausibility. In the revised version of LFG (cf. Bresnan 2001), a(rgument) structure has been formally incorporated as one of a set of three parallel structures entailed in LFG. In fact, a-structure corresponds neatly with conceptual structure in Levelt's (1989) model of language generation. In the context of this summary we will not utilise the new features of LFG since the purpose of the summary is to present PT in its 1998 format which was based on the original version of LFG. In Chapter 7 of this volume the revised and extended LFG framework will be utilised to extend the PT hierarchy.

All c-structures are generated directly by phrase structure rules without any intervening transformations. Hence the mapping of predicate-argument structures onto surface forms is achieved without any intervening levels of representation. Grammatical functions assume the role of grammatical primitives, and major constituents are annotated for their grammatical function. The c-structure of the sentence "Peter owns a dog", for instance is shown in Figure 2 which can be generated by the annotated phrase structure rules shown in Figure 3. A simplified account of the lexical entries relating to Figure 2 is given in Figure 4.

As is obvious from these simplified examples, lexical entries specify a number of syntactic and other properties of lexical items by assigning values to features (e.g. NUM = SG). In most cases such equations *define* the value of features. In some cases they may also "demand" certain values elsewhere in the functional description of a sentence. One example for such a constraining equation would be

$$WH =_c +$$

This equation stipulates that the phrase to which it is attached must be a WH-WORD.

The functional structure or "f-structure" of a sentence is a list of those pieces of grammatical information needed to semantically interpret the sentence. It is generated by the interaction between c-structure and the lexicon. The f-structure of the sentence in Figure 2 is given in Figure 5.

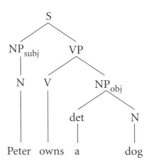

Figure 2. Constituent structure

$$
\begin{array}{lll}
\text{S} & \rightarrow & \text{NP}_{\text{subj}}\ \text{VP} \\
\text{NP} & \rightarrow & (\text{det})\ \text{N} \\
\text{VP} & \rightarrow & \text{V}\ (\text{NP}_{\text{obj}}).
\end{array}
$$

Figure 3. C-structure rules

Peter:	N,	PRED	=	"Peter"
owns:	V,	PRED	=	"own" (SUBJ, OBJ)
		TENSE	=	present
		SUBJ PERSON	=	3
		SUBJ NUM	=	SG
a:	DET,	SPEC	=	"a"
		NUM	=	SG
dog:	N,	PRED	=	"dog"
		NUM	=	SG

Figure 4. Lexical entries

PRED	"own" (SUBJ, OBJ)	
TENSE	present	
SUBJ	PRED	"Peter"
OBJ	SPEC	"a"
	NUM	SG
	PRED	"dog"

Figure 5. Functional structure

The predicate entry [PRED "own" (SUBJ, OBJ)] is taken from the lexical entry of the verb. Listing the stem of the verb in quotation marks ("own") is simply a short-hand convention for a semantic representation of the word. The slots to the right of the verb which are filled by SUBJ and OBJ in Figure 5 list the arguments of the predicate: first the *owner*, then the *item owned*.

The PRED entry of the f-structure therefore makes it possible to relate the different constituents to the "players" described by the sentence (actor, patient, etc.). This forms the link between the syntactic form and its underlying predicate-argument relations.

In the context of this summary of PT the reader may wonder what motivated the author to implement the above hierarchy of processing procedures into a theory of grammar rather than directly into IPG which *is* a processing grammar. I decided against this option for several reasons. I demonstrated in Pienemann (1998) that feature unification, which is one of the main characteristics of LFG, captures a psychologically plausible process that involves (i) the identification of grammatical information in the lexical entry, (ii) the temporary storage of that information and (iii) its utilisation at another point in the constituent structure. I also demonstrated that feature unification is one of the key processes in morphology and word order, the two areas to be studied in the empirical sections of this book. Every level of the hierarchy of processing procedures can be represented through feature unification. In other words, the essence of that hierarchy can be captured through feature unification in LFG.[7] I will use the LFG system with the informal assumption that unification occurs at the lowest node which the two 'sources' of the unification share.

A theory of second language acquisition has to be typologically plausible since it has to apply to any pair of L1 and L2 from amongst the languages of the world. One of the great strengths of LFG is its proven typological plausibility. In this respect, LFG is a 'tried and tested' framework with extensive studies on typologically diverse languages (e.g. Simpson 1991; Bresnan & Kanerva 1989).

A further reason for the suitability of LFG in defining processability in the context of language acquisition is the fact that the acquisition process itself can most plausibly be viewed as a lexically driven process. The main reason for this assumption is an epistemological one: the inferential process is more powerful if it is based on lexical learning, because the learner can assimilate grammatical features with lexical items on the basis of positive evidence. Roeper, Lapointe, Bing and Tavakolian (1981) point out that a lexical acquisition theory has two advantages: (i) it eliminates many potential grammars which would be logically possible if acquisition was based on the generation of structural hypotheses only, and (ii) it provides a solution for the learning of optional rules which cannot otherwise be inferred from positive evidence (Roeper et al. 1981: 38).

In short, LFG promises to afford a valid application of the PT hierarchy of processing procedures; it is readily available, compatible with Levelt's model and attractive from a typological point of view.

2.   Second language development: ESL

The explanatory potential of Processability Theory will become clearer when the theory is applied to a particular case of language development. In this section I will apply Processability Theory to explaining the sequence found in the second language acquisition of English as a second language. I will focus on the development of the following morphological and syntactic structures in ESL learners.

In the area of morphology, *plural marking* on nouns, *possessive pronouns* and *S-V-agreement marking* (3sg-s) (e.g. He eat-*s* at home) will be examined.

In the area of syntax I will concentrate on word order. The phenomena I will look at are the following:

- One-word utterances
- Do-Fronting
- Topicalisation (Topi)
- Yes-no Inversion
- Copula Inversion
- Tense agreement
- Do/Aux 2nd
- Cancel Inversion
- Canonical word order
- Neg + V
- Adverb Fronting (ADV)
- Particle Verbs

One-word utterances are typical of early learner English. For instance, the learner might say "home." Within the given context one might interpret this utterance as meaning "I am going home." Canonical word order (SVO) can be found in most affirmative sentences in English. ADV refers to the occurrence of adverbs and adverbials in initial position of sentences. Neg + V refers to an interlanguage form of negation where a lexically invariable form of a negator is used in preverbal position, for instance "*He no like coffee."

By 'Do-Fronting' I do *not* refer to what is traditionally described as 'do-support'. While the latter implies one type of SV-agreement and is operational in negation and direct questions without auxiliary, 'do-fronting' isolates only one single aspect of this amalgamation of structural phenomena, namely the appearance of 'do' in initial position in the sentence for the purpose of marking direct questions. 'Do-fronting' therefore covers sentence (3) as well as (4) and (5):[8]

(3) Do you like it?

(4) *Do he like it?

(5) *Do he have lunch yesterday?

Topicalisation refers to the initial position of non-subject noun phrases as in (6):

(6) That I didn't like.

Yes/no-Inversion refers to the syntactic pattern found in 'direct yes/no-questions' in which the subject and the auxiliary are inverted as in (7).

(7) Has he seen you?

Copula Inversion refers to wh-questions with a copula. In such cases the grammatical subject is in final position (e.g. "where is John?"), while in wh-questions with lexical verbs the subject is followed by the lexical verb (e.g. "where does John live?").

An example of Particle Verbs is "*take off*" in "take that off".

"Tense agreement" refers to the agreement of the modal and lexical verbs and the auxiliary in the marking of such diacritic features as tense, person and number (i.e. "he has seen him" rather than "he has sees him" or "he has seed him", etc.)

"Do/Aux2nd" refers to inversion in Wh-questions as in (8) to (10):

(8) Why did he sell that car?

(9) Where has he gone?

(10) What is she eating?

"Cancel inversion" describes the fact that in indirect questions subject auxiliary inversion does not apply. This is illustrated in (11) to (13).

(11) I wonder why he sold that car.

(12) I wonder where he has gone.

(13) I wonder what she is eating.

Table 2. Adult learners of ESL

Stage	Structure	van	IS	my	ks	tam	long	vinh	jr	sang	bb	ka	es	ij	ja	dung	phuc
6	Cancel Inversion	–	–	–	–	–	–	–	–	–	–	–	–	–	–	–	–
5	Aux2nd/ Do2nd	–	–	–	–	–	–	–	–	–	–	–	–	–	–	+	+
	3 sg-s	–	–	–	–	–	–	–	–	–	–	–	–	+	+	+	+
4	Y/N Inversion	–	–	–	–	–	–	–	–	+	+	+	+	/	/	+	+
	Copula Inversion	–	–	–	–	+	+	+	+	/	+	+	+	+	+	/	/
3	Neg+V	–	–	–	+	+	+	+	+	+	+	+	+	+	+	+	+
	Do Front.	–	–	+	+	+	/	+	+	+	+	+	+	+	+	+	+
	Topi	–	–	+	+	+	+	+	+	+	+	+	+	+	+	+	+
	ADV	–	–	+	+	+	+	+	+	+	+	+	+	+	+	+	+
2	SVO	–	+	+	+	+	+	+	+	+	+	+	+	+	+	+	+
	Plural	–	+	+	+	+	+	+	+	+	+	+	+	+	+	+	+
1	single words	+	/	/	/	/	/	/	/	/	/	/	/	/	/	/	/

Legend: + acquired   – not acquired   / no context
van, IS, my etc. = names of informants

The development of the above morpho-syntactic structures in ESL learners has been examined in several comparable empirical studies. The first study is that by Johnston (1985) which consists of a total of 24 samples from Polish and Vietnamese adult immigrants in Australia. The results of Johnston's study for the 12 grammatical structures listed in Table 1 which is based on a sub-set of 16 informants were summarised by Johnston in Pienemann, Johnston and Brindley (1988). This summary is replicated with some amendments by Johnston (personal communication) in Table 2.

The full distributional analysis of this study is available in Johnston (1985). I will therefore focus on the summary of his analysis in which the raw frequency counts have been interpreted on the basis of the emergence criterion for acquisition.[9] The true size of the corpus may not be obvious from the compact format of Table 2. I would therefore like to point out that each of the 16 interviews was between 40 and 60 minutes in length, resulting in a 60,000 word corpus.

Table 2 contains 12 of the 14 grammatical structures of English and learner English which we discussed above. Table 2 is laid out as an implicational table. Grammatical structures are listed on the left-hand side. For each learner and structure a '+' marks structures which have been acquired according to our emergence criterion; a '–' marks those structures which have not been acquired, and a '/' marks those structures for which there is no linguistic context in the sample.

Table 3. Bio-data of Child learners of ESL

Subject ID	Sex	Age	L1	Length of residence
1.1	F	9	Polish	7 months
1.2	F	8	Hindi	8 months
1.3	F	8	Syrian	11 months
1.4	F	8	Khmer	6 months
1.5	M	9	Spanish	11 months
1.6	M	8	Khmer	8 months
1.7	M	8	Polish	8 months
2.1	M	8	Spanish	9 months
2.2	M	9	Spanish	11 months
2.3	M	8	Spanish	60 months
2.4	F	8	Spanish	22 months
2.5	F	10	Spanish	44 months
2.6	F	9	Spanish	22 months

The key issue in reading this implicational table is to check to what extent the hypothesised implicational relationships hold, i.e. to check if it is true that for every structure and learner the acquisition of the highest structure in the hierarchy implies the acquisition of all lower-level structures. The reader will recall that the implicational relationship is contradicted if there is 'negative evidence' (marked '−' above) for any structure in the hierarchy in the presence of positive evidence (marked '+') for any higher-level structure.

The scalability of Table 2 is 100%. This means two things: (i) the twelve grammatical structures described above are acquired in the order in which they are presented in Table 1 (from bottom to top), and (ii) There is not a single piece of evidence to contradict this implicational pattern.

The richness of the database adds to the strength of this study. This is evident in the small number of slashes ('/') in Table 2. A slash indicates that there were no contexts for an obligatory structure or, in the case of an optional structure,[10] that there were no instances. Cases marked in this way have to be considered gaps in the corpus. Leaving aside one constituent utterances,[11] such gaps occur in merely 3.125% of Johnston's corpus.

The second ESL study to be summarised here is based on samples collected from 13 children aged 8 to 10 years (Pienemann & Mackey 1993).[12] The samples were collected using a range of communicative tasks. Table 3 sets out some of the key bio-data of this group of informants.

Table 4 displays the implicational analysis of this corpus. Table 4 is set out in the same way as Table 1 for the Johnston study. The only difference is that in the child ESL study, all 14 structures are included that were introduced above.

Table 4. Child learners of ESL – implicational table

Stage	Structure	1:7	1:4	1:2	1:3	2:3	1:5	2:2	2:1	2:5	2:4	1::6	2.6	1:1
6	Cancel Inversion	/	/	/	/	/	/	/	/	/	/	–	/	+
5	Aux2nd/ Do2nd	/	/	–	/	–	/	+	+	+	+	+	+	/
	3 sg-s	–	–	–	–	+	+	+	+	+	+	+	+	+
4	Y/N Inversion	/	/	/	/	+	/	+	+	+	+	/	+	/
	Particle verbs	/	/	/	+	+	+	+	+	+	+	+	+	+
	Copula Inversion	/	/	/	/	+	/	+	+	+	+	+	+	/
3	Neg+V	+	+	+	+	+	+	+	+	+	+	+	+	+
	Do Front.	/	/	+	/	/	/	+	+	+	+	/	+	/
	Topi	+	+	+	+	+	/	+	+	+	+	+	+	+
	ADV	+	/	+	+	+	+	+	+	+	+	/	+	+
2	SVO	+	+	+	+	+	+	+	+	+	+	+	+	+
	Plural	+	+	+	+	+	+	+	+	+	+	+	+	+
	possessive pronoun	+	+	+	+	+	+	+	+	+	+	+	+	+
1	single words	+	+	/	/	/	+	/	/	/	/	/	+	/

Legend: + acquired   – not acquired   / no context

As in the Johnston study, the scalability of Table 4 is 100%, i.e. there is no contradictory evidence to the sequence found in Johnston's study, and this includes the two additional structures. While this study lends strong additional support to the universality of the acquisition sequence, the internal consistency of this study is not quite as strong as that of Johnston's study.

Firstly, the gaps in this corpus amount to some 24%. This means that in about a quarter of all structures per informant there is no evidence for or against the hypothesis to be tested. While this in no way disqualifies the hypothesis, it highlights the fact that this corpus is not as rich as that in Johnston's study.

The second limitation is that not all structures are documented by at least one learner who displays evidence that the structure marks a developmental step. Again, this does not falsify the hypothesised sequence, but the data are not sufficiently rich to support all of the structures. One very clear example is that of one constituent utterances. While these do appear in the data, there is no individual learner who produces this structure and no other structures. To prove that one constituent utterances mark a developmental level one would have to 'supply' such an informant. The reader will notice that the Johnston study does indeed discriminate between all the structures of the hierarchy, except for Cancel Inversion. However, the latter is documented in the child ESL study.

Table 5. Processing procedures applied to English

Processing procedure	L2 process	morphology	syntax
6 – subord. cl. procedure	main and sub cl		Cancel INV
5 – S-procedure	inter-phr info	SV agreement ($= 3sg$-s)	Do2nd, Aux2nd
4 – VP-procedure	inter-phr info	tense agreement	Y/N inv, copula inv
3 – phrasal procedure	phrasal info.	NP agr Neg+V	ADV, Do-Front, Topi
2 – category procedure	lex morph possessive pro	plural[13]	canonical order
1 – word/lemma	'words'	invariant forms	single constituent

Summing up, the two studies provide strong evidence in support of a specific sequence in the acquisition of English morphosyntax. In the remainder of this paper I will try to explain this sequence from a language processing perspective, to be more precise from the perspective of Processability Theory (Pienemann 1998).

To provide the intended psycholinguistic explanation of ESL development one needs to apply the above general hierarchy of language processing procedures to the morphological and syntactic structures found in the acquisition of English as a second language. I will proceed as follows: I will characterise the structures found in ESL development within LFG. This characterisation serves as a basis for the analysis for transfer of grammatical information required for the production of these structures. The analysis of information transfer allows a prediction of the processability of these structures by L2 learners. Ideally, the processability hierarchy will coincide with the sequence found in the empirical studies.

Table 5 gives an overview of how these morphological and syntactic structures can be accounted for in the proposed processability framework.

The morphological forms of English included in this hierarchy relate to processing procedures in a straightforward manner. Diacritic features such as 'possessive' and 'number' are listed in the lexical entries of words. They can therefore be matched directly from conceptual structure and no exchange of grammatical information is required for this process as long as the diacritic feature is to be marked in one constituent only. This process can therefore occur at level 2.

Once diacritic features are to be marked in several constituents, their value information has to be matched between constituents. Hence grammatical information needs to be exchanged requiring phrasal or other procedures as repositories. Therefore phrasal agreement, such as plural agreement, is predicted to occur at level 3. For instance, the relevant lexical entries for the phrase "many dogs" are as follows:

> many: DET, (SPEC) = MANY
>   (NUM) = PL
> dogs: N,   (PRED) = DOG
>   (NUM) = PL

To achieve agreement marking, the value for the diacritic feature 'number' has to be unified between Det and N. Phrasal procedures need to be in place for this operation to be executable.

The situation is rather different with Subject-Verb *agreement* marking. The features for Number and Person have to be unified across constituent boundaries and the grammatical information consisting of the values of the diacritic features 'person' and 'number' have to be deposited in the S-procedure to be placed in the specified constituent of S. This is illustrated below:

$$[\text{This man}]_{NP_{subj}} \quad [\text{owns}]_{V}\ldots \text{(Present)}$$

> $\quad$ | $\qquad\qquad$ |
> Person = 3 $\qquad$ Person = 3
> NUM = SG $\qquad\quad$ NUM = SG

In other words, SV-agreement marking requires the presence of the S-procedure and is therefore located at level 5 of the hierarchy. In other words, the observed sequence of acquisition (lexical before phrasal before inter-phrasal morphemes) is predicted by the processability of the morphological structures under investigation.

Let us now look at how the syntactic phenomena contained in the ESL processability hierarchy can be accounted for by LFG and how this treatment justifies the position of the individual rules in the hierarchy. The general line of argument followed here is very similar to that of Kaplan and Bresnan (1982) and Pinker (1984).

Since there is only one level of c-structure in LFG (and no intervening transformations), the canonical SVO order follows directly from c-structure rules such as R1 below:

(R1) $S \rightarrow NP_{subj}$ V (NP_{obj}) (ADJ) (S)

In other words, no exchange of grammatical information is needed here which places this rule at level 2 of the hierarchy – as found in the data. Note that no

S-procedure has been developed at this point, and the learner can be expected to use a simplified version of that procedure which I argued elsewhere (Pienemann 1998) to be based on a direct mapping of conceptual structures onto linguistic form.

ADV and the initial position of Wh-words can also be derived from c-structure by allowing adverbs (and other lexical categories) to appear in focused positions (i.e. in XP position) – as shown in R2 below:

(R2) S' → (XP)   S
$$\left\{ \begin{array}{l} wh =_c + \\ adv =_c + \end{array} \right\}$$

Note that (R1), together with (R2), allows for sentences such as (14).

(14) *Where you have been?

This type of sentence structure does indeed occur in learner data.

The constraint equations in (R2) ensure that the XP position can only be filled by lexical material which is either a member of the class "*wh*-word" or "adverb". This notation further allows the researcher to trace the lexical nature of the acquisition process by describing the transition from a lexically to a categorically defined rule system. This would be possible by annotating the lexical elements permitted by the equation (e.g. *wh* $=_c$ '*who*'). This annotation will then at some stage become categorical (i.e. wh $=_c$ +) allowing for all words of that category.

In terms of processability, the structures ADV and Wh-Front are a modification of the serial order principle which allows the learner to map conceptual structures directly onto linguistic form:

   agent action patient
    N   V   N

The new structure (ADV S) modifies the seriality principle utilising the general cognitive principle of saliency which identifies initial and final positions and allows the canonical order principle to apply once the salient positions have been processed:

   INITIAL]   agent action patient [FINAL
   PP/wh/adv NP   V   NP

These additional word order options allow the learner to produce a range of L2 syntactic phenomena without acquiring the full range of L2 word order.

Also note that in the above representation of the canonical schema the constituents of the canonical sequence are described as phrases. This is so, because phrasal procedures are operational at this stage. This makes it possible for the canonical schema to allow a definition of 'position' in terms of phrases rather than words.

Do-FRONT can be generated if one assumes the following modification of (R1):

(R3) S → ($V_{aux = c\,'do'}$) NP$_{subj}$ V (NP$_{obj}$) (ADJ) (S)

The constraint equation *aux* $=_c$ *'do'* ensures that only the auxiliary 'do' can appear in the position of the first V. This treatment of Do-FRONT is similar to Bresnan's (1982) treatment of Aux-2nd, which is also based on a constraint equation at the level of c-structure. Note that this account of Do-FRONT only deals with the *position* of the aux not with its morphological form or that of the lexical verb. It therefore permits structures as in (15) and (16).

(15) *Do she see him?

(16) *Do he going home?

These are indeed structures that one finds at the same relative point in time as the first occurrences of Do-FRONT.

By generalising the above equation to *aux* $=_c$ ± all auxiliaries are possible in initial position. This form of the rule then describes the *positional* facts of yes/no-inversion, while the morphological forms of AUX and V are untouched.

To achieve 'tense agreement' the morphological component has to be informed about the INF value for V. For this purpose the feature values for INF and PARTICIPLE have to be unified between the auxiliary and the lexical verb, before any verb can be selected for the verb positions. The lexical entries for verbs would contain, amongst other things, the following features:

seen: V,   PRED = 'see' (SUBJ, OBJ)
                PARTICIPLE = PAST
                INF = +
                AUX = −

has: V,   PRED = 'have, V-COMP (SUBJ)'
                TENSE = PAST
                AUX = +
                NUM = SG
                PERSON = 3RD

$$\text{V-COMP PARTICIPLE} = \text{PAST}$$
$$\text{V-COMP INF} =_c +$$

In this example the constraint equation V-COMP INF $=_c$ + listed under the entry for 'has' is checked against the INF value in the entry for 'seen'. This ensures that the complement does not define any tense. In other words, this provision rules out sentences such as (17) and (18).

(17) *He has sees him.

(18) *He has see him.

Such errors do, however, occur in ESL data. This means that not all the necessary features are listed in the entries to the learner's lexicon. In other words, the unification of INF values described above accounts for this aspect of the learning process which constitutes phrasal agreement within the verb phrase, and the latter occurs at level 4 (cf. Table 9).

To account for auxiliaries in second position (Aux2nd) after preposed question words or preposed adverbs such as "never", (R2) needs to be modified along the lines of Kaplan and Bresnan's (1982) and Pinker's (1984) original proposal:

(R2a)   S" → (XP)   S'
$$\left\{ \begin{array}{l} \text{wh} =_c + \\ \text{adv} =_c + \\ \text{SENT MOOD} = \text{INV} \end{array} \right\}$$

(R3) then has to be modified as follows:

(R3a)   S' → (V)   S
$$\left\{ \begin{array}{l} \text{aux} =_c + \\ \text{ROOT} =_c + \\ \text{SENT MOOD} =_c \text{INV} \end{array} \right\}$$

In this way it is guaranteed that (i) only auxiliaries appear in this position, that (ii) this position is filled only in matrix sentences and (iii) only after the constraints expressed in (R2a), i.e. in the context of preposed question words and some other lexical items.

Again, it is possible to account not only for structures that occur in mature English, but also for the dynamics of the learning process, i.e. for structures created by the learner on the way to acquiring target structures. For instance, it is known that Aux2nd is first acquired in the context of a limited number of preposed question words and certainly not in the context of preposed adverbs like "never". As I indicated above, the formalism used here can express this through an alteration of the constraint equations appended to XP.

In the same way it is possible to account for the application of Aux2nd to a limited set of auxiliaries or the over-application of this position to subordinate clauses (i.e. indirect questions). In the latter case the distinction +/− ROOT has not been appended to (R3a).

In terms of the processability hierarchy, Do/Aux2nd occurs at level 5 because grammatical information needs to be exchanged between sentence constituents, namely the equation SENT MOOD $=_c$ Inv.

Cancel Inversion can be accounted for by assuming a linear c-structure for subordinate clauses – similar to that of stage 1 clauses.

(R4)   S → (COMP)$_{ROOT=-}$ NP$_{subj}$ (V$_{INF=+}$) (V$_{INF=-}$) (NP$_{obj1}$) (NP$_{obj2}$) (ADJ)

This ensures that Aux2nd, Do-Fronting and ADV are blocked in subordinate clauses.

It is worth noting that this treatment again allows for a gradual acquisition of properties of English subordinate clauses. Learner data are full of seemingly unsystematic examples such as the following:

(19)   *I asked if could he come home.

(20)   I asked when he could come home.

The seeming unsystematicity is nothing but a reflex of the lexical nature of the acquisition of Cancel Inversion. This imaginary learner has not properly classified question words and complementisers. In (19) "if" is not classified as a complementiser so that the clause "if he could come home" is treated as a main clause, while in (20) "when" is classified as a complementiser and consequently the 'when-clause' is treated as being subordinate. The reader will recall that in the processability hierarchy the distinction between main and subordinate clauses occurs at level 6.

3.   Second language development: German as L2

The developmental trajectory found in ESL acquisition is rather similar to that found in the acquisition of German as L2. This is not surprising given the close genetic relationship between the two languages.

Because the L1-L2 comparison presented in the following section is based on German as L2, it may be useful to briefly sketch GSL development in the

PT framework. The German L2 sequence is well-documented in the literature and has been the object of much of the debate on explaining developmental phenomena in SLA. The acquisitional sequence in question is based on a series of longitudinal and cross-sectional studies by the ZISA research group[14] (Clahsen 1980; Clahsen, Meisel & Pienemann 1983; Meisel, Clahsen & Pienemann 1981; Pienemann 1980, 1981). Similar findings have emerged in studies of the acquisition of German in formal contexts (Jansen 1991; Pienemann 1988; Westmoreland 1983). In all cases, the basic sequence of acquisition can be summarised as follows:

> Stage x = Canonical Order
> *die kinder spielen mim ball*
> 'the children play with the ball'
>
> Stage x + 1 = Adverb Preposing (ADV)
> *da kinder spielen*
> 'there children play'
>
> Stage x + 2 = Verb Separation (SEP)
> *alle kinder muß die pause machen*
> 'all children must the break have'
>
> Stage x + 3 = INVERSION (INV)
> *dann hat sie wieder die knoch gebringt*
> 'then has she again the bone bringed'
>
> Stage x + 4 = Verb Final (V-END)
> *er sagt, daß er nach hause kommt*
> 'he says that he home comes'

It should be noted that, in the process of L2 acquisition, the learner accumulates these rules. This means that the structure of a given IL can be described as the sum of all the rules the learner has acquired up to a certain point.

The application of Processability Theory to this sequence will occur in two steps: first a brief account of the word order phenomena concerned will be given in a somewhat simplified LFG framework, and then I will demonstrate that the process of feature unification required for each of the structures is predicted by the above hierarchy of processability.

As mentioned above, in LFG possible word orders of languages are defined through c-structure rules (Kaplan & Bresnan 1982: 175ff.).

(R1)   S → NP_{subj} V (NP_{obj1}) (NP_{obj2})

(R1) allows for a basic SVO order (i.e. NP_{subj} V NP_{obj1} NP_{obj2}), as it occurs at stage x. The occurrence of Wh-words, PPs and NPs in focus position, the characteristic of stage x+1, can be accounted for by (R2) which is adapted from Pinker (1984:278):

$$(R2) \quad S' \rightarrow (XP) \qquad S$$
$$\begin{Bmatrix} wh =_c + \\ adv =_c + \\ NP =_c + \\ PP =_c + \end{Bmatrix}$$

The constraining equations in (R2) (e.g. $wh =_c +$) ensure that only Wh-words, adverbs, NPs and PPs can occur in focus position. Standard German also allows lexical verbs to occur in this position, but such structures appear later than x+1.[15] Also, note that at stage x+1 structures like "*hat-ge-sag-en*" (have-past-*sag*-infinitive) may occur. I analyse this as "PAST-PAST-V" and thus as a single verb entry, which can be inserted into the V-slot in (R1).

Hence (R2) allows for the possibility that the topic position becomes available separately to wh-words, adverbs, etc., because each of these categories requires separate constraining equations, which may be acquired individually.

The German "split verb" position (i.e. stage x+2 or "PART") can be described as a gradual lexical acquisition process which is based on a number of alterations of the existing c-structure rule as shown in (R3). One alteration concerns the introduction of VP as a constituent, which is necessary to account for a range of phenomena in German, as we will see below. The other alteration is concerned with the position of the verb. VP rewrites alternatively into the structure known from R1, or as V-COMP, and the latter constituent rewrites as (NP_{obj1}) (NP_{obj2}) V. This ensures that V will only occur in second position unless licensed by a V that takes V-COMP.

$$(R3) \quad S \rightarrow \qquad NP_{subj} \quad VP$$
$$VP \rightarrow \qquad V \quad \begin{Bmatrix} (NP_{obj1}) \ (NP_{obj2}) \\ V\text{-COMP} \end{Bmatrix}$$
$$V\text{-COMP} \rightarrow (NP_{obj1}) \ (NP_{obj2}) \ V$$

Apart from this change in c-structure rules, I assume that the learner gradually re-analyses the verbs of his/her interlanguage, by analysing AUX and V as two separate entries and by adding the feature AUX to the lexical features of V.

To achieve the split verb effect, the newly created auxiliaries and modals are treated as main verbs (with the feature AUX that takes the value '+'), which

getrunken: V,	PRED = '*trinken* (SUBJ) (OBJ)'
	PARTICIPLE = PAST
	INF = *ge*
	OBJ CASE = accusative
	AUX = −
hat: V,	PRED = '*haben*, V-COMP (SUBJ)'
	TENSE = PAST
	AUX = +
	NUM = SG
	PERSON = 3RD
	V-COMP PARTICIPLE = PAST
	V-COMP INF =$_c$ *ge*

Figure 6. Lexical entries for the German verbs 'getrunken' and 'hat'

take VP complements (as in Kaplan & Bresnan 1982; Netter 1987). Let us take sentence (21) as an example:

(21) er *hat* ein Bier *getrunken*
    he has a   beer drunk
    'he has drunk/drank a beer'.

The simplified lexical entries for the verbs in (21) are as shown in Figure 6.

This set of entries and rules, etc., ensures two things which are of relevance here. (i) A particular (at this stage, not necessarily the correct) morphological form of the main verb is used with the auxiliary to express the intended grammatical function. This is achieved by functional well-formedness conditions which ensure that functional annotations match across related constituents. In this case it is the value PAST in (PARTICIPLE) = PAST and (V-Comp PARTICIPLE) = PAST which allows a unification of these two functions and thus legitimates these two constituents in this particular sentence.

(ii) The second point is that the c-structure rules, in conjunction with the unification processes mentioned under (i), ensure that the two verbs appear in a split position and that only the lexical verb can appear in the final position. Figure 6 illustrates why, according to the rule system developed above, only lexical verbs can occur in the final position: the PRED value for '*hat*' contains V-COMP and SUBJ, while that of '*getrunken*' contains SUBJ and OBJ. The SUBJ of '*getrunken*' needs to be unified with the SUBJ of '*hat*' since it is not directly linked to any argument. Because of these differences in the lexical entries of the verbs, and the way they interact with c-structure, '*hat*' cannot be inserted under that V that is dominated by V-COMP, i.e. '*hat*' in the final position is excluded.

In essence, this means that the positioning of verbs is controlled by the unification of the feature PARTICIPLE. This grammatical system can account for what seems to be an unsystematic behaviour on the part of the learner, who applies PART (= split verb) only in a certain percentage of all contexts. In other words, the rule is applied with some verbs but not with others. This phenomenon can be accounted for by the fact that some AUX-V combinations can continue to be analysed as one lexical entry while others are not. What determines this variational phenomenon, then, is whether the verbs in question have been analysed as single lexical entries and whether the feature AUX has been appended and annotated correctly.[16]

To account for German Subject-Verb INVERSION, c-structure has to be modified further. The modifications suggested here are adaptations from Kaplan and Bresnan's (1982) and Pinker's (1984) treatment of inversion in English, which assumes that there is an optional Verb to the left of S as illustrated below:

$$S' \rightarrow (V)\ S$$

Pinker adds the constraining equation $ROOT =_c +$ to the verb position in this rule to ensure that inversion only applies to matrix sentences (i.e. the feature ROOT is constrained to be + in matrix and as – in embedded clauses). This distinction is also relevant to the analysis of Standard German, where INVERSION is blocked in embedded clauses. Pinker (1984) further adds the constraining equation $SENT\ MOOD =_c INV$ to the verb position in order to be able to allow the rule to constrain INVERSION *lexically* in elements which can occur in topicalised position (cf. (R2) above). The resulting rule is given in (R4).

(R4) $S' \rightarrow (V)$ S
$$\left\{ \begin{array}{l} ROOT =_c + \\ SENT\ MOOD =_c Inv \end{array} \right\}$$

In essence, the same rule also operates in German. It is the interaction of (R2) and (R4) which creates the correct word order: a lexical entry for adverbs such as "*selten*" (seldom) or a lexical redundancy rule for wh-words and prepositional phrases etc. ensures that the filling of the focus position creates the information "sentence MOOD = inv". This information then feeds into the equation in (R4) which licences a verb in a position left of NP_{subj}. In other words, grammatical information is created through the processing of one constituent, and that information is being utilised during the processing of another constituent.

On the basis of the picture that has emerged so far, word order in subordinate clauses has been treated in exactly the same way as in matrix clauses. However, at stage x+5 the learner starts to distinguish between matrix and subordinate clauses. This is evidenced by the final positioning of verbs: $[X \; V_{INF=-} \; V_{INF=+} \;]_S$, where $INF = -$ refers to verbs not marked for person or number and $INF = +$ refers to verbs which are marked for those features. At the same time, INVERSION disappears (sometimes gradually) from subordinate clauses. To account for these facts, the feature ROOT has to be introduced, i.e. the distinction between matrix and subordinate clause. This has the effect that INVERSION would be ruled out in subordinate clauses, assuming that Pinker's constraining equation $ROOT = c +$ is appended to V in (R4).[17]

If one accepts this rough proposal for the treatment of German interlanguage word order, then the next point in my argument will be to show that the hierarchy of processing resources developed in Section 1 can be incorporated into this description and that the combination of the two elements accounts for the orders of acquisition discussed above.

My account of German word order development started with phase 2 of the acquisition process which is characterised by a strict SVO word order. Since grammatical functions are assigned at the level of c-structure, a strict canonical order does not involve any feature unification and therefore corresponds to level 2 of the hierarchy of processing resources developed in Section 1. In other words, the LFG account of this structure positions it correctly in the hierarchy of processability and its actual phase of acquisition.

German stage 3 syntax was accounted for by a modification of the stage 2 c-structure rule. This modified rule also does not involve any exchange of grammatical information. From a processing point of view, the difference between SVO and ADV is the following. While SVO is a completely linear structure with NPsubj in a predictable and invariable position, there is a degree of non-linearity in ADV where the sequence of constituents may deviate somewhat from a strictly canonical sequence. In the latter case, the canonical sequence starts after the topicalised phrase. To achieve this process the learner can utilise the general cognitive mechanism of saliency which allows the developing grammatical encoder to process a position that is external to the canonical sequence. However, in contrast to structures which are acquired later, in the structure ADV-SVO, grammatical functions can be read directly off c-structure and no cross-constituent unification is required.

For the German split-verb construction to occur, the PARTICIPLE value of the main verb and that of V-COMP in the auxiliary entry have to be unified. This exchange of information occurs across constituent boundaries and the matching of the PARTICIPLE value occurs in the VP procedure. Therefore PART requires processing resources which are located higher on the implicational hierarchy than SVO and ADV, i.e. level 4 of the processability hierarchy.

Subject-verb inversion (INV), then, involves a process that depends on the unification of the feature SENT MOOD across XP and V in the S-procedure. Since the S-procedure is hypothesised to become available at level 5 in the processability hierarchy, INV is positioned at that level.

The German structure V-Final is one of the features distinguishing embedded from matrix clauses in the target language. In the above LFG description this structure is accounted for by the introduction of the feature ROOT into the IL grammar and a separate c-structure for embedded sentences. This description accounts for the fact that in the processability hierarchy, features of embedded clauses which distinguish those from matrix clauses are acquired after word order constraints in the matrix clause have been acquired. In other words, the above account of V-Final is in line with the processability hierarchy which predicts that V-Final occurs at level 6.

In summary, I characterised the sequence in the acquisition of German L2 word order in terms of unification of lexical features in a modified LFG framework. I showed that the unification processes involved follow the sequence predicted by Processability Theory. Hence the theory accounts for the observed sequence.

4.   Comparing L1 and L2 acquisition

A number of rationalist approaches to SLA have in common that they assume *fundamental differences* in first and second language acquisition (Felix 1984; Clahsen 1990; Meisel 1991; cf. also Bley-Vroman 1990). They assume that L1 learners have access to UG and L2 learners[18] do not. To account for L2 acquisition, these authors therefore make recourse to a processing-oriented alternative to UG. This position has become known as the Fundamental Difference Hypothesis (Bley-Vroman 1990). Clahsen and Meisel are the scholars who have produced the most explicit accounts of explanations of L2 acquisition which are conceived as learning and processing strategies. Clahsen and Muysken (1986) view the relationship of explanandum and explanans roughly as in Figure 7.

Figure 7. Clahsen and Muysken's view of the relationship between explanandum and explanans

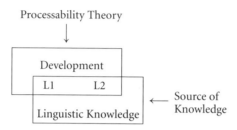

Figure 8. Author's view of the relationship between explanandum and explanans

In this section I will argue for a different relationship. In particular I will argue that the notions of universal grammar and language processing do not form a dichotomy in the context of explaining differences between L1 and L2 acquisition. In Section 1, I made the case that the fundamental principles of language processing apply to native and non-native language use. I therefore argue that the architecture of human language processing will have a bearing on any type of language acquisition. In fact, the two explanatory devices, UG and strategies, are on quite a different scale and address different aspects of the acquisition process.

UG has been productive mostly as a property theory, addressing the issue of the origin of linguistic knowledge (i.e. the 'logical problem') and has been far less successful in accounting for the 'developmental problem' (cf. Section 1) for which a transition theory is needed. I made the point above that Processability Theory is designed exclusively to address the developmental problem, and I will show that it accounts for development, not only in the L2 context but also for L1 and that it can interact with other theory modules which do address the logical problem. I therefore view the relationship of explanandum and explanans roughly as in Figure 8 where the processability components address the developmental problem while linguistic knowledge is created by a source that I leave unspecified for the time being. Some researchers would see UG in its place. This view allows the Fundamental Difference Hypothesis to be maintained without attributing the L1-L2 differences to a processing factor that applies equally to both types of acquisition.

Before I apply Processability Theory to L1 acquisition, let us first have a brief look at an account of the key descriptive facts relating to L1 acquisition. Long (1988, 1990) presents extensive evidence in support of the view that there are marked differences between L1 and L2 acquisition in *ultimate attainment*. He demonstrates that the age of onset "... is a robust predictor of their [the L2 learners', MP] long-term success ..." (Long 1988: 197). Remarkable differences between L1 and L2 acquisition also exist in the developmental schedule. In his 1982 study, Clahsen found the following developmental pattern in the acquisition of German as a first language:

> L1 sequence
> (1) variable word order
> (2) SOV
> (3) V-2nd and SV-agreement marking
> (4) subordinate clauses (without any mistakes in the positioning of the verb).

Quite clearly, this developmental pattern differs markedly from the one observed in the acquisition of German as a second language which was discussed in the previous section.

It is important to note that the differences between L1 and L2 go beyond that of the developmental path to include the following phenomena:

− The virtually error-free learning of the position of the verb in subordinate clauses. Clahsen observed that as soon as the child uses complementisers, the position of verbal elements in subordinate clauses is completely in line with the structure of the adult language.
− The interlocking of different rules in the acquisitional process. Clahsen found that in German child language development SV-agreement is acquired exactly at the same point in time as the V-2nd position. This is not the case in the acquisition of German as L2. The two rules were not found to closely interlock. I found the same in a longitudinal study of the acquisition of child GSL (Pienemann 1981).

The issue is how to explain these differences. In Clahsen and Muysken's (1986) view, all of these differences are due to the fact that children have access to universal grammar while adults do not. Instead, adults use inductive learning strategies, which enable them to reconstruct the canonical sentence schema of the target language. This implies that L1 learners are able to discover the underlying word order for German, whereas L2 learners simply infer the canonical sentence schema of German which reflects a syntactic feature of the surface structure of the target language.

Clahsen (1984) and Clahsen and Muysken (1986) account for the developmental path of L2 acquisition using a set of processing strategies. The latter have been subject to serious criticism of which I will mention only three key issues. White (1989) points out that Bever's (1970) strategies were designed for language comprehension. However, Clahsen applied these to production data. White further demonstrates that the assumed strategies do not contain any information or mechanisms that allow for their further development. This is known as the property of extensibility that a theory of learnability must entail (Pinker 1984). In addition, Clahsen's strategies were conceptualised as processing constraints on transformations as described in 'transformational grammar'. However, it is now accepted that transformations are psychologically implausible concepts (Altmann 1990; Horrocks 1987; Levelt 1989; cf. also Ingram 1971). As a result of this, it is illogical to assume that processing constraints can operate on linguistic structures which have no psychological plausibility. In short, the processing explanation invoked for L2 acquisition by Clahsen in support of the Fundamental Difference Hypothesis is not viable. In the previous section I demonstrated that it can be replaced by Processability Theory in the L2 context.

Clahsen and Muysken (1986) argue that the interlocking of different rules in the acquisitional process can be attributed to the setting of the INFL parameter, which is responsible for the distinction of finite and non-finite verbal elements, the crucial distinction that is the prerequisite for both rules. They further claim that the grammatical systems produced by L2 learners are not possible grammars, and in particular that the rules necessary to derive the above L2 patterns from an underlying SVO order are not possible in terms of UG. This claim has inspired du Plessis, Solin, Travis and White (1987) and Schwartz (1988) to propose a re-analysis of the above L2 sequences which is indeed based on an underlying SVO order.

However, Meisel (1991:237) points out that "... [d]u Plessis et al. (1987), in order to be able to write a grammar for L2 learners compatible with UG, have to postulate the existence of two more parameters ...". He notes that Schwartz's analysis implies a similar requirement and that in addition, both proposals rely on a poorly defined process of restructuring. Meisel quotes Chomsky (1981) in showing that the *ad-hoc* nature of these proposals runs counter to the fundamental nature of parameters to form clusters of a number of seemingly unrelated grammatical phenomena. In view of these shortcomings he concludes that the above counter-proposals remain unconvincing.

Let us recoup. Clahsen and Muysken (1986) and Meisel (1991) present evidence in favour of access to UG for L1 acquisition and evidence of limited access for L2 acquisition. I have shown that the developmental problem in SLA can be explained by processability. It is therefore quite logical to ask if Processability Theory also accounts for the developmental problem in L1 acquisition.

To test this hypothesis it has to be demonstrated that the above L1 sequence is positioned within the constraints of hypothesis space. Formally, this is achieved by showing that the L1 sequence is predictable by the hierarchy of processing resources on which Processability Theory is based.

Similarly to SVO structures in L2 acquisition, the initial word order hypothesis in L1 acquisition (i.e. SOV – after variable word order) can be accounted for simply by a c-structure rule along the lines of (R5). Since grammatical functions can be read off c-structure canonical orders and do not involve any transfer of grammatical information, the SOV order is positioned at the lowest level in the processability hierarchy.

$$(R5) \quad S \rightarrow \quad NP_{subj} \ VP$$
$$VP \rightarrow (NP_{obj1}) \ (NP_{obj2}) \ V \ (V)$$

$$(R6) \quad S'' \rightarrow (XP) \hspace{4cm} S'$$
$$\left\{ \begin{array}{l} wh =_c + \\ adv =_c + \\ N =_c + \\ SENT \ MOOD = Inv \end{array} \right\}$$

$$(R7) \quad S' \rightarrow (V) \hspace{4cm} S$$
$$\left\{ \begin{array}{l} ROOT =_c + \\ SENT \ MOOD =_c Inv \end{array} \right\}$$

The Verb-2nd phenomenon can be produced by (R6) and (R7) in a way similar to German and English INVERSION. Note that the constraint equation ROOT $=_c$ + is not appended to V at this stage. For the V-2nd position to be produced, the grammatical information SENT MOOD has to be exchanged by two constituents (XP and V). This places V-2nd at the same level in the processability hierarchy as INVERSION (in the L2 sequence) and SV-agreement.

One reviewer commented that one might conclude from this that Processability Theory entails the prediction that the above structures are acquired simultaneously. However, it would be incorrect to derive such a prediction from the theory, since it does not predict that whatever can be processed will indeed be acquired. Instead, the theory predicts that what cannot be processed will not be acquired. In other words, processability acts as a constraint on development and therefore does not entail the prediction that the above structures are acquired simultaneously.[19]

The sentence-final position of the verb in subordinate clauses can be accounted for by appending the constraint equation $ROOT =_c +$ to V in (R-c). Since the feature $\pm ROOT$ emerges at level 6 of the processability hierarchy, the final stage of the L1 sequence is also in line with Processability Theory.

In other words, SOV, V2nd and V-Final (as well as SV-agreement) do indeed fall within the constraints of hypothesis space and the L1 sequence is explained by the same hierarchy of processability as the L2 sequence. I hasten to add that this does not imply that the two processes are one and the same thing. To start with, the routes of acquisition are different. The reader will notice that the rule SEP is absent from the L1 sequence. To explain why this is structurally possible one has to consider the effect of the rules R5-R7: starting (developmentally) with an SOV c-structure, these three rules have the same effect as the combined application of PART and INVERSION on the basis of an SVO c-structure. Since in (R5) the verb is in the final position, and (R6) jointly with (R7) permit the finite verb to appear in second position, the "split verb" position is also permitted.

The rule ADV is also absent from the L1 sequence. This means that L1 learners do not produce the ungrammatical structure X S V Y which is typical of L2 learners. The processability hierarchy allows for ADV to emerge at level 3. However, it does not predict that it will necessarily develop.

Table 6 gives an overview of this comparison of grammatical development in the acquisition of German as a second and as a first language which shows at a glance that both developmental paths fall within the confines of Hypothesis Space. In other words, there are no differences in the temporal order in which processing resources are activated. All grammars are processable at the time they develop, and each grammar builds upon the processing resources acquired at the previous stages in a cumulative fashion. However, the L1 learner achieves this in two key 'moves', SOV and V2nd (with SV agreement) while the L2 learner takes five 'moves' most of which introduce ungrammatical structures which have to be modified in later moves.

We now find ourselves in a situation where strikingly different developmental routes in L1 and L2 acquisition have been accounted for within one and the same hierarchy of processing resources. Therefore the formula "UG for L1 and processing factors for L2" no longer holds. And one has to ask one-

Table 6. Comparing development in L1 and L2

stage	exchange of information	resources	GSL	German L1
6	within subordinate clause	+/– ROOT	V-End	V-End (no errors)
5	inter-phrasal	S-Procedure	INV	V2nd
			±agr	+agr
4	phrasal	VP-Procedure	PART	–
3	none	lexical categories	ADV	–
				b SOV
2	none	lex. categories	SVO	a variable word order
1	none	lexical entries	words	words

self what causes the apparent differences between L1 and L2 that exist despite the common basis in language processing.

5.   Developmental dynamics and generative entrenchment

My basic thesis is that different outcomes and developmental paths in language development are, at least partly, due to different developmental dynamics, caused by differences in the initial hypotheses and that the process of development can be fundamentally similar, with respect to language processing, despite fundamentally different outcomes and different developmental paths.

The basic mechanism behind developmental dynamics is the principle that developmentally early decisions bias the further development of the interlanguage system. This percolation of structural properties in developmental processes is known in biology and philosophy and has been termed "*generative entrenchment*" by Wimsatt (1986, 1991).

The concept of generative entrenchment is exemplified, for instance, by the embryonic development of animals where sections of the fertilised egg take on more and more specialised structures (e.g. Gehring 1985; Coen & Carpenter 1992; Wolpert 1992). The segmentation of the body plan occurs very early in these processes for all animals. In other words, the position of head, limbs, etc. is determined very early. These structural features are maintained throughout the developmental process, and they do not have to be decided on every time a refinement of parts of the structure is made. One can say that these features are "developmentally entrenched."

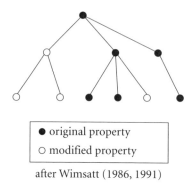

after Wimsatt (1986, 1991)

Figure 9. Generative entrenchment illustrated

We also know that incorrect information on the positioning of segments can have serious consequences for the ultimate shape of the organism (Gehring 1985; Coen & Carpenter 1992; Wolpert 1992). This sometimes unfortunate phenomenon illustrates the concept of the *depth* of generative entrenchment. The earlier a decision is made in structural development, the more far-reaching the consequences for the ultimate stage in structural development.

Figure 9 illustrates how development can be understood as a generative process where structures increase in complexity, starting with a minimal number of structural properties to which other properties are added throughout development. Figure 9 displays structural options that exist in the development of structure as a tree diagram where each node represents a point at which more specialised structures can develop. The top node contains the initial structural information. The tree allows for different developmental paths. However, once a decision has been made and a new structure has been added, it is very costly, if not impossible, for the developmental process to move to a different developmental path. In effect, changing the developmental path would mean that all developmental steps up to the node that gives access to the alternative path would have to be cancelled. As a result, a great deal of structural information would be lost in such a move. Many physical processes of development are indeed irreversible, as the example of developmentally misformed organisms shows.

The key explanatory point that can be derived from the concept of generative entrenchment for language acquisition is that a massive computational saving can be made if structural decisions do not have to be revised in the developmental process every time a structural change occurs. In this model initial structural features propagate in the developing system and thus determine the ultimate structure without being invoked again and again. The basic 'body plan' stays the same. In other words, a computational saving is made by laying structures down and keeping them. The alternative would be a developing system in which all processes of structural refinement have to be orchestrated globally for every developmental step, and this would require far more computational resources than the preservation of structures once they have developed.

The aspect of computational saving inherent in generative entrenchment is captured by Wimsatt (1986, 1991) in his "developmental lock" metaphor which is based on Herbert Simon's (1962) classic paper, "The Architecture of Complexity" where he demonstrates that solutions of complex problems can be found more effectively by using the heuristic of factorising sub-problems which are solved independently, and the solutions to sub-problems are strung together to produce the solution to the overall problem.

Wimsatt's developmental lock is an idealised set of complex problems. The lock consists of ten wheels with ten positions each, very much like an extended version of a combination lock. Obviously, the total number of possible combinations on this lock is 10^{10}, which, according to Wimsatt, requires 10^9 trials to find the correct combination. In this form of unconstrained hypothesis testing, the lock is referred to as a "complex lock". In the developmental lock, Wimsatt constrains hypothesis testing by allowing the problem solver to factorise the combination problem. Rather than having to get all ten digits right before the combination can be subjected to an empirical test, each wheel can be tested individually in a left-right sequence. This additional ability to test the wheels individually from left to right mimics the cumulative nature of developmental processes: old solutions can be kept.

The computational advantage of factorising the complex problem is remarkable. Only fifty trials are necessary to find the solution to the developmental lock problem, providing a strict left-right sequence is followed. In other words, in this metaphor later decisions depend on earlier decisions. If an error is made earlier it will be very costly to recover from it, because all intervening solutions will be lost.

Summing up, the assumption that underlies the notion of generative entrenchment is that, in the course of development, structures are preserved and further refined. The dynamics of this process have a constraining effect on development: because of the preservation constraint, early decisions exclude whole branches on the "developmental tree".[20] In other words, generative entrenchment can be understood as a constraint on development that derives from the dynamics of development itself. In this way it complements the notion of processability which also acts as a constraint on language development.

Hence, the concept of generative entrenchment is a general logical-mathematical set of constraints that applies to any continuous developmental process in which structures diversify developmentally. It has been applied to many cases of biological development in ontogenesis and phylogenesis as well as population development. It is also applicable to the development of physical phenomena. Since language acquisition is another case in which structure diversifies developmentally from an initial state, the dynamics of generative entrenchment apply. An anonymous reviewer objected that language acquisition is different from cases of biological and physical development, because the role of input and environment is different in the case of language development. However, this objection missed the point. Generative entrenchment models nothing but the dynamics of cumulative developmental processes, no matter where they occur. All of the non-language cases of development are also placed in an environment, be it the distribution of matter in space or the location of a body segment of the fruit fly embryo in an acidic environment. Generative entrenchment should be seen on the same scale as the logical problem where one looks at the logic of developmental dynamics.

The continuity assumption that underlies the notion of Generative Entrenchment can be verified in the two developmental paths under discussion. Table 7 reveals a great deal of continuity in both developmental paths. The initial word order hypothesis of the L2 learner is maintained and refined in four developmental steps until it is finally modified to reflect the structure of the TL. It is evident from distributional analyses of large bodies of data (cf. Clahsen, Meisel & Pienemann 1983) that the SVO pattern continues to be produced in tandem with INVERSION and V-End. Looking at the L1 perspective, a similar picture emerges: the initial SOV pattern is maintained and refined throughout the developmental process.

In other words, pattern conservation is evident in the two developmental paths, and this gives a first indication of the initial hypothesis being a determining factor for the later course of development. However, there is also direct evidence of this. The need for the separate rule PART arises only if the initial syntactic hypothesis is SVO. In order to modify the initial SVO order to match German main clause patterns, two developmental 'moves' are needed: one that ensures that V_i is in final position and one that constrains V_f into second position. INV on its own would not be the solution. If INV were applied without PART, ungrammatical structures like $X\ V_f\ S\ V_i\ Y$ would result.[21] In

Table 7. Generative entrenchment of linguistic structures

	L2	L1
subordinate clause	comp SOV [comp *S V O*]	comp *SOV*
use of S-procedure for storage across constituents in S	X Vf S O Vi ±agr [(X) *S V O*]	X Vf *S O* Vi +agr
use of VP-procedure for storage across constituents in VP	X *S* Vf*O* Vi	—
use of saliency principle to relax canonical order constraint	X *S V O*	—
word order con-strained into canonical order	*S V O*	*S O V*

other words, both PART and INV are necessitated by the initial SVO word order and the initial SVO hypothesis is propagated in the development of these rules.

Based on an SOV order, V2nd produces the same effect as PART and INV combined, namely the correct target structure $X V_f S Y V_i$. This means that the development from SOV to V2nd renders the acquisition of PART and the two developmental steps PART and INV superfluous.

A further developmental saving is made in the acquisition of the verb final position in subordinate clauses. In L1 acquisition, where the initial fixed word order is SOV, the position of the verb does not have to change, when the distinction between main and subordinate clauses is acquired. All that has to happen is that V2 is blocked in subordinate clauses. This allows verb-final positions to be acquired with less effort than in the L2 sequence where every complementiser has to be marked for the feature ±ROOT until a lexical redundancy rule is formed for subordinate clauses. And yet again this developmental twist is brought about by the moves that followed from the initial structural hypothesis. This explains why in L1 acquisition the verb-final position is acquired virtually without errors while in L2 acquisition the development of the rule can be traced along the path of an increasing set of complementisers with the effect of an error-ridden acquisition process.

In summary, the initial hypothesis for word order in L1 acquisition renders the acquisition of PART and V-End as separate c-structure rules superfluous and results in a grammatically more correct output during development. Hence, the L1 initial hypothesis is far more economical, and so is the development that follows from it.

One might, of course hypothesise that L2 learners fundamentally restructure the developing grammar and switch to the assumption that German is an SOV language (e.g. Tomaselli & Schwartz 1990). However, it is hard to see, in the absence of negative evidence, on the basis of which structural evidence the learner would arrive at such a conclusion, since the SVO structures they produce form a subset of the input data. But even if the learner were able to arrive at such a conclusion by some yet unknown means, a total restructuring of the interlanguage would be computationally very costly since all rules developed until the restructuring would have to be abandoned to start a new developmental path. Neither SVO, nor PART nor INV are compatible with the SOV assumption. In this way, the developmental path known in L1 acquisition becomes inaccessible once the initial syntactic hypothesis has been formed, and the development that follows is determined by the initial hypothesis, because the structure of the target language can be mapped only by the set of rules ADV, PART, INV and V-END, and these rules emerge in this sequence because of their processability.

From the above discussion, we can summarise the following points:

–   There are two distinct developmental paths;
–   Each of them falls within Hypothesis Space;
–   One of the paths is superior to the other;
–   Each is determined by the initial hypothesis.

One can conclude from this that one of the main reasons for L1-L2 differences is the superior initial hypothesis of the L1 learner which propagates through the entire developmental process. This raises the obvious question as to what it is that causes the initial hypothesis. However, this question goes well beyond the developmental problem which I set out to address with Processability Theory. The source of the initial hypothesis is an epistemological issue which requires not a transition theory (such as Processability Theory) but a property theory (cf. Gregg 1996).

6.   Variation and processing constraints

Perhaps the strongest doubts about the universality of grammatical development have been expressed by scholars who study L2 variation and by language testers. For instance, Bachman (1988) voices the following concern about acquisition-based profiling procedures: "… to what extent is the procedure sensitive to individual variations that may result from different elicitation contexts, and to what extent will this affect the determination of the developmental stage?" (Bachman 1988:204). Similarly Douglas (1986) is concerned about "… the problem of characterising a learner's competence when it would appear that 'competence' varies with task." (Douglas 1986:158)

Indeed, there is ample evidence that the shape of an interlanguage varies within one and the same learner on one and the same day depending on which linguistic task the learner performs in which context (e.g. Tarone 1983; Crookes 1989; Crookes & Gass 1993; Selinker & Douglas 1985). For instance, Tarone (1989) observed that the frequency of producing /r/ may vary between 50% and almost 100% where the latter occurs in the reading of word lists and the first in 'free speech.'

However, the issue at stake is not whether interlanguages are constant across tasks, but if the developmental stage is constant across tasks. Obviously, if the stage can change from situation to situation, the concept of universal routes of development becomes vacuous.

The question of the stability of stages is one that can be answered empirically. In Pienemann (1998) I put forward the 'steadiness hypothesis' which predicts that the basic nature of the grammatical system of an IL does not change in different communicative tasks as long as these are based on the same skill type in language production (such as 'free conversation'). In Pienemann (1998) I tested the steadiness hypothesis in a sample containing six ESL learners, each of whom carried out six different communicative tasks. The IL profiles of all learners were found to be *perfectly consistent* across all tasks in the area of syntax according to the emergence criterion. For the area of morphology, a total of three out of 324 possible cases of 'under-production' and not a single case of 'over-production' were found. This amounts to a 99.1% fit of the data in this area. In other words, these data constitute strong support for the steadiness hypothesis.

I further demonstrated that fluctuations in correctness levels across tasks do not reflect different levels of acquisition (Pienemann 1998) and that they are instead brought about by the specific lexical needs of individual tasks and the status of morphological marking in different entries to the learner's lexicon. In all these analyses it is essential to compare learner behaviour with measures that are well-defined, theoretically motivated and that are applied consistently across different corpora. For all measurements of learner behaviour my above study provided quantified distributional analyses for each individual speaker.

I further used the emergence criterion because of its suitability as a measure of the in-principle acquisition of processing skills. In addition, implicational scaling was used for determining developmental stages.

It should be added that within Processability Theory interlanguage variation is not merely defined as fluctuations in correctness levels. Instead it is defined in an *a priori* manner by the learner's current level of processing. In other words, it is defined as a specific range of structural options that are available to the learner. This range of structural options results from the fact that the learner's limited processing resources constrain the way in which he or she can avoid structures which have not yet been acquired. An example is the acquisition of English inversion. As noted above, this rule is acquired at stage 4 in the ESL hierarchy. This rule describes the observational fact that auxiliaries are placed in second position in English Wh-questions as in the following example:

(22)   Where is he going?

Variability occurs in Wh-questions before this rule is acquired. At the prior stage some learners leave out one or more constituents, e.g.

(23)   Where he going?

(24)   Where is going?

Other learners produce Wh-questions using canonical word order:

(25)   Where he is going?

The range of possible solutions to the formation of wh-questions simply derives from the state of the learner's grammar before stage 4. The ESL processability hierarchy specifies the following for stage 4:

$$S'' \rightarrow (XP) \qquad\qquad S'$$
$$\left\{ \begin{array}{l} \text{wh} =_c + \\ \text{adv} =_c \text{'seldom, rarely ...'} \\ \text{SENT MOOD} = \text{INV} \end{array} \right\}$$

$$S' \rightarrow (V) \qquad\qquad S$$
$$\left\{ \begin{array}{l} \text{aux} =_c + \\ \text{ROOT} =_c + \\ \text{SENT MOOD} =_c \text{INV} \end{array} \right\}$$

In other words, the information "SENT MOOD = INV" has to be exchanged between XP and V to achieve the desired position of the auxiliary in second position. However, before stage 4 the interlanguage processor cannot carry out this operation and, quite logically, the learner has only a limited number of options to resolve this problem: (i) Leaving out one of the constituents involved in the exchange of grammatical information. This ensures that the impossible information exchange becomes obsolete. (ii) Applying a canonical sentence schema to the sentence (S → wh NP$_{subj}$ V X). This too makes the crucial exchange of information obsolete. (iii) Avoiding the context for this structure (i.e. no wh-questions). This also avoids the impossible operation. However, these are all the options that are available. There is no alternative way to exchange the crucial grammatical information and thus to produce inversion anyway (except in rote memorised chunks). In other words, the full range of solutions to the developmental problem is dictated by the learner's current state of the production grammar.

This brief summary of the treatment of variation within the processability approach highlights a key feature of that approach, namely the fact that it provides a coherent formal framework for the treatment of the dynamics of second language development. On the one hand it makes testable predictions about stages of development across languages by defining those classes of grammars that are processable at each stage. On the other hand, processability leaves a certain amount of leeway which allows the learner to develop a range of solutions to developmental problems. However, this range is strictly constrained.

Mentioning testable predictions triggers the question as to how Processability Theory can be falsified. The simple answer is: "when it makes incorrect predictions". To be more specific, predictions on processability involve implicational hierarchies such as (i) before (ii) before (iii). If such a prediction is made and it can be demonstrated in a corpus with sufficient data on (i), (ii) and (iii) that (iii) is acquired before, say (ii), then the prediction is falsified.

7. Ultimate attainment and stabilisation

In Section 4 above I compared L1 and L2 developmental trajectories and demonstrated that the different developmental paths found in these different contexts for language acquisition can be accommodated within the overall constraints of human language processing as specified in PT and that the different trajectories are due to different initial states. This nevertheless leaves a number of questions unanswered, including the following: Why do some L2-learners appear not to progress in development?

To address this question, one needs to consider the notion "learner variation" as defined within PT. A summary discussion of this notion is given in

Section 4. The reader will recall that for each level of processing PT defines a specific limited range of structural options that are available to the learner. These limited options give rise to learner variation. In Pienemann (1998) I discuss the inter-relation between different structural domains in L2 development and demonstrate that for every grammatical rule there are structural prerequisites. I further show that there is a window of time during which the rule can develop. Many L2 structures serve as the context for other L2 structures, and different types of solutions to developmental problems arise from a varying utilisation of the time window in structural development which leads to different types of learner language characterised by different sets of variational features.

This interdependence goes further than the relationship of structural environment and rule. This is exemplified particularly well in the observation that learners who produce English equational sentences without inserting the copula ("*me good*") are deprived of the context for the most easily processable form of INV which occurs in direct equational questions ("*Where is he?*"). Given that affirmative equational sentences develop before questions in equational sentences, the learner's 'decision' to develop equational sentences without the copula biases the acquisition of the second rule.

This situation is depicted in Figure 10. When the learner develops equational sentences s/he has to 'decide' whether they contain a copula or not. Learners who put their bet on the copula-free structure, lose out in discovering a prototypical form of English inversion when question formation is developed. In other words, their structural choice was inferior, though easier to achieve and impedes further development.

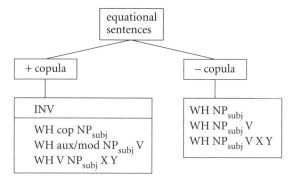

Figure 10. Equational sentences and inversion in English: A case of generative entrenchment

The earlier decision then has repercussions for the acquisition of question formation, and a developmentally early decision biases the further development of the interlanguage system. In other words, variational features can get developmentally entrenched in the interlanguage.

What we see here is a repetition of the L1-L2 differences on a smaller scale, based on the same developmental dynamics. When a structural choice has to be made (within the confines of the hypothesis space defined by PT) the different options each have their own structural repercussions which vary in quality when measured against their potential for further development. The copula example demonstrates that the wrong choice can lead to a developmental dead-end.

When a learner accumulates many inferior choices, each of which becomes generatively entrenched, one can predict that further development is structurally impeded. This phenomenon of lack of progress despite exposure is well-attested in many of the large empirical studies of SLA (e.g. Clahsen, Meisel & Pienemann 1983). Some scholars refer to this phenomenon as 'fossilisation' (Selinker 1972). In his lucid review of research on fossilisation, Mike Long (2003) points out that one needs to distinguish clearly between non-native ultimate attainment, stabilisation and fossilisation and that each of these notions in turn require empirically testable definitions. He adds that classifying these phenomena needs to be clearly differentiated from developing explanatory approaches. In fact, Long shows that most studies on fossilisation do not meet these requirements for a variety of reasons. He is certainly right in pointing out that fossilisation (defined as the terminal but non-native level of acquisition) can only be studied on the basis of longitudinal data covering long periods of time. If stabilisation is defined as the temporary stagnation of L2 development, it is somewhat easier to test empirically.

In this section I do not want to enter into the fossilisation debate. Instead, I will confine my analysis to a contribution to explaining one cause of variation in L2 ultimate attainment that is inherent in the very dynamics of the developmental process. Based on the L2 developmental dynamics described above, I hypothesise that L2 development may be impeded when a learner accumulates inferior choices for developmental problems. This hypothesis can be tested by specifying the two notions (i) 'inferior choices' and (ii) 'developmental problem'. The latter term is defined above. At this point I define 'inferior choice' as the omission option described in Section 6.

The 'bad-choice hypothesis' can be tested empirically in a major SLA study (Clahsen, Meisel & Pienemann 1983). This study is based on one-hour interviews with 45 adult learners of German as a second language. In a distributional analysis of this corpus the six word order stages were found through implicational scaling. In addition, 14 variational features were identified which included the omission of obligatory constituents such as the subject pronoun, lexical verbs, modals, auxiliaries, prepositions and determiners. These variational features are also distributed implicationally. This means that a learner with the most highly simplifying feature also displays all other variational features. In this way, the population of the study fell into four groups of learners, measured according to the variational features contained in their interlanguage. These four groups can roughly be described as ranging from highly simplifying (group 3) to highly norm-oriented (group 1a).

When one considers the group of learners below the stage SEP, one finds that about half of these learners were recent arrivals. Their low level of acquisition can be attributed to limited exposure. However, the other half had between seven and fifteen years of exposure. One has to bear in mind that the level of acquisition attained by these learners corresponds to level 3 (ADV) at the very most. After seven to fifteen years of exposure one may conclude with certainty that L2 development has been greatly impeded in these learners. My point is not that this is the learners' ultimate level of development. To make such a statement one would have to analyse longitudinal data.

However, this data set does permit one to test my hypothesis that cumulative inferior choices correlate with low levels of acquisition after long periods of exposure. If my hypothesis is correct and the protracted development in these learners is caused by the developmental dynamics, one would have to find that these learners all produce highly simplifying and thus inferior varieties of the IL. Table 8 gives an overview of this group of informants.

Table 8 does confirm the 'bad-choice hypothesis': all learners below level SEP and with seven or more years of exposure belong to the highly simplifying group 3 in learner variation. The only exception is Montse S who is the most simplifying learner of group 2; i.e. at the transition to group 3. All other learners are distributed across variation groups 1 to 3 with a proportion of group membership that is similar to that of the whole population of 45 informants. In other words, one does indeed find that all learners who do not progress far along the developmental axis after a long period of exposure develop a highly simplifying variety of the L2, while beginning learners develop a wide range of learner varieties, including non-simplifying ones.

As in the case of L1-L2 differences, the 'bad-choice hypothesis' identifies the developmental dynamics as one cause for the lack of progress in particular L2 learners. However, it does not offer an answer to the question as to why

Table 8. Informants from the ZISA study (Clahsen, Meisel & Pienemann 1983) below level SEP

Name	years in G	type of variation	male/female
Dolores S	15	3	F
Zita P	1	3	F
Manuel P	1	3	M
Montse S	14	2+	F
Pascua S	7	3	F
Miguel S	1	1b	M
Estefania P	3	2	F
Eliseo I	12	3	M
Maria P	5	3	F
Pepita S	14	3	F
Rosemarie S	1	2	F
Antonio S	11	3	M
Francisco S	2	3	M
Pasquale I	7	3	F
Rosa I	7	3	F

the inferior option was chosen in the first place. Again, this epistemological question is deliberately not addressed here.

One can take the 'bad-choice hypothesis' one step further and apply it to L2 acquisition generally. This would mean that the more 'inferior choices' a learner makes, the more the progress of further development is affected by the fact that those structural choices are generatively entrenched. This hypothesis serves to explain why there is variation in ultimate attainment in L2 acquisition.

Notes

* Parts of this chapter are based on an extended and revised version of my paper (1998) "Developmental dynamics in L1 and L2 acquisition: Processability Theory and generative entrenchment." in *Bilingualism: Language and Cognition* 1: 1–20. I would like to thank Avery Andrews, Bruno Di Biase, Gisela Håkansson, Jürgen Meisel, Bonnie Schwartz and four anonymous reviewers for their invaluable input into this chapter. All remaining errors are mine. I gratefully acknowledge the financial assistance from the Australian Research Council and the University of Paderborn which I received for the research presented in this paper.

1. The term "target language" is used here to cover L1 and L2.

2. It has been noted that the potential components of a theory of learnability interact: the stronger the first, the weaker the second and vice versa or, in the words of Bates, MacWhinney, and Smith (1982:15):

...as Pinker (1979) and Braine (1978) both noted, the Wexler and Culicover conclusion is not the only one that can be reached with learnability analysis. The strength of their (W & C's) fourth parameter (i.e. innate hypotheses) is required only because of the value they have assigned to the other three.

3. Kempen and Hoenkamp conceptualise the matching of diacritic features as a process of 'feature-copying' where features have a source and a destination. Vigliocco, Butterworth and Garrett (1996) demonstrate in cross-linguistic experiments on subject-verb agreement in Spanish and English that it is psychologically more plausible to view the matching of diacritic features as a process of 'feature-merging' (or unification) in which both constituents involved in the matching process can derive features independently from conceptual structure. They show that the advantage of the merging process is that it can account for null-subject languages such as Spanish and for certain distributivity effects of conceptual structure on agreement phenomena. Vigliocco, Butterworth, and Garrett (1996) therefore assume a version of Incremental Procedural Grammar in which the feature copying mechanisms are replaced by feature merging mechanisms. In Lexical Functional Grammar this feature merging process is managed through the 'unification' of features found in lexical entries. Vigliocco, Butterworth and Garrett's modification is psychologically more plausible and creates a tighter fit with LFG.

4. Appointment rules which were mentioned in the text above are not productive for the phenomena discussed in this paper. They do therefore not appear in this hierarchy.

5. Note that the sequence of generation of the preverbal message in the conceptualiser does not have to coincide with the constraints on word order.

6. A proviso on this is that the procedures that underlie LFG cannot be understood to represent psychological procedures themselves. Instead, they can be considered a short-hand notation which contains the necessary elements to relate structures to a hierarchy of processability. The LFG formalism is designed to be highly noncommittal as to when unifications are performed. They can be done incrementally, as each phrase is built, or at the end, when an entire c-structure has been constructed. (See Maxwell & Kaplan 1995 for some discussion). Since Processability Theory assumes strict limits on grammatical memory, it would follow that unifications ought to be done as soon as possible.

7. In my use of a modified and somewhat simplified LFG formalism I will focus on the implementation of the processability hierarchy in morphology and word order. I do not claim that all other formal aspects of LFG are related in a similar way to the processes modelled in IPG. In particular, psychological plausibility is, at present, attibuted only to the unification of lexical features, not unification generally. It may well be that other adjustments will have to be made to the formalism at a later stage.

8. Example sentences (3)–(10) have been taken from Johnston's (1985) ESL corpus.

9. The emergence criterion identifies the point of first emergence of a structure in an interlanguage system. The criterion was developed by Meisel, Clahsen and Pienemann (1981) in contrast to more ambiguous accuracy-based criteria. Pienemann (1998) adapted this criterion and the related analytical approach to morphological interlanguage development.

10. The 14 structures that are considered in this paper can be classified as follows:

obligatory	optional
Plural-s (with det)	possessive pronoun
Subject-verb agreement	Neg+V
	one word utterances
canonical word order	adverb fronting
Do-fronting	topicalisation
Wh-fronting	
Yes/no inversion	
PS inversion	
Do/Aux 2nd	
Cancel inversion.	

11. One constituent utterances do not form part of the implicational relationship in the same way as the other interlanguage rules do since all other rules *accumulate* in the course of the acquisition process, while this basic pattern will be replaced by other rules.

12. This study was carried out at the Language Acquisition Research Centre at the University of Sydney under the direction of Manfred Pienemann and was funded by a grant from the National Languages and Literacy Institute of Australia to Manfred Pienemann.

13. Here I refer to plural marking on nouns only. At the next level I refer to plural agreement.

14. ZISA stands for 'Zweitspracherwerb Italienischer und Spanischer Arbeiter' (Second Language Acquisition of Italian and Spanish Workers). The group was founded and directed by Jürgen Meisel at the University of Wuppertal in 1974.

15. In a more explicit treatment of these facts one would have to append a further equation to the XP position which shows that XP controls the gap created by topicalisation (e.g. in "*was er hat gegessen* (gap)?" as compared with "*er hat gegessen ein Kuchen*" (both examples in x+1 interlanguage)). For the purpose of this paper I will not include this aspect of the description.

16. Note that while these rules account for the facts observed in L2 acquisition, the reality of German word order is far more complex.

17. In Pienemann (1998) I developed a more differentiated approach to this problem that accounts for the gradual nature of the acquisition of 'verb final'. However, the details of that argument are not crucial here.

18. I use the term 'L2 learner' here to keep the text readable. However, it should be noted that most authors base their hypotheses on the critical age of around 6 years. I will return to this point later in the text.

19. In contrast, parametrization is a property theory which addresses epistemological issues in language acquisition. It specifies which bits of linguistic knowledge the learner has access to through UG. Since the latter theory links the two phenomena in question to a single parameter, the setting of this parameter necessarily includes the prediction of the simultaneous acquisition of the two structures.

20. There is ample evidence for this in biological development (cf. Gehring 1985; Coen & Carpenter 1992; Wolper 1992).

21. This structure has not been reported in GSL acquisition studies.

References

Altmann, G. T. M. (1990). Cognitive models of speech processing: An introduction. In G. T. M. Altmann (Ed.), *Cognitive models of speech processing. Psycholinguistic and computational perspectives* (pp. 1–23). Cambridge, MA: The MIT Press

Bachman, L. F. (1988). Language testing – SLA interfaces. *Review of Applied Linguistics, 9*, 193–209.

Baddeley, A. (1990). *Human Memory: Theory and practice.* Hillsdale, NJ: Lawrence Erlbaum.

Bates, E., MacWhinney, B., & Smith, S. (1982). Pragmatics and syntax in psycholinguistic research. In S. W. Felix & H. Wode (Eds.), *Language Development at the Crossroads: Papers from the interdisciplinary conference on language acquisition at Passau* (pp. 11–30). Tübingen: Narr.

Berwick, R. & Weinberg, A. (1984). *The Grammatical Basis of Linguistic Performance: Language use and language acquisition.* Cambridge, MA: The MIT Press.

Bever, T. G. (1970). The cognitive basis for linguistic structures. In J. Hayes (Ed.), *Cognition and the Development of Language.* New York, NY: Wiley.

Bley-Vroman, R. (1990). The logical problem of second language learning. *Linguistic Analysis, 20*, 3–49.

Bock, M. (1978). *Wort-, Satz- und Textverarbeitung.* Stuttgart: Kohlhammer.

Braine, M. P. S. (1978). On the relation between natural logic of processing and standard logic. *Psychological Review, 85*, 1–21.

Bresnan, J. (Ed.). (1982). *The Mental Representation of Grammatical Relations.* Cambridge, MA: The MIT Press.

Bresnan, J. (2001). *Lexical-Functional Syntax.* Oxford: Blackwell.

Bresnan, J. & Kanerva, J. M. (1989). Locative inversion in Chichewa: A case study of factorization in grammar. *Linguistic Inquiry, 20*(1), 1–50.

Broadbent, D. E. (1975). The magic number seven after fifteen years. In A. Kennedy & A. Wilkes (Eds.), *Studies in Long Term Memory.* London: Wiley.

Chomsky, N. (1981). *Lectures on Government and Binding.* Dordrecht: Foris.

Clahsen, H. (1980). Psycholinguistic aspects of L2 acquisition. In S. W. Felix (Ed.), *Second Language Development* (pp. 57–79). Tübingen: Narr.

Clahsen, H. (1982). *Spracherwerb in der Kindheit. Eine Untersuchung zur Entwickung der Syntax bei Kleinkindern.* Tübingen: Narr.

Clahsen, H. (1984). The acquisition of German word order: A test case for cognitive approaches to L2 development. In R. Anderson (Ed.), *Second languages* (pp. 219–242). Rowley, MA: Newbury House.

Clahsen, H. (1990). The comparative study of first and second language development. *Studies in Second Language Acquisition, 12*, 135–153.

Clahsen, H. (1992). Learnability theory and the problem of development in language acquisition. In J. Weissenborn, H. Goodluck, & T. Roeper (Eds.), *Theoretical Issues in Language Acquisition: Continuity and change* (pp. 53–76). Hillsdale, NJ: Lawrence Erlbaum.

Clahsen, H. & Muysken, P. (1986). The availability of universal grammar to adult and child learners: A study of the acquisition of German word order. *Second Language Research, 5*, 93–119.

Clahsen, H., Meisel, J., & Pienemann, M. (1983). *Deutsch als Zweitsprache: Der Spracherwerb ausländischer Arbeiter.* Tübingen: Narr.

Coen, E. & Carpenter, R. (1992). The power behind the flower. *New Scientist, 25,* 26–29.

Cooper, W. E. & Zurif, E. B. (1983). Aphasia: Information-processing in language production and reception. In B. Butterworth, *Language Production* (Vol. 2). London: Academic Press.

Crookes, G. (1989). Planning and interlanguage variation. *Studies in Second Language Acquisition, 11*(4), 367–383.

Crookes, G. & Gass, S. (Eds.). (1993). *Tasks and Language Learning. Integrating theory and practice.* Multilingual Matters: Clevedon.

de Bot, K. (1992). A bilingual production model: Levelt's speaking model adapted. *Applied Linguistics, 13,* 1–24.

Dewaele, J.-M. & Veronique, D. (2001). Gender assignment and gender agreement in advanced French interlanguage: A cross-sectional study. *Bilingualism. Language and Cognition, 4*(3), 275–297.

Douglas, D. (1986). Communicative competence and the tests of oral skills. In C. W. Stansfield (Ed.), *TEFOL Research Reports, 21. Toward communicative competence testing: Proceedings of the Second TEFOL Invitational Conference* (pp. 157–175). Princeton, NJ: Educational Testing Service.

du Plessis, J., Solin, D., Travis, J., & White, L. (1987). UG or not UG, that is the question: A reply to Clahsen and Muysken. *Second Language Research, 3,* 56–75.

Engelkamp, J. & Zimmer, H. D. (1983). *Dynamic Aspects of Language Processing.* Heidelberg: Springer.

Engelkamp, J. (1974). *Psycholinguistik.* München: UTB.

Felix, S. W. (1984). Maturational aspects of universal grammar. In A. Davies, C. Criper, & A. Howatt (Eds.), *Interlanguage.* Edinburgh: Edinburgh University Press.

Felix, S. W. (1991). Accessibility of UG in second language acquisition. In L. Eubank (Ed.), *Point-counterpoint*: *Universal Grammar in the second language* (pp. 89–104). Amsterdam: John Benjamins.

Garman, M. (1990). *Psycholinguistics.* Cambridge: CUP.

Garrett, M. F. (1976). Syntactic process in sentence production. In R. Wales & E. Walker (Eds.), *New approaches to language mechanisms* (pp. 231–256). Amsterdam: North Holland.

Garrett, M. F. (1980). Levels of processing in sentence production. In B. Butterworth (Ed.), *Language Production: Speech and talk,* Vol. 1 (pp. 177–220). London: Academic Press.

Garrett, M. F. (1982). Production of speech: Observations from normal and pathological language use. In A. W. Ellis (Ed.), *Normality and Pathology in Cognitive Functions* (pp. 19–76). London: Academic Press.

Gehring, W. J. (1985). The molecular basis of development. *Scientific American, 253*(4), 137–146.

Gregg, K. (1996). The logical and the developmental problems of second language acquisition. In W. C. Ritchie, *Handbook of Second Language Acquisition* (pp. 49–81). San Diego, CA: Academic Press.

Håkansson, G. (2001). Tense morphology and verb-second in Swedish L1 children, L2 children and children with SLI. *Bilingualism: Language and Cognition, 4,* 85–99.

Horrocks, G. (1987). *Generative Grammar.* London: Longman.

Huter, K. (1996). Atarashii no kuruma and other old friends – the acquisition of Japanese syntax. *Australian Review of Applied Linguistics, 19,* 39–60.

Ingram, E. (1971). A further note on the relationship between psychological and linguistic theories. *IRAL, 9*(4), 335–346.

Jansen, L. (1991). The development of word order in natural and formal German second language acquisition. *Australian Working Papers in Language Development, 5,* 1–42.

Johnston, M. (1985). *Syntactic and Morphological Progressions in Learner English.* Canberra: Commonwealth Dept of Immigration and Ethnic Affairs.

Kaplan, R. & Bresnan, J. (1982). Lexical-Functional Grammar: A formal system for grammatical representation. In J. Bresnan (Ed.), *The Mental Representation of Grammatical Relations* (pp. 173–281). Cambridge, MA: The MIT Press.

Kempen, G. & Hoenkamp, E. (1987). An incremental procedural grammar for sentence formulation. *Cognitive Science, 11,* 201–258.

Kintsch, W. (1974). *The Representation of Meaning in Memory.* Hillsdale, NJ: Lawrence Erlbaum.

Levelt, W. J. M. (1983). Monitoring and self-repair in speech. *Cognition, 14,* 41–104.

Levelt, W. J. M. (1989). *Speaking. From intention to articulation.* Cambridge, MA: The MIT Press.

Long, M. H. (1988). Second language acquisition as a function of age: Research findings and methodological issues. In K. Hyltenstam & Å. Viberg (Eds.), *Progression and Regression in Language* (pp. 196–221). Cambridge: CUP.

Long, M. H. (1990). Maturational constraints on language development. *Studies in Second Language Acquisition, 12*(3), 251–286.

Long, M. H. (2003). Stabilisation and fossilisation in interlanguage development. In C. J. Doughty & M. H. Long (Eds.), *The Handbook of Second Language Acquisition* (pp. 487–535). Oxford: Blackwell.

Marinis, T. (2003). Psycholinguistic techniques in second language acquisition research. *Second Language Research, 19*(2), 144–161.

Marslen-Wilson, W. D. & Tyler, L. K. (1980). The temporal structure of spoken language understanding. *Cognition, 8,* 1–71.

Maxwell, J. T. & Kaplan, R. M. (1995). The interface between phrasal and functional constraints. In M. Dalrymple, R. M. Kaplan, J. T. Maxwell, & A. Zaenen (Eds.), *Formal Issues in Lexical-Functional Grammar.* Stanford, CA: CSLI.

Meisel, J. M. (1991). Principles of Universal Grammar and strategies of language use: On some similarities and differences between first and second language acquisition. In L. Eubank (Ed.), *Point -Counterpoint: Universal Grammar in the second language* (pp. 231–276). Amsterdam: John Benjamins.

Meisel, J. M. (1996). *The acquisition of the syntax of negation in French and German: Contrasting first and second language development.* MS. Hamburg: University of Hamburg and Nedlands Institute for Advanced Study, March.

Meisel, J. M., Clahsen, H., & Pienemann, M. (1981). On determining developmental stages in natural second language acquisition. *Studies in Second Language Acquisition, 3,* 109–135.

Netter, K. (1987). Wortstellung und Verbalkomplex im Deutschen. In U. Klenk, P. Scherber, & M. Thanller (Eds.), *Computerlinguistik und Philologische Datenverarbeitung.* Hildesheim: Olms.

Paradis, M. (1987). *The Assessment of Bilingual Aphasia.* Hillsdale, NJ: Lawrence Erlbaum.

Paradis, M. (1994). Neurolinguistic aspects of implicit and explicit memory: Implications for bilingualism and SLA. In N. C. Ellis (Ed.), *Implicit and Explicit Language Learning* (pp. 393–419). London: Academic Press.

Penfield, W. & Roberts, L. (1959). *Speech and Brain-Mechanisms.* Princeton, NJ: Princeton University Press.

Pienemann, M. (1980). The second language acquisition of immigrant children. In S. W. Felix (Ed.), *Second Language Development: Trends and issues* (pp. 41–56). Tübingen: Narr.

Pienemann, M. (1981). *Der Zweitspracherwerb ausländischer Arbeiterkinder.* Bonn: Bouvier.

Pienemann, M. (1998). *Language Processing and Second Language Development: Processability theory.* Amsterdam: John Benjamins.

Pienemann, M. & Mackey, A. (1993). An empirical study of children's ESL development and rapid profile. In P. McKay (Ed.), *ESL Development. Language and literacy in schools*, Vol. 2 (pp. 115–259). Commonwealth of Australia and National Languages and Literacy Institute of Australia.

Pienemann, M. & Håkansson, G. (1999). A unified approach towards the development of Swedish as L2: A processability account. *Studies in Second Language Acquisition, 21*, 383–420.

Pienemann, M., Johnston, M., & Brindley, G. (1988). Constructing an acquisition-based procedure for second language assessment. *Studies in Second Language Acquisition, 10*, 217–224.

Pinker, S. (1979). Formal models of language learning. *Cognition, 7*, 217–283.

Pinker, S. (1984). *Language Learnability and Language Development.* Cambridge, MA: Harvard University Press.

Roeper, T., Lapointe, S., Bing, J., & Tavakolian, S. (1981). A lexical approach to language acquisition. In S. Tavakolian (Ed.), *Language Acquisition and Linguistic Theory* (pp. 35–58). Cambridge, MA: The MIT Press.

Schwartz, B. D. (1988). Testing between UG and Problem-solving Models of SLA: Developmental sequence data. Ms., University of Geneva.

Selinker, L. (1972). Interlanguage. *International Review of Applied Linguistics, 10*, 209–231.

Selinker, L. & Douglas, D. (1985). Wrestling with 'context' in interlanguage theory. *Applied Linguistics, 6*, 190–204.

Simon, H. A. (1962). The architecture of complexity. *Proceedings of the American Philosophical Society.* Reprinted in Simon, H. A. 1981. *The Science of the Artificia* (pp. 192–229). Cambridge, MA: The MIT Press.

Simpson, J. H. (1991). *Warlpiri Morpho-Syntax: A lexicalist approach.* Dordrecht: Kluwer Academic.

Sridhar, S. N. (1988). *Cognition and Sentence Production.* New York, NY: Springer.

Tarone, E. (1983). On the variability of interlanguage systems. *Applied Linguistics, 4*, 142–163.

Tarone, E. (1989). On the variability of interlanguage systems. In F. Eckman, L. H. Bell, & D. Nelson (Eds.), *Universals in Second Language Acquisition* (pp. 9–23). Rowley, MA: Newbury House.

Tomaselli, A. & Schwartz, B. (1990). Analysing the acquisition stages of negation in L2 German: Support for UG in adult SLA. *Second Language Research, 6*(1), 1–38.

Tulving, E. (1990). In M. W. Eysenck (Ed.), *The Blackwell Dictionary of Cognitive Psychology*. Oxford: Blackwell.

Vigliocco, G., Butterworth, B., & Garrett, M. F. (1996). Subject-verb agreement in Spanish and English: Differences in the role of conceptual constraints. *Cognition, 61*, 261–298.

Westmoreland, R. (1983). L2 German Acquisition by Instructed Adults. Ms., University of Hawaii at Manoa.

Wexler, K. (1982). A principle theory for language acquisition. In E. Wanner & L. R. Gleitman (Eds.), *Language Acquisition: The state of the art* (pp. 288–315). Cambridge: CUP.

Wexler, K., & Culicover, P. (1980). *Formal Principles of Language Acquisition*. Cambridge, MA: The MIT Press.

White, L. (1989). *Universal Grammar and Second Language Acquisition*. Amsterdam: John Benjamins.

Wimsatt, W. C. (1986). Developmental constraints, generative entrenchment and the innate-acquired distinction. In W. Bechtel (Ed.), *Integrating Scientific Disciplines* (pp. 185–208). Dordrecht: Martinus Nijhoff.

Wimsatt, W. C. (1991). Generative entrenchment in development and evolution. Ms., Dept of Philosophy, University of Chicago.

Wolpert, L. (1992). The shape of things to come. *New Scientist, 134*(1827, June), 38–42.

CHAPTER 2

Discussing PT

Manfred Pienemann
University of Paderborn and University of Newcastle upon Tyne

The previous chapter gave an overview of most of the key notions developed in the original version of PT. This chapter focuses on developments that took place in the years between the original publication (1998) and the publication of this volume. This includes new empirical research, especially relating to the typological plausibility of PT and the discussion of a number of key issues that have been raised by critics. This chapter also contains a rough sketch of the development of ideas that underly PT because some textbooks on second language acquisition fail to differentiate them clearly.

1. Typological plausibility

What has been presented in Chapter 1 is a principled approach to the interface between linguistic theory and the acquisition of language processing procedures. This approach was exemplified on the basis of two closely related languages (German and English). The goal of an explanatory theory of SLA must, of course, be to provide a mechanism which has the capacity of making predictions for ANY human language. It would therefore be desirable to demonstrate the applicability of the proposed theory for a range of typologically different languages. If it can be demonstrated that the actual course of L2 development follows the route predicted by the theory (stated in universal terms), then the status of that theory must be beyond a mere generalisation of observational facts for the languages in the context of which the theory was first developed.

Examining the typological plausibility of PT is, of course, the overarching theme of this volume. First steps were made in this direction in Pienemann (1998) and Pienemann and Håkansson (1999) by demonstrating that the developmental trajectories found in the acquisition of Swedish and Japanese as second languages follow the course predicted by PT. The research on Swedish

Table 1. Processing procedures applied to Swedish word order, morphology and negation

Processing procedures	L2 structure	morphology	syntax	negation
5 – subord.clause procedure	main and sub cl		Cancel INV	neg V_f
4 – S-procedure/WO Rules	inter-phr info	pred. agr	INV	X V_f NP_s neg
3 – phrasal procedure	phrasal info.	NP agr	ADV	
		VPagr	WH fronting	V_f neg
2 – category procedure	lexical morph	pl, def	canonical	(Aux) V neg
		past, pres	order	neg V
		(Aux)		neg V
1 – word/lemma	'words'	invariant forms	single const.	neg+X

SLA was based on an extensive overview of the majority of studies carried out on Swedish SLA over a period of more than two decades (cf. Pienemann & Håkansson 1999). Pienemann and Håkansson (1999) applied the PT hierarchy to Swedish morpho-syntax. An overview is given in Table 1 which constitutes a prediction of the developmental trajectory for Swedish as L2 that is based solely on the internal architecture of the theory. Testing this set of predictions in the large number of studies reviewed by Pienemann and Håkansson produced very solid empirical support for the overall approach.

Glahn, Håkansson, Hammerberg, Holmen, Hvenekilde and Lund (2001) tested this framework with specific reference to affixation in attributive and predicative adjectives in Scandinavian languages (cf. also Hammerberg 1996). When intervening variables, such as gender assignment, are "factored out" (cf. Pienemann 1998: 159ff.) the data strongly support the predictions made by the theory.

Dewaele and Veronique (2001) applied PT to agreement in French adjectives, focusing on levels of accuracy in gender assignment. Unfortunately, PT is not a suitable conceptual framework for such a study. First of all, in LFG gender is a lexical feature and thus has to be acquired for every lexical item. Therefore, one can test a person's ability to transfer grammatical information at the PT levels only if gender assignment has been established for every item in the given learner's lexicon. Obviously, such a step would render the application of PT to this phenomenon in French superfluous for an explanation of this very set of facts. Secondly, PT does not make any predictions on levels of accuracy. Instead, the theory utilises the emergence criterion. In addition, I showed in Pienemann (1998) that accuracy rates do not relate to levels of acquisition in a linear manner and are not a valid measure of development.

The research on Japanese SLA reported in Pienemann (1998) was based on Kawaguchi's initial work which is presented in more detail in Di Biase and Kawaguchi (2002). Kawaguchi's extended framework is presented in her chapter of this volume. The application of PT to Japanese SLA constitutes a crucial test case for the theory because all other languages PT had been applied to (German, English and Swedish) are closely related to each other and share a number of typological features. For instance, they are all configurational languages with verb-second constraints. In contrast, Japanese is a non-configurational, agglutinative language. The crux of the typological plausibility test for PT is to demonstrate that the universal architecture of grammatical information flow entailed in PT can make testable and correct predictions for the course of Japanese L2 development. Kawaguchi demonstrated that the developmental predictions she made for Japanese as L2 on the basis of PT are borne out by longitudinal and cross-sectional learner data.

Most studies of Japanese SLA focused on adult university learners of Japanese. However, recent PT-based studies also inluded natural learners. For example, Itani-Adams (2003) studies bilingual first language acquisition of a Japanese-Australian child. Her work utilises the developmental trajectory of English as a second language established by Pienemann (1998) and the developmental trajectory of Japanese as a second language established by Di Biase and Kawaguchi (2002). Itani-Adams found that both languages develop following the hierarchy predicted by PT (lexical > phrasal > inter-phrasal). She used PT as a matrix for a comparison of language development across the two first languages of the informant. She found the three different types of morphology (i.e., lexical, phrasal and interphrasal morphology) did not develop in synchrony in two languages. This finding supports De Houwer's (1990) Separate Development Hypothesis. Iwasaki (2003) studied the acquisition of Japanese morphosyntax by a seven-year-old Australian boy in a naturalistic environment and found the same developmental trajectory as Di Biase and Kawaguchi (2002).

Zhang (2001) applied PT to modern standard Chinese, another language that is typologically distant from Germanic languages. Modern standard Chinese is an isolating and topic-prominent language. Zhang identified five grammatical morphemes and related them to three different PT levels. Her data show that the morphemes are acquired in the sequence predicted by PT. The results of her study are summarised in Chapter 5.

Gao (2004) is an extensive empirical study of the acquisition of key grammatical morphemes and topic marking in Mandarin as a second language by adult language learners in formal and informal contexts with a range of different source languages. This study replicates the Zhang study with a different and wider database and also includes additional aspects of Mandarin grammar, espcially topic marking. All of these aspects of Mandarin are postioned within the PT framework, and the resulting developmental trajectory is supported by the data. Using data from a number of typologiclly different source languages, Gao also provides strong empirical evidence against full transfer at the initial state.

Di Biase (cf. Di Biase & Kawaguchi 2002) applied the PT hierarchy to Italian as L2. One important corollary of his research is the conclusion that the mechanics of subject-verb agreement may vary between typologically different languages. This analysis is not only congruent with the data presented by Di Biase and with his implementation of PT into Italian, but also with cross-linguistic on-line studies of agreement in English and Romance languages by Vigliocco, Butterworth and Garrett (1996) and Vigliocco, Butterworth and Semenza (1995).

Harada (2004) explores the relationship between the acquisition of modality and PT stages of development in three Japanese learners of English L2. She finds that only lexical modality (e.g. as expressed in 'maybe' or 'I think') appears in early learners (stage 1 and 2) while modal verbs (e.g. can + lexical verb) seem to coincide with the appearance of the VP procedure.

Taylor (2004) uses PT to compare IL development in two high-intermediate English-speaking learners of Spanish L2 over a period of six months (pre-test/post-test) with one learner continuing formal instruction and the other undertaking in-country study in Spain. Her findings are consistent with a PT hierarchy for pro-drop Romance languages and confirm S-procedure resources as a requirement for topicalized objects as in Di Biase & Kawaguchi (2002).

Empirical research carried out in the PT framework yielded precise descriptions of ESL and other developmental trajectories and of learner variation. This research has been used as an objective psycholinguistic basis of measurement in educational evaluation studies. For instance, Keßler (in press) compared levels of attainment in primary and secondary ESL programs in German schools utilising PT-based descriptions of ESL development. Liebner (in press) studied the acquisition of English as L2 by German and Swedish primary school students in immersive and non-immersive contexts and compared learner variation in the different contexts demonstrating that non-immersive and non-communicative contexts are more likely to be associated with simplified varieties of learner language. The study by Berti and Di Biase (2002) shows the effectiveness of L2 teaching based on a syllabus informed by the PT hierarchy in conjunction with form-focused teaching method. PT has also been used as a basis for profiling natural and formal L2 learners of Italian as L2 (Bettoni & Di Biase 2005).

Håkansson, Salameh and Nettelblatt (2003) produced a highly innovative application of PT that capitalises on its cross-linguistic capacity. Håkansson et al. studied the acquisition of Swedish-Arabic bilingual children with and without specific language impairment. Based on the above PT hierarchy for Swedish, Mansouri's (2000) Arabic PT levels and further development of this research by Håkansson and Mansouri, these authors (Håkansson, Salameh & Nettelblatt 2003) were able to measure the language development of bilingual informants using compatible scales for both languages. This was possible because of the universal nature of the underlying PT framework. In other words, this approach to the measurement of bilingual language development affords us a description of the current state of the learner's bilingual system in which both languages can be compared on the same developmental scale despite their typological distance. Key issues arising from the comparison between impaired and non-impaired language development is taken up in Håkansson's chapter in this volume. The application of PT to Arabic is discussed in Mansouri's chapter in this volume.

Özdemir (2004) applies the comparative approach developed by Håkansson et al. to the study of trilingual language development in Turkish-German children learning English. She uses the existing PT hierarchies for English (L3) and German (L2) and develops a Turkish PT hierarchy. All three languages are profiled on the basis of PT hierarchies. This permits a comparison of their levels of development across all three languages.

2. Feature unification and the case of perceptual salience

The reader will recall from the previous section and from Chapter 1 that, within the framework of Processability Theory, Lexical Functional Grammer (or a somewhat simplified version thereof) serves to formally model several aspects of language generation, in particular feature unification. Hence the "mechanics" of PT are driven by the exchange of lexical feature information within and across constituents, and the PT hierarchy results from the nature of this exchange of grammatical information. Within this framework all operations are specific to language – with one exception: PT also utilised the general cognitive principle of *perceptual saliency*.

The inclusion of two unrelated sets of principles in the design of PT was critically reviewed by Hammarberg (1996) and Hulstijn (1987, 1998). Hammarberg comments critically on how to formally define saliency particularly in morphology, and Hulstijn comments that saliency appears to be included in PT on an *ad hoc* basis and needs to be integrated formally in the theory.

We developed our own misgivings about the inclusion of the saliency principle when trying to apply the PT framework to typologically different languages. This process amplified Hulstijn's claim about the *ad hoc* nature of the inclusion of this principle. The design of PT was based on the assumption that in theory construction one should aim for theoretical parsimony. The inclusion of any *ad hoc* principle, however well justified it may be in isolation, jeopadises parsimonious explanations. In the case of perceptual saliency this principle is general cognitive in nature, whereas everything else in PT rests upon an LFG-specific modularity assumption. This contradiction needs to be resolved in a principled way before we set out to extend the scope of PT.

It may be useful to first review the way in which the saliency principle has been used in PT. There are two instances in the German L2 hierarchy in which it was utilised: (i) the sentence-initial position of adverbials (ADV) and (ii) the distance position of German verbs.[1]

The distance or "split verb" position in German is exemplified in (1).

(1)   *Er hat den Saft getrunken.*
      He has the juice drunk.
      'He drank the juice'.

Orginally, we argued as follows. Following Kaplan and Bresnan (1982) and Netter (1987), auxiliaries and modals are treated as V with the feature AUX that takes the value '+' and which take VP-complements (cf. Pienemann 1998). The lexical entries of the verbs are given in Figure 1, and the following (simplified) c-structure rules are assumed:

(2) $S \rightarrow$ NP_{subj} VP

      $VP \rightarrow$ V $\left\{ \begin{array}{l} (NP_{obj1})\ (NP_{obj2}) \\ \text{V-COMP} \end{array} \right\}$

      V-COMP $\rightarrow$ $(NP_{obj1})\ (NP_{obj2})$ V

With this treatment the verbs need to exchange information on tense (i.e. PARTICIPLE = PAST and V-COMP PARTICIPLE = PAST) to be inserted in the correct position in c-structure.

We argued that in this case grammatical information was exchanged across constituents – as in SV-agreement marking. We further argued that in the case of split verbs one of the constituents that exchanges information is in a per-

getrunken: V,   PRED = 'trinken (SUBJ) (OBJ)'
                PARTICIPLE = PAST
                INF = ge
                OBJ CASE = accusative
                AUX = –

      hat: V,   PRED = 'haben, V-COMP (SUBJ)'
                TENSE = PAST
                AUX = +
                NUM = SG
                PERSON = 3RD
                V-COMP PARTICIPLE = PAST
                V-COMP INF $=_c$ ge

Figure 1. Lexical entires for the German verbs *getrunken* and *hat*

ceptually salient position while in the case of SV agreement both constituents (subject and verb) may be in sentence-internal position. The processor is therefore unable to rely on the perceptual saliency of one of the constituents. This difference was seen as the reason for the two structures to develop at different stages.

In Chapter 7 Pienemann, Di Biase and Kawaguchi propose that the revised version of LFG (Bresnan 2001) contains a set of principles that permit a parsimonious explanation of the phenomena previously explained with reference to the saliency principle. To achieve this, we will utilise the process of mapping a(rgument)-structure onto f(unction)-structure which can be formally modelled in LFG. The inclusion of this additional set of explanatory principles in PT will also allow us to extend the scope of explananda in PT.

In the context of this chapter, it may be worthwhile noting that in some cases reference to the saliency principle turned out to be quite unnecessary. For instance, the case of German 'split verbs' can very well be handled relying solely on feature unification as the underlying principle (as in the summary of PT in Chapter 1). To illustrate this point, we refer the reader to Figure 2 which shows graphically that the position of the two verbs can be accounted for by the unification of the information "PART = PAST", that is present in both verb entries, in VP. This account also explains the developmental schedule PART before SV-agreement, because German SV-agreement depends on feature unification in S, i.e. one level higher than VP, and this corresponds precisely with the observed order of acquisition.

However, this type of explanation cannot be extended to the initial position of adverbials and related phenomena in other languages. In the original

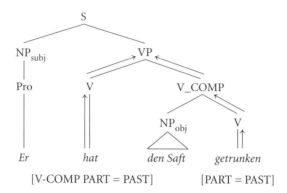

Figure 2. German verbs in "split position"

version of PT we therefore made recourse to the serial order principle (cf. Bever 1970; Bever & Townsend 1979; Slobin & Bever 1982) and perceptual saliency (originally Murdock 1962; cf. also Sridhar 1988; Kintsch 1974). The reader will recall that in the acquisition of all configurational languages as L2 (and even in the case of some non-configurational languages such as Japanese), word order is initially strictly canonical.

In subsequent stages, learners gradually adjust the interlanguage to match target language word order constraints. In many cases, this strictly canonical pattern is followed by the appearance of adverbials and wh-words in focus position as a distinct second step. This is where PT utilised the saliency principle. Pienemann (1998: 173f.) reasoned as follows:

> In terms of processability, the structures ADV and WH-Front are a modification of the serial order principle which allows the learner to map conceptual structures directly onto linguistic form:
>
> agent action patient
> N   V   N
>
> The new structure ... modifies the seriality principle utilising the general cognitive principle of saliency which identifies initial and final positions and allows the canonical order principle to apply once the salient positions have been processed:
>
> INITIAL]   agent action patient [FINAL
> PP/wh/adv NP   V   NP
>
> These additional word order options allow the learner to produce a range of L2 syntactic phenomena without acquiring the full range of L2 word order".

As this quotation illustrates, the serial order principle does tap into fundamental aspects of language generation. However, it is not formally connected to the architecture of LFG nor to the notion of feature unification nor to any aspect of the model of sentence generation on which PT is based. In Chapter 7 precisely this connection will be made, based on LFG-style correspondence principles.

3.   Competence and performance

Most authors who have dealt with theory construction in SLA would agree on one issue: a coherent theory of SLA is not in sight, even though many attempts have been made to tackle aspects of such a theory (cf. Berretta 1991; Berretta & Crookes 1993; Crookes 1992; Long 1990, 1993). This is due mainly to the enormous complexity of the task in hand. It was for this reason that Processability Theory was designed from the start as a modular approach that can be extended by other necessary modules. Given the modular nature of PT, it *intentionally* does not address the logical problem of language acquisition in its original format (i.e. Pienemann 1998). However, the theory is designed to include this extension at a later stage. The outlines of this extension are presented in Chapter 7 of this volume.

In the discussion of processing approaches to SLA the relationship between competence and performance has been critically examined. As I have shown in Pienemann (1998), most of the key points of criticism of processing strategies such as Clahsen's (1984) have been addressed in later work on L2 processing.

One key point that is of interest in the current discussion of language processing and SLA is the relationship between the processor and linguistic knowledge. White (1991) equates research on acquisition with research on linguistic knowledge only, and she relegates everything else to the domain of language use.

Kaplan and Bresnan (1982) have a different view. In the context of language acquisition they put research on language processing on an equal footing with research on linguistic knowledge as the following quotation illustrates:

> [Children] acquire knowledge and skills that enable them to produce and comprehend an infinite number of novel utterances .... The major goal of psycholinguistic research is to devise an explanatory account of the mental operations that underlie these linguistic abilities. (Kaplan & Bresnan 1982: 177)

Processability Theory is positioned in this tradition. It therefore does not fit into White's dichotomy. As Kaplan and Bresnan (1982) point out, the various components of a theory of language acquisition can be studied separately as long as they ultimately fit together in a coherent model. And it is for reasons of overall coherence that LFG was chosen as the grammatical framework for Processability Theory because it provides a basis for relating linguistic knowledge to the processor.

In other words, PT is constructed in a modular fashion, and the study of the relationship between the processor and grammatical knowledge is one that can be pursued within the processability framework since the language processor is seen as the computational routines that operate on, but are separate from linguistic knowledge (cf. Kaplan & Bresnan 1982).

Indeed such an integrative line of research could prove highly productive. For instance, White (1991) is concerned that production data may not reveal a learner's linguistic knowledge because the learner may fail to produce certain structures for reasons to be found in the production routines rather than in his or her linguistic knowledge. In fact, White's concern highlights the fact that the interface between the processor and linguistic knowledge is of particular relevance to those SLA researchers who focus on the study of linguistic knowledge. As Chomsky (1978: 10) pointed out, we do not know *a priori* which aspects of linguistic data are attributable to grammatical competence or to innumerable other factors. Language acquisition studies that focus on linguistic competence therefore ought to place special emphasis on the interface between the processor and grammatical knowledge, since the latter is accessible only through the former, especially in SLA where it cannot be taken for granted that individual utterances are representative of the structure of the underlying linguistic system.

Utilising an explicit production grammar and a compatible theory of linguistic representation would allow one to explore this issue in detail. Such a study could potentially shed light on the relationship between production routines and linguistic representation.

4.   A rough sketch of the development of PT ideas

The conceptual development from the Multidimensional Model (Meisel, Clahsen & Pienemann 1981) to Processability Theory (Pienemann 1998) and beyond has a reasonably long history, now spanning more than 20 years, and this may be the reason why some authors (e.g. Cook 2001; Jordan 2004) inadvertently blend some of these developments in their accounts of PT. The reader will appreciate that these conceptual developments were aimed at increasing the precision of formally modelling the dynamics of language acquisition and at extending our ability to formally account for a larger range of phenomena within a typologically and psychologically plausible framework.

In other words, there is a substantial difference between PT and ideas that precede it. In the 1998 volume I took stock of the ideas pre-dating PT, including the Multidimensional Model (Meisel, Clahsen & Pienemann 1981), Clahsen's (1984) Strategies Approach, the Teachability Hypothesis (Pienemann 1984, 1989) and the Predictive Framework (Pienemann & Johnston 1987). Each of these models and frameworks was reviewed and evaluated in detail. Particularly the Strategies Approach was reviewed in the light of the limitations discussed during the 1980s and 1990s, and PT was designed to overcome these limitations. Authors such as Cook (2001) nevertheless treat Processability Theory merely as a new label for the Multidimensional Model. Therefore a brief sketch of the the development of the main ideas may be in order. For more detail the reader is referred to the 1998 volume (cf. Pienemann 1998).

As illustrated in Table 2, the Multidimensional Model (MM) (Meisel, Clahsen & Pienemann 1981) focused on the issue of determining developmental sequences in SLA. One has to bear in mind that the paper addressed some of the key issues discussed in the late 1970s and early 1980s which focused on the relationship between data and their proper description. The issue was whether every change found in an interlanguage constitutes evidence of interlanguage development and if the changes that can be found need to be measured in native language terms. As the name suggests, the Multidimensional Model assumes that interlanguage development is not linear and that instead interlanguages contain at least two dimensions. This assumption has repercussions for determining stages of development, and IL differences can now be understood to represent either development or inter- or intra-learner variation. The MM utilises implicational scaling and probabilistic rules to operationalise the emergence criterion for acquisition. In other words, the MM is first and foremost a *descriptive* framework for interlanguage dynamics.

The MM has been criticised for a lack of falsifiability. Larsen-Freeman and Long (1991) note that there is no independent motivation for variational interlanguage features and that as a result there is a problem in not being able to falsify a developmental sequence because any deviation from a predicted sequence can be considered a variational feature. This shortcoming has been rectified in PT which now formally constrains development as well as variation in a predictable and testable manner.

The Strategies Approach was developed by Clahsen (1984) to explain the development of German L2 word order. It is based on a set of processing strate-

Table 2. PT and its predecessors and relatives

Model	Key references	Key concepts	Scope
Multidimensional Model	– Meisel, Clahsen & Pienemann 1981, – Pienemann, Johnston & Meisel 1996	– implicational scaling, – probabilistic rules, – emergence criterion, – two dimensions in L2 dynamics: (1) development (2) variation	*descriptive* framework for dynamic processes in L2 development
Strategies Approach	Clahsen 1984	development of L2 German word order determined by shedding of processing constraints	explanation of German L2 word order development
Teachability Hypothesis	Pienemann 1984, 1989	stages of acquisition cannot be skipped through instruction, variation can be altered, speed can be accelerated	explains constraints on teachability, originally German L2 word order development, based on strategies, universal since based on PT
Predictive framework	Pienemann & Johnston 1987	development of ESL morpho-syntax determined by incremental development of processing resources	explains developmental patterns in ESL and GSL morpho-syntax
PT	Pienemann 1998, 2003	– processability hierarchy modelled in linguistic theory (LFG), – hypothesis space constrains development and variation (testable), – factorisation and other refined descriptive methods, – partial transfer hypothesis (DMT), – task variation: steadiness hypothesis, – stabilisation: bad choice hypothesis, – L1-L2 differences, – basis for L2 profiling	Universally explains L2 development in syntax and morphology

gies which are assumed to be shed as interlanguage development progresses. In this way, the strategies approach complements the MM by providing an *explantion* of the developmental dimension. Nevertheless, the MM and the Strategies Approach constitute two separate conceptual entities. In several introductions to SLA research the strategies approach has been presented as part of the Multidimensional Model (e.g. Larsen-Freeman & Long 1991; Ellis 1994). This is probably due to the fact that the Strategies Approach forms an excellent explanatory complement to the descriptive framework of the MM. Meisel (1983) produced his own version of the Strategies Approach that is more closely related to Slobin's (1973) and Anderson's (1984) acquisition strategies. Clahsen's strategies approach was subject to severe criticism (e.g. White 1991). Some aspects of this criticism have been refuted. The main limitations that remained, however, were its confinement to word order permutations and its undefined relationship to grammatical representation. These limitations have been overcome in PT.

The Teachability Hypothesis (Pienemann 1984, 1989) was based on the MM and the Strategies Approach. It predicts that stages of SLA cannot be skipped (through teaching intervention) because of the cumulative nature of the processing stategies. It also predicts that variational features are not subject to the same constraints on teachability. In other words, the Teachability Hypothesis defines CONSTRAINTS on teachability. It does not predict sufficient conditions for teaching to be successful. The Teachability Hyothesis was later (Pienemann 1998) put on a PT basis.

As I noted in the preface to the 1998 volume (Pienemann 1998), the Predictive Framework (Pienemann & Johnston 1987) was only short-lived, because it was quickly outdated by new developments present in PT. The Predictive Framework tried to stretch the Strategies Approach to include aspects of L2 morphology and to apply them to an additional target language, English. It thus attempted to widen the scope of the Strategies Approach. However, it soon became clear that speech processing strategies failed to connect to grammatical knowledge and that they were conceptualised too close to specific languages, thus lacking typological plausibility.

All of the critical points listed so far gave rise to the development of Processability Theory, especially the lack of falsifiability in the MM and the inability of the Strategies Approach to link up to grammatical knowledge and its lack of typological plausibility.

PT was designed to be able to address the two key issues of a theory of language acquisition, (i) the developmental problem and (ii) the logical problem. The 1998 volume on PT focused on the first issue. However, the overall design of PT does allow for both issues to be addressed. This is possible mainly because of the inclusion of a grammatical theory (i.e. LFG) that has a high degree of psychological and typological plausibility and that allows one to model several key aspects of language generation using feature unification. This approach also permitted a clear and falsifiable differentiation between the two dimensions of SLA postulated by the MM. Both dimensions are constrained by the hypothesis space defined by PT.

PT has been designed to be universally applicable to any L2, and it is the focus of this volume to put this to the test. This wide scope of PT required the development of new descriptive and analytical methods, including the notion of "factorisation" and an operationalisation of the emergence criterion. PT also contains an explicit view on L1 transfer at the initial state and in later L2 development, a testable hypothesis on interlanguage variability, a hypothesis on the stabilisation of interlanguage development and a view on L1-L2 differences. In addition, work in PT serves as a basis for the development of an L2 profiling procedure.

As this briefest possible summary illustrates, PT made the Strategies Approach and the Predictive Framework obsolete, and the MM and the Teachability Hypothesis are re-defined in this approach thus gaining a far wider scope and technical operationalisation.

5.   The explanatory power of PT

By the 1990s, SLA research had focused on explanatory issues. This gave rise to an extensive debate of the underlying assumptions in the philosophy of science (cf. Berretta 1991; Berretta & Crookes 1993; Crookes 1992; Long 1990, 1993). In his monograph, Jordan (2004) systematises this discussion by providing an overview of the main trends in the philosophy of science and by relating these to the debate in SLA. Jordan develops a set of criteria from a rationalist position that he uses to evaluate the explanatory adequacy of a number of theories of SLA. In particular, Jordan sets out the following criteria for the evaluation of SLA theories (Jordan 2004: XVIII):

– "Research, hypotheses, and theories should be coherent, cohesive, expressed in the clearest possible terms, and consistent."
– "Theories should have empirical content . . . and should not fly in the face of well-established empirical findings."

- "Theories should be fruitful. Theories should make daring and surprising predictions, and should solve persistent problems in their domain."
- "Theories should be broad in scope."
- "Theories should be simple."

Jordan applied these criteria to a number of SLA theories, including PT (Jordan 2004:221–227). This evaluation is highly productive for the SLA field because it contributes to our understanding of what constitutes an explanation and it provides a point of reference for relating SLA to other scientific fields. Jordan makes it clear from the outset that he assumes a rationalist position, and he makes a strong case for this position. This may be annoying for non-rationalists, but it seems to me that there is no neutral ground in the philosophy of science. At the same time it is obvious from the outset that the most recognisably rationalist theory will win the race. I will take this as an opportunity to reflect on the philosophy of science position that is implicit in PT and to respond to Jordan's evaluation.

In his evaluation of PT, Jordan identifies two main strengths of PT, namely (i) that it is not merely a description but that it constitutes an explanation of L2 development that can be tested (with some limitations) and (ii) the theory makes strong and widely applicable predictions.

His evaluation also contains a considerable number of critical points. One point of critique is directed at the use of the saliency principle which was discussed in Section 3 above. As I noted above, I have developed my own misgivings on this point, and steps have been taken to remedy this shortcoming.

Unfortunately, Jordan's evaluation of PT is somewhat obscured by the fact that he does not properly distinguish between PT, the Multidimensional Model and the Strategies Approach. Jordan devotes more space to what he sees as the Multidimensional Model, most of which in fact turns out to be the Strategies Approach, than to the actual Processability Theory. He states that "Pienemann (1998) expands the Multidimensional Model into a Processability Theory which predicts which grammatical structures an L2 learner can process at a given level of development" (Jordan 2004:223). As this quotation highlights, Jordan does not show what this assumed 'expansion' consists of nor which aspects of the MM and the Strategies Approach were dismissed and replaced by linguistic theory. In this context it is worth noting that the 1998 volume (Pienemann 1998) contains a whole subsection entitled "limitations of the strategies approach".

Jordan claims that in the MM developmental and variational features are not defined *a priori*. This is a point that was previously raised by

Larsen-Freeman and Long (1991) and that is indeed addressed in PT. Jordan (2004:225) states that "[by] extending the scope of the model to include grammatical forms, Pienemann has to some extent answered these criticisms."[2] It is not clear what Jordan means by 'the inclusion of grammatical forms', because they had been included in the MM all along. However, this does not capture the way in which Larsen-Freeman and Long's criticism was answered. Instead, PT formally constrains development AND variation, and the theory is sufficiently precise to allow these constraints to be formally modelled for every level of development thus predicting the exact confines within which variation may occur, and this is supported by an extensive empirical study on task variation in Pienemann (1998).

Jordan goes on to relate the alleged lack of clarity in the emergence criterion[3] to one of the guidlines for the evaluation of SLA theories, namely the clarity of operational definitions. He claims that in PT there is still the problem of defining emergence. Jordan does not support this claim by any argument or observation in the PT literature, and it appears without even mentioning the extensive discussion of this issue in two subsections of Pienemann (1998) where the emergence criterion is indeed operationalised. Jordan comments on a lack of operational definitions in PT in the face of one of the most explicit efforts in the field of operationalising not only emergence, but also form-function relationships, implicational relationships, probabilistic rules and developmental dynamics. All of this is situated in the historical context of related criteria and based on very extensive sets of data. It is hard to understand why the same author has no problems accepting very simplistic and conceptually highly questionable accuracy criteria in other theories he reviews in the same volume.

Jordan (2004:225) further claims that the "Processability Theory suggests that transfer is not important." Again, it is hard to reconcile this with my knowledge of PT. In Pienemann (1998:81ff.) I argue explicitly against full transfer at the initial state and for a partial transfer model which is developed into the Developmentally Moderated Transfer Hypothesis in Håkansson, Pienemann and Sayheli (2002). It is therefore not correct to claim that transfer 'is not important' for PT. On the contrary, PT has a very explicit position on transfer and, I might add, a rather daring and highly falsifiable one.

Jordan goes on to claim that PT's stance on transfer is challenged by empirical data. He then switches back to the MM to make an inference about the role of transfer at the initial state. He claims that the MM predicts canonical word order at the initial state and points out that the study of Dutch learners of French by Hulk (1991) cited in Towell and Hawkins (1994) shows ". . . in the earliest stages the learners adopted Germanic word order not the Canonical order [sic.] suggested by the Multidimensional Model" (Jordan 2004: 226).

There are a number of points that need to be considered here. First of all, one cannot simply switch between two different theories/models in the course of their evaluation. What is true for PT does not automatically apply to the MM and vice versa. The reader will recall that the MM is merely a descriptive framework and not a theory. It does not make any predictions for the initial state. Instead, predictions have been made by such authors as Clahsen and Muysken (1986) and Meisel (1983, 1991). Clahsen and Meisel were co-authors of the MM. However, their assumptions on strategies are different from each other and from the MM. What these authors have in common is the assumption that L2 learners do not have full access to UG. This is compatible with my own position (e.g. Pienemann 1998b). However, this overlap does not automatically imply identical views about what is contained in the initial state.

Secondly, the study by Hulk does not have the most suitable design for a test of the initial hypothesis of L2 syntax from a developmental perspective because (i) it is based on grammaticality judgements rather than on production data, (ii) it uses group mean scores for groups of learners, not individualised data, thus making it impossible to draw inferences for developing interlanguage sytems, and (iii) the alleged earliest stages of acquisition are defined merely by the point of data collection in a school class of formal learners, not by systematic features of developing interlanguages. In the end, the alleged hard-and-fast initial L2 hypothesis is merely a statistical trend in group mean scores in responses to grammaticality judgement tasks taken in three school classes of Dutch learners of French.

Thirdly, one wonders if Jordan assumes that theories may not be contradicted by *any* set of data. In fact, elsewhere in the book he points out that a certain amount of contradictory evidence cannot be avoided. Therefore other theories find themselves in the same position. What appears to be crucial is to evaluate how the empirical evidence relates to the assumptions made by the theory.

And there is a fourth point. In the case of the Hulk study, Clahsen's and Meisel's hypotheses about the L2 initial state (which Jordan must have in mind here, not PT) are based on assumptions that are rather different from the ones made by Hulk. The first two authors make claims about the syntax of individual learners, whereas Hulk focuses on statistical trends in group mean scores. This illustrates that empirical evidence is not theory-neutral. Instead, it needs to be collected and analysed with the assumptions in mind that one tries to falsify. In other words, one can only test predictions on the terms defined by the theory.

The final point of Jordan's critique concerns the scope of PT. Jordan (2004: 227) states that

> ... the domain [of PT] is limited; the theory restricts itself to an account of processing that accounts for speech production, and while it suggests that a certain type of linguistic theory should complement it, it does not go into the details.

This is not quite correct. Jordan is right in pointing out that the scope of the 1998 format of PT is limited. It focuses on the developmental problem and does not address the logical problem. However, this limitation is part of the design of the overall research programme, and PT is operationalised through a formal theory of grammar, Lexical Functional Grammar (cf. Bresnan 2001). The LFG interface ensures that the logical problem can be tackled as the next step in the construction of PT. In other words, a modular approach was taken in the construcion of PT, using a design that has provisions for the inclusion of modules that will be constructed later. Chapter 7 of this volume contains the first components of this extension. This modular strategy in theory construction was chosen because I did not want to compromise on the precision the theory would be able to achieve in delineating formally processable grammars in the two dimensions found in SLA.

This modular approach has also been applied to the comparison of L1 and L2 acquisition (cf. Pienemann 1998b) where I demonstrated that L1 and L2 developmental trajectories may be structurally different, but they are nevertheless positioned within the overall constraints on L2 development defined by PT. The differential developmental trajectories can be explained within PT on the basis of the developmental dynamics and the differential initial hypothesis. This difference in the initial hypothesis is the only epistemological issue that remains in the L1-L2 comparison within the PT framework. Hence PT serves to reduce the 'burden' placed on universal grammar (not necessarily the PP or Minimalist version) and the learning device in a theory of SLA. Therefore it makes sense to first construct the module that constrains the learner's hypothesis space and then to extend the theory to account for the remaining epistemological issues.

The second reason for this modular approach is practical. If one wants to construct a theory that can be formally modelled and that is fully operationalised and testable, one has to be explicit in the use of formalisms and in the theory-data interface. This creates a very considerable demand on detail which in turn converts into an enormous amount of work. Given the limitation of human processing resources, the researcher therefore faces a choice between covering a wide scope or a high degree of precision. My choice was high precision within a modular approach.

I cannot see that this strategy contradicts anything that is known about sound theory construction. The charge that PT is 'incomplete' would be very strange indeed for a rationalist outlook on SLA research. After all it is the rationalists and their alleged 'reductionism' that has to defend itself against similar charges from the empiricist camp. Jordan gives many examples of this in his book. For instance, he quotes Firth and Wagner (1997) claiming that SLA research has ignored the social context. As we know, Chomsky's approach to formal grammar has been charged with the same omission. The rationalist position to this charge is that one first needs to demonstrate that the abstraction made by formal theory negates an essential part of the explanandum and that it is thus illegitimate. The same logic applies to the modular approach chosen by PT.

In fact, it turns out that already the original version of PT addresses all of the explananda that Jordan (2004:10) quotes from Towell and Hawkins (1994:15):

1. Transfer → developmentally moderated transfer
2. Staged development → processability hierarchy
3. Systematicity → processability hierachy
4. Variability → hypothesis space
5. Incompleteness → generative entrenchment.

PT accounts for these phenomena not merely by use of vague metaphors or with a few illustrative examples, instead it constitutes a generic approach that covers the above phenomena across wide areas of linguistic structure and across typologically different languages. This is the advantage of the precision that can be achieved through a modular approach. The alternative would be a grand sketch of an overall theory that covers everything at the price of remaining vague and making few or no testable predictions.

The modular approach pursued in the construction of PT also recognises the relationship between the developmental and the logical problem and between the different components of learnability theory. As Pinker (1979) noted, the four standard components of such a theory compete against each other, and what is not contained in the initial state must be in the input or in the learning device. If we first construct a theory that defines the constraints that are imposed on hypothesis space then this will naturally constrain our assumptions about the initial state. I therefore assume that it is a reasonable sequence to first construct the theory module that defines those constraints. This way of proceeding has the advantage that the burden on the epistemelogical basis can be reduced, and this will result in a simpler and therefore more parsimonious explanation.

Notes

1. This is one aspect in which the summary of PT given in Chapter 1 differs from the original exposition of the theory. For reasons of readability no reference was made in Chapter 1 to perceptual saliency to explain the distance position of German verbs.

2. Jordan also claims that the MM's handling of morpheme acquisition is not falsifiable because of the undefined status of 'chunked morphemes'. Unfortunately, no reference is provided for this claim, and I find it hard to reconcile this with my own knowledge of the MM. This claim is now irrelevant anyway.

3. In his evaluation of PT Jordan also quotes R. Ellis (1994) who is said to claim that the original acquisition criterion used by the ZISA group (in the 1970s) was an 85% criterion. Again, no original reference is given, and I cannot reconcile this claim with my knowledge of the group's use of the criterion. The key paper here is the one by Meisel, Clahsen and Pienemann (1981), and this paper has two core messages: (1) 'there are two dimensions in SLA' and (2) 'in order to find them we need to look at emergence'. The paper did not apply the 85% criterion nor any other quantitaitve criterion.

References

Andersen, R. (1984). The one-to-one principle. *Language Learning, 34*, 77–95.

Berretta, A. (1991). Theory construction in second language acquisition. Complementarity and opposition. *Studies in Second Language Acquisition, 13*(3), 451–512.

Berretta, A. & Crookes, G. (1993). Cognitive and social determinants of discovery in SLA. *Applied Linguistics, 14*(3), 250–275.

Berti, P. & Di Biase, B. (2002). Form-focused instruction and the acquisition of nominal morphology in primary school learners of Italian L2. *Italiano e Scuola NSW Italian Teachers Bulletin, 7*(1), 10–14.

Bettoni, C. & Di Biase, B. (2005). Sviluppo obbligato e progresso morfosintattico – un caso di Processabilità in italiano L2. *ITALS* (*Italiano Lingua Seconda*).

Bever, T. G. (1970). The cognitive basis for linguistic structures. In J. R. Hayes (Ed.), *Cognition and the Development of Language*. New York, NY: Wiley.

Bever, T. G. & Townsend, D. (1979). Perceptual mechanisms and formal properties of main and subordinate clauses. In W. Cooper & E. Walker (Eds.), *Sentence Processing: Psycholinguistic studies presented to Merrill Garret* (pp. 159–226). Hillsdale, NJ: Erlbaum.

Bresnan, J. (2001). *Lexical-Functional Syntax*. Blackwell: Oxford.

Chomsky, N. (1978). A theory of core grammar. *GLOT, 1*, 7–26.

Clahsen, H. (1984). The acquisition of German word order: A test case for cognitive approaches to L2 development. In R. Anderson (Ed.), *Second Languages: A cross-linguistic perspective.* Rowley, MA: Newbury House.

Clahsen, H. & Muysken, P. (1986). The availability of universal grammar to adult and child learners: A study of the acquisition of German word order. *Second Language Research, 5,* 93–119.

Cook, V. (2001). Second Language Learning and Language Teaching. (3rd edition). London: Arnold.

Crookes, G. (1992). Theory format and second language acquisition theory. *Studies in Second Language Acquisition, 14*(4), 425–449.

De Houwer, A. (1990). *The Acquisition of Two Languages from Birth: A case study.* Cambridge: CUP.

Dewaele, J.-M. & Veronique, D. (2001). Gender assignment and gender agreement in advanced French interlanguage: A cross-sectional study. *Bilingualism: Language and Cognition, 4*(3), 275–297.

Di Biase, B. & Kawaguchi, S. (2002) Exploring the typological plausibility of Processability Theory: Language development in Italian second language and Japanese second language. *Second Language Research, 18*(3), 274–302.

Ellis, R. (1994). *The Study of Second Language Acquisition.* Oxford: OUP.

Firth, A. & Wagner, J. (1997). On discourse, communication and (some) fundamental concepts in SLA research. *Modern Language Journal, 81*(3), 285–300.

Glahn, E., Håkansson, G., Hammarberg, B., Holmen, A., Hvenekilde, A., & Lund, K. (2001). Processability in Scandinavian second language acquisition. *Studies in Second Language Acquisition, 23,* 389–416.

Håkansson, G., Pienemann, M., & Sayehli, S. (2002). Transfer and typological proximity in the context of L2 processing. *Second Language Research, 18,* 250–273.

Håkansson, G., Salameh, E.-K., & Nettelbladt, U. (2003). Measuring language development in bilingual children: Swedish-Arabic children with and without language impairment. *Linguistics, 41,* 255–288.

Hammarberg, B. (1996). Examining the processability theory: The case of adjective agreement in Swedish. In E. Kellerman, B. Weltens, & T. Bongaerts (Eds.), EUROSLA 6. A selection of papers. *Toegepaste taalwetenschap in artikelen, 55*(2), 75–88.

Harada, A. (2004). The Acquisition of English Modal Verbs by Japanese learners. MA Dissertation, University of Western Sydney.

Hulk, A. (1991). Parameter setting and the acquisition of word order in L2 French. *Second Language Research, 7,* 1–34.

Hulstijn, J. (1987). Onset and development of grammatical features: Two approaches to acquisition orders. Paper presented at *Interlanguage Conference,* La Trobe University, Melbourne 1987.

Hulstijn, J. (1998). Semantic/informational and formal processing principles in proc-essability theory. *Bilingualism: Language and Cognition, 1*(1).

Itani-Adams, Y. (2003). From word to phrase in Japanese-English bilingual first language acquisition. Paper presented at The MARCS seminar in 15 September 2003, University of Western Sydney.

Iwasaki, J. (2003). The acquisition of verbal morpho-syntax in JSL by a child learner. Paper presented at 13th Biennial Conference of the JSAA, Brisbane.

Jordan, G. (2004). *Theory Construction in Second Language Acquisition*. Amsterdam: John Benjamins.

Kaplan, R. & J. Bresnan. (1982). Lexical-functional grammar: A formal system for grammatical representation. In J. Bresnan (Ed.), *The Mental Representation of Grammatical Relations* (pp. 173–281). Cambridge, MA: The MIT Press.

Keßler, J. (in press). Englischerwerb im Anfangsunterricht der Primar- und Sekundarstufe. In M. Pienemann, J. Keßler, & E. Roos (Eds.), *Englischerwerb in der Schule*. Paderborn: UTB-Schöningh.

Kintsch, W. (1974). *The Representation of Meaning in Memory*. Hillsdale, NJ: Lawrence Erlbaum.

Larsen-Freeman, D. & Long, M. H. (1991). *An Introduction to Second Language Acquisition Research*. London: Longman.

Liebner, M. (in press). Variationsverhalten in verschiedenen Lernergruppen. In M. Pienemann, J. Keßler, & E. Roos (Eds.), *Englischerwerb in der Schule*. Paderborn: UTB-Schöningh.

Long, M. H. (1990). The least a second language theory needs to explain. *TESOL Quarterly, 24*(4), 654–666.

Long, M. H. (1993). Assessment strategies for SLA theories. *Applied Linguistics, 14*(3), 225–249.

Mansouri, F. (2000). *Grammatical Markedness and Information Processing in the Acquisition of Arabic as a Second Language*. München: Lincom Europa.

Meisel, J. M. (1983). Strategies of second language acquisition: More than one kind of simplification. In R. W. Andersen (Ed.), *Pidginisation and Creolisation as Language Acquisition* (pp. 120–157). Rowley, MA: Newbury House.

Meisel, J. M. (1991). Principles of Universal Grammar and strategies of language use: On some similarities and differences between first and second language acquisition. In L. Eubank (Ed.). *Point – Counterpoint. Universal grammar in the second language* (pp. 231–276). Amsterdam: John Benjamins.

Meisel, J. M., Clahsen, H., & Pienemann, M. (1981). Determining developmental stages in natural second language acquisition. *Studies in Second Language Acquisition, 3*, 109–135.

Murdock, B. B. Jr. (1962). The serial position effect in free recall. *Journal of Experimental Psychology, 62*, 618–625.

Netter, K. (1987). Wortstellung und Verbalkomplex im Deutschen. In U. Klenk, P. Scherber, & M. Thanller (Eds.), *Computerlinguistik und Philologische Datenverarbeitung*. Hildesheim: Olms.

Özdemir, B. (2004). Language development in Turkish-German bilingual children and implications for English as a third language. MA thesis. University of Paderborn.

Pienemann, M. (1984). Psychological constraints on the teachability of languages. *Studies in Second Language Acquisition, 6*(2), 186–214.

Pienemann, M. (1989). Is language teachable? Psycholinguistic experiments and hypotheses. *Applied Linguistics, 1*, 52–79.

Pienemann, M. (1998). *Language Processing and Second Language Development: Processability theory*. Amsterdam: John Benjamins.

Pienemann, M. (2003). Language processing capacity. In C. Doughty & M. H. Long (Eds.), *Handbook of Second Language Acquisition Theory and Research* (pp. 679–714). Oxford: Blackwell.

Pienemann, M. & Håkansson, G. (1999). A unified approach towards the development of Swedish as L2: Processability account. *Studies in Second Language Acquisition, 21*, 383–420.

Pienemann, M. & Johnston, M. (1987). Factors influencing the development of language proficiency. In D. Nunan (Ed.), *Applying Second Language Acquisition Research* (pp. 45–141). Adelaide: National Curriculum Research Centre, Adult Migrant Education Program.

Pienemann, M., Johnston, M., & Meisel, J. M. (1993). The multidimensional model, linguistic profiling and related issues: A reply to Hudson. *Studies in Second Language Acquisition, 15*, 495–503.

Pinker, S. (1979). Formal models of language learning. *Cognition, 7*, 217–283.

Slobin, D. I. (1973). Cognitive prerequisites for the development of grammar. In C. A. Ferguson & D. I. Slobin (Eds.), *Studies of Child Language Development* (pp. 175–208). New York, NY: Holt, Rinehart and Winston.

Slobin, D. I. & Bever, T. (1982). Children use canonical sentence schemes: A cross-linguistic study of word order and inflections. *Cognition, 12*(3), 229–265.

Sridhar, S. N. (1988). *Cognition and Sentence Production*. New York, NW: Springer.

Taylor R. (2004). Spanish L2 from a Processability Perspective: Two developmental case studies. BA (Honours) Dissertation, University of Western Sydney.

Towell, R. & Hawkins, R. (1994). *Approaches to Second Language Acquisition*. Clevedon: Multilingual Matters.

Vigliocco, G., Butterworth, B., & Semenza, C. (1995). Constructing subject-verb agreement in speech. The role of semantic and morphological factors. *Journal of Memory and Language, 34*, 186–215.

Vigliocco, G., Butterworth, B., & Garrett, M. F. (1996). Subject-verb agreement in Spanish and English: Differences in the role of conceptual constraints. *Cognition, 61*, 261–298.

White, L. (1991). Second language competence versus second language performance: UG or processing strategies? In L. Eubank (Ed.), *Point – counterpoint. Universal grammar in the second language* (pp. 167–189). Amsterdam: John Benjamins.

Zhang, Y. (2001). Second Language Acquisition of Chinese Grammatical Morphemes: A Processability perspective. PhD Dissertation, The Australian National University.

CHAPTER 3

Processability, typological distance and L1 transfer

Manfred Pienemann[*], Bruno Di Biase[**], Satomi Kawaguchi[**] and Gisela Håkansson[+]

*University of Paderborn, Germany and
University of Newcastle upon Tyne
**University of Western Sydney
+Lund University, Sweden

This chapter focuses on the interplay between L1 transfer and psycholinguistic constraints on L2 processability. The theoretical assumptions underlying this paper are those made in Processability Theory (Pienemann 1998) which include, in particular, the following two hypotheses: (i) that L1 transfer is constrained by the processability of the given structure and (ii) that the initial state of the L2 does not necessarily equal the final state of the L1, because there is no guarantee that the given L1 structure is processable by the under-developed L2 parser. In other words, it is assumed that L1 transfer is constrained by the capacity of the language processor of the L2 learner (or bilingual speaker) irrespective of the typological distance between the two languages.

Using the PT hierarchy as a comparative matrix, we will demonstrate on the basis of empirical studies of SLA that learners of closely related languages do not necessarily transfer grammatical features at the initial state even if these features are contained in L1 *and* L2, providing the features are located higher up the processability hierarchy. We will further demonstrate that such features *will* be transferred when the IL has developed the necessary processing prerequisites. In addition, we will demonstrate that typological distance and differences in grammatical marking need not constitute a barrier to learning if the feature to be learned is processable at the given point in time. All of this demonstrates that processability is a key variable in L1 transfer.

1.   Competing theoretical approaches to L1 transfer

This paper focuses on the interplay between L1 transfer and psycholinguistic constraints on L2 processability. The basic thesis of this paper is that L1 transfer is constrained by the capacity of the language processor of the L2 learner (or bilingual speaker) irrespective of the typological distance between the two languages.

Before we lay out our argument it may be useful to briefly characterise the nature of the various competing approaches to L1 transfer and their theoretical basis.

In the study of language contact, bilingualism and second language acquisition, cross-linguistic influence appears to be one of the key phenomena that has caught the attention of scholars for over one hundred years. For instance, Sweet (1899) and Palmer (1917) both discuss L1 interference in relation to what would now be termed typological distance. Weinreich (1953) in his seminal treatment of interference in language contact places great emphasis on operationalising this concept in the context of the overall 'linguistic system' as conceptualised in structuralist theory of communication of his time. And in his own review of research on the study of interference in bilingualism he complains that "... all these studies suffer ... from a lack of linguistic advice" (Weinreich 1974 (1953): 12). Indeed, his review contains many examples of anecdotal approaches. One of Weinreich's achievements was to place the notion of interference in the context of the overall design of structuralist linguistics. In other words, L1 influence was not considered an accidental or irregular accumulation of L1 'borrowings' in an individual bilingual, but was placed firmly within the overall system of the source and the target language. Other scholars established a theoretical link between behaviourist theories of learning and the notion of L1 interference (e.g. Lado 1957) establishing an influential paradigm that was ultimately damaged by the rationalists' critique of behaviourist concepts of language learning.

By the 1970s the outlook on L1 transfer had changed under the influence of the newly emerging discipline of Second Language Acquisition (SLA) research which initially was fuelled in particular by the idea that learners construct their own linguistic systems that may be quite independent of L1 and L2. With the new emphasis on the 'creative construction process' (e.g. Dulay & Burt 1974) in SLA the notion of L1 interference appeared a less attractive explanatory concept, and it became clear that one needed to develop specific SLA theories to predict the exact conditions for creative construction on the one hand and for L1 transfer on the other hand, since these explanations compete with each other. In this context Felix (1977) argued that the role of L1 transfer can be determined in empirical studies only if the null-hypothesis is tested in a typological manner. This requires a systematic typological comparison of the given linguistic feature in L1, L2 and IL in the following constellation:

	L1	L2	IL
feature x	+	–	+
feature x	–	–	–

Felix argued as follows: in cases where the IL contains an L2-deviation which is structurally similar to the L1, one can assume that this structure has been transferred from the L1 only if this structure does not appear in ILs (with the same L2) where the L1 does not contain the feature in question. Using this matrix in empirical studies, Felix demonstrated, however, that in the above constellation features are often assigned as follows:

	L1	L2	IL
feature x	+	–	+
feature x	–	–	+

When this is the case, the null-hypothesis (for L1 transfer) cannot be rejected. Instead, one has to conclude that one is dealing with a genuine IL feature. Unfortunately, this logic has not always been adhered to in later research. However, in making a case for developmental constraints on L1 transfer we will apply exactly this logic to evaluating the significance of empirical evidence for or against competing theoretical positions including our own.

Scholars who accept that 'universal grammar' (UG) plays a role in SLA attribute different roles to it. These roles vary according to the degree to which L2 learners are thought to have access to UG and according to the degree to which L1 knowledge is transferred to the L2.

The most radical position is that of Schwartz and Sprouse (1994, 1996) who propose the "Full Transfer/ Full Access model". These authors assume that "... the initial state of L2 acquisition is the final state of L1 acquisition." (Schwartz & Sprouse (1996:40f.). In other words, L2 learners have full access to UG. However, parameters have already been set as in the L1. In this perspective, L2 acquisition is seen as the process of restructuring the existing grammatical knowledge. This implies that when positive evidence in the input is needed to restructure aspects of L1 knowledge and this evidence is not available or 'obscure', then this can lead to fossilisation. The latter process is thought to explain why, contrary to child language, in L2 acquisition "... convergence with the TL grammar is not guaranteed" Schwartz and Sprouse (1996:42).

The position of Vainikka and Young-Scholten (1994, 1996) might be labelled "Full Access/ Minimal Transfer". In other words, it differs from that of Schwartz & Sprouse's Full Transfer/ Full Access position in the amount of transfer that is assumed to occur from the L1 to the L2 setting of parameters. For Vainikka & Young-Scholten (1994, 1996) transfer is limited to lexical categories; they assume that there are no functional projections in the L2 initial state. They therefore describe their position as the 'minimal tree' position which in effect amounts to the assumption that L1 word order is transferred.

A further position is proposed by Eubank (1993) who hypothesises that lexical and functional categories can be transferred to the L2, but the strength of inflection associated with functional categories is not transferred. Eubank argues that the strength of the inflection will not be transferred because the affixes themselves may be fundamentally different from language to language. Meisel (1995) gives a detailed review of the positions summarised above.

Platzack (1996) proposes a universal "initial hypothesis of syntax" based on the Minimalist Program. His study focuses on the acquisition of Swedish word order, and he demonstrates that word order constellations can be captured by the weak/ strong distinction in functional heads.[1] He assumes that the default value of functional heads is 'weak'. If all functional heads are weak in a sentence, a universal default word order 'Subject-Verb-Complement' will be generated. Only if a functional head is strong, can the position of constituents change.

Platzack (1996: 375) claims that "... the initial syntactic hypothesis of the child must be that all syntactic features are weak," furthermore that "... the child has access to the full range of functional categories already at the time of first sentence-like utterances ..." (Platzack 1996: 377). In other words, "... every human being is expected to assume from the outset that any unknown language s/he is exposed to, including the first language, has the word order subject-verb-complement: this is the order obtained if there are no strong features at all" (Platzack 1996: 378). With regard to second language acquisition he claims that "... we initially go back to ... [the initial hypothesis of syntax] when trying to come to grips with a second language" (Platzack 1996: 380).

The above views all have in common that L2 learners are believed to have full access to universal grammar. However, several scholars hold other views. Felix (1984), Clahsen (1986) and Meisel (1983, 1991) have all developed models in which L2 learners have limited or indirect access to universal grammar. This assumption is congruent with the observation that L2 acquirers do not necessarily become native speakers of the L2. Given that the limited availability of universal grammar creates an explanatory void, these authors all make proposals for a more general cognitive substitute that can account for the somewhat deficient process that is present in second language acquisition.

The Competition Model (Bates & MacWhinney 1981, 1982, 1987; MacWhinney 1997) represents a fundamentally different approach to language acquisition from the rationalist tradition. It is a functionalist approach that is based on the assumption that linguistic behaviour is constrained, among other things, by general cognition (and not by a language-specific cognitive module) and communicative needs. Following the functionalist tradition, Bates and MacWhinney assume that "the surface conventions of natural languages are created, governed, constrained, acquired, and used in the service of communicative functions" (Bates & MacWhinney 1981:192).

The Competition Model has been applied to child language, language processing and second language acquisition. According to this model it is the task of the language learner to discover the specific relationship between linguistic forms of a given language and their communicative functions. The linguistic forms used to mark grammatical and semantic roles differ from language to language. For instance, agreement marking, word order and animacy play a different role in the marking of subjecthood and agency in different languages. Linguistic forms are seen as 'cues' for semantic interpretation in on-line comprehension and production, and different cues may compete as in the above case of the marking of subjecthood, hence the name 'competition' model.

In the Competition Model the process of learning linguistic forms is driven by the frequency and complexity of form-function relationships in the input. In this context the majority of L2 learning problems is modelled in connectionist terms. MacWhinney (1987) exemplifies this with the preverbal positioning of a linguistic form as a (processing) cue for the semantic actor-role. He states that the strength of this cue "... can be viewed as the weight on the connection between the preverbal positioning node (an input node) and the actor role (an output node). If the preverbal positioning node is activated, it then sends activation to the actor node in proportion to the weight on the connection" MacWhinney (1987:320).

The Competition Model has formed the conceptual basis of experiments on bilingual sentence processing (e.g. Gass 1987; Harrington 1987; Kilborn & Ito 1989; Sasaki 1991). In these studies bilingual speakers of different languages need to identify the function of different 'cues' in L1 and L2. The input material is designed to reflect the coordination and competition of cues. For instance, Harrington (1987) studies the (competing) effects of word order, animacy and stress on the comprehension of Japanese and English sentences by native speakers and non-native speakers of the two languages who are all speakers of both languages. Obviously, the three cues have different weights in the two target languages concerned. The results show that L2 learners transfer their L1 processing strategies (i.e. weighting of cues) when interpreting L2 sentences. This overall result is predicted by the Competition Model, since within this framework processing cues are not initially separated by languages and their weighting is therefore predicted to be transferred.

MacWhinney (1997) attributes a key role to L1 transfer also in the acquisition (as opposed to the processing) of a second language. This is motivated mainly by the stark contrast in learning outcomes in first and second language acquisition that was also noticed by many rationalist researchers (e.g. Clahsen & Muysken 1989; Meisel 1991; Bley-Vroman 1990). The logic behind this is straightforward: both first and second language learners rely on cue strength in acquisition. The reason why the outcomes are different is because in the case of second language learners first language patterns interfere with second language learning. On the basis of the above assumptions MacWhinney develops a strong view on L1 transfer that is in effect similar to the "Full Transfer/ Full Access" hypothesis by Schwartz and Sprouse (1996) – despite their fundamentally different theoretical orientation:

> ... the early second language learner should experience a massive amount of transfer from L1 to L2. Because connectionist models place such a strong emphasis on analogy and other types of pattern generalization, they predict that all aspects of the first language that can possibly transfer to L2 will transfer. This is an extremely strong and highly falsifiable prediction.
>
> (MacWhinney 1997:119)

MacWhinney (1997) illustrates his point on structurally 'impossible transfer' using German and English as an example. German nouns are implicitly marked for grammatical gender, English nouns are not. He concludes that German learners therefore have no basis for transferring the German gender system to English. Therefore this set of features is not included in the list of things that will be transferred.

Our own approach to cross-linguistic influences in second language acquisition does not take the initial state but processing constraints as its point of departure (e.g. Pienemann 1998; Håkansson, Pienemann & Sayehli 2002). The theoretical assumptions underlying our approach are those made in Processability Theory (PT) (Pienemann 1998) which include, in particular, the following two hypotheses: (1) that L1 transfer is constrained by the processability of the given structure and (2) that the initial state of the L2 does not necessarily equal the final state of the L1 (contrary to the assumption made by Schwartz & Sprouse 1996), because there is no guarantee that the given L1 structure is processable by the under-developed L2 parser.

The key assumption of the processing perspective in SLA is that L2 learners can produce only those linguistic forms for which they have acquired the necessary processing prerequisites (Pienemann 1998). Therefore PT predicts that, regardless of linguistic typology, only those linguistic forms that the learner can process can be transferred to the L2. These claims are operationalised in PT by being embedded in a coherent theoretical framework of L2 processing.

The assumption that L1 transfer may be developmentally constrained is not new in SLA research. Wode (1976, 1978) demonstrates such constraints for the acquisition of negation and interrogatives. He shows that German learners of English produce certain L1 forms only after they have developed the structural prerequisites in the L2. Zobl (1980) shows similar phenomena, as does Kellerman (1983). What Processability Theory (Pienemann 1998) adds to the concept of developmental constraints on transfer is an explicit formal framework for specifying these constraints. This framework will be tested in sets of data that allow us to test the null-hypothesis for transfer in typological 'minimal pairs'.

2. Processing constraints on L1 transfer

The internal mechanics of PT imply processing constraints on L1 transfer because in the given architecture of the language generator there is no guarantee that one can simply utilise L1 procedures for the L2. Pienemann (1998: 80f.) argues that such "bulk transfer" would lead to internal problems

> ... because all of the above processing procedures need to be orchestrated in a language-specific way. If any one of them is missing or incompatible with the rest, the Formulator is inoperable. If, for instance, the lexical category information is missing, category and phrasal procedures cannot be called. If diacritic features are missing or have no values or values which are not compatible with those listed in agreeing phrases or if they are incompatible with the Functorisation Rules, then the processor will be inoperable.
>
> (Pienemann 1998: 80)

PT does not imply, however, that the learner will never attempt to form diacritic features and Functorisation Rules that reflect L1 regularities. Instead, the theory does imply processing constraints on L1 transfer:

... 'bulk-transfer' of the L1 Formulator would lead to very unwieldy hypotheses. German learners of English, for instance, would have to invent large sets of diacritic features for nouns, verbs and adjectives without any evidence of their existence in the L2, since German definite determiners express a complex set of diacritic features of the noun (three genders and two numbers). Since English nouns do not contain these diacritic features in nouns the complex system of definite determiners presented in Table [1] corresponds to merely one English grammatical morpheme ('the').

In this case the simplest structural solution would be to abandon the L1 diacritic features altogether. This would in fact reproduce a situation which is close to the English determiner system. However, the relationship between L1 and L2 diacritic features may be more complex than in the above example, with two intersecting sets of diacritic features and different form-function relationships in L1 and L2. In other words, there is potentially a multitude of L1 features only some of which are applicable to the L2."   (Pienemann 1998:81)

In essence the lack of psychological plausibility present in the 'bulk transfer' approach forms a logical argument in favour of processing constraints on L1 transfer, the position assumed by PT:

> ... I hypothesise that the L1 Formulator will not be 'bulk-transferred'. Instead, the learner will re-construct the Formulator of the L2. This would not exclude that in the course of this process L1 procedures be utilised. However, I hypothesise that such L1 transfer always occurs as part of the overall reconstruction process.   (Pienemann 1998:81–82)

The case of constraints on the transfer of morphological and lexical regularities is relatively straightforward as the example of the determiner illustrates. It may be less obvious why the same constraints should also be operational on word order, particularly in the case of two languages that share several identical features. To appreciate this point it may be useful to consider the lexical nature of word order regularities within an LFG framework and indeed in Levelt's model of language generation.

Table 1. The German definite article

| | masculine | | feminine | | neuter | |
	sgl	pl	sgl	pl	sgl	pl
nominative	der	die	die	die	das	die
genitive	des	der	der	der	des	der
dative	dem	den	der	den	dem	den
accusative	den	die	die	die	das	die

This point has been illustrated by Pienemann (1998:99–102) with the acquisition of German separable verbs. This has been described as a gradual lexical acquisition process that is based on a number of alterations of the initial c-structure rule (R1) for canonical word order when it is modified in later development into (R2). One alteration concerns the introduction of VP as a constituent, which is necessary to account for a range of phenomena in German, as we will see below. The other alteration is concerned with the position of the verb. VP rewrites alternatively into the structure known from R1, or as V-COMP, and the latter constituent rewrites as $(NP_{obj1})(NP_{obj2})$ V. This ensures that V will only occur in second position unless "licensed" by a V that takes V-COMP.

(R1)   S   → NP_{subj} V (NP_{obj1}) (NP_{obj2})

(R2)   S   → NP_{subj} VP

  VP → V $\left\{ \begin{array}{l} (NP_{obj1})\ (NP_{obj2}) \\ \text{V-COMP} \end{array} \right\}$

  V-COMP → (NP_{obj1}) (NP_{obj2}) V

Apart from this change in c-structure rules, Pienemann (1998) assumes that the learner gradually re-analyses the verbs of his/her interlanguage, by analysing AUX and V as two separate entries and by adding the feature AUX to the lexical features of V.

The relevant part of that analysis is as follows:

> To achieve the split verb effect, the newly created auxiliaries and modals are treated as main verbs (with the feature AUX that takes the value '+'), which take VP complements (as in Kaplan & Bresnan 1982; Netter 1987). Let us take sentence (1) as an example:

> (1)   *er hat ein Bier getrunken*
>   he has a   beer drunk
>   'he has drunk/drank a beer'.

The c-structure of (1) is represented in the form of a simplified tree diagram in Figure 1. The simplified lexical entries for the verbs in (1) are as shown in Figure 2.

This set of entries and rules, etc. ensure two things which are of relevance here: (1) that a particular (at this stage not necessarily the correct) morphological form of the lexical verb is used with the auxiliary to express the intended grammatical function. This is achieved by functional well-formedness conditions which ensure that functional annotations match across related constituents. In this case it is the value PAST in (PARTICIPLE) = PAST and (V-Comp PARTICIPLE) = PAST which allows a unification of these two functions and thus legitimates these two constituents in this particular sentence.

(2) The second point is that the c-structure rules, in conjunction with the unification processes mentioned under (1), ensure that the two verbs appear in a split position and that only the lexical verb can appear in the final position. ... [A]ccording to the rule system developed above, only lexical verbs can occur in the final position [because] the PRED value for 'hat' contains V-COMP and SUBJ, while that of *getrunken* contains SUBJ and OBJ. The SUBJ of *getrunken* needs to be unified with the SUBJ of 'hat' since it is not directly linked to any argument. Because of these differences in the lexical entries of the verbs, and the way they interact with c-structure, 'hat' cannot be inserted under that V that is dominated by V-COMP, i.e. 'hat' in final position is excluded.

In essence, this means that the positioning of verbs is controlled by the unification of the feature PARTICIPLE.   (Pienemann 1998:100–102)

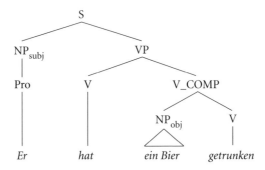

Figure 1. C-structure for the sentence 'Er hat ein Bier getrunken'

getrunken: V,   PRED = 'trinken (SUBJ) (OBJ)'
PARTICIPLE = PAST
INF = ge
OBJ CASE = accusative
AUX = –

hat: V,   PRED = 'haben, V-COMP (SUBJ)'
TENSE = PAST
AUX = +
NUM = SG
PERSON = 3RD
V-COMP PARTICIPLE = PAST
V-COMP INF =$_c$ ge

Figure 2. Lexical entries for the German verbs 'getrunken' and 'hat'

This unification process is the key point in our discussion of L1 transfer. The above example illustrates that word order phenomena depend crucially on the correct annotation of lexical entries which differ in their diacritic features even between related languages.

Cross-linguistic differences in diacritic features are further illustrated by the following comparison of two lexical classes and their diacritic features in closely related languages.

	German	Swedish	English
noun	2 numbers	2 numbers	2 numbers
	3 genders	2 genders	–
	4 cases	–	–
verb	2 numbers	–	–
	3 persons	–	2 persons
	tense	tense	tense

In other words, the procedures that achieve the different positions are highly language-specific, and the lexical information involved is not necessarily compatible even between two closely related languages.

In the case of the Swedish-German contrast there is also a host of syntactic phenomena which apply to one of the languages only, as for instance a complex array of constraints on the placement of negation that apply to Swedish only (cf. Pienemann & Håkansson 1999). The Swedish learner of German is therefore faced with the following situation: the phonology of the two languages is markedly different; the lexical items are not mutually intelligible, and the structure of the lexicon is different despite certain overlaps. A similar overlap also applies to syntax.

In this situation the learner has the task of discovering which lexical features and which syntactic patterns are shared by the two languages. Pienemann (1998) points out that the existing similarities between the languages are not obvious to the learner, because they are distributed amongst a host of typological differences:

> While it may be clear to the linguistic analyst which of the diacritic features of the L1 apply to the L2, and which syntactic patterns are shared between the languages, there is no obvious *a priori* way for the learner to know this. A random choice of features would be likely to generate procedures which are incompatible with the rest of the Formulator. Unless the learner simply limits herself or himself to the L1 Formulator, thus re-lexifying the L1 (as it may be possible in mutually intelligible languages) and not acquiring the L2, there is

> no other obvious choice than to re-construct the set of diacritic features and
> syntactic routines specific to the L2.   (Pienemann 1998: 81)

In other words, according to PT, the re-construction of the L2 and developmental constraints on L1 transfer follow from the hierarchical nature of the learning task. In this scenario there is no other logical point of departure for this reconstruction process than the beginning of the processability hierarchy because it is stripped of all language-specific lexical features and syntactic routines. It would therefore be logical for this reconstruction process to follow the path described in the processability hierarchy and for L1 knowledge and skills to become accessible once they are processable in the developing system.

Summing up, PT implies the hypothesis that the L1 Formulator will not be bulk-transferred, because the processing of syntax is lexically driven and the processor relies on highly language-specific lexical features. Instead, the learner will re-construct the Formulator of the L2. This would not exclude that in the course of this process L1 procedures will be utilised. However, it is hypothesised that such cases of L1 transfer occur as part of the overall reconstruction process. This means that L1 transfer is *developmentally moderated* and will occur when the structure to be transferred is processable within the developing L2 system.

3.   Typological proximity without an advantage

The notion of "developmentally moderated transfer" basically implies that certain grammatical structures which are identical in L1 and L2 require the development of certain processing prerequisites before the L1 procedures can be utilised in the L2. In this section we will review a number of key studies in support of this hypothesis. What these studies have in common is that they all focus on L1 transfer in the context of typological proximity. In other words, we will provide empirical evidence to show that typological proximity does not guarantee L2 learners ready access to L1 knowledge or to L1 processing skills.

Håkansson, Pienemann and Sayehli (2002) provide empirical evidence to demonstrate that L1 transfer is developmentally moderated as predicted by PT. The study focuses on the acquisition of German by Swedish school children. The L1 and the L2 share the following word order regularities in affirmative main clauses:

SVO

Peter mag Milch (German)
Peter gillar mjölk (Swedish)
'Peter likes milk'[2]

adverb fronting (ADV)
*Heute Peter mag Milch
*Idag Peter gillar mjölk
'Today Peter likes milk'

subject-verb inversion (INV) after ADV
Heute mag Peter Milch.
Idag gillar Peter mjölk
'Today likes Peter milk'

In order to place this developmental sequence in the overall context of the processability hierarchy, an overview of the implementation of key morpho-syntactic features of German and Swedish is provided in Tables 2 and 3. (For a full exposition of this implementation process and supporting empirical evidence, we refer the reader to Pienemann 1998; and Pienemann & Håkansson 1999).

The results of the study by Håkansson, Pienemann and Sayehli (2002) are summarized in Table 4 which treats all learner samples as parts of a cross-sectional study. Therefore Table 4 represents an implicational scale[3] (cf. Hatch

Table 2. Processing procedures applied to German word order and morphology

Stage	Exchange of information	Procedures	Word order	Morphology
5		Sub cl procedure	V-final	
4	Inter-phrasal	S-procedure	INV	SV-agreement
3	Phrasal	Phrasal procedure	ADV	Plural agreement
2	None	Lex. categories	SVO	Past – te etc.
1	None			'words'

Table 3. Processing procedures applied to Swedish word order and morphology

Stage	Exchange of information	Procedures	Word order	Morphology
5		Sub cl procedure	neg V_f	
4	Inter-phrasal	S-procedure	INV	Predicative agr.
3	Phrasal	Phrasal procedure	ADV	Attributive agr.
2	None	Lex. categories	SVO	Past. etc.
1	None			'words'

Table 4. Implicational scale based on all learners in the study by Håkansson, Pienemann and Sayheli (2002)

Name	SVO	ADV	INV
Gelika (Year 1)	+	−	−
Emily (Year 1)	+	−	−
Robin (Year 1)	+	−	−
Kennet (Year 1)	+	−	−
Mats (Year 2)	+	−	−
Camilla (Year 2)	+	−	−
Johann (Year 1)	+	+	−
Cecilia (Year 1)	+	+	−
Eduard (Year 1)	+	+	−
Anna (Year 1)	+	+	−
Sandra (Year 1)	+	+	−
Erika (Year 1)	+	+	−
Mateus (Year 2)	+	+	−
Karolin (Year 2)	+	+	−
Ceci (Year 2)	+	+	−
Peter (Year 2)	+	+	−
Johan (Year 2)	+	+	+
Zandra (Year 2)	+	+	+
Zofie (Year 2)	+	+	+
Caro (Year 2)	+	+	+

& Farhady 1982) of the data which demonstrates that the learners follow the
sequence (1) SVO, (2) ADV and (3) INV. In other words, ADV and INV are not
transferred from the L1 at the initial state although these rules are contained in
the L1 and the L2. This implies that for a period of time the learners produce
the constituent order

  *adverb + S + V + O

which is ungrammatical in the L1 as well as in the L2 (e.g. *Heute Peter mag
Milch).

Håkansson et al. (2002) argue on the basis of PT that the L2 system can
utilize L1 production mechanisms only when the L2 system has developed the
necessary prerequisites to process the L1 forms and that therefore the INV-
procedure of the L1 cannot be utilized before the full S-procedure has been
developed in the L2.

Given that in this study German was in fact the third language of the informants and that English was the second, it may be easy to conclude that the
non-application of INV (or V2) was due to transfer from English. In fact, this

explanation is popular amongst Swedish school teachers of German and has also been suggested by Ruin (1996) and Naumann (1997). Swedish teachers of German disrespectfully termed this phenomenon the "English illness".

However, such a proposal is not quite conclusive. In the above study ADV did not appear at the early stage although it is also part of English grammar and could therefore be transferred. In other words, one would need to consider how the transfer-from-L2 hypothesis would be testable. Logically, the hypothesis would have to predict that all L2 word-order constraints would be transferred, or at least all those that are shared by the L1, the L2 and the L3. Otherwise the transfer hypothesis would have no predictive power and could not be falsified, unless one added a separate theory predicting which items are to be transferred and which are not.

In the absence of such a theory one can only test the transfer-all hypothesis. To follow this line of argument it is important to remember that the data from the above study show a strictly implicational development. It is evident from this analysis that six of the twenty learners produce SVO only and no ADV. If one followed the transfer-from-L2 view, they would appear to have transferred selectively only one word-order pattern known from their L2 (English). This clearly falsifies the transfer-all hypothesis and leaves the selective-transfer-from-L2 hypothesis with the problem of making no testable prediction as to when transfer will take place.

Bardel & Falk (2004) assume that the 'Developmentally Moderated Transfer Hypothesis' (DMTH) implies a principled position on transfer from the L2, and these authors claim to have found counter-evidence to the DMTH. Bardel and Falk present data on negation in an attempt to demonstrate that L2 learners can acquire high-stage structures without first acquiring the lower-stage structures, if their second language contains the higher structure. To demonstrate this point, they collected speech data from five learners with the following constellations of L1s, L2s and L3s:

	L1	strongest L2	L3
Group 1 (2 informants)	English	German	Swedish
	Hungarian	Dutch	Swedish
Group 2 (3 informants)	Dutch	English	Swedish

First of all, we need to point out that the DMTH does not imply a position on transfer from L2. Instead, we argued that in the specific case of the study by Håkansson, Pienemann and Sayehli (2002) transfer from the L2 is not a plausible hypothesis. For their own proposal Bardel and Falk fail to provide any explicit reason why transfer from L2 should be privileged over transfer from L1. And no explicit and testable proposal is developed for a model of transfer from the L2.The learners in Bardel and Falk's database have several L2s. No reason is given why the other L2s would not show an effect on L3 acquisition.

Bardel and Falk (2004) calculated group mean scores of the use of preverbal and postverbal negation. They found that Group 1 has a higher rate in the use of postverbal negation than Group 2. They interpret this in terms of transfer from the strongest L2 to the L3.

First of all, one needs to consider the minimal size of database of this study which is based on a total of merely 121 sentences for all five learners over 10 interviews each. This is little more than two sentences per informant for each interview. In other words, the database does not even cover every context of negation for every interview. Therefore one cannot carry out a meaningful distributional analysis on the basis of this limited set of data.

Even if one ignored these serious reservations about the validity of the database, it is impossible to evaluate its implications for the DMTH because Bardel and Falk (2004) do not report whether their informants also produced structures at lower levels. If the learners were able to produce structures at the lower levels, the early correct placement of negation would be fully com-patible with the DMTH. In this case transfer from the L2 would have been developmentally moderated.

Further evidence supporting the hypothesis that L1 transfer is develop-mentally constrained comes from Johnston's study of the acquisition of English by learners of Polish and Vietnamese. Johnston's study consists of a total of 24 samples from Polish and Vietnamese adult immigrants in Australia and focuses on the acquisition of 12 grammatical rules. The full distributional analysis of this study is available in Johnston (1997) and is also reported on in Pienemann, Johnston and Brindley (1988). We will therefore focus on the summary of his analysis, i.e. after the application of the emergence-based acquisition criterion. The true size of the corpus may not be obvious from the compact format of the tables below. We would therefore like to point out that each of the 16 interviews was between 40 and 60 minutes in length, resulting in a 60,000 word corpus.

Now to the test of the hypothesis that L1 transfer is developmentally con-strained: Polish uses subject-verb agreement marking, Vietnamese does not. According to the Full Transfer/Full Access Hypothesis, AGR ought to be trans-ferred from Polish to English. The Polish learners therefore ought to have an advantage over the Vietnamese learners concerning this structure. However, a separate implicational analysis of the two groups reveals that both groups follow the same pattern, and in both groups AGR is acquired late. This can be seen from the perfect implicational pattern in Tables 5 and 6 below.

Tables 5 and 6 are laid out as implicational tables. The 12 grammatical rules of English discussed above are listed on the left-hand side in their order of processability. For each learner and rule a '+' marks rules which have been acquired according to the emergence criterion (cf. Pienemann 1998); a '–' marks those rules which have not been acquired, and a '/' marks those rules for which there is no linguistic context in the sample.

The scalability of Tables 5 and 6 is 100%. It therefore fully supports the predicted sequence of acquisition for English. The late acquisition of SV-agreement is predicted by the processability hierarchy, as outlined above. Within this framework one would not expect agreement to be transferred because the process is lexically driven and highly language-specific.

Klein Gunnewiek (2000) believes her study to contradict the predictions made by PT. She investigated the acquisition of German word order by Dutch learners. The typological scenario of this study is therefore the same as that in the study by Håkansson, Pienemann and Sahyli (2002). In both cases the critical structures are the same in L1 and L2.

The structures in question were elicited by a number of specifically designed written and oral tests. The written tests consisted of a multiple choice test, a 'domino test' with scrambled word order, two types of grammaticality judgement tests, one with explanations of errors, one with just the identification of errors. The oral tests was based on various communicative tasks including role play, 'negotiation', picture narration, 'sports rules', translation

Table 5. Vietnamese learners of English

Stage	Structure	van	tam	long	vinh	sang	dung	phuc
6	Cancel Inversion	–	–	–	–	–	–	–
5	Aux2nd/ Do2nd	–	–	–	–	–	+	+
	3 sg-s	–	–	–	–	–	+	+
4	Y/N Inversion	–	–	–	–	+	+	+
	PS Inversion	–	–	+	+	/	/	/
3	Neg+V	–	+	+	+	+	+	+
	Do Front.	–	+	+	/	+	+	+
	Topi	–	+	+	+	+	+	+
	ADV	–	+	+	+	+	+	+
2	SVO	–	+	+	+	+	+	+
	Plural	–	+	+	+	+	+	+
1	single words	+	/	/	/	/	/	/

Table 6. Polish learners of English

Stage	Structure	IS	my	ks	jr	bb	ka	es	ij	ja
6	Cancel Inversion	–	–	–	–	–	–	–	–	–
5	Aux2nd/ Do2nd	–	–	–	–	–	–	–	–	–
	3 sg-s	–	–	–	–	–	–	–	+	+
4	Y/N Inversion	–	–	–	–	+	+	+	+	+
	PS Inversion	–	–	–	+	+	+	+	+	+
3	Neg+V	–	–	+	+	+	+	+	+	+
	Do Front.	–	+	+	/	+	+	+	+	+
	Topi	–	+	+	+	+	+	+	+	+
	ADV	–	+	+	+	+	+	+	+	+
2	SVO	+	+	+	+	+	+	+	+	+
	Plural	+	+	+	+	+	+	+	+	+
1	single words	/	/	/	/	/	/	/	/	/

and structured interviews with lists of questions. Data from 24 learners were collected over a period of 7 months.

In the data analysis, percentages of correctness of selected structures were calculated. The results shown are interpreted in terms of supporting development over time. The crucial point in the context of the current discussion of L1 transfer is the following. Klein Gunnewiek notes that subject-verb inversion is based on the same syntactic regularities in German and in Dutch. She therefore sets up an analysis of her data to test if this regularity is transferred from L1 to L2. To test this hypothesis she compares the level of grammatical accuracy in the use of subject-verb inversion and verb-final, the structure acquired after subject-verb inversion according to PT. She found that in her data subject-verb inversion is produced at a higher level of accuracy than verb-final and concludes that this constitutes a falsification of the predictions made by PT.

In assessing the implication of this study for the notion of psychological constraints on L1 transfer, one has to bear in mind that the learners in Klein Gunnewiek's study used subject-verb inversion 40% correctly in the first week and improved to 70% in the 28th week. Applying the emergence criterion (Pienemann 1998) as required for PT, one has to conclude that they had clearly acquired this rule when data collection began, and her data set does not permit her to test the hypothesis that her learners acquire inversion before verb-end. In other words, Klein Gunnewiek tested the following hypothesis: "V-End before INV", and in her data INV is already present from the outset. Therefore it is impossible to prove that V-End had been acquired before INV applying the required criteria. Nevertheless the Dutch learners of German appear to reach higher levels of accuracy more quickly than Romance learners (cf. Clahsen,

Meisel & Pienemann 1983). This may indeed be the kind of advantage the next section is dealing with.

4. Typological proximity with an advantage

The rationale of the previous section was the following: typological proximity does not guarantee L2 learners ready access to L1 knowledge or to L1 processing skills. In this section we will show that typological proximity *may* have an advantage – if it implies that the L1-L2 similarity is based on a structure that is located low on the processability hierarchy.

Haberzettl (2000) studied the acquisition of German word order by Russian and Turkish learners. Turkish is an agglutinative language with SOV as the preferred word order, whereas Russian has post-verbal objects and follows a VX pattern. Haberzettl focuses on the acquisition of the German split-verb position (cf. our discussion above) which creates an SVXV pattern with the inflected verb in second and the uninflected verb in final position.

Haberzettl carried out a longitudinal study of 12 child learners of German aged six to eight years over a period of two to four years based on monthly sessions of 20 to 60 minutes in length. The key finding in the present context is that the Russian learners acquired the split-verb position gradually over several months whereas the Turkish learners acquired it categorically and with native-like correctness once the structure emerged. This point can be illustrated by contrasting one of the Turkish and one of the Russian learners as in Tables 7 and 8.

Tables 7 and 8 give the percentage of correct split-verb positions in the interlanguage of the two informants as opposed to the ungrammatical adjacency position (*SVVX), and one can easily see the contrast between the two types of learners, i.e. the gradual acquisition process in the Russian learner and the sudden emergence in the Turkish learner.

Haberzettl concluded from these findings and their replication with the other learners in her study that the Turkish learners benefit from the structural overlap in word order constellations in German and Turkish. This conclu-

Table 7. Turkish learner of German L2

	session 15	session 16	session 17	session 18	session 19
X V Y V	100	100	99	98	100
*X V VY	0	0	1	2	0

Table 8. Russian learner of German L2

	session 3	session 5	session 8	session 10
X V Y V	0	20	42	97
*X V VY	100	80	58	3

sion is fully compatible with the predictions that can be made on the basis of the processability hierarchy and the notion of developmentally moderated transfer. As the above discussion has shown, the split-verb construction is associated with level four of the hierarchy, and both types of learners follow the predicted sequence. However, the Turkish learners can take advantage of their L1 processing skills once their interlanguage has developed to the point at which they can be integrated into the L2 processor. In other words, this type of study constitutes evidence in support of the productive nature of developmentally moderated transfer while the studies reviewed in the previous section demonstrated the constraining nature of the same notion.

5. Typological distance without a disadvantage

Above we reviewed studies carried out in the context of typological proximity and demonstrated that typological proximity does not guarantee L2 learners ready access to L1 knowledge or to L1 processing skills. In this section we will reverse the typological constellation and will review studies in the context of typological distance. We will demonstrate that typological distance does not necessarily imply a learning barrier. In other words, L2 structures that are absent from the L1 may nevertheless be positioned at the bottom of the processability hierarchy and may therefore be readily learnable.

Kawaguchi (1999, 2002, submitted) studied the acquisition of Japanese syntax by native speakers of English. One aspect she studied is the acquisition of word order by Australian university students of Japanese. The study examined a typological contrast in which native speakers of a highly configurational, head-first language with SVO word order (English) acquire a less configurational, head-last language (Japanese, cf. Shibatani 1990) with preferred SOV word order.

Kawaguchi's study constitutes a prime test case for the "Full Access/ Full Transfer Model" (Schwartz & Sprouse 1994, 1996) as well as for the Competition Model (MacWhinney 2005). These two models would both predict the

Table 9. The position of the verb in main clauses by second language learners of Japanese (Jaz and Lou)

Interview No.	T1		T2		T3		T4	
	Jaz	Lou	Jaz	Lou	Jaz	Lou	Jaz	Lou
Verb in clause final position	3	10	12	19	17	12	13	27
Verb in clause non-final position	0	0	0	0	0	0	0	0

Australian learners of Japanese to transfer English SVO word order. However, this prediction is clearly falsified by Kawaguchi's study.

The results of Kawaguchi's study for the initial word order hypothesis are displayed in Table 9, which is based on a longitudinal corpus collected from two informants without any previous exposure to the target language. The informants were interviewed four times in their first year of learning Japanese as a second language starting at the very beginning of the learning process.

Table 9 affords a distributional analysis of the corpus in relation to the positioning of the verb in clauses. The third line in Table 9 lists the number of target-like occurrences of the verb in clause-final position, and the fourth line lists the number of occurrences of the verb in non-target positions. It is easy to see from this analysis that from the very beginning of their acquisition of Japanese neither of the learners ever produces verbs in a non-final position, despite the fact that this is in stark contrast to the structure of their first language.

Summing up, we find that both learners of Japanese studied longitudinally by Kawaguchi start with SOV word order although their first languages follow an SVO pattern. Obviously, these findings falsify the hypothesis that first language features are transferred to the second language at the initial state.

This raises the question as to why second language learners would start out with a structure that is typologically rather distant from their first language. The answer is implied in PT, and more specifically, in the 'developmentally moderated transfer hypothesis' advocated in this chapter. In relation to the initial hypothesis for word order, PT predicts the use of a canonical word order pattern. Japanese follows a canonical SOV word order, which requires no exchange of grammatical information within the sentence as it can rely on direct mapping of semantic roles onto surface structure (cf. our discussion above and Chapters 7 and 8). In other words, because of the low demands on processability, this word order pattern can be processed at the initial stage of clause development despite the typological distance between the first and the second language (for a more detailed and formal account of information distribution in Japanese syntax see Kawaguchi, Chapter 8, this volume; and Di Biase & Kawaguchi 2002).

This analysis of the initial word order in the acquisition of Japanese as a second language also highlights a key difference between Clahsen's (1984) strategies and the processability approach. As Vainikka and Young-Scholten (1994) and Towell and Hawkins (1994) point out, Clahsen's strategies would predict that the initial hypothesis in L2 acquisition is formed on the perceptual array 'actor, action, acted-upon', thus producing universal SVO patterns for all L2s. No such assumption is made in PT. The only stipulation that exists at this level is that no grammatical information be exchanged within the sentence. This constrains the language processor to produce only structures that can be processed without such information exchange. SVO and SOV both satisfy this condition.

Di Biase (in preparation) studied another typological constellation of the same kind as Kawaguchi. In his study he focused on the acquisition of a 'pro-drop' language (Italian) as L2 by speakers of a non pro-drop language (English). According to White's (1989: 87) analysis, this type of learner has to learn two things: 1) the fact that null subjects are permitted, and 2) the circumstances in which the language makes use of null subjects. These assumptions are derived from the more general assumption that L2 learners transfer the setting of the L1 parameter to the L2.

Di Biase (in preparation) carried out a longitudinal study with two Australian informants over a one-year period. Both informants were university students of Italian. One informant (Ernie) was a beginning learner who had had no previous exposure to the language. The first set of data (= t1) was collected as soon as the learner started producing utterances with more than one constituent. The second informant (Lisa) was an intermediate student when the first set of data was collected.

Table 10 compares the three different types of realization of grammatical subjects, null, pronominal and referential, in both informants. It is easy to see that, contrary to White's prediction, both learners start with a high level of null realizations of grammatical subjects. In fact, the level of null-subject realizations found in these data is not unlike that found by Bates (1976) in her study of Italian first language acquisition, namely about 70%.

In terms of the processability hierarchy, null-subjects are placed at the same level as pronominal subjects because both are directly derived from c-structure (for a detailed analysis of information distribution in these structures see Di Biase & Kawaguchi 2002). Therefore Di Biase's finding supports the prediction that the acquisition of a typologically distant L2 does not necessarily cause a

Table 10. Realization of grammatical subjects with lexical verbs in percent

	t1	t2	t3	t4
Ernie				
Null	54	64	67	84
Pronominal	4	24	4	2
Referential	43	12	29	14
Lisa				
Null	71	52	59	79
Pronominal	24	45	30	11
Referential	6	3	11	13

learning barrier as long as the structure in question is located at the lower end of the processability hierarchy – even if it does not exist in the L1.

This finding is supported by other studies with the same typological constellation as in Di Biase (in preparation). For instance, Phinney (1987) studied the acquisition of null subjects in English learners of Spanish (i.e., L1 = - pro-drop, L2 = + pro-drop) and also found an early appearance of null subjects. Liceras and Diaz (1999) studied the acquisition of L2 Spanish (+ pro-drop) by speakers of Chinese, English, French, German and Japanese (i.e., speakers of both types of languages) and found a consistent early appearance of null-subjects in all informants.

6. Typological distance with an advantage

Above we reviewed studies carried out in the context of typological proximity and demonstrated that typological proximity does not guarantee L2 learners ready access to L1 knowledge or to L1 processing skills. In the previous section we reversed the typological constellation and reviewed studies in the context of typological distance and demonstrated that typological distance does not necessarily imply a learning barrier. In this section we will focus on a variant of the typological constellation examined in the previous section. This time the L2 structure does exist in the L1, is positioned at the bottom of the processability hierarchy and is therefore readily learnable.

Rahkonen (1993) studied the acquisition of word order in Finnish learners of Swedish and Swedish learners of Finnish. In the context of this study one has to bear in mind that Finland has two official languages, Finnish and Swedish. The Finnish-speaking majority students take Swedish in school and the Swedish-speaking minority students take Finnish. As mentioned above, Swedish has a verb-second constraint, whereas Finnish does not. The latter language is non-configurational and follows an SVO pattern as the preferred word order.

The material for the study consisted of written essays by 999 learners of Swedish and 173 learners of Finnish. The aim was to investigate whether it is easier to go from Finnish XSV to Swedish XVS word order than the other way around. The results showed a significant difference between the two directions of L1 transfer. The Swedish learners of Finnish were more successful in their use of Finnish word order, than the Finnish learners of Swedish. Rahkonen calculated the proportion of Swedish-Finnish transfer and Finnish-Swedish transfer based on a minimum of one example from any given learner. This analysis shows that 34.8% of the Finnish learners of Swedish transferred the XSV structure whereas for the Swedish learners of Finnish the proportion was only 6.9%. Rahkonen discusses the results in terms of markedness and difference in status of Swedish and Finnish word order. He points out that Swedish word order is grammatically determined while Finnish word order is governed by functional principles.

A similar typological constellation was present in a study of simultaneous bilingualism by Schlyter (1993) in which six children were studied who acquired Swedish (XVS) and French (XSV) simultaneously in a natural context. The children were recorded from the age of about 2 to the age of 4 years. Three of the children were considered dominant in French and three were dominant in Swedish. An examination of word order patterns in the children's production showed that all children transferred French XSV order to Swedish, but there was not a single case of transfer of the Swedish XVS order to French in the data (Schlyter & Håkansson 1994).

The typological constellation 'L1 with V2' and 'L2 without V2' was present in a study by Fearch (1984) who studied word order in oral and written production of 24 Danish-speaking learners of English. In the oral production there was not a single case of transfer of Danish word order (subject-verb inversion) to English. None of the sentences with a preposed constituent showed inversion in English, but all followed the target XSVO order.

As the above discussion of subject-verb inversion has shown, Finnish and French SVO word order follows the canonical principle and can thus be expected to be found early on in SLA, whereas the processing of the Swedish verb-second constraint requires the exchange of grammatical information between constituents and can thus be acquired only later. In other words, the processability hierarchy accounts for the directionality of L1 transfer in this typological scenario.

7. Summary and conclusion

In this paper we proposed that L1 transfer is developmentally moderated. This hypothesis follows from the internal design of Processability Theory, which provides a framework for relating specific L1 and L2 structures to a universal hierarchy of processability based on grammatical information transfer in the production process. This overall framework predicts which processing procedures are required for the processing of specific L2 structures. This is the basis for the general prediction that L1 knowledge and skills can be utilised for L2 processing only if the necessary processing resources have developed. This implies that processability may override typological proximity and distance in L1 transfer.

Our developmentally-moderated-transfer hypothesis was tested empirically in the context of typological proximity and typological distance. We demonstrated that in both types of context transfer may or may not occur. The key predictive factor is always processability. In other words, processability acts as a constraint on L2 transfer and may override typological distance. In addition to this constraining effect, processability also has a facilitating effect which sets in (given structural L1-L2 overlap) once the L2 has developed to the point at which the L1 structure is processable. This is evident in the advantage of Turkish learners of German over Russian learners of the same L2 with respect to word order (cf. Haberzettl 2000).

The empirical studies discussed in this paper also shed light on the validity of the set of competing approaches to L1 transfer discussed in Section 1 above. We can state now that the "Full Transfer/Full Access" hypothesis by Schwartz and Sprouse is falsified boldly by all cases of non-transfer reported above since the latter authors assume that the final state of the L1 is the initial state of the L2. The falsification of this assumption is particularly obvious in the study by Håkansson, Pienemann and Sayehli (2002) which shows that Swedish learners of German do not transfer V2 although both languages contain this structure.

The so-called "minimal tree hypothesis" predicts that L1 word order is transferred to L2. This is falsified by Kawaguchi's (in preparation) observation that Australian learners of Japanese start with an initial SOV hypothesis. This observation and the study of Swedes learning German both also falsify the transfer hypothesis implied in the Competition Model (cf. MacWhinney 2005) according to which all transferable structures will be transferred at an early stage. The above studies show that this prediction is not borne out by empirical data. Swedish learners of German do not transfer V2 to German (which would yield a correct result) and Australian learners of Japanese do not transfer SVO to Japanese (which would yield an incorrect result).

The strong initial transfer assumption inherent in MacWhinney's (1997) competition model also produces predictions which are falsified by empirical data, particularly by the Swedish-German study (Håkansson, Pienemann & Sayehli 2002) which shows that verb-second is not transferred from Swedish to German even though this structure exists in the L1 *and* in the L2. All other cases of non-transfer discussed above prove the same point.

In addition, it may be useful to consider the explanatory parsimony of MacWhinney's assumption that "…all aspects of the first language that can possibly transfer to L2 will transfer" (MacWhinney 1997: 119). The reader will recall that MacWhinney (1997) illustrates his point about structurally 'impossible transfer' using German and English as an example. German nouns are implicitly marked for grammatical gender, English nouns are not. He concludes that German learners therefore have no basis for transferring the German gender system to English. Therefore this set of features is not included in his list of things that will be transferred.

Our point is the following. Whereas L1-L2 contrasts are transparent to the linguist, the question remains as to how the learner recognizes these differences. The reader will recall that at the beginning of this chapter we argued that the relationship between German and English diacritic features (of nouns) is not obvious to the learner and that a full transfer hypothesis would lead to unwieldy hypotheses. Conversely, it is precisely this lack of transparency in the relationship between L1 and L2 that makes a radical no-transfer hypothesis equally unlikely.

Assuming a lexically driven model of language production such as the one proposed by Levelt (1989), gender is one of several diacritic features residing in the lexical entry for (German) nouns, and the learner will have to discover for all lexical classes (such as noun, verb etc.) which of the L1 diacritic features are also marked in the second language, using known or unknown linguistic means, and which additional diacritic features are marked using which linguistic means. This is a monumental learning task. Assuming that diacritic features such as 'gender' are not transferable for structural reasons would amount to a classical conditioning assumption within the competition model, which would assume a strictly linear relationship between input and output, following the motto 'if it is not in the input it cannot occur in the output'. As noted above, empirical data falsify such an assumption. This is also illustrated by the well-attested example of over-generalization in English regular past marking, such as in Cazden's "She holded the baby rabbits..." (1972:96).

As these examples show, the assumption of a strictly linear relationship between input and output and a rich transfer assumption produce predictions which are falsified by empirical data – at least for the domain of morphosyntax.

A rich transfer assumption is not supported in the area of bilingual first language acquisition either. According to De Houwer (2005) no studies have empirically backed up the existence of the sort of language repertoires that would be predicted to develop in bilingual children in line with a transfer theory. Indeed she maintains that the interpretation of morphosyntactic features of the two input languages would assume that processing mechanisms in bilingual children would enable them to "approach each input language as a morphosyntactically closed set."

The gist of the cross-linguistic survey of L1 transfer presented in this chapter can be summed up in two fundamental trends:

i.   Structures higher up the processability hierarchy are never transferred at the initial state – regardless of typological constellation.
ii. Initial word order may vary as long as the flow of grammatical information is restricted to the initial stage of processability.

These trends clearly contradict any theory that places emphasis on extensive L1 transfer at the initial state and support a view on transfer that is sensitive to the developmental state of the learner's language.

Notes

1. In the pre-minimalist as well as in the minimalist framework, a distinction is made between lexical and functional heads. Lexical heads are heads of one of the four lexical phrases VP, AP, NP or PP. Functional heads are heads of functional phrases such as IP (inflectional phrase) or CP (complementiser phrase). Functional phrases may contain lexical material, such as affixes, but are not required to do so (cf. Cook & Newson 1996: 136ff.)

2. The English transliteration is a word-by-word gloss that follows the same word order as the German and Swedish example sentences.

3. The implicational scaling technique was developed by Guttman (1944) and applied to linguistic dynamics by DeCamp (1973) and to dynamics in second language acquisition by Meisel, Clahsen and Pienemann (1981) (for further information see Pienemann 1998). The basic point behind implicational scales is this: cumulative learning processes can be represented by successive additions of linguistic rules to the interlanguage system: rule 1 +

rule 2 + rule 3 etc. In this way changes in the interlanguage system can be accounted for by the addition of rules. When analysing interlanguage corpora one can apply the following logic of implicational scales to individual interlanguage samples. For any set of rules that is learnt in a cumulative fashion the following is true: if sample A contains rule 3, then it will also contain rule 2 and rule 1. This fact is usually expressed in tables of the following kind.

	time 1	time 2	time 3	time 4
rule 1	–	+	+	+
rule 2	–	–	+	+
rule 3	–	–	–	+

In other words, rules which are learned later imply the presence of rules which are learned earlier: rule 3 > rule 2 > rule 1. This notation has a number of advantages for the description of linguistic dynamics. Implicational scales make it possible to describe complex acquisition processes on a continuum. The rules of the interlanguage system are listed on one axis while the samples (here identical with points in time) are listed on the other axis. This presentation amounts to a systematic account of a linguistic system (grammar axis) in relation to developmental time. In other words, this system is a non-static grammar which describes many aspects of the learning process.

References

Bardel, C. & Falk, Y. (2004). Can processability be transferred? Paper given at The *Fourth International Symposium on Processability*, Second Language Acquisition and Bilingualism University of Sassari, 13–15 April 2004.

Bates, E. (1976). *Language and Context: The acquisition of pragmatics*. New York, NY: Academic Press.

Bates, E. & MacWhinney, B. (1981). In H. Winity (Ed.), *Native Language and Foreign Language Acquisition* [Annals of the New York Academy of Sciences 379] (pp. 190–214). New York: Academy of Sciences.

Bates, E. & MacWhinney, B. (1982). Functionalist approaches to grammar. In E. Wanner & L. R. Gleitman (Eds.), *Language Acquisition: The state of the art* (pp. 173–218). Cambridge: CUP

Bates, E. & MacWhinney, B. (1987). Competition, variation and language learning. In B. MacWhinney (Ed.), *Mechanisms of Language Acquisition* (pp. 157–193). Hillsdale, NJ: Lawrence Erlbaum.

Bley-Vroman, R. (1990). The logical problem of second language learning. *Linguistic Analysis, 20*, 3–49.

Cazden, C. (1972). *Child Language and Education*. New York: Holt, Reinhart and Winston.

Chomsky, N. (1981). *Lectures on Government and Binding*. Dordrecht: Floris.

Clahsen, H. (1984). The acquisition of German word order: A test case for cognitive approaches to L2 development. In R. Anderson (Ed.), *Second Languages: A cross-linguistic perspective*. Rowley, MA: Newbury House.

Clahsen, H. (1986). Connecting theories of language processing and (second) language acquisition. In C. W. Pfaff (Ed.), *First and Second Language Acquisition Processes* (pp. 103–116). Rowley, MA: Newbury House.

Clahsen, H., Meisel J., & Pienemann, M. (1983). *Deutsch als Zweitsprache. Der Spracherwerb ausländischer Arbeiter*. Tübingen: Narr.

Clahsen, H. & Muysken, P. (1989). The UG paradox in L2 acquisition. *Second Language Research, 2*, 1–29.

Cook, V. J. & Newson, M. (1996). *Chomsky's Universal Grammar. An introduction* (2nd ed.). Oxford: Blackwell.

DeCamp, D. (1973). Implicational scales and sociolinguistic linearity. *Linguistics, 73*, 30–43.

De Houwer, A. (1990). *The Acquisition of Two Languages from Birth: A case study*. Cambridge: CUP.

Di Biase, B. (in preparation). Processability and subject-verb agreement in a pro-drop language.

Di Biase, B. & Kawaguchi, S. (2002). Exploring the typological plausibility of Processability Theory: Language development in Italian L2 and Japanese L2. *Second Language Research, 18*(3), 274–302.

Dulay, H. & Burt, M. (1974). Natural sequences in child second language acquisition. *Language Learning, 24*, 37–53.

Eubank, L. (1993). On the transfer of parametric values in L2 development. *Language Acquisition, 3*, 183–208.

Faerch, C. (1984). Giving transfer a boost – describing transfer variation in learners' interlanguage performance. *Scandinavian Working Papers on Bilingualism, 2*, 1–22.

Felix, S. W. (1977). Interference, interlanguage and related issues. In C. Molony, H. Zobl, & W. Stölting (Eds.), *German in contact with other languages* (pp. 237–258). Kronberg.

Felix, S. W. (1984). Maturational aspects of universal grammar. In A. Davies, C. Criper, & A. Howatt (Eds.), *Interlanguage* (pp. 133–161). Edinburgh: Edinburgh University Press.

Gass, S. M. (1987). The resolution of conflicts among competing systems: A bidirectional perspective. *Applied Psycholinguistics, 8*, 329–350.

Guttman, L. (1944). A basis for scaling qualitative data. *American Sociological Review, 9*, 139–150.

Haberzettl, S. (2000). Der Erwerb der Verbstellung in der Zweitsprache Deutsch durch Kinder mit typologisch verschiedenen Muttersprachen. Eine Auseinandersetzung mit Theorien zum Syntaxerwerb anhand von vier Fallstudien. PhD dissertation, Potsdam University.

Håkansson, G., Pienemann, M., & Sayehli, S. (2002). Transfer and typological proximity in the context of L2 processing. *Second Language Research, 18*(3), 250–273.

Harrington, M. (1987). Processing transfer: Language-specific processing strategies as a source of interlanguage variation. *Applied Psycholinguistics, 8*, 351–377.

Johnston, M. (1997). Development and Variation in Learner Language. PhD Dissertation, Australian National University.

Kaplan, R. & Bresnan, J. (1982). Lexical-functional grammar: A formal system for grammatical representation. In J. Bresnan (Ed.), *The Mental Representation of Grammatical Relations* (pp. 173–281). Cambridge, MS: The MIT Press.

Kawaguchi, S. (1999). The acquisition of syntax and nominal ellipsis in JSL discourse. In P. Robinson (Ed.) *Representation and Process: Proceedings of the 3rd Pacific Second Language Research Forum*, Vol. 1 (pp. 85–93).

Kawaguchi, S. (submitted). L1 transfer in Japanese L2 in learners of typologically distant languages. Submitted for the proceedings of CAESS (College of Arts, Education and Social Sciences) Research Conference 2005 at the University of Western Sydney. 7–9 October 2005.

Kellerman, E. (1983). Now you see it, now you don't. In S. Gass & L. Selinker (Eds.), *Language Transfer in Language Learning* (pp. 112–134). Rowley, MA: Newbury House.

Kilborn, K. & Ito, T. (1989). Sentence processing in a second language: The timing of transfer. *Language and Speech, 32*, 1–23.

Klein Gunnewiek, L. (2000). *Sequenzen und Konsequenzen. Zur Entwicklung niederländischer Lerner im Deutschen als Fremdsprache*. Amsterdam: Rodopi.

Lado, R. (1957). *Linguistics across Cultures: Applied Linguistics for language teachers*. Ann Arbor, MI: University of Michigan.

Levelt, W. J. M. (1989). *Speaking. From intention to articulation*. Cambridge, MA: The MIT Press.

Liceras, J. M & Diaz, L. (1999). Topic-drop versus pro-drop: Null subjects and pronominal subjects in the Spanish L2 of Chinese, English, French, German and Japanese speakers. *Second Language Research, 15*, 1–40.

MacWhinney, B. (1987). The competition model. In B. MacWhinney (Ed.) *Mechanisms of Language Acquisition*. Hillsdale, NJ: Lawrence Erlbaum.

MacWhinney, B. (1997). Second language acquisition and the competition model. In A. M. B. de Groot & J. Kroll (Eds.), *Tutorials in Bilingualism* (pp. 113–142). Mahwah, NJ: Lawrence Erlbaum.

MacWhinney, B. (2005). A unified model of language acquisition. In J. Kroll & A. M. B. de Groot (Eds.), *Handbook of Bilingualism. Psycholinguistic approaches* (pp. 49–67). Oxford: OUP

Meisel, J. M. (1983). Strategies of second language acquisition: More than one kind of simplification. In R. W. Anderson (Ed.), *Pidginisation and Creolisation as Language Acquisition* (pp. 120–157). Rowley, MA: Newbury House.

Meisel, J. M. (1991). Principles of Universal Grammar and strategies of language use: On some similarities and differences between first and second language acquisition. In L. Eubank (Ed.), *Point -counterpoint. Universal Grammar in the second language* (pp. 231–276). Amsterdam: John Benjamins.

Meisel, J. M. (1995). Parameters in acquisition. In P. Fletcher & B. MacWhinney (Eds.), *The Handbook of Child Language* (pp. 10–35). Oxford: Blackwell.

Meisel, J. M., Clahsen, H., & Pienemann, M. (1981). On determining developmental stages in natural second language acquisition. *Studies in Second Language Acquisition, 3*, 109–135.

Naumann, K. (1997). Svenska som främmande språk i Schweiz. In Håkansson, G., Lötmarker, L., Santesson, L., Svensson, J., & Viberg, Å. (Eds.), *Svenskans beskriving* 22 (pp. 318–334). Lund: Studentlitteratur.

Palmer, H. (1917 [1968]). *The Scientific Study and Teaching of Language* [Language and Language Learning Series]. London: OUP.

Phinney, M. (1987). The pro-drop parameter in second language acquisition. In T. Roeper & E. Williams (Eds.), *Parameter Setting* (pp. 221–238). Dordrecht: Reidel.

Pienemann, M. (1998). *Language Processing and Second Language Development: Processability Theory*. Amsterdam: John Benjamins.

Pienemann, M., Johnston, M., & Brindley, G. (1988). Constructing an acquisition-based procedure for second language assessment. *Studies in Second Language Acquisition, 10*, 217–224.

Pienemann, M. & Håkansson, G (1999). A unified approach towards the development of Swedish as L2: A processability account. *Studies in Second Language Acquisition, 21*, 383–420.

Platzack, C. (1996). The initial hypothesis of syntax: A minimalist perspective on language acquisition and attrition. In H. Clahsen (Ed.), *Generative Perspectives on Language Acquisition* (pp. 369–414). Amsterdam: John Benjamins.

Rahkonen, M. (1993). Huvudsatsfundamentet hos svenska inlärare av finska och finska inlärare av svenska [Main clause foundation in Swedish learners of Finnish and Finnish learners of Swedish]. In V. Muittari & M. Rahkonen (Eds.), *Svenskan i Finland 2. Meddelanden från institutionen för nordiska språk vid Juväskyllä universitet, 9*, 199–225.

Ruin, I. (1996). *Grammar and the Advanced Learner. On learning and teaching a second language*. Stockholm: Almqvist and Wiksell International.

Sasaki, Y. (1991). English and Japanese Interlanguage comprehension strategies: An analysis based on the competition model. *Applied Psycholinguistics, 6*, 190–204.

Schlyter, S. (1993). The weaker language in bilingual Swedish-French children. In K. Hyltenstam & Å., Viberg (Eds.), *Progression and Regression in Language* (pp. 289–308). Cambridge: CUP.

Schlyter, S. & Håkansson, G. (1994). Word order in Swedish as the first language, second language and weaker language in bilinguals. *Scandinavian Working Papers in Bilingualism, 9*, 49–66.

Schwartz, B. D. & Sprouse, R. A. (1994). Word order and nominative case in non-native language acquisition. A longitudinal study of (L1 Turkish) German interlanguage. In T. Hoekstra & B. D. Schwartz (Eds.), *Language Acquisition Studies in Generative Grammar: Papers in honour of Kennth Wexler from the 1991 GLOW workshops* (pp. 317–368). Amsterdam: John Benjamins.

Schwartz, B. D. & Sprouse, R. A. (1996). L2 cognitive states and the Full Transfer/Full Access model. *Second Language Research, 12*(1), 40–72.

Shibatani, M. (1990). *The Languages of Japan*. Cambridge: CUP.

Sweet, H. (1899 [1964]). *The Practical Study of Languages* [Language and Language Learning Series]. London: OUP.

Towell, R. & Hawkins, R. (1994). *Approaches to Second Language Acquisition*. Clevedon: Multilingual Matters.

Vainikka, A. & Young-Scholten, M. (1994). Direct access to X'-theory: Evidence from Korean and Turkish adults learning German. In T. Hoekstra & B. D. Schwartz (Eds.), *Language Acquisition Studies in Generative grammar: Papers in honour of Kenneth Wexler from the 1991 GLOW workshops* (pp. 7–39). Amsterdam: John Benjamins.

Vainikka, A. & M. Young-Scholten (1996). Gradual development of L2 phrase structure. *Second Language Research, 12*, 7–39.

Weinreich, H. (1953 [1974]). *Languages in Contact. Findings and problems.* The Hague: Mouton.

White, L. (1987). Against comprehensible input: The Input Hypothesis and the development of L2 competence. *Applied Linguistics, 8,* 95–110.

White, L. (1989). *Universal Grammar and Second Language Acquisition.* Amsterdam: John Benjamins.

Wode, H. (1976). Developmental sequences in naturalistic L2 acquisition. *Working Papers on Bilingualism, 11,* 1–12.

Wode, H. (1978). The L1 vs L2 acquisition of English negation. *Working Papers on Bilingualism, 15,* 37–57.

Zobl, H. (1980). The formal and developmental selectivity of L1 influence on L2 acquisition. *Language Learning, 30,* 43–57.

CHAPTER 4

Agreement morphology in Arabic as a second language

Typological features and their processing implications*

Fethi Mansouri

Deakin University, Australia

This study attempts to establish the developmental stages for agreement morphology in the acquisition of Arabic as a second language (henceforth Arabic SLA) from a Processability Theory (PT) perspective (Pienemann 1998). More specifically, the paper will provide a systematic account of the developmental features of structures within Stage 3 (phrasal agreement morphology) and Stage 4 (inter-phrasal agreement morphology) on the PT predicted developmental sequence. The empirical testing of these stages is based on data produced by English-speaking learners of Arabic in a classroom context (Mansouri 2000). The paper builds on Mansouri's previous findings (1999, 2000) by further refining the linguistic description of agreement structures in Arabic SLA taking into account key typological features such as form function relationships, class type of the head NP, word order variation and directionality of encoding. These typological features discussed at length in Arabic grammar theories (Kremers 2000; Fassi Fehri 1983, 1988, 1993; Moutaouakil 1985; Bahloul 1993; Benmamoun & Aoun 1999) will be analysed in terms of key patterns of grammatical information exchange (Bresnan 2001) in order to define their processing requirements and, consequently, their predicted developmental order. The paper will conclude by discussing the issue of intra-stage sequencing and the potential for this to be examined on the basis of a combination of language-specific typological features and differing processing requirements.

1. Introduction

The chapter has two inter-related objectives, the first to provide a typological account for phrasal and inter-phrasal agreement morphology in Arabic, and the second to establish their developmental sequence on the basis of the Processability Theory's predictions (Pienemann 1998). The former is essential for an accurate formulation of the latter. The choice of Arabic for cross-linguistic validation is theoretically important because it provides a unique typological testing context for theoretical claims that have been initially developed on the basis of research carried out on Indo-European languages such as German and English.

One of the difficulties in cross-linguistic testing of theoretical claims in SLA is the specific typological peculiarities of the target language (TL) and its methodological implications for establishing comparable structures at different developmental stages. The contribution of PT in this context is that its processing procedures hierarchy reflects the universal concept of feature unification in different patterns of grammatical information exchange and, therefore, this hierarchy is testable in any language. However, applying the notion of grammatical information exchange in different languages requires a careful selection of optimal structures for SLA testing. In considering why some structures may or may not be optimal candidates for SLA testing, this study will rely on the concept of grammatical information exchange as outlined in Lexical Functional Grammar (LFG) and adopted in PT (Pienemann 1998). This concept is crucial in generating predictions across typologically different languages: the higher the syntactic level of this information exchange (phrasal > inter-phrasal > inter-clausal), the later its development/emergence in the learner language is predicted.

Another important point that will be discussed in this paper is the multiplicity of structures within individual acquisition stages and their role in analysing the learner language. This is especially the case in Arabic phrasal (Stage 3 in PT) and inter-phrasal agreement morphology (Stage 4 in PT) where their multiple structures exist. The importance of the intra-stage range of structures is that it will have implications for interpreting certain developmental 'gaps' that are otherwise categorised as 'inconsistent' with the predicted developmental order. This paper will examine the various typological phenomena within a particular stage, establish whether structures belonging to the same stage are all processable in the same manner, and (if so) whether such an analysis can form the basis for an intra-stage learning sequence.

2.   Studies on Arabic SLA

As far as research on the acquisition of Arabic as a second language is concerned, the few studies carried out in the past two decades are either too narrow in focus (e.g., Nielsen 1997) and, therefore, cannot claim to establish acquisition stages for Arabic grammar, or are essentially descriptive studies (e.g., Bakalla 1980; Kuntz 1996) that focus mainly on the major difficulties facing learners of Arabic as a second language. The latter studies, in particular, are typically undertaken from a traditional error analysis approach where certain types of the learner's errors are analysed, accounted for and classified into various lexical, phonological and grammatical categories. Much of this research ignores the key developmental issues in Arabic second language acquisition and as such will not be discussed any further in this paper.

The main concern of Mansouri's (1995) study was to investigate: (i) the effect of grammatical encoding on the acquisition of subject-verb agreement marking in terms of the amount and direction of encoding between the subject (source of information) and the verb (target of information); and (ii) the effect of discourse information on the acquisition of grammatical agreement. The learners were 15 Australian tertiary students enrolled in three different levels of Arabic courses offered at an Australian tertiary institution. The main hypothesis of the study was that directionality of encoding (the degree to which the source's grammatical information is morphologically marked onto the target) would correlate with learning difficulty in a systematic manner. It was predicted that:

i.   when the source's features (i.e. person, number and gender) are fully mapped onto the target [Source = Target] learning is expected to be easy;
ii.   when there is an under-specification of source's features onto the target as with non-humans [Source > Target], learning is expected to be less easy; and
iii. when there is an over-specification, i.e. the target is marked for features that the source does not explicitly exhibit as in the case of collectives [Source < Target], then learning is expected to be the least easy.

A linguistic analysis of data revealed that the main source of difficulty for learners was the correct identification of the pragmatic roles of 'subject' head nouns. This is especially the case when the 'subject' NP exhibits the feature [–Human] resulting in reduced agreement marking. The study has shown that the developmental order of subject-verb agreement goes along the following path:

[Source<Target] > [Source>Target] > [Source=Target]
(Time 3)   (Time 2)   (Time 1)

This study, however, was interested in linguistic complexity as the basis for learning predictions. This is different from Mansouri's (2000) study, which attempts to establish the full developmental hierarchy for Arabic SLA syntax and morphology from a general PT perspective. The study explored the connection between linguistic (e.g. word order and semantic class), cognitive (e.g. learner's processing procedures) and educational (e.g. formal objectives of instruction) factors. The findings of the study for syntax resulted in the formulation of the following simplified implicational developmental sequence with SVO being the first to emerge:

[*Anaphora*] > [*Subordination*] > [*VSO*] > [*SVO*]
(Time 4)   (Time 3)   (Time 2) (Time 1)

The detailed analysis shows that this sequence is invariably similar across all learners and that all the structures are acquired in a cumulative and implicational manner. The findings in relation to the acquisition of morphology are less coherent, with a greater degree of inter-learner variability, in particular with regard to clitics, grammatical gender, case marking and irregular plurals. These four structures, not surprisingly, are among the latest structures to be acquired by all learners.

Nielsen (1997) attempted to test the Processability Theory's prediction in the context of Arabic as a second language. The focus of Nielsen's study is the acquisition of agreement procedures within (phrasal) and across (inter-phrasal) constituents. The structures selected to test Processability Theory in the context of Arabic SLA are noun phrases (phrasal agreement) where the head nouns and their modifiers are marked for definiteness, gender and optionally preceded by a demonstrative article, and subject-verb agreement (inter-phrasal agreement) with number and gender being the variant features.

This study suggests that phrasal agreement in Arabic SLA (in particular, the definite article /al/ in mid point and the *idafa* structure /N1 al-N2/) occurs later than inter-phrasal morphology (subject-verb agreement). There are a few methodological issues that need to be clarified before a clear interpretation of these findings is achieved. The first issue is the lack of a clear formal account of the selected target language structures which is necessary for the empirical testing of the predictions outlined in Processability Theory. This is essential in the context of processability research in order to outline why certain structures would be processed differently or at different times from other structures.

This is a key aspect of linguistic and psychological plausibility articulated in PT which accounts for the processing operations required for different structures (with different patterns of information exchange).

The second methodological issue relates to the misunderstanding and, therefore, (mis)application of the emergence criterion which adds an element of methodological confusion to the conceptual basis of the study in question. Processsability Theory states clearly that the emergence criterion can only be applied to "morphological development through more refined analyses which 'neutralise' the effect of un-analysed entries into the learner's lexicon" (Pienemann 1998:144). Furthermore, Pienemann suggests that the emergence criterion can be applied effectively only once a distributional analysis, i.e. a detailed linguistic description of the context in which the morpheme is produced, is undertaken. It is, therefore, clear that it would be difficult to interpret any research findings correctly if there is a lack of a formalised account of the target language structures selected for testing the theory and the misunderstanding of the emergence criterion as applied within PT.

Keeping in mind these methodological constraints, the objective of this paper is to provide a detailed analysis of phrasal and inter-phrasal agreement structures in Arabic and their processability requirements. This linguistic analysis is based on the concept of grammatical information exchange and will yield a PT-generated set of predictions that will be tested empirically among learners of Arabic as a second language. The following section, therefore, provides a systematic linguistic analysis of the key structures in Arabic agreement morphology making use of key notions in LFG.

3.   An LFG approach to agreement marking in Arabic language

Formal analyses of agreement phenomena in Arabic language have tended to focus on syntactic structures, their typological properties and their grammatical marking (c.f, Fassi Fehri 1983, 1988; Bahloul 1993; Mahfoudhi 2001; Benmamoun & Aoun 1999; Bolotin 1995). Many of these analyses have been undertaken from a broad government and binding (GB) perspective focusing, among other things, on structural properties of agreement relations in deep structure and their realisation in the surface structure. This is in sharp contrast to the approach adopted in this study, namely, Lexical Functional Grammar (Bresnan 2001) in which feature unification is used to capture agreement relations and speech generation. A key aspect of LFG is the interaction of the three structures (c-structure, f-structure and lexical entries) governed by a set of well-formedness conditions. This interaction constrains the process of feature unification ensuring that all properties of an f-structure are compatible with each other. Many types of ungrammatical speech in the learner's language (learner's errors) can be accounted for on the basis of compatibility between the different components of the functional structure. Constituent structures are generated by phrase structure rules with major constituents being annotated for their grammatical functions.

4. Agreement marking in Arabic

Any account of grammatical agreement marking should be able to account for the appropriate constraints on the main sub-components of the agreement system. These relate to the nature of the agreeing lexical expressions, the features involved, and the domain in which the agreeing constituents are located. As far as Arabic morphology is concerned, the features included in this definition are gender (GEND), number (NUM), person (PERS), case (CASE), definiteness (DEF), and humanness (HUM). Other features such as MOOD are also relevant, but will not be included in this paper. Fassi Fehri offers the following definition of agreement: "Two expressions are said to agree if some of their features match by virtue of a linking relationship." (Fassi Fehri 1988:129). Unification within LFG implies feature sharing (and in some cases merging) rather than simply copying. This feature 'sharing' aspect of agreement relations will prove crucial in Arabic agreement marking where often there are no one-to-one relationships between forms and their functions. This is because functional specifications such as the NP types [± Hum] and word order variation (e.g. SV(O) as opposed to VS(O) order) affect the morphological marking of diacritics in certain agreement relations.

4.1 Phrasal agreement (agreement within constituent)

Phrasal agreement refers to the process of feature unification (also referred to as feature matching) across the head noun and its modifier(s). This matching process in Arabic involves key features such as number, person and gender, which are unified (in agreement) by means of feature specification within their respective lexical entries. Before dealing with the NP structures selected for this study, let us briefly describe Arabic NPs and their complex typological features. The modifiers in Arabic NPs may be either post-nominal or pre-nominal (or a combination of both) as in the following two structures adopted from Kremers (2000: 13):

    a.   (Ord)-(Card)- **Def-N.Gend**-(Adj)[1]
    b.   **Def-N.Gend**-(Adj)-(Card)-(Ord)

The positioning of modifiers in Arabic NPs (pre-nominal vs post-nominal) is not governed by whether the adjectival phrase is used in a predicative or attributive manner, but rather by pragmatic choice and discourse considerations. Pre-nominal positioning of modifiers occur only with cardinals, ordinals and superlatives (used in the same manner as other adjectives), whilst post-nominal positioning is not restrictive in the range of modifiers that can be included. However, the basic sequence [Def-N.Gend][2] is a fixed combination that cannot be split.

Different agreement rules govern pre-nominal and post-nominal agreement in Arabic NPs. Given that the focus of this paper is not linguistic analysis *per se* but rather the learner language, the following analysis will not include the full spectrum of NP combinations and their complex agreement patterns. The focus of this paper will be on the basic sequence [Def-N.Gen] with post-nominal modifiers (i.e. NPs of the pattern b listed above) as well as the basic structure [Card-N-Adj] which is a frequent NP structure in the target language. The four basic structures to be tested in this study are: (i) NPs with head nouns and their modifiers; (ii) NPs containing possessive pronouns; (iii) NPs containing *Idafa* i.e. possessive constructions of the order Noun-Noun; and (iv) NPs preceded by cardinals. Let us consider the following illustrative examples for the relevant NP structures for this study:

i.   [N-Adj] (Singular Number marked by means of affixation)

   (1) *al-kalb-u*   *al-kabi:r-u*
        the-dog-.SG.NOM the-big.SG.NOM
        'The big dog.'

   [N-Adj] (Plural Number marked by means of affixation)

   (2) *qa:bal-tu* *al-mudarris-i:n*   *al-faransiyy-i:n*
        met-I   the-teachers-M.PL.ACC the-French-M.PL.ACC
        'I met the French teachers.'

ii.   [N-Pron-Adj] (Definiteness marked by means of an attached possessive pronoun)

(3)   *bayt-i:*   *al-qadi:m*
house-my the-old
'My old house.'

iii.   [N-N] (*Idafa:* Possessive Construction)

(4)   *qalam-u*   *al-'usta:ð -i*
pen-Nom   the-teacher-Gen
'The teacher's pen.'

iv.   [Card-N-Adj] (Gender polarity with cardinals 3 to 9)

(5)   *xamsa-t-u riʒa:l-in ṭiwa:l-in*
five-FEM-Nom   men-Gen tall.MASC.PL-Gen
'Five tall men.'

The structures discussed in the above examples exhibit a combination of typological features relating to the architecture of the target language and their processing requirements. The combination of these two sets of factors will prove highly useful in determining the structural options and their hierarchical order of development in the learner language (Pienemann 1998).

Two key structures will be analysed within LFG to demonstrate the type of information exchange involved between the head noun and its modifier/complement.

4.1.1 *Full noun-adjective agreement marking:* [N-Adj]
The basic type of noun-phrase agreement in Arabic has an extensive set of agreeing features that include number, gender, definiteness and case. Full noun-adjective agreement refers to instances where all the features of the head nouns have the same values as those of their modifiers, as illustrated in example (6) below:

(6)   *qa:bal-tu al-mudarris-i:n*   *al-faransiyy-i:n*
met-I   the-teachers-M.PL.ACC the-French-M.PL.ACC
'I met the French teachers.'

The f-structure and c-structure for the 'French teachers' noun phrase are outlined in Figure 1.

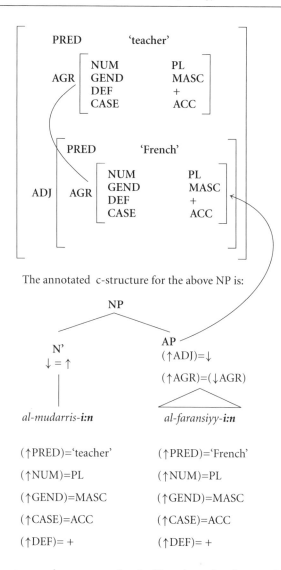

The annotated c-structure for the above NP is:

Figure 1. f-structure and c-structure for the 'French teachers' noun phrases

4.1.2 *Idafa or possessive construction: [N-N]*

(7)   *darra:ʒ-at-u   al-'usta:ð -i   al-ʒadi:d-at-u   gha:liyat-un*
bicycle-F.Nom the-teacher-Gen the-new-F.NOM expensive-NOM
'The teacher's new bicycle (is) expensive.'

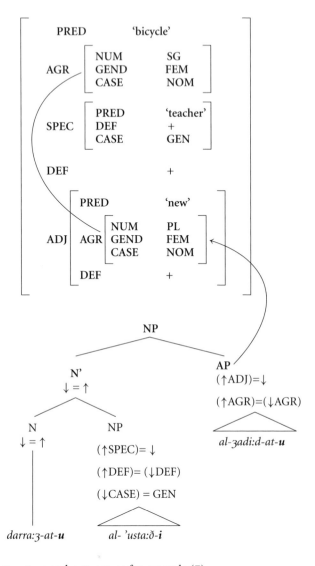

Figure 2. F-structure and c-structure for example (7)

Because nouns in Arabic must agree with their specifiers first before any other dependents (Malouf 1998:5), the following f-structure and annotated c-structure for the above example are represented in Figure 2.

The possessive (*idafa*) construction represented in the above c-structure can be explained in terms of one phrase structure rule (adopted from Thomann 2002):

$$NP \rightarrow N' \quad NP$$
$$\uparrow = \downarrow \quad (\uparrow DEF) = \downarrow DEF$$
$$\downarrow CASE = GEN$$

This complex rule for agreement within the *idafa* construction can be explained as follows: an NP can consist of an N', followed by an NP receiving CASE, NUM and GENDER from the head N ('bicycle') and DEF from the N' ('the teacher's bicycle').

To sum up, phrasal agreement in Arabic is characterised by several features as illustrated above. The feature matching between head noun and its modifier, as is the case in (1) and (2), marks definiteness across head nouns and their modifiers by different affixes. In (3) definiteness is marked on the head by means of an attached possessive pronoun, whilst it is marked on the modifier by the determiner /al-/. The marking of definiteness across the head noun and its complement Noun (in *idafa* possessive structure) is signalled by means of a Head-Complement order rule as is the case in example (4), with the complement being matched for the genitive case. And in (5), the marking of agreement between cardinals and head nouns by means of gender polarity is demonstrated.

4.2 Inter-Phrasal Agreement (agreement across constituents)

For the purposes of this paper, inter-phrasal agreement will be restricted to subject-verb agreement structures within which information exchange occurs across two syntactic constituents represented by an NP and a VP. Given that Arabic belongs to the *pro drop* type of languages, an emphasis on merging of features will be adopted as in Vigliocco, Butterworth and Garret (1996). However, before dealing with the *pro drop* phenomenon, let us examine full agreement in Arabic.

For the purpose of this study full inter-phrasal agreement in Arabic will be analysed in terms of the morphological marking of the features number, person and gender across the subject NP and the verb. The following example illustrates this information exchange within S-V-O sentences with both the NP and the verb being lexically realised.

(8) *al-la:ʕib-u:n*   *al-mumta:z-u:n*   *na:l-u:*   *ʒa:ʾizat-an*
    the-players.   the-excellent.   received-   prize-
    3MASC.PL   3MASC.PL   3MASC.PL   Acc.SG
    'The excellent players received a prize.'

Given the agglutinative nature of Arabic morphology, the affixes can denote more than one single feature as is the case with /-*u:n*/ in example (8) which marks the features number, gender, person as well as case (nominative case in this example). The general phrase structure rule for the syntactic order of Arabic sentences is listed below, with the comma between the NP and the VP indicating that these can be freely ordered. Bracketed NP indicates that Arabic is a *pro drop* language where the SUBJECT need not be lexically realised:

$$(R1): \quad S \quad \rightarrow \quad (NP), \qquad VP$$
$$(\uparrow SUBJ)=\downarrow \quad \uparrow = \downarrow$$

$$(R2): \quad VP \rightarrow \quad V \qquad\qquad (NP)$$
$$\uparrow = \downarrow \qquad (\uparrow OBJ) = \downarrow$$

As a definite determiner within an NP will be treated as a clitic, the following rules will apply:

$$(R3): \quad N' -> \quad Det \quad N$$
$$\uparrow = \downarrow$$

$$(R4): \quad A' -> \quad Det \quad A$$
$$\uparrow = \downarrow$$

The LFG analysis of Arabic inter-phrasal agreement structures will be limited to two types of subject-verb agreement discussed below.

4.2.1 *Full subject-verb agreement marking*

This type of agreement involves SVO type sentences where agreement between the nominal head and the verbal phrase is full.

(9) *al-la:ˤib-u:n*   *al-mumta:z-u:n*
the-players-3MASC.PL   the-excellent-3MASC.PL
na:l-u:ʒa:'izat-an
received-3MASC.PL prize-ACC.SG
'The excellent players received a prize.'

The complex information exchange for (9) is illustrated in terms of lexical entries, c-structures and f-structures displayed below respectively:

al-	DET	$(\uparrow DEF) = +$
la:ˤib	N	$(\uparrow PRED) = $ 'player'
		$(\uparrow AGR) = \downarrow$
		$(\downarrow PERS) = 3$
		$(\downarrow GEND) = MASC$
		$(\downarrow CASE) = NOM$

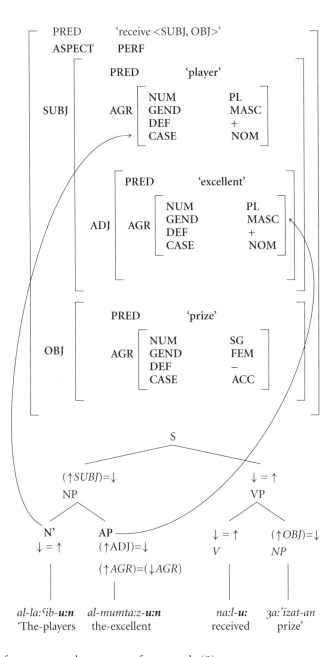

Figure 3. f-structure and c-structure for example (9)

mumta:z A   ($\uparrow$PRED) = 'excellent'
　　　　　　($\uparrow$AGR) = $\downarrow$
　　　　　　　　　　($\downarrow$PERS) = 3
　　　　　　　　　　($\downarrow$GEND) = MASC
　　　　　　　　　　($\downarrow$CASE) = NOM

na:l　　V　　($\uparrow$PRED) = 'receive'
　　　　　　($\uparrow$ASPECT) = PERF
　　　　　　($\uparrow$ SUBJ) = $\downarrow$
　　　　　　　　　　($\downarrow$ AGR NUM) = PL
　　　　　　　　　　($\downarrow$ AGR PERS) = 3
　　　　　　　　　　($\downarrow$AGR GEND) = MASC

ʒa:'izat　N　　($\uparrow$PRED) = 'prize'
　　　　　　($\uparrow$AGR) = $\downarrow$
　　　　　　　　　　($\downarrow$PERS) = 3
　　　　　　　　　　($\downarrow$GEND) = FEM
　　　　　　　　　　($\downarrow$CASE) = ACC

The f-structure and c-structure for (9) are as above.

The above formal representations illustrate the basis for information exchange between the subject NP and the verb of the sentence. The features listed in the above lexical entries for both the subject NP and the verb are specified in the f-structure under <f1> ensuring that the appropriate information is shared across both constituents.

4.2.2 *Reduced SV agreement marking*

The multiple lexical entries for affixes allow an account for agreement relations where the SUBJ has the feature [–Hum; +PL] or belongs to either a collective noun or the irregular plural class of nouns (also known in Arabic grammar as Broken Plural). Let us first consider the following examples for Subject NPs with the feature [–Hum]:

(10)　*al-kila:b-u*　　　　*harab-**at***
　　　the-dogs.PL-NOM　escaped-FEM.SG
　　　'The dogs escaped.'

The subject in the above example has the usual AGR features but in this case – reduced SV-agreement marking – it appears with a non-agreeing form of the verb. The lexical entries for this example are listed below:

al-	DET	$(\uparrow DEF) = +$
kalb	N	$(\uparrow PRED) = \text{'dog'}$
		$(\uparrow AGR) = \downarrow$
		$\quad (\downarrow PERS) = 3$
		$\quad (\downarrow GEND) = MASC$
		$\quad (\downarrow NUM) = PL$
		$(\uparrow HUM) = -$
harab	V	$(\uparrow PRED) = \text{'escape'}$
		$(\uparrow SUBJ\ AGR) = \downarrow$
		$\quad (\downarrow PERS) = 3$
		$\quad (\downarrow NUM) = PL$
		$\quad (\downarrow GEND) = MASC$
		$(\uparrow SUBJ\ HUM) = -$
		$(\uparrow FORM) = \downarrow$
		$\quad (\downarrow PERS) = 3$
		$\quad (\downarrow GEND) = FEM$
		$\quad (\downarrow NUM) = SG$

This suggests that the verb has two sets of features: SUBJ AGR and FORM. Normally, for a verb, FORM = SUBJ AGR; in other words, if it is a '3rd plural masculine verb' then it agrees with a 3rd plural masculine subject. In these cases of reduced agreement, this does not happen and, therefore, it results in a verb whose f-structure and annotated c-structure are represented in Figure 4.

The above formal representations illustrate the basis for information exchange between the subject NP and the verb of the sentence. The features listed in the above lexical entries for both the subject NP and the verb are specified in the f-structure under <f1> ensuring that the appropriate information is shared across both constituents.

4.3 The pro drop phenomenon in Arabic agreement marking

As far as PT is concerned, perhaps the most important of these typological features is the *pro drop* nature of Arabic. This is because in *pro drop* languages, the verb may occur without an explicit lexical or pronominal subject constituent. Yet, the verb is still marked for such grammatical features as person, gender and number expressed by means of a combination of prefixes and suffixes. Bresnan (2001:117) suggests that "pro drop refers to the functional specification of a pronominal argument by a head; this entails the absence of the structural expression of the pronoun as a syntactic NP of DP." Such analysis has been

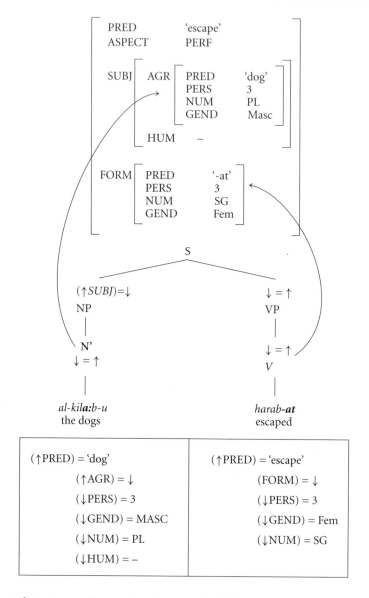

Figure 4. f-structure and c-structure for example (10)

applied to other non-configurational languages such as Italian (c.f. Di Biase &
Kawaguchi 2002:276) where it is argued the "morphology of a head verb may
incorporate its pronominal arguments." The position adopted in this paper follows that of Vigliocco, Butterworh and Garret (1996) who propose a "feature

merging process" rather than a "feature copying process" in accounting for the null subject phenomenon in languages such as Spanish. This is because in LFG merging can be managed through unifying morpho-syntactic features located in the relevant lexical entries. Let us consider the following examples:

(11)   ʒaː' -uː
       came-3.MASC.PL
       'They came.'

(12)   ʒiʔ- tu
       came-I
       'I came.'

(13)   ʒaː' -uː   bi-lqitaːr
       came-3.MASC.PL by train
       'They came not by train.'

The important question in the above examples ((11), (12) and (13)) is the nature of the affixes attached to the verb and their respective features. Based on LFG, the lexical entry, the c-structure and the f-structure for the affix $[-uː]$ in example (11) are as illustrated by Figure 5.

(14)   -uː: (↑ SUBJ)=↓
$$\begin{bmatrix} (↓ PRED)=PRO \\ (↓ AGR\ NUM)=PL \\ (↓AGR\ GEND)=MASC \\ (↓AGR\ PERS)=3 \end{bmatrix}$$

The above analysis makes use of two crucial assumptions (Fassi Fehri 1988: 109): (a) that the affix $[-uː]$ does not have a corresponding syntactic category at constituent structure (c-structure); and (b) that it is pronominal, i.e. it has an attribute PRED whose value is 'PRO'. Hence, we see the important role of the lexical entry specifications listed in (14) above which would serve as the basis upon which the 'merging process' is undertaken to fulfil the agreement requirements, for example (11).

4.4 A typological account of inter-phrasal agreement patterns

On the basis of the typological discussion of agreement in Arabic above, one can identify a set of three distinct types of agreement relations governed by the nature of agreeing features (in terms of grammatical functions) and the domain in which they occur (this is assumed to be governed by f-structure). These

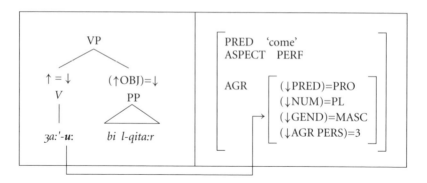

Figure 5. c-structure and f-structure for example (11)

are: (a) internal agreement; (b) anaphoric binding; and (c) external agreement, all of which are briefly described below.

4.4.1 *Internal agreement*
The core structures of such agreement relations in Arabic are realised when:

i.   Verbs agree with their SUBJ (as in example (15)).
ii.   Head NPs agree with their arguments (as in example (16)).

   (15) *akal-at*   *al-bintu*   *al-ʒubna*
          ate-3F.SG the-girl.3FEM.SG the-cheese
          'The girl ate the cheese.'

   (16) *al-ban-a:t-u*   *ðakiy-a:t-u-n*
          the-girl-PL-NOM smart-PL.FEM-NOM.Indef
          'The girls (are) smart.'

The agreement relation in example (16) relates to a topic NP and a predicative AP within an equative sentence marked grammatically by means of a definiteness polarity: a definite [+ DEF] topicalised NP and an indefinite [–DEF] predicative AP. The other features (number, gender and case) are unified across the two constituents.

4.4.2 *Agreement with local anaphoric binding*
This type of agreement takes place in a larger domain (f-nucleus) that contains not only argument functions such as SUBJ and OBJ but also non-argument ones such as adjunct (ADJ) and modifier (MODIF). Thus the adjunct is not directly lexically governed by a predicate P but rather indirectly linked to P

because it contains a pronominal controlled by an argument of the predicate P. This is what examples (17 and 18) below illustrate:

(17) *laqi:-tu   zayd-an   ya-qra'u*
      found-I zayd-ACC 3.MASC.SG- read.
      'I found Zayd reading.'

(18) *laqi:-tu   zayd-an   na:' im-an*
      found-I zayd-ACC sleeping.3.MASC.SG-ACC
      'I found Zayd sleeping.'

In (17) the OBJ of the matrix verb controls the pronominal subject of the adjunct clause: the PRO is anaphorically bound by the object (a case of local anaphoric binding, c.f. Fassi Fehri 1981). Similarly in (18) the pronominal subject of the participial AP can be controlled by the subject or the object of the matrix verb. Anaphoric agreement is characterised by the fact that:

i.   the two agreeing expressions are of the same category (nominal expressions);
ii. the direction of agreement is from an argument function to a nonargument function (e.g., (17)); and
iii. the features involved are all pronominal including NUM, PERS, HUM and GEND.

4.4.3 *External agreement*

The term 'external' in this instance refers to the controller of agreement being external to the f-nucleus where the agreement target is found. External agreement shares some properties with local anaphoric agreement most notably as in (c) above. For the purposes of this paper, the core characteristics of external agreement that will be investigated are the following:

i.   left dislocation: agreement between a THEME,[3] in simple LFG terms a case of topicalisation, and the co-referential (resumptive) pronominal inside the clause;
ii. relativisation: agreement between the relative marker and the head noun in gender, number and case;[4]
iii. equative sentences: agreement between the topic NP and the predicative AP (more precisely a pronominal contained in the AP); and
iv. questioning with pronominalisation: agreement between the question word and the co-referential (resumptive) pronominal.

Consider the following illustrative examples for (i), (ii), (iii) and (iv) respectively:

(19)   *zayd-un   laqi:-tu aba:-hu*
       zayd-NOM   met-I   father-his
       'Zayd, I met his father.'

What looks like an agreement marker above is, in fact, a pronominal affix that is anaphorically related to a THEME in a left dislocation construction.

(20)   *laqi:-tu a-lwalad-ayni   allað-ayni   darras-ta*
       met-I   the-boy-DUAL.ACC who-DUAL.ACC taught-you
       'I met the two boys whom you taught.'

(21)   *ayy-at-u   laʒn-at-in   asdar-at*
       which-FEM-NOM committee-FEM-GEN issued-FEM
       ha:ð aal-qara:r-a
       this the-decision-ACC
       'Which committee issued this decision?'

In examples (20) and (21) the information exchange in the agreement relationship is shared between a resumptive pronominal on the one hand, and a relative pronoun and a question word on the other. In example (20) the features marked are number and case, while in example (21) it is gender.

4.5 A summary of inter-phrasal agreement structures in Arabic

The following table includes a summary of the key structures discussed so far in this paper and highlights their relevant typological features. Given the *pro drop* aspect of the Arabic language, the only instances of subject-verb agreement included in this study are those where the subject is lexically realised in the agreement relationship in either an SV(O) or VS(O) word order combination. Another important typological issue taken into consideration in this table is the semantic type of the head NP (i.e. –Hum) as it results in agreement marking where the feature number on the verbal constituent is always set for the value (–PL) even if the feature number is set as (+PL) on the head NP.

Relativisation (as in example (20)), which is indicative of inter-clausal rather than inter-phrasal agreement, is listed in the above table for inter-phrasal agreement structures because of the similar typological feature (external agreement) it shares with more typical inter-phrasal structures. However, when formulating the general predictions for Arabic SLA, relativisation will be placed at the higher inter-clausal stage.

Table 1. An account of inter-phrasal agreement in Arabic

Type of Agreement Relation	Typological issue
Internal Agreement: word order variation	VS(O): Marked for Natural Gender only (i.e. reduced agreement marking) SV(O): Marked for Number and Natural Gender (i.e. full agreement marking)
Internal Agreement: with [−Hum] referents	Non Human NP type (Gram Gender) Collective NP Type (Gram Gender)
Anaphoric Agreement: left dislocation	AP controlled by matrix Vb e.g. (18) OBJ of matrix Vb controls agreement e.g. (17) Question words e.g. (21) Topicalisation: Left dislocation e.g. (19) Relativisation e.g. (20)

5. PT and Arabic agreement marking

The process of exchange of grammatical information (agreement marking), according to Pienemann (1998:76) is not possible unless: 1) the lexicon is annotated for the features in question; and 2) the syntactic procedures have specialised to hold specific grammatical information. Pienemann (1998) goes on to argue that it is feasible to predict that learners in the initial stages of acquisition will be unable to produce structures where there is exchange of grammatical information specific to the target language using syntactic procedures (or in LFG terms 'feature unification') at the early stages of acquisition.

The two levels of grammatical information exchange investigated in this study (phrasal vs inter-phrasal) require different processing resources ranging from utilisation of phrasal procedures for phrasal agreement to s-procedure for inter-phrasal agreement. These two types of information exchange correspond to phrasal agreement and subject-verb agreement marking in Arabic. If these different patterns of information exchange are acquired in a manner which reflects their processing requirements and complexities, then the argument that (a) learners can only acquire what they can process and (b) that the processing operations form an implicational hierarchy will be validated. A developmental pattern which does not reflect these processing realities is likely to raise questions about the status of processing prerequisites in SLA and the availability of an implicational processing hierarchy able to predict developmental sequences in learner language.

From a processing perspective, agreement between the noun phrase of a sentence and its verbal phrase is differentiated from agreement between noun phrases and their modifiers on the basis of syntactic boundaries and processing procedures. In the former, the morpho-syntactic information number and gender is exchanged or transferred within the same constituent, i.e. noun phrase, and in the latter this same process takes place across two distinct syntactic constituents, namely, a noun phrase and a verbal phrase. Agreement across constituents involves the marking of the subject's syntactic features (person, number and gender) onto the verbal phrase (cf. Fassi Fehri 1988). This agreement is, in most cases, a straightforward feature – copying process whereby the subject's features are marked onto the verb. This holds for those types of agreement relations where the syntactic word order of the constituents is the basic SV(O) and the semantic class of the nominal heads (subjects) exhibits the feature [+ HUM]. However, when there are different syntactic (i.e. different word order combinations) and semantic (i.e. NPs involving [–HUM] referents) parameters, agreement marking is affected primarily in its scope, i.e. reduction in the range of features that can still be unified across constituents. The typological discussion of agreement marking in Arabic can be summarised within three central features: multiplicity and complexity of form-function mappings (Pienemann 1998); multiplicity of information sources (as in the Competition Model, MacWhinney & Bates 1987), which learners need to consider in real-time processing of the target language; and the affixation process (i.e. form, location and order, if more than one).

The various typological features and the resulting patterns of agreement relationships can have a significant impact on the processing load of key target language structures and, therefore, their processability in a specific implicational order. The objective of the previous linguistic analysis and description of the target language structures was to enable us to identify the processing requirement of different Arabic structures. In undertaking this task, the analysis incorporated general processing issues (e.g. phrasal vs inter-phrasal marking) and language-specific features such as the semantic type of the head noun and word order variation.

6.   Predictions for Arabic SLA

As far as this study is concerned, the focus is on the incremental generation of phrasal procedure, S-procedure and subordinate clause procedure by learners of Arabic as a second language. The processing procedures outlined in PT provided the predictive framework for Arabic SLA structures, resulting in Table 2 below:

Table 2. Predictions for Arabic agreement structures

Level of information exchange	Linguistic context for structures	Processing procedures	Typological features
Inter-clausal	Relativisation	Subordinate clause procedure	Referential coherence (feature unification across clauses)
Inter-phrasal	Left Dislocation (object clitic)	S-procedure	Topicalisation: feature unification across constituents
	[–Hum]; / [+BP]	S-procedure	Semantic type of NP: feature mismatch across constituents
	[+Hum] in VS(O)	S-procedure	Reduced agreement: Feature unification across constituents (Gender only)
	[+Hum] in SV(O)	S-procedure	Full agreement: Feature unification across constituents
Phrasal	[Card[5] -N-Adj]	Phrasal procedure	Feature mismatch: gender polarity
	[N-N] (Idafa/Complement Construction)	Phrasal procedure	Cancel Det marker
	[N-Pro-Adj]	Phrasal procedure	Partial Cancel Det marker
	[N-Adj] (Number)	Phrasal procedure	Feature unification
	[N-Adj] (Natural Gender)	Phrasal procedure	Feature unification

It is important to state here that the general hierarchy of PT is flexible enough to incorporate language-specific typological features (such as gender polarity and humanness). Such language-specific typological features are important because they yield multiple structures at each developmental stage with intra-stage ordering of structures being driven by form-function relationships, which introduce additional processing tasks for the learner. For example in Table 2 above, the first two structures involving number and gender within phrasal agreement exhibit one-to-one form function mappings while the others (e.g. gender polarity with cardinals) do not.

7. Empirical evidence for the PT-generated predictions

Let us first look at the data-generated acquisition sequences for the key structures in Arabic SLA (Mansouri 2000) as defined in PT and using the emergence criterion as the key developmental indicator. This study is based on a stratified sample of individual learner data gathered from two learners studying Arabic in a formal classroom environment. The two English-speaking background (ESB) learners were selected on the basis of their developmental level in Arabic, having started to learn Arabic without any prior knowledge or exposure. The main data-eliciting procedures were eight spontaneous oral interviews conducted over four semesters of classroom language learning, which consisted of a total of 52 instruction weeks. Data collection commenced with both learners after they completed their first introductory module of formal study of the Arabic language. Individual interviews were conducted four times over a two-semester period.

7.1 Acquisition criteria and data analysis

Although the data for this study was collected from learners of Arabic as a second language in a classroom environment, the fact that only oral data elicited through conversational interviews is used ensures that the key feature of time-constrained production is maintained. The learners in this study "produced the data in conversational setting, thus being subject to the same constraints on word access and the computing of syntactic structures etc: as any other speaker. Therefore, whatever they produce must be taken as evidence of their language processing skill and their underlying linguistic knowledge" (Håkansson, Pienemann & Sayehli 2002: 255).

In line with PT's emergence criterion and its emphasis on morphological and lexical variation for the production of structures by the learner, the position taken in this study is that at least one minimal pair of a given structure is produced before a judgment on emergence, or lack of it, can be formulated. Pienemann (1998: 146) categorises quantitative observations of the learner language into four types, namely: "(1) no evidence, i.e. no linguistic contexts; (2) insufficient evidence, i.e. very small number of contexts; (3) evidence for non-application, i.e. non-application in the presence of contexts for rule x; and (4) evidence of rule application, i.e. examples of rule application in the presence of contexts."

Following Pienemann's approach, this study relies primarily on type (4) observations as the basis for applying the emergence criterion. The figures reported in the following tables indicate the number of linguistic contexts for rule application and the number of suppliance. A ratio is also included in the same cell indicating the learner's developmental progression along the time axis.

7.2 Empirical findings

The learner data will be reported individually with quantitative displays of the production of all the key TL structures at different points along the developmental time axis. The data is summarised in terms of quantitative figures and ratios to give the reader an approximate indication of the learner's dynamic interlanguage system. However, this is by no means an indication that quantitative measures are taken as a strict criterion for acquisition. On the contrary, it is the qualitative criteria and careful analyses of linguistic contexts and the obligatory minimal pair rule that allow us to include in these figures only those structures which have been produced in morphologically and lexically variable contexts. Let us first look at both learners' data summarised in Tables 3 and 4 below.

A quick first look at the data reported in this table reveals an overall pattern of developmental hierarchy predominantly, but not entirely, consistent with the predictions generated in Table 2. In fact, Louise's[6] language reveals an inter-

Table 3. The development of agreement morphology in ASL (Louise's data)

	Structures	T1	T2	T3	T4
Phrasal	[N-Adj] (feature: Natural Gender)	6/6	7/7	9/9	8/8
		1	1	1	1
	[N-Adj] (feature: Number)	14/16	15/17	22/22	25/25
		0.87	0.88	1	1
	[N-Pron-Adj]	2/4	2/3	4/4	5/5
	(Def marked by possessive pronouns)	0.5	0.66	1	1
	[N-N-(AP)] Idafa (Possessive construction)	0	1/3	2/2	2/2
			0.33	1	1
	[Card-N-Adj]	0	0	2/3	2/2
				0.66	1
Inter-Phrasal	SV(O); NP [+Hum]	0	2/3	4/5	5/5
			0.66	0.8	1
	VS(O); NP [+Hum]	2/3	1/4	1/2	2/2
		0.66	0.25	0.5	1
	SV(O): NP [−Hum] / [+BP]	0	0	1/1	1/2
				1	0.5
	Anaphoric binding: Left Dislocation (object clitic)	0	0	0	1/3
					0.33
Inter-clausal	Relativisation	0	0	2/4	1/2
				0.5	0.5

Table 4. The development of agreement morphology in ASL (George's data)

	Structures	T1	T2	T3	T4
Phrasal	[N-Adj] (feature: Natural Gender)	5/5	6/7	6/6	7/8
		1	0.85	1	0.87
	[N-Adj] (feature: Number)	6/12	12/14	18/19	21/22
		0.5	0.85	0.95	0.96
	[N-Pron-Adj]	1/3	2/4	2/3	3/3
	(Def marked by possessive pronouns)	0.33	0.5	0.66	1
	[N-N-(AP)] Idafa (Possessive construction)	0	1 /2	2/2	2/2
			0.5	1	1
	[Card-N-Adj]	0	1 /2	2/3	2/2
			0.5	0.66	1
Inter-phrasal	SV(O); NP [+Hum]	1 /4	1/3	2/3	4/5
		0.25	0.33	0.66	0.8
	VS(O); NP [+Hum]	1/2	1/3	1/1	2/2
		0.5	0.33	1	1
	SV(O): NP [–Hum] / [+BP]	0	0	0	1/2
					0.5
	Anaphoric binding: Left Dislocation (object clitic)	0	0	0	0
Inter-clausal	Relativisation	0	0	1/3	1/3
				0.33	0.33

esting, but not totally unexpected, pattern of quantitatively large samples for certain structures and rules but not others within the same stage. This is the case for phrasal morphology where structures 1 and 2 seem to be produced far more frequently than structures 3, 4 and 5. Similar observations can be made for inter-phrasal agreement with regard to structure 6 being produced more frequently than the others. This may be a useful observation both for the idea of differing processing requirements for structures within the same stage, but also for the notion of the optimal structure to be tested in SLA studies.

George's data reveals many similar patterns found in Louise's data, namely, the relatively larger quantitative samples in certain structures rather than others within the same stage. This issue will be addressed in the discussion section below where it will be shown that the concept of form-function relationships (Pienemann 1998: 155) can be used successfully to account for such variation. Overall, and despite the lack of any productive use of certain structures such as object clitics in left dislocation, George's data exhibits features of an implicational hierarchy that largely reflects the predicted sequence.

It should be noted that the linguistic analysis of the learner language is not undertaken from a traditional target language approximation exercise, which can end up looking more like an error analysis than a systematic developmental analysis of inter-language. On the contrary, even grammatically erroneous utterances have been taken as evidence of emergence when containing the basic structure. Only when the structure and the rule for producing the structure are missing altogether, do we conclude that the structure is still not processable at that particular point in time. Let us now consider the following examples from both learners, which will be followed by a theoretical discussion:

i.   [N-Adj]

  (22) "*al*-*walad*-*u*   *al*-*kabi:r*-*u*   *huna:*"
       the-boy-NOM.SG the-big-NM.SG here
       'The older boy is here.'

  (23) "*al*-*bint*-*u*   *al*-*kabi:r*-*at*-*u*   *huna:*"
       the-girl.FEM-Nom the-big-FEM.Nom here
       'The older girl is here.'

Examples (22) and (23) above are an indication of both learner's ability to produce this basic NP structure productively and accurately, marking both the Determiner and the Gender accordingly. The agglutinative nature of Arabic morphology can be seen here with example (22) where the form /-*u*/ exhibits a classical case of one-to-many form function relationships (cf. Pienemann 1998; Håkansson 1996b). While still at the phrasal agreement stage, examples (24) and (25) below show that when this basic NP structure is compounded by additional syntactic features such as possessive pronouns in (24) and cardinals in (25), the learners are consequently unable to mark agreement.

ii.   [N-Pro-Adj]

  (24) *"*askunu*   *fi:* *ʃaqqat*-*i:*   *saɣi:ra*"
       live.1SG in flat-**my**   small
       'I live in my small flat.'

For example (24) this would require merging the possessive pronoun with the determiner [al-] thus producing the NP structure: /ʃaqqat-i: as-saghi:ra/ (my flat the small).

iii. [N-Card-(Adj)]

(25) "*na-skun ʒami:ʕan fi al-wa:ḥid da:r"
      we-live all   in the-one   house
      'We all live in one house.'

Similarly, for the NP structure in (25) the cardinal presence results in the following structure: /ad-da:r al-wa:ḥid-at/ (the-house the-one.Fem).

iv. [N-N-(Adj)] *Idafa* structure (Possessive Construction)

(26) "*a-skun fi: al-madi:nat Melbourne"
      I-live   in the-city   Melbourne
      'I live in the city of Melbourne.'

(27) "*yaʕmal abi: fi   al-ja:miʕat   Melbourne"
      works   my father in the-university Melbourne
      'My father works at Melbourne University.'

(28) "*al-mana:x muʕtadil fi: **al-faṣl**   fita:"
      the-weather moderate in the-season   winter
      'The weather is moderate in winter.'

An interesting pattern is observed in examples (26), (27) and (28), whereby the learner in an *idafa* construction (Noun Complement) incorrectly produces the determiner on the head noun to mark definiteness. This is a case where the determiner should be cancelled (cancel determiner) as it becomes redundant in a noun-complement NP structure. This point will be picked up in the discussion section. Let us now examine some examples relating to inter-phrasal agreement marking.

SV(O); NP [+Hum]

(29) "*Susan wa Nicole wa Lynda taktub-**u:n**   ʕala al-waraqa"
      Susan and Nicole and Lynda FEM-write-3**MASC.PL** on   the-paper
      'Susan, Nicole and Lynda wrote on the paper.'

(30) "*Sally wa Lynda wa Susan ta-'kul-**u**   al-bitza"
      Sally and Lynda and Susan F-eat-**3SG** the-pizza
      'Sally, Lynda and Susan eat pizza (at lunch time).'

In (29) and (30) the learner language exhibits a feature mismatch relating to gender and number respectively. In fact, the verbal agreement suffix in both (29) and (30) should be [-na] indicating the features /Plural; Feminine/.

VS(O); NP [+Hum]

(31) "*ka:n-u: al-'asa:tiða   ḥazi:nØ"
     was.3MASC.PL the-teacher.3MASC.PL sad.3MASC.SG
     'The teachers were sad (about the 3 students not finishing the course).'

(32) "*askun-u ab-i: wa umm-i: fi ashwood"
     live-1SG   father-my and mother-my in Ashwood
     'My father and mother live in Ashwood.'

Similarly, in (31) the learner produces VS-agreement patterns with full merging of the feature number. This seems to be a case of over-generalisation from
the SV-agreement rule where features of the subject, including number and
gender, are expected to be unified with the verbal agreement suffix. In example
(32) it is the feature /person/ that is marked incorrectly with the learner repro-
ducing the verbal morphology in the first person instead of third person. This
can be a case of undifferentiated 'chunk learning', or simply a lexically driven
strategy to communicate in the target language using available forms (in this
case the verb *askun* being in the first person).

SV(O); NP [−Hum]

(33) "al-imtiḥa:n-a:t   ta-ʃɣalu   ba:l-i:"
     the-exams-3FEM.PL 3FEM.SG-occupy mind-my
     'The exams occupy my mind.'

Anaphoric binding: Left Dislocation (object clitic)

(34) "*as-suḥuf   al-ʕarabiy-at   al-luɣa
     the-newspapers.PL the-Arabic-3FEM.SG the-language
     fi:-haya-xtalifØ"
     in-it.3FEM.SG3MASC.SG-differ
     '(As for) the Arabic newspapers, the language in it differs (from colloquial
     Arabic).'

Example (33) provides a good illustration that a rather complex agreement
rule relating to non-human subject NPs is at play. The learner here is correctly
identifying the semantic type of the NP (−Hum) and holding this feature in
memory before mapping the appropriate agreement marker onto the verb. In
example (34) we notice a rare instance in the learner language (in this case
George) where object clitics are marked correctly in a left dislocated subject-
verb agreement relationship. However, since there was only one example, it
would be insufficient evidence to argue that this signals the emergence of this
type of complex agreement marking.

Relativisation

(35) "al-*muʃkil-at*   *alla-ti:*   *ta-fɣalu -hu*
     the-problem-FEM.SG which-FEM.SG FEM.SG-occupy-him
     la:zim yaʕmal wa yadrus"
     must work and study
     'The problem that is occupying him is that he must study and work (at the
     same time).'

Example (35) provides a rare instance of inter-clausal structure in Louise's language with the relative pronoun /*alla-ti:*/ correctly 'governed' in the marking of its features by the head subject NP. However, we notice the lack of a resumptive pronoun (*hiya*) which is necessary to ensure the overall coherence of the sentence.

8. A processability perspective on the findings

From a PT perspective a number of concepts can be drawn upon to account for this seemingly inconsistent developmental sequence. Although the basic idea in PT is that processing procedures at each stage are necessary for the processing of the target language structures, there is no absolute guarantee nor a logical argument that all processable structures at a given stage must be acquired before the learner is able to process structures from the next developmental stage. 'Developmental trailers' can be viewed as a possible explanation for the temporal gap between the capacity to produce the linguistic context for a certain TL structure and the production of the structure itself (cf. Larsen-Freeman & Long 1991; Pienemann 1998). To put it simply, the fact that learners are producing a representative structure of the relevant stage should not be equated with his/her ability to produce all potential structures irrespective of typological and functional constraints. This is where an operationalised definition of the target language optimal structures for establishing developmental sequences is useful.

   A common phenomenon that is noticeable across both learners is what appears to be a case of 'developmental gaps' in phrasal agreement relating to possessive structures (*Idafa* structures) and gender polarity with NP involving cardinals (numbers between 3 and 9). Neither of these structures were produced by either learner at Time 1 (T1) of data collection, though the basic form of subject-verb agreement was. On the surface, this finding would seem to contradict PT's prediction in a manner similar to Nielsen's (1997) findings. However, not all structures within a given stage share exactly the same typological features in terms of form-function relationships. Therefore, it is not imperative that all structures within such a developmental sequence emerge before the next stage emerges. In fact, Pienemann (1998) already indicated that multiplicity of form-function relationships can be a source of additional processing complexity and, therefore, delay the emergence of certain structures in the learner language. Such structures with multiplicity of form-function mapping should not be the prime choice for the optimal test structure in SLA research.

Let us now apply the emergence criterion to the statistical results displayed in Tables 3 and 4 above in order to establish the developmental path for both learners. The emergence criterion represented by the [+] symbol is assigned to structures (in the learner language) which meet the minimal pair requirement with lexical and morphological variation being the key indicator. In other words, only when a structure is produced at least twice with different morphological markers and with different lexical items, do we conclude that it has emerged in the learner language. In most cases, both learners have produced more than one minimal pair of the same structure. When structures were produced only once, these are represented with the Figure 1 between brackets. Tables 5 and 6 below provide a developmental summary of agreement structures in both learners' language.

The empirical results show that, overall, both learners have acquired the various ASL structures in the predicted order with phrasal structures clearly emerging before inter-phrasal ones. This is despite the fact that certain phrasal

Table 5. The development of agreement morphology in ASL (Louise's data)

	Structures	T1	T2	T3	T4
Phrasal	[N-Adj] (feature: Natural Gender)	+	+	+	+
	[N-Adj] (feature: Number)	+	+	+	+
	[N-Pron-Adj] (Def marked by possessive pronouns)	+	+	+	+
	[N-N-(AP)] Idafa (Possessive construction)	–	–	+	+
	[Card-N-Adj]	–	–	+	+
Inter-Phrasal	SV(O); NP [+Hum]	–	+	+	+
	VS(O); NP [+Hum]	+/–[7]	–	–	+
	SV(O): NP [–Hum] / [+BP]	–	–	(1)	(1)
	Anaphoric binding: Left Dislocation (object clitic)	–	–	–	(1)
Inter-clausal	Relativisation	–	–	+	(1)

Table 6. The development of agreement morphology in ASL (George's data)

	Structures	T1	T2	T3	T4
Phrasal	[N-Adj] (feature: Natural Gender)	+	+	+	+
	[N-Adj] (feature: Number)	+	+	+	+
	[N-Pron-Adj] (Def marked by possessive pronouns)	–	–	+	+
	[N-N-(AP)] Idafa (Possessive construction)	–	–	+	+
	[Card-N-Adj]	–	–	+	+
Inter-phrasal	SV(O); NP [+Hum]	–	–	+	+
	VS(O); NP [+Hum]	-	-	(1)	+
	SV(O): NP [–Hum] / [+BP]	–	–	–	–
	Anaphoric binding: Left Dislocation (object clitic)	–	–	–	–
Inter-clausal	Relativisation	–	–	–	–

Table 7. Conflated statistical summary for all structures (Louise's data)

	Structures	T1	T2	T3	T4
Phrasal	All phrasal structures	22/26 .84	25/30 .83	38/40 .95	42/42 1
Inter-Phrasal	All inter-phrasal structures	2/3[8] .66	5/7 .71	6/8 .75	9/12 .75
Inter-clausal	Relativisation as inter-clausal structure	–	–	2/4 .5	1/2 .5

Table 8. Conflated statistical summary for all structures (George's data)

	Structures	T1	T2	T3	T4
Phrasal	All phrasal structures	22/26 .84	25/30 .83	38/40 .95	42/42 1
Inter-Phrasal	All inter-phrasal structures	2/3[8] .66	5/7 .71	6/8 .75	9/12 .75
Inter-clausal	Relativisation as inter-clausal structure	–	–	2/4 .5	1/2 .5

structures such as *idafa* [N-N-(Adj)] and NPs preceded by cardinals [Card-N-(Adj)] were only produced by both learners at Time 3 of the data collection timeline. One of the most striking findings of this study is the emergence of VS(O) structures in Louise's data as early as Time 1. This result needs to be treated cautiously in the light of the reduced agreement-making required in such structures. In fact, the feature number here does not unify across subject and verb with only the feature gender being marked. Given that gender, in particular semantic gender, has a conceptual basis, it is not therefore totally surprising that gender in VS(O) – type structures is easier to mark and hence emerge early in the learner language (cf. Vigliocco & Franck 1999).

Given that there are multiple structures in both phrasal and inter-phrasal stages, it would be useful to conflate the findings for both learners whereby all structures within each of the stages are represented statistically together. This will provide a more complete picture of inter-stage hierarchy and also their scalability ratio which is a good indicator of data validity.

The conflated statistical summary displayed above shows that the structures appear in both learners in the implicational order predicted in PT. Both learners have clearly acquired phrasal structures before inter-phrasal structures. To put it differently, by the time inter-phrasal structures emerged in both learners (i.e. Time 3), phrasal structures had already been produced productively and consistently as early as Time 1. The empirical data displayed above does not provide counter-evidence or significant gaps (i.e. stage gaps) for the predicted developmental hierarchy. This means that the all important scalability ratio for both sets of data is 1.0 indicating a perfect implicational relationship between lower stage structures (phrasal) and higher stage ones (inter-phrasal).

9. Conclusion

This study provides an empirical test for an acquisition hierarchy of agreement marking in Arabic SLA based on Processability Theory (Pienemann 1998). A detailed analysis of the target language structures was undertaken which resulted in a complex and multi-layered typology of agreement structures in Arabic for both phrasal and inter-phrasal agreement. When implemented into an LFG framework, this typology of agreement structures reveals a systematic pattern of agreement relations that are influenced by language-specific typological features such as the semantic class of the head noun, word order and topicalisation. The findings clearly support the predicted developmental hierarchy and, overall, provide robust evidence of its implicational nature. An important issue that emerged from this study relates to the order/sequencing of structures within a particular stage and whether this requires additional explanatory tools. In fact, a combination of tools, most notably form-function complexity, i.e. one-to-one as opposed to one-to-many or many-to-one relationships (Bates et al. 1982; Bates & MacWhinney 1987), language-specific typological features including semantic and classificatory information (Bybee 1991), as well as morpheme types ranging from zero morpheme to bound and free morphemes, can be used to account for intra-stage developmental order. The general architecture of Processability Theory does, in fact, allow for such analysis since it clearly differentiates between "the core of processability, namely the processing of procedures needed for different kinds of affixation ... [and] the learning of morphological forms in relation to their functions" (Pienemann 1998: 154). In other words, the task of undertaking information exchange or distribution within different grammatical structures is a separate and different task when compared to the learning of the morphological form of a given affix. As such, the hierarchy of processing resources and the relevant patterns of information exchange reflects the former, whilst language-specific morphological features (including form-function relationships and classificatory information), reflects the latter. In fact, feature mismatch involving grammatical gender (i.e. where there is no conceptual basis for gender encoding) is supported by psychological experiments on gender processing and production (cf. Vigliocco & Franck 1999).

To conclude, let us return to the two core objectives of this study, namely, establishing the developmental hierarchy for agreement marking in Arabic SLA and testing this hierarchy against predictions extrapolated on the basis of Processability Theory. As far as the first objective is concerned, a hierarchy including the main structures in the target language was established with a systematic account for their typological features and their implications for processability and processing requirements. More importantly, the study generated strong empirical evidence in support of the developmental hierarchy formulated within Processability Theory with clear implicational sequences observed in both learners, despite some inconsistencies with regard to the lack of emergence evidence for *idafa* structures (possessive noun phrases) and cardinal numbers (gender polarity within NP) at the first time of data collection (T1). Both learners, however, were able to produce these structures in subsequent interviews. Overall, the findings of this study demonstrate that the developmental sequences in both learners follow that predicted in PT, despite the delayed emergence of certain structures which, nevertheless, did not amount to violation of the implicational hierarchy articulated in PT.

Key phonetic symbols

Phonetic description	Conventional/IPA transcription
voiced alveolar stop	d
voiceless alveolar stop	t
emphatic voiced alveolar stop	*d̲*
emphatic voiceless alveolar stop	t̲
voiceless velar stop	k
uvular stop	q
glottal stop	’
voiceless glottal fricative	h
voiceless pharyngeal fricative	ħ
voiced pharyngeal fricative	ʕ
voiceless palato-alveolar fricative	ʃ
voiced palato-alveolar fricative	ʒ
voiceless dental fricative	θ
voiced dental fricative	ð
voiceless velar fricative	*x*
voiced velar fricative	ɣ
voiceless alveolar fricative	s
emphatic voiceless alveolar fricative	s̲
voiceless labio-dental fricative	f
bilabial nasal	m
alveolar nasal	n
alveolar lateral	l
alveolar trill	r
short low back vowel	a
long low back vowel	a:
short high front vowel	i
long high front vowel	i:
short high back vowel	u
long high back vowel	u:
Zero morpheme	∅

Notes

* In writing this paper, I have benefited from interactions and discussions with Manfred Pienemann whose feedback helped in the overall conceptualisation of the paper. I am grateful to Peter Sells who provided excellent detailed feedback on the LFG analysis of Arabic structures. Other colleagues working within Processability Theory including Gisela Håkansson, Yanyin Zhang and Satomi Kawaguchi have been a source of insightful discussions on

many occasions. I would like to thank Bruno DiBiase in particular who provided constructive feedback on the final draft. Needless to say, any shortcomings are the author's sole responsibility.

1. The feature Gender is always marked in Arabic nouns and therefore is obligatorily shared between the head noun and its modifier.

2. Definiteness in Arabic is a marked by means of an attached prefix /al-/.

3. Functions and definitions adopted from Dik (1978) and Fassi Fehri (1988):

> THEME: information with respect to which the predication can be relevant,
> TOPIC: old information in the relevant discourse structure,
> FOCUS: most salient information in the relevant discourse structure.

4. For the purpose of the study, relative pronouns are treated as instances of inter-clausal agreement marking, and as such are predicted to emerge in the learner language at final stage 5.

5. This rule applies to cardinals 3 to 10 only.

6. The names used for both learners are pseudonyms.

7. This cell needs to be treated cautiously in light of the reduced agreement required: number does not unify across subject and verb; semantic gender does unify but this has a conceptual basis and is easy to mark (cf. Vigliocco & Franck 1999).

8. See previous note.

References

Bahloul, M. (1993). The copula in Modern Standard Arabic (SA). In M. Eid (Ed.), *Perspectives on Arabic Linguistics V* (pp. 209–229). Amsterdam: John Benjamins.

Bakalla, M. H. (1980). *Proceedings of the First International Symposium on the Teaching of Arabic to Non-Arabic*. Riyadh: University of Riyadh.

Bates, E. S., McNew, B., MacWhinney, A., Devescove, & Smith, S. (1982). Functional constraints on sentence processing: A cross-linguistic study. *Cognition 11*, 245–299.

Bates, E. & MacWhinney, B. (1987). Language universals, individual variation, and the competition model. In B. MacWhinney & E. Bates (Eds.), *Mechanism of Language Acquisition*. Cambridge: CUP.

Benmamoun, E. & Aoun, J. (1999). Patterns of partial agreement in Arabic. In S. Lappin & E. Benmamoun (Eds.), *Fragments: Studies in ellipsis and gapping*. Oxford: OUP.

Bresnan, J. (2001). *Lexical Functional Syntax*. Oxford: Blackwell.

Bolotin, N. (1995). Arabic and parametric VSO agreement. In M. Eid (Ed.), *Perspectives on Arabic Linguistics VII* (pp. 7–27). Amsterdam: John Benjamin Publishing Company.

Bybee, L. J. (1991). *Morphology: A study of the relation between meaning and form*. Amsterdam: John Benjamins.

Di Biase, B. & Kawaguchi, S. (2002). Exploring the typological plausibility of Processability Theory: Language development in Italian second language and Japanese second language. *Second Language Research, 18*(3), 274–302.

Dik, S. (1978). *Functional Grammar*. Amsterdam: North Holland.

Fassi Fehri, A. (1981). Complémentation et anaphore en arabe moderne. Une approache lexical fonctionelle. PhD Disseration, University of Paris III.

Fassi Fehri, A. (1983). Binding, agreement and typology. In A. Fassi Fehri & D. Serghouchni (Eds.), *Issues in Grammar and Discourse*. Rabat: Publications of the Moroccan Society of Philosophy. (In Arabic).

Fassi Fehri, A. (1988). Agreement in Arabic, binding and coherence. In M. Barlow & C. Ferguson (Eds.), *Agreement in Natural Languages*. Standford, CA: CSLI.

Fassi Fehri, A. (1993). *Issues in the Structure of Arabic Clauses and Words*. Dordrecht: Kluwer Academic.

Håkansson, G., Pienemann, M., & Sayehli, S. (2002). Transfer and typological proximity in the context of second language processing. *Second Language Research, 18*(3), 250–273.

Håkansson, G. (1996). Bilingualism in children in Sweden. Ms. Lund, Sweden: Department of Linguistics. (In Swedish).

Kremers, J. (2000). *A Recursive Linearization Approach to Arabic Noun Phrases*. Nijmegen: University of Nijmegen.

Kuntz, P. (1996). Students of Arabic: Beliefs about foreign language learning. *Al-Arabiyya, 29*, 153–177.

Larsen-Freeman, D. & Long, M. H. (1991). *An Introduction to Second Language Acquisition Research*. London: Longman.

Mahfoudhi, A. (2001). Agreement lost, agreement regained!: A minimalist account of word order and agreement variation in Arabic. Ms., University of Ottawa.

Malouf, R. (1998). Coherent nominalizations. Unpublished paper, Stanford University.

Mansouri, F. (1995). The acquisition of Subject-Verb agreement in Arabic as a second Language. *The Australian Review of Applied Linguistics, 18*(2), 65–85.

Mansouri, F. (2000). *Grammatical Markedness and Information Processing in the Acquisition of Arabic as a Second Language*. München: Lincom Europa.

Mansouri, F. (1999). *The acquisition of Arabic as a second language: From theory to practice*. Sydney: Language Australia.

Moutaouakil, A. (1985). Topics in Arabic: Towards a functional analysis. In A. M. Bolkestein, C. de Groot, & J. L. Mackenzie (Eds.), *Syntax and Pragmatics in Functional Grammar*. Dordrecht: Foris.

Nielsen, H. L. (1997). On acquisition order of agreement procedures in Arabic learner language'. *Al-Arabiyya, 30*, 49–95.

Pienemann, M. (1998). *Language Processing and Second Language Development: Processability theory*. Amsterdam: John Benjamins.

Thomann, J. (2002). LFG as a pedagogical grammar. In M. Butt & T. Hooloway King (Eds.), *Proceedings of the LGF02 conference*. Athens: National Technical University of Athens.

Vigliocco, G. & Franck, J. (1999). When sex and syntax go hand in hand: Gender agreement in language production. *Journal of Memory and Language, 40*, 455–478.

Vigliocco, G., Butterworh, B., & Garret, M. F. (1996). Subject-verb agreement in Spanish and English: Differences in the role of conceptual constraints. *Cognition, 61*, 261–298.

Chapter 5

Processing and formal instruction in the L2 acquisition of five Chinese grammatical morphemes*

Yanyin Zhang
University of Canberra

Using Processability Theory (Pienemann 1998) as the theoretical framework, the present longitudinal study investigates the L2 developmental process of five Chinese grammatical morphemes. The morphemes are: the progressive marker *zhengzai-*, the experiential marker *-guo*, the possessive marker *-de*, the classifier, and the relative clause marker *de*. These five morphemes represent three levels of information distribution according to Processability Theory: lexical (aspectual and possessive markers), phrasal (classifier), and inter-phrasal (relative clause marker). The data for the study was collected from three English-speaking university students of Chinese over a period of one academic year. Through distributional analysis and emergence criterion as described in Pienemann (1998), an acquisition sequence was found in accordance with the predicted developmental hierarchy: the lexical morphemes were acquired before the phrasal morpheme, which in turn was acquired before the inter-phrasal morpheme. Formal instruction was shown to have had a positive influence on the acquisition, but it did not seem to overrule the processing-based developmental constraint.

1. Chinese: A brief sketch

Modern Standard Chinese (i.e., *Putonghua* 'Common Speech') is an isolating or analytic language with a low degree of morphological complexity. The grammatical relations are marked largely by word order or by structural particles (Li & Thompson 1981; Norman 1988). Such grammatical categories as gender and case are absent. The plural is either not marked (e.g., *Wo you bi*, 'I have pen(s)'), or is realized through lexical means (e.g., numerals, quantifiers) rather than through the plural marker *-men*(PL). Chinese does not have an article system. The contrast between definiteness, indefiniteness and specificity is largely expressed through context and demonstrative pronouns (*zhe* 'this,' *zhexie* 'these'). There is no grammatical tense in Chinese. Time reference is indicated pragmatically or lexically (e.g., *zuotian* 'yesterday', *san nian hou* 'three years later'). Verbs do not have conjugations and the pronouns do not have cases. Grammatical agreement through morphological markings (e.g., subject-verb agreement) is absent.

Although the basic word order in Chinese is SVO, this order is frequently permuted in spoken discourse where the object and other constituents are often fronted. Furthermore, subject and object ellipsis is very common at both sentence and discourse levels. It is also common for a stretch of discourse to form a "sentence group" (*juqun*) which consists of a topic-like constituent at the beginning, followed by one or more comment-like *xiaoju* "small sentence(s)" or clause(s) (Chu 1996) with or without a subject. Because of this feature, Chinese is often described as a topic-prominent language as opposed to subject-prominent languages such as English (Li & Thompson 1981).

Structurally, Chinese is a left-branching language. The modifier, be it a single word, a phrase, or a clause, occurs before the modified constituent. Grammatical particles are frequently employed to mark such relationships. The structure of constituents exhibiting a modification relationship can be broadly described by the following formula (DeFrancis, personal communication):

> A   -*de* B
> modifier -*de* modified (head)

While tense is not grammatically realized in Chinese, aspect is. There are four main aspects in Chinese (Li & Thompson 1981).

i.   Progressive aspect *zhengzai*-V: indicating an action in progress, as in (1).

(1)   *Wo zhengzai- kan   dianshi.*
      I   PROG-   watch   TV
      'I am watching TV'.

ii. Experiential aspect V-*guo*: indicating an action having been experienced at least once in the past, but the experience is no longer current, as in (2).

(2)   *Wo dang -guo   laoshi.*
      I   be   -EXP   teacher
      'I've been a teacher before. / I used to be a teacher'.

iii. Durative aspect V-*zhe*: indicating the durative nature of an action, as in (3).

(3) *Wo na -zhe yi shu hua.*
I   hold -DUR one CL flower
'I have a bouquet in my hand'. / 'I'm holding a bouquet of flowers'.

iv. Perfective aspect V-*le*: indicating (mainly) the state of completion of an action[1] as in (4).

(4) *Wo xie -le liang ge zi.*
I   wrote PERF two CL word
'I wrote / have written two words.'

Finally, one feature which Chinese shares with many of the Southeast Asian languages is the use of classifiers. The classifier occurs in the presence of a quantifier in an NP, as shown in (5). It is optional with demonstrative pronouns, as (6) illustrates.

(5) *san ge ren.*
three CL person
'three persons'.

(6) *na (ge) ren*
that (CL) person
'that person'.

This brief sketch of Chinese serves to accentuate some of the basic grammatical features of Chinese. It aims to provide a general background for the present study on the formal L2 acquisition of the following five Chinese grammatical morphemes:

i.   Progressive marker *zhengzai-* (PROG)
ii.   Experiential marker *-guo* (EXP)
iii. Possessive marker *-de* (POSS)
iv.   Classifier (CL)
v.   Relative clause marker *de* (RC)

These five morphemes are among the most common grammatical particles in Modern Standard Chinese. Furthermore, they form a developmental hierarchy based on the processing procedures detailed in Processability Theory (Pienemann 1998). It is this hierarchy and the underlying theoretical prediction of the developmental order of these morphemes that the present study aims to test. The focus of the study centers on the developmental process of the five morphemes, as well as the role of formal instruction in this process.

The study is presented in the following structure. Section 2 is a Lexical-Functional Grammar (LFG)-based grammatical description of the five morphemes. This is followed, in Section 3, by an analysis of the grammatical information exchange involved in the morphological processing of each of the five morphemes. The outcome of the analysis leads to a formal prediction of their developmental sequence. Research methods including data collection and analysis, acquisition criterion and informants' details are presented in Section 4. Empirical evidence is reported in Section 5, followed by a discussion of the findings in Section 6 and a conclusion in Section 7.

2.   Grammatical description

The LFG-based description of the five grammatical particles in this section largely follows Bresnan (2001), Falk (2001), Dalrymple (2001), Sells (1985), and Horrocks (1987).

2.1 Aspect markers

According to Levelt (1989), aspect is one of the diacritic features residing in the lexical entries of the verb. Figures 1 and 2 show the c-structure of (7) and (8) in their respective progressive and experiential aspects. The lexical information is also provided.

(7)   *Wo zhengzai- kan   dianshi.*
       I   PROG   watch TV
       'I am watching TV'.

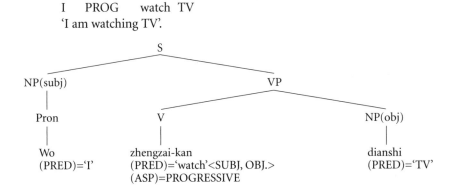

Figure 1. c-structure of *Wo zhengzai-kan dianshi*

(8) *Wo dang -guo   laoshi.*
      I   be   -EXP teacher
     'I've been a teacher before'.

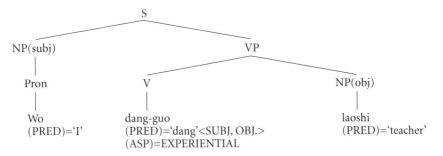

Figure 2. c-structure of *Wo dang-guo laoshi*

2.2 Classifier

The classifier is structurally obligatory in an NP when the head noun is enumerated (Dobson 1974) as shown in (9).[2] When the head noun is not enumerated, as in (10), the classifier must not be used. This means that the classifier is licensed by the numeral in an NP, and that the lexical entry of a classifier contains the feature of quantification (QUAN). The classifier is also a semantic expression. It encodes such information as shape, function, and size of the noun referent with which it co-occurs in an NP (Li & Thompson 1981). For example, the classifier for objects which are flat in shape (e.g., photo, paper, bed) is *zhang*, as (9) shows. This type of information must be mapped from the head noun to the classifier in order for the NP to be semantically well-formed. Due to the presence of the quantifier information and the semantic feature of the head noun in the classifier, the classifier is often used in an NP in which the head noun is not overt as, for example, in a shopping situation. Figure 3 shows the c-structure of (9) and the lexical entries of the NP constituents.

(9) [*yi zhang zhaopian*]ₙₚ
      one CL.   photo
     'one/a photo'

(10) [*zhaopian tai da le.*]ₙₚ
      photo   too big MOD.PAR[3]
     'The photo(s) is(are) too big'.

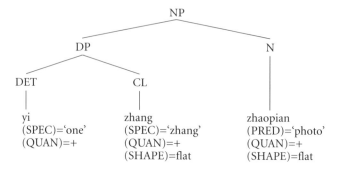

Figure 3. c-structure of *yi zhang zhaopian*

2.3 Particle *de*

The grammatical particle *de* is multi-functional in Chinese. Within an NP, it marks various semantic and grammatical relations between the head and its modifier in the scheme

> NP -> A *de* B(head).

In the following, an LFG analysis of two NP structures is presented. One is the possessive NP in which *de* is a possessive marker (POSS). The second NP structure contains a relative clause (RC) in which *de* is a relative clause marker (RC).[4]

2.3.1 *Possessive marker*

As a possessive marker, *-de*(POSS) can be seen as a diacritic feature of a noun whose referent is capable of ownership. In (11), the *-de*(POSS)-marked noun *laoshi* 'teacher' is the possessor, and *shu* 'book' is the item being possessed. Figure 4 shows the c-structure of (11) in which the possessive NP contains the DP, the possessor *laoshi-de* 'teacher's'.

> (11) *zhe   shi   laoshi   -de   shu.*
>   This is   teacher -POSS book
>   'This is teacher's book'.

2.3.2 *Relative clause marker de(RC)*

Consistent with the "modifier-modified" word order in an NP, the head noun of a relative clause is placed after the modifying clause, and the particle de(RC) is used to mark the relationship. The head is related to its within-clause syn-

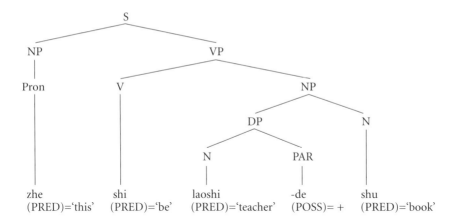

Figure 4. c-structure of *zhe shi laoshi-de shu*

tactic function such as subject or object. In (12) and (13), the head nouns *ge* 'song' and *ren* 'person' (underlined) are object and subject in their respective relative clauses.

(12) *Ta   chang de ge   haoting.*
      He/She sing   RC <u>song</u> good-hear
      'The song he/she sings is nice'.[5]

(13) *Chang ge   de   ren   bing le.*
      sing   song RC <u>person</u> sick MOD.PAR
      'The person who sang / sings is sick'.

Following the LFG analysis of the English relative clause by Falk (2001) and Dalrymple (2001), the relative clause marker *de*(RC) is part of ADJ(unct) (i.e., relative clause) and it is assigned the TOPIC function. The reason for treating the particle *de*(RC) the same way as the relative pronoun in English is the following. In English, the within-clause function of the displaced head noun (often represented by a gap) is linked to the relative pronoun. The relative pronoun in turn represents the head noun modified by the relative clause. In a parallel fashion, the relative clause marker *de*(RC) in Chinese also represents the head noun in that its presence nominalizes the relative clause in such a way that the head noun can be omitted. In a morphologically less transparent way (compared to the English relative pronoun), *de*(RC) is related to the within-clause function (or gap) of the displaced head noun on the one hand, and to the head noun itself on the other, similar to the English relative pronoun. The c-structure and f-structure of (12) and (13) is displayed in Figures 5 and 6.

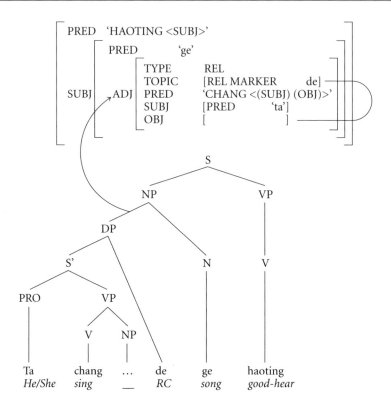

Figure 5. c-structure and f-structure of *Ta chang de ge haoting*

(12)   a.   *Ta chang de ge haotin.*
            'The song he/she sings is nice'.

(13)   a.   *Chang ge de ren bing le.*
            'The person who sang is sick'.

3.   Information exchange and processing hierarchy

The LFG analysis above shows that the five grammatical markers exhibit information exchange in different structural contexts. The aspectual and possessive information is generated directly from the conceptual structure or the pragmatic context. As a result, the insertion process of the progressive and the experiential aspect markers as well as the possessive marker during sentence production is motivated by the speaker's need to express the concepts of "action in progress" (progressive marker), "action having been experienced" (experi-

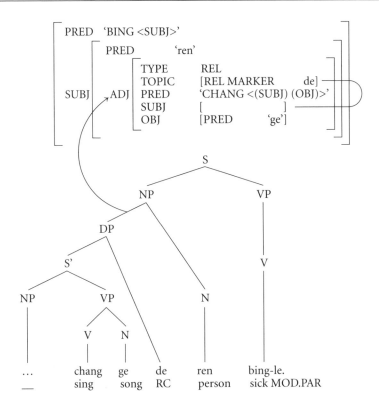

Figure 6. c-structure and f-structure of *Chang ge de ren bing le*

ential marker), and "possession/ownership" (possessive marker). This process does not involve any grammatical feature unification between constituents in their structural context. According to Processability Theory, they are "lexical morphemes", which require the Category Procedure (Stage 2) to implement.

In contrast, the classifier is activated by the presence of the numeral in an NP, which in turn is called for by the numerative feature in the head noun. This process can be best represented by information exchange in which the QUAN(tity) feature is being distributed across all three constituents of the NP (see Figure 3). Because this process occurs within a phrase, the classifier is a "phrasal morpheme" and the Phrasal Procedure (Stage 3) must be in place to handle the process.

The structural requirement above does not necessarily guarantee the semantic appropriateness of the classifier chosen for the NP. The semantic "agreement" is a separate process which largely involves the lexical analysis of the noun and the classifier which comes with it. The present study is concerned

Table 1. Processing procedures applied to Chinese

Processing procedures	L2 processes	Chinese morphosyntax
4. S-procedure	Inter-phrasal information	relative clause marker *de*(RC)
3. Phrasal procedure	Phrasal information	classifier (CL)
2. Category procedure	Lexical morphemes	progressive *zhengzai*-(PROG) experiential -*guo*(EXP) genitive -*de*(POSS)
1. Word/Lemma	None	single words / invariant forms

with structural well-formedness, i.e., the morphological process of the classifier insertion in an NP.

Finally, the c-structures and f-structures of the relative clauses in Figure 5 and Figure 6 show that the particle *de*(RC) links different kinds of structural elements. In Figure 5, it is linked to the gap created by the displaced object head noun in the ADJ(junct), while in Figure 6, it is linked to the gap created by the displaced subject head noun in the ADJ(unct). The grammatical information flows between the gap in the ADJ(unct) clause and the head noun in the main clause through *de*(RC), exhibiting inter-phrasal information exchange.[6] The particle *de*(RC) is therefore an inter-phrasal morpheme.

In Table 1, the five Chinese grammatical morphemes are displayed in a processing hierarchy based on the information exchange processes described above. This hierarchy serves as the prediction of the developmental sequence of these morphemes. If the analysis and the prediction are correct, the acquisition of these five morphemes should proceed from the lexical to the phrasal, and finally, to the inter-phrasal. Furthermore, this sequence should not be altered by external intervention such as formal instruction (Pienemann 1984, 1998).

4. Methodology and findings

4.1 Informants

The informants of the study were three English native speakers, Kate, Sharon, and Dave.[7] They were in their late teens and early twenties, and were enrolled in a first-year Chinese language course at an Australian University. All three informants had zero proficiency in Chinese when being selected, but each had studied a foreign language before (Kate: German; Sharon: Indonesian; Dave: Korean). They reported having had a positive and successful experience in their previous foreign language learning. They attended the same Chinese lectures during the entire data collection period. Kate and Dave were in the same Chinese tutorial group.

4.2 Syllabus and textbook

The first-year Chinese language course at the university where the data was collected comprised a total of 10 classroom contact hours per week, divided equally between lectures and tutorials. The syllabus covered all 50 units of the first two volumes of the structure-based textbook: *Practical Chinese Reader* (Liu, Deng & Liu 1991). In each unit, there was a section called *Yufa* 'Grammar' which explains in both Chinese and English the focal grammatical point(s) of the unit. Detailed structural analysis was often shown in tables, followed by examples and exercises. All five grammatical particles in this study were part of the teaching objectives in the textbook and syllabus.

The classroom teaching followed the syllabus closely. The essentials of a unit – vocabulary, grammar, and reading passages – were dealt with in the lecture, while consolidation of the essentials through practice was handled in the tutorial. Both the lecturer and the tutor were native speakers of Chinese and highly experienced Chinese language instructors.

4.3 Data collection

Textbook materials were analyzed prior to each data collection session in order to target those structures that had appeared in the classroom input. Regular classroom observation and data collection sessions were carried out over one academic year (36 weeks). The first data collection session was held five weeks into the first semester. Subsequent sessions took place every three weeks except during the class-free periods (two weeks within each semester and five weeks between the two semesters). Each session lasted from 15 to 50 minutes, with later sessions considerably longer than early ones. A total of nine data sets were obtained from Kate and Dave, and eight from Sharon (who missed one session).

The data collection session was structured, and except for the last group session, the informants and the researcher met individually, working on tasks which required the informants to respond to different situations or scenarios spontaneously. The tasks were communicative, consisting of such activities as problem-solving, role-play, picture-based oral composition, story-retelling, and various kinds of description. Each task was designed to elicit certain linguistic forms. Of the five morphemes, two (*-de*(POSS) and the classifier) were

Table 2. Data statistics

Data information	Kate	Sharon	Dave	Total
Date set	8+1*	7+1	8+1	24
Length (min)	235	248	300	783
Utterance	1,262	1,615	1,664	4,541
Suitable utterance	1,060	1,094	1,255	3,409

* +1 refers to the last group session.

not specifically targeted in the elicitation tasks. Each session ended with a conversation in which some of the linguistics forms, notably the aspectual markers and the relative clause, were elicited again in a casual and implicit manner (for details of the technique, see Zhang 2001).

The interview sessions were audio-taped and later transcribed. A total of 4,541 utterances were produced by the informants, of which 3,409 were suitable for the purpose of this study. Unsuitable utterances are verbatim repetitions, translations of previous utterances, interjections, and non-lexical fillers (ah, mmh). These speech features had discourse functions, but they did not provide useful information for the study of the acquisition of L2 grammar. Table 2 displays the basic statistics of the data.

4.4 Data analysis and emergence criterion

The utterances were coded for grammatical features along with their functional and structural contexts. A distributional analysis was then performed and the emergence criterion was applied to the result to determine the status of the grammatical forms in the L2 of the informants. A form was considered to have emerged if there was a minimum of three tokens in lexically varied contexts. For example, if the progressive marker *zhengzai-*(PROG) occurred exclusively with the verb *tiaowu* 'dance', it would not be viewed as having emerged regardless of the number of tokens found in the data set. On the other hand, if it occurred with different verbs, it was counted as having emerged provided that there were no fewer than three tokens. This measure reduced the chance of mistaking possible morphomorphemic chunks for productive occurrences.

The emergence criterion established above operated as a general guideline for the qualitative aspect of the data analysis. In order for the emergence criterion to be meaningful, certain structural contexts specific to a form needed to be taken into consideration. For example, in the data, the possessive marker was found to have occurred in five contexts, displayed in Table 3.

Table 3. Contexts of -*de* (POSS)

-de(POSS)	Examples
1. pron-de	*wo-de shu* my book
2. personal name-de	*Gupo-de shu* Gupo's book
3. lexical N-de	*xuexiao-de shu* school's book
4. NP-de	*Wo(-de) baba-de shu* my father's book
5. locative proper noun-de*	*Zhongguo-de renkou* China's population

* locative proper noun refers to names of countries, cities and institutions.

By itself, the first environment, i.e., the pronoun -*de*, is not reliable in determining the emergence status of the possessive marker because it is possible to learn Chinese possessive pronouns, all formed as 'pronoun -*de*(POSS)', as single lexical items without knowing the morphological status of -*de*. The productive nature of -*de*(POSS) can be reasonably determined when -*de*(POSS) also occurs with lexical nouns, or when the optional deletion rule (i.e., delete -*de*(POSS) when the head noun is a kinship term) is applied in the pronoun context, as shown in (14). Such evidence would demonstrate that -*de*(POSS) is structurally separable from the pronoun, hence productive.

(14)   *wo mama* my mother
       'I mother'

With regard to the classifier, the analysis focused on its structural context, not its actual form. Both obligatory and optional rule contexts were considered relevant in the analysis.

4.5 Findings

Tables 5 to 7 display the composite quantitative results of the distributional analysis. Each decimal figure represents the ratio between the number of tokens of a particular morpheme (second column) and the structural context in which they occurred. When less than three tokens were found in a data set, the token number is given before the slash (/). The parentheses indicate less than three contexts. Non-productive instances (e.g., the exclusive use of the pronoun -*de*(POSS) form) were not counted. The slash sign (/) in an otherwise empty cell means no rule application context was present in the given set of data. The emergence point is marked by a plus sign.

The tables show a three-tier progression in the overall acquisition profiles of Kate and Dave: the lexical particle -*de*(POSS) emerged before the phrasal

Table 5. Kate: Development of grammatical morphemes

Morpheme type	Session-> Morpheme	1 wk 5	2 wk10	3 wk13	4 wk16	5 wk23	6 wk26	7 wk29	8 wk34	9 wk36
Lexical	-de (POSS)	0. *	.52+	.71	1/.06	1/.07	.81	.55	.75	1.
	zhengzai- (PROG)	/	(0.)	0.	2/.13	2/.29	0.	.38+	(0.)	/
	-guo (EXP)	/	/	/	/	.79+	2/.5	/	/	/
Phrasal	CL	/	2/(1.)	1.+	1.	1.	.95	.88	1.	1.
Inter-phrasal	de (RC)	/	/	(0.)	.60+	(0.)	(0.)	/	/	/

* Exclusive use of pron-de(POSS). For details, see Section 4.3.

Table 6. Sharon: Development of grammatical morphemes

Morpheme type	Session-> Morpheme	1 wk 5	2 wk10	3 wk13	4 wk16	5 wk23	6 wk26	7 wk29	8 wk34	9 wk36
Lexical	-de (POSS)	2/(1.)	.55+	.84	.53	.26	nd	.74	.68	.89
	zhengzai- (PROG)		(0.)	.42+	.40	1/.25	nd	2/.29	/	(0.)
	-guo (EXP)		/	/	(0.)	2/.12	nd	1/(1.)	.80+	/
Phrasal	CL		1.+	.83	.89	1.	nd	1.	.96	.78
Inter-phrasal	de (RC)			1.+	.90	/	nd	1.	2/(1.)	/

Table 7. Dave: Development of grammatical morphemes

Morpheme type	Session-> Morpheme	1 wk 5	2 wk10	3 wk13	4 wk16	5 wk23	6 wk26	7 wk29	8 wk34	9 wk36
Lexical	-de (POSS)	.67+	.94	.84	.65	.60	1.	.67	1.	1.
	zhengzai- (PROG)		(0.)	.50+	.95	.78	1/(1.)	1/.17	.90	/
	-guo (EXP)					.75+	.60	2/.67	2/(1.)	/
Phrasal	CL		1.+	.71	.84	1.	1.	1.	.95	1.
Inter-phrasal	de (RC)			1.+	1.	1.	1.	1.	1.	1.

particle *CL*, which in turn developed before the inter-phrasal particle *de*(RC). Kate's emergence schedule was always one session behind that of Dave. Sharon's profile, however, showed a two-tier progression: the lexical particle *-de*(POSS) and the phrasal particle *CL* emerged at the same time. Finally, the two aspectual markers (lexical particle) developed later than the classifier (phrasal particle), and sometimes even after the inter-phrasal particle (*de*(RC)).

5.   Discussion

The discussion in this section focuses on two issues arising from the findings shown in Tables 5–7, namely (1) the acquisition sequence of the five grammatical morphemes in terms of the PT-based prediction and (2) the role of formal instruction in the observed acquisition sequence.

5.1   Developmental sequence

The question of whether second language acquisition of grammar follows a certain systematic and sequenced course of development has prompted much research interests and effort over the years. From the morpheme order studies of the 1970's (e.g., Dulay & Burt 1973/74) to the strategies approach of the 1980's (Clahsen 1984), the attention and focus were shifted from the discovery of the order to the explanation of the order. Processability Theory (Pienemann 1998) goes one step further in that it employs the general language processing mechanisms underlying speech production to construct a universal hierarchy of procedural skills which can be used in describing and predicting the development of a second language grammar.

The observed developmental course as shown in Kate's and Dave's samples (Table 5 and Table 7) is compatible with the theory-motivated processing hierarchy and prediction. The ordered and step-by-step progression from the Category Procedure (-*de*(POSS)) to the Phrasal Procedure (CL) and finally to the S-Procedure (*de*(RC)) was observed in the samples. Kate and Dave differed from each other in the rate of the progression as well as the quantity of morpheme suppliance, but not in their overall acquisition profile.

Sharon's developmental course was somewhat different. As Table 6 shows, two of the developmental stages (Stage 2 and Stage 3) were found to be indistinguishable: the possessive marker -*de*(POSS), a lexical form, emerged at the same time as the classifier, a phrasal morpheme. Both forms met the emergence criterion in Session 2 (week 10).

Unlike Kate who produced the possessive marker exclusively in the pronoun context (see Table 3) in Session 1 (week 5), Sharon did produce two NPs which contain multiple possessive relationships, shown in (15) and (16).

(15)   "...*ni-de*   *pengyou-de   mama*"
　　　 ...you-GEN   friend-GEN   mom
　　　 '...your friend's mom'　　　　　　　　　　　　　　(Sharon, T1.4, #7)[8]

(16) "...*ni-de*   *pengyou-de*   *baba*"
      ...you-GEN friend-GEN dad
      '...your friend's dad'   (Sharon, T1.4, #8)

These two NPs were produced in two consecutive utterances, and they were identical in both structure and lexical component. In the absence of more lexical nouns marked by *-de*(POSS), it was difficult to rule out the possibility that the *-de*(POSS)-marked component in (15) and (16) was a chunk and nonproductive. On the other hand, a further check of Sharon's data in Session 1 revealed that both the bare form *pengyou* 'friend' and the possessive form *pengyou-de*(POSS) 'friend's' were present (see (17) and (18)), meaning that the possessive marker might not have been an integral part of *pengyou-de*(POSS) 'friend's' after all, and that *pengyou-de*(POSS) 'friend's' might not have been a chunk. However, since there were only two such tokens and no lexical variation, it did not satisfy the emergence criterion stipulated for this study.[9] Even though two stages did not show a clear developmental distinction in Sharon's samples, they did not violate the prediction or the processing hierarchy.

(17) "...*ni* -*de*   *pengyou*   *ma*?"
      ...you -GEN friend   Q-par
      '...your friend?'   (Sharon, T1.3, #2)

(18) "...*ni* -*de*   *pengyou*."
      ...you -GEN friend
      '...your friend'   (Sharon, T1.4, #1)

In an earlier study (Zhang 2001), Dave's acquisition profile also exhibited a similar phenomenon to that of Sharon. The classifier (phrasal morpheme) and the relative clause marker *de* (inter-phrasal morpheme) were found to have emerged at the same time (Session 3, week 13). A re-examination of the data revealed that the assessment of the classifier in Dave's second set of data (Session 2, week 10) was partly based on the accuracy measure: the suppliance of the classifier in cases such as (19) was not counted as relevant because the NP was ungrammatical. As mentioned in Section 2.2 (Note 2), some nouns are themselves measure words, and as such they do not take classifiers. However, the structural context in which they occur is identical to that of the classifier – in the presence of a quantifier and/or a demonstrative pronoun. Suppliance of the classifier in such a context by a learner is to be expected before he/she is able to carry out an adequate lexical analysis of such words. In terms of acquisition, however, the insertion of the classifier in such contexts does demonstrate to a certain degree the productive nature of the classifier in the L2 system, albeit immature. For this very reason, the present study gave credit to such cases as shown in (19), resulting in a different conclusion from that of Zhang (2001).

(19)   "...*si   ge   dian*"
       ...four CL   o'clock
       '... four o'clock'   (Dave, T2.8. #66)

While the overall developmental profiles of the informants were sequenced according to the processing hierarchy proposed in Processability Theory (Pienemann 1998), the acquisition of the two aspectual markers, both lexical morphemes, did not appear to keep pace. Tables 5–7 show that their emergence in the L2 Chinese of all three informants was quite late, creating a gap within Stage 2. Although the cause of their delayed emergence needs to be investigated, the phenomenon itself does not violate the central idea of Processability Theory (Pienemann 1998: 250–252). At this point, the question to be asked is: to what extent is the overall developmental profile (including the delayed development of the aspectual markers) the product of formal teaching as opposed to the processing constraints? This question is dealt with in the next section.

5.2 Instructional syllabus and language processing

There is a large body of research dealing with the role of formal instruction in second language acquisition. These studies vary in their concerns. Some are interested in the general pedagogical efficacy (e.g., Lightbown & Spada 1990; Doughty 1991; Ellis 1984), while others take a psycholinguistic stance, focusing on the implicit vs. explicit dichotomy in second language acquisition. (For an overview, see Norris & Ortega 2000). The general findings of these studies are in favour of formal instruction for L2 learners.

The question in the context of the present study is not whether formal instruction is effective, but whether it overrides the psycholinguistic constraints in the form of PT-based processing procedures on the L2 learning process of the five Chinese grammatical morphemes discussed above.

In order to investigate this issue, the syllabus of the Chinese language course in which the informants were enrolled was examined. Table 8 displays the teaching schedule of the five morphemes. The possessive marker (lexical) was introduced first, in week 2, six weeks before the classifier (phrasal). The relative clause marker (inter-phrasal) was taught last, in week 11, four weeks after the classifier. The two aspectual markers (lexical) were taught in week 12 (*zhengzai*(PROG)) and week 22 (*guo*(EXP)) respectively, after the classifier and the relative clause. In so far as the unfolding of the processing skills is

Table 8. Instructional sequence of the five morphemes

Processing Procedures	L2 Process	Week -> Morpheme	2	8	11	12	13	22
1. Category Procedure	lexical	-de (POSS)	x					
		zhengzai-(PROG)				x		
		-guo(EXP)						x
3. Phrasal Procedure	phrasal	CL		x				
4. S-Procedure	inter-phrasal	-de (RC)					x	

Table 9. Teaching schedule and emergence point[10]

Week ->	2	3	5	8	10	11	12	13	16	22	23	26	29	34	37
Interview->			1		2			3	4		5	6	7	8	9
-de (POSS)	x		s/d		k										
PROG							x	s/d					k		
EXP										x	k/d			s	
CL						x		s/d	k						
-de (RC)						x		s/d	k						

concerned, the instructional sequence is by and large in accordance with the developmental hierarchy proposed in Processability Theory.

The findings shown in Tables 5–7 also show that the observed acquisition sequence parallels the developmental hierarchy. The identical sequence across the developmental hierarchy, the syllabus, and the acquisition may have settled the question regarding the contributing factor for the acquisition pattern observed in the L2 samples of the learners. One can say that both the syllabus and the processing skills contributed to the acquisition process.

However, if one looks more closely at the issue again, there seems more to it than meets the eye. Table 9 combines the time of instruction of the five morphemes and their respective point of emergence in the L2 data of the informants. The time of the instruction is marked by a shaded cross sign (x), while the emergence point of a form is indicated by the initials of the informants.

The most obvious revelation in Table 9 is that learning occurred invariably after classroom instruction. This is not surprising given the foreign language learning setting and the informants' zero extracurricular contact with Chinese language and its speakers. In fact, instruction was the only source of Chinese language input in the life of the informants.[11]

A second observation based on Table 9 is that the learners showed considerable differences in their responsiveness to instruction as well as to individual grammatical forms. Dave was the most responsive, while Kate was the least.

In four of the five morphemes (the possessive marker, the progressive marker, the classifier and the relative clause marker), there was invariably a delay of three to sixteen weeks between the instruction of the form and its emergence in Kate's L2 Chinese. Unlike Dave who learned each form as soon as it was taught, as judged by the data collected at the first session after the instruction, Kate's "intake" schedule was rather unpredictable, and sometimes even in reverse to the teaching sequence. This was illustrated by the relationship between instruction and acquisition of the two aspectual markers. Table 9 shows that the experiential marker -*guo*(EXP) was taught 10 weeks later than the progressive marker *zhengzai*-(PROG), yet it emerged in Kate's data six weeks earlier than the latter. This unpredictable response to teaching was also found in Sharon to some extent (see -*guo*(EXP) in Table 9).[12] It seems that the instructional sequence did not have the binding force on Kate's, and to some extent, Sharon's acquisition process.

Logically, Kate's delayed response to teaching, together with her unpredictable acquisition schedule, meant that the emergence of an L2 form could have materialized in her L2 Chinese at any moment after it was taught. In other words, it was possible for the possessive marker to emerge after the classifier, or the classifier after the relative clause in her Chinese. The reality, however, was not so. When these forms did emerge in Kate's L2 Chinese, they did so in an order consistent with the processing hierarchy: the lexical morpheme (possessive marker) precedes the phrasal morpheme (classifier), and the inter-phrasal morpheme (relative clause marker) was learned last. The delay did not disrupt this fundamental, incremental sequence.

It is necessary to point out, however, that Kate was by all accounts a good student. Her grades in Chinese were consistently "High Distinction" (or A) throughout the first year. According to her Chinese tutor (personal communication), Kate was a relatively quiet student in class, "but when she speaks", said her tutor, "she does not make mistakes. Everything she says is correct".

Regarding the delayed emergence of the two aspectual markers, there are at least two contributing factors, (1) the syllabus and (2) the linguistic realization of aspect. Table 8 shows that the two aspectual markers were taught after the classifier and the relative clause marker. In the informants' learning environment where the source of the target language input was limited to the classroom, the informants had no other opportunities to learn L2 specific encoding of certain functions before formal instruction. Consequently, even if the necessary procedural skills for acquiring a given target language form were in place, the form would not have been acquired due to the knowledge gap in the informants' L2 system.

Secondly, linguistic "aspect" is largely a pragmatic concept. Its linguistic realization is dependent upon the viewpoint of the speaker. When to use the progressive or perfective aspect in the description of an action depends on the speaker's view of the action (Comrie 1976; Jacobs 1995). Consequently, the same situation or task in the eyes of two speakers may result in different linguistic realizations of aspectual marking. The following examples are cases in point. The three informants viewed the situation depicted in a picture in three different ways. Dave was focusing on the action-in-progress (20c), while Sharon was attending to the general event of "visiting a doctor" (20b). Kate seemed to view the situation as a general fact (20a).

Picture 1:   In a doctor's surgery. A few students are being examined by the doctor. Some are at the back and one is at the front.

(20)   a.   Kate: "*Gupo kanbing.*"
              Gupo   see-illness
              'Gupo visits a doctor'.   (Kate, T5.2, #1)
         b.   Sharon: "*Zhe zhang hua,   ta   qu kan daifu.*"
                  this   CL   picture, he   go   see   doctor
                  'In this picture, he goes to see a doctor.' (Sharon, T5.2, #1)
         c.   Dave: *"*Zhe xuesheng -men zhengzai kan daifu   ne.*"
                  this   student   -PL   PROG   see   doctor PROG
                  *'This students are visiting a doctor.'   (Dave, T5.2, #1)

Although tasks targeting both progressive and experiential markers were used for data collection, these opportunities were not always taken, at least not consistently, by the informants. In contrast, the same tasks elicited one hundred percent aspectual marking from two native speakers. Viewed from this perspective, Kate and Sharon's acquisition of the two aspectual markers as shown in Tables 5 and 6 was delayed, but the nature of the delay might be more conceptual than procedural.

In summary, the evidence and discussion above support the conclusion that although teaching plays an important role in the L2 learning of Chinese, learning itself is not absolutely determined by teaching. Taking into consideration the syllabus, the PT-based prediction, and the acquisition profiles of the three informants, it appeared reasonably certain that the processing constraints had played a central role in the L2 acquisition of the five Chinese grammatical morphemes.

6.   Limitation and conclusion

Arguably, the strongest case for processability-driven acquisition instead of syllabus-driven acquisition comes from the evidence that acquisition follows the developmental hierarchy in spite of a syllabus which is at odds with the hierarchy (e.g., Pienemann 1984). Given the design of the present study – non-experimental and non-interventional – it is not possible to prove this point categorically.

However, the overall findings of the study demonstrate that the acquisition of the five Chinese grammatical forms, defined by the emergence criterion, proceeded in an orderly sequence as predicted in Processability Theory (Table 1) (Pienemann 1998). This sequence was not violated by delayed emergence, nor was it invalidated by indistinguishable stages found in the data. Furthermore, this sequence was not strongly motivated by the syllabus either. One does not always learn what one is taught. The syllabus facilitates learning rather than defines it and, consequently, the identical order between the syllabus and the developmental course of the five grammatical markers in the L2 Chinese of the informants was more likely coincidental.

Notes

* I am grateful to Manfred Pienemann for his encouragement as well as comments and suggestions on an earlier version of this paper. I am indebted to Bruno Di Biase and Satomi Kawaguchi who spent hours patiently discussing with me the LFG analysis of Chinese. The critical input from the anonymous reviewer and the participants of the 3rd Australian Symposium on Processability Theory (University of Western Sydney, February 2003), especially Fethi Mansouri and Gisela Håkansson, helped me rethink many of the issues discussed in the paper. I wish to thank Karl Rensch who proofread and edited the paper at various stages, and Lesley Cioccarelli who eliminated many of the non-native features from the paper. The errors that remain are entirely mine.

1. The particle *le* has multiple aspectual functions. The perfective function is a major one. For an early account of *le*, see Li and Thompson (1981). For the lastest, see Jin (2001, 2002).

2. In speech, the numeral *yi* 'one' is often omitted (e.g., *Wo you (yi) zhang zhaopian*. 'I have (a) CL photo'). When associated with a singular demonstrative pronoun (*zhe* 'this,' *na* 'that'), the classifier is optional. When a noun denotes a measurement such as length (*mi* 'meter'), weight (*jin* 'tae'), frequency (e.g., *tian* 'day'), the noun is regarded as a measure word and no classifier is necessary in the presence of a quantifier (Li & Thompson 1981).

3. Modal particle.

4. For a complete discussion of *de*, see Li & Thompson (1981), Zhu (1998), Chao (1968).

5. The Chinese relative clauses in (12) and (13) could be translated into English in a number of ways using simple present tense and simple past tense. The head noun *ge* and *ren* can be either singular or plural.

6. I wish to thank Bruno Di Biase for his help on this point.

7. These are fictitious names.

8. The notation stands for interview session, task and utterance number. T1.4, #7 means session 1, task 4, and utterance 7 respectively.

9. Applying a different emergence criterion, e.g., the structural variation or the "minimal pair" criterion (Håkansson, personal communication 2003) would have rendered the status of -*de*(POSS) in Sharon's first data set entirely different: the possessive marker would be deemed to have emerged in session 1.

10. Weeks 8–9, 16–20 and 30–31 were class-free periods.

11. According to self -reports by the informants at every session.

12. In Zhang (2001, 2004), it was observed that the adjective marker emerged in Sharon's L2 Chinese 21 weeks after the instruction, while it never did in Kate's throughout the entire observation period (36 weeks).

References

Bresnan, J. (2001). *Lexical-Functional Syntax*. Oxford: Blackwell.

Chao, Y.-R. (1968). *A Grammar of Spoken Chinese*. Berkeley, CA: University of California Press.

Chengdu Jin, L. (2002). Ciwei "zhe" "le" "gip" he juwei "le" shiti yiyi de duili jiqi zai jufa xingshi shang de tiaonjian [The time and aspectual meaning and contrast of word final "zhe" "le" and "guo" and their syntactic conditions]. In *Selected conference papers for the 7th International Conference on Teaching Chinese as a Foreign Language*. Shanghai: Institute of Cultural Exchange, Shanghai Foreign Languages University.

Chu, C. (1996). Hanyu zhong juzi de dingyi jiqi diwei [The sentence: Its definition and its place in Chinese grammar]. *Shijie Hanyu Jiaoxue* [*World Chinese Teaching*] 4, 16–23.

Clahsen, H. (1984). The acquisition of German word order: A test case for cognitive approaches to second language acquisition. In R. Andersen (Ed.), *Second Languages*. Rowley, MA: Newbury House.

Comrie, B. (1976). *Aspect*. Cambridge: CUP.

Dalrymple, M. (2001). *Syntax and Semantics: Lexical functional grammar*. San Diego, CA: Academic Press.

Dobson, W. (1974). *A Dictionary of the Chinese Particles*. Toronto: University of Toronto.

Doughty, C. (1991). Second language instruction does make a difference. *Studies in Second Language Acquisition, 13*, 431–469.

Dulay, H. & Burt, M. (1973). Should we teach children syntax? *Language Learning, 23*, 245–258.

Dulay, H. & Burt, M. (1974). Natural sequences in child second language acquisition. *Language Learning, 24*, 37–53.

Ellis, R. (1984). Can syntax be taught? A study of the effects of formal instruction on the of WH-questions in children. *Applied Linguistics, 5*(2), 138–155.

Falk, Y. (2001). *Lexical-Functional Grammar: An introduction to parallel constraint- based syntax*. Stanford, CA: CSLI.

Horrocks, G. (1987). *Generative Grammar*. London: Longman.

Jacobs, R. (1995). *English Syntax*. Cambridge: CUP.

Jin, L. (2001). "S-le" de shiti tezheng jiqi jufa tiaojian [The time and aspect features of "S-le" and its syntactic conditions.] Paper presented at the *7th Academic Conference of Chinese Association of Teaching Chinese as a Foreign Language.*

Levelt, W. J. M. (1989). *Speaking: From intention to articulation*. Cambridge, MA: The MIT Press.

Li, C. & Thompson, S. (1981). *Mandarin Chinese: A functional reference grammar*. Berkeley, CA: University of California Press.

Lightbown, P. & Spada, N. (1990). Focus-on-form and corrective feedback in communicative language teaching: Effects on second language learning. *Studies in Second Language Acquisition, 12*(4), 429–448.

Liu, X., Deng, E., & Liu, S. (1991). *Practical Chinese Reader*. Vols. 1&2. Beijing: Commercial Press.

Norman, J. (1988). *Chinese*. Cambridge: CUP.

Norris, J. & Ortega, L. (2000). Effectiveness of L2 instruction: A research synthesis and quantitative meta-analysis. *Language Learning, 50*(3), 417–528.

Pienemann, M. (1984). Psychological constraints on the teachability of languages. *Studies in Second Language Acquisition, 6*, 186–214.

Pienemann, M. (1998). *Language Processing and Second Language Development: Processability Theory*. Amsterdam: John Benjamins.

Sells, P. (1985). *Lectures on Contemporary Syntactic Theories*. Stanford, CA: CSLI.

Zhang, Y. (2001). Second Language Acquisition of Chinese Grammatical Morphemes: A processability perspective. PhD Dissertation, The Australian National University.

Zhang, Y. (2004). Processing constraints, categorial analysis and the second language acquisition of the Chinese adjective suffix -*de*(ADJ). *Language Learning, 54*(3), 437–468.

Zhu, D. (1998). *Yufa Jiangyi* [Lectures on Grammar]. Beijing: Commercial Press.

Chapter 6

Similarities and differences in L1 and L2 development

Opening up the perspective: Including SLI*

Gisela Håkansson
Lund University

By tradition, comparisons between first and second language acquisition involve data from child or adult L2 learners and data from young L1 children. However, there is a subgroup of L1 children, namely children with Specific Language Impairment (SLI), which is rarely accounted for in these comparisons. These are children with significant problems in acquiring their mother tongue despite growing up in a monolingual environment. In this chapter, Processability Theory (Pienemann 1998a, b) is used as a framework to compare the development of morphosyntax in three groups of children: L1 children, L2 children and children with SLI. Contrary to expectations, the results show that the development of grammar in children with SLI sometimes is more similar to the grammatical development in L2 acquisition than that in L1 acquisition. A similarity between these two groups has implications for theories about language acquisition and language impairment.

1. Introduction

The question of similarities and differences between first and second language acquisition is a complex issue with many problems involved. Differences in the-oretical paradigms, views on what counts as reliable data, acquisition criteria and which linguistic areas to measure all contribute to the complexity. Very few studies contain comparable data from both L1 and L2 learners, where the data have been collected within the same study and elicitation methods, analyses and interpretation have been held constant. In this chapter, results from a lon-gitudinal project on three groups of Swedish-speaking children: L1 children,

L2 children and children with SLI, will be discussed (Håkansson & Nettelbladt 1993, 1996). The empirical data will be analyzed from a perspective of language processing.

Processability Theory (Pienemann 1998a, b) provides a theoretical framework for conceptualising a unified view of human language development. Processability Theory (henceforth PT) deals with the dynamics of language development. The central assumption is that the architecture of human language processing works as a constraint on grammatical development and there is no reason to believe that L1 acquisition and L2 acquisition would not follow the same process of development. The Theory focuses on the dynamic character of language acquisition and spells out in detail the processing prerequisites that are needed for the automatisation of grammatical rules on different developmental levels. By choosing a psycholinguistic theory of language development I want to stress that I regard SLI grammar from a learning perspective. The children with SLI are analysed as language learners, building their own grammar and not as having an impaired variety of the target language.

Earlier L1-L2 comparisons

A lot of the research comparing L1 and L2 acquisition has been focussing on the acquisition of German. One of the most interesting and much discussed differences that has been found is the close relationship between verbal morphology and verb placement in L1 development of German, and the lack of this relationship in L2 German (e.g. Clahsen & Muysken 1986, 1989; Meisel 1991, 1997; Pienemann 1981). In L1 acquisition the form and the correct placement of the verb are acquired simultaneously, whereas L2 learners go through an extended period of variability in both verb form and verb placement.

> The second and most important difference between the two types of acquisition concerns the developmental relationship, in L1 acquisition, between the emergence of the +/– finite distinction and verb placement and consequently also target-like placement of the finite verb with respect to the negative element. This generalisation clearly does not hold for L2 acquisition.
>
> (Meisel 1997: 257)

Interestingly, there is a universal tendency of L1 learners and L2 learners to differ when it comes to the acquisition of word order in verb-second languages. Verb-second has been reported to be problematic to all L2 learners, irrespective of their L1 (for an overview of studies, see Håkansson, Pienemann & Sayehli

2002). L1 learners, on the other hand, seem to have no problems in acquiring verb-second. Similarly to German L1 children, Dutch L1 children use variable word order or verb-final structures in the initial stages and as soon as they start using finite verbs these are placed correctly in the second position of the clause (Wijnen & Verrips 1998). Likewise, Swedish L1 children start with variable word order and use verb-second as soon as they produce finite verbs (Håkansson & Nettelbladt 1993, 1996).

Different explanations for this L1-L2 difference have been suggested. Clahsen & Muysken (1986, 1989) and Meisel (1994, 1997) argue that L2 learners do not have access to Universal Grammar but use other learning strategies. Eubank (1992) and Vainikka & Young-Scholten (1994) claim that L2 learners in fact use Universal Grammar in a way similar to L1 learners, the difference being that the L2 learners can transfer certain properties of the L1 into the L2.

An alternative view presents itself in Processability Theory (Pienemann 1998a, b). According to this theory, transfer of the L1 into the L2 is of minor importance and it is developmentally moderated. L1 and L2 acquisition have in common that they are constrained by what can be processed at a given stage. The differences that have been observed in empirical studies have their cause in the different initial hypotheses that L1 and L2 learners have.

2. Research on children with SLI

Research on monolingual children with language problems dates back to the 1850s and different labels for the condition have been used, e.g. congenial aphasia, infantile aphasia, developmental aphasia, delayed speech and dysphasia. Today, the terms Specific Language Impairment (SLI) or Language Impairment (LI) are used to cover language development in children with significant deficits in language ability, but no other problems (Leonard 1998).

> These [children with SLI] are children who show a significant limitation in language ability, yet the factors usually accompanying language problems – such as hearing impairment, low non-verbal intelligence test scores, and neurological damage – are not evident. This is a real curiosity, especially in the light of the many language acquisition papers that begin with a statement to the effect that "all normal children" learn rapidly and effortlessly. The only thing clearly abnormal about these children is that they don't learn language rapidly and effortlessly. (Leonard 1998:9)

The design usually used in SLI research is one where a group of children diagnosed with SLI is compared to a group of normally developing children. The groups are matched according to age and/or according to MLU (mean length of utterance). The results from such studies are informative when it comes to similarities and differences at group level, but it does not capture the dynamics of language development nor individual variation between children.

2.1 Nature or nurture?

The underlying assumption is that SLI is a syndrome with one single cause and much of today's research aims at discovering this cause. The cause most widely discussed today is related to *nature*, and the possibility of SLI being a hereditary deficit. One of the most discussed studies reporting genetic factors is a paper by Gopnik, published in *Nature*. Gopnik (1990) investigated a whole family of 30 members in three generations. Sixteen members of the family had been diagnosed with some kind of language disorder, their main problem being inflection paradigms, e.g. tense morphology.

If it were the case that genetic factors influence parts of grammar, this would have large implications for linguistic theory. As Gopnik & Crago (1991: 10) formulate it, "this would be support for a hypothesis that language is made up of several autonomous subparts that may have evolved at different times." However, there has been a lot of controversy around the relationship between genes and grammar. For example, Gilger (1996) casts serious doubts upon the idea that one specific gene can be linked to one specific language feature, given the fact that human neurology is very complex.

Another cause for SLI that has been explored is related to *nurture*. For example, one may expect that diseases such as otitis media, with shorter periods of impaired hearing, may affect the child's language abilities. However, studies of children with frequent otitis media have shown that this cannot be the single cause of SLI (e.g. Harsten, Nettelbladt, Schalén, Kalm & Prellner 1993). The dynamics of parent-child interaction makes it problematic to compare between groups, but by and large, parents of children with language impairment use similar child-directed speech modifications as are used by parents of normally developing children (Conti-Ramsden 1994). Thus, no causal relationship between linguistic environment and language impairment has been detected.

2.2 What is the linguistic problem?

As mentioned earlier, the diagnosis SLI is made upon observations of atypical language behaviour, i.e. the children exhibit behaviour that is different from normally developing children. This difference is manifested by a lower percentage of correct structures in the language production and/or comprehension of these children, and by some structures being disproportionately vulnerable. The vulnerable structures differ between languages and the identification of them is an important step towards finding a common denominator of SLI.

A number of different explanations have been offered to explain the linguistic problems in children with SLI. Some researchers propose that there is a deficit in the linguistic representations. The *feature blindness hypothesis*, introduced by Gopnik (1990) assumes that grammatical features such as person and tense are missing from the underlying grammars of children with SLI. Clahsen (1991) suggested the *missing agreement account*, according to which children with SLI have problems in establishing agreement relationships, e.g. subject-verb agreement. The *extended optional infinitive hypothesis* (EOI), suggested by Rice and Wexler (1996), claims that children with SLI have an extended period where finiteness is only optionally marked. For normally developing children the period of optional infinitives is short and disappears as the child matures. Rice and Wexler (1996) suggest that the optional infinitive period is part of a biologically determined program and that children with SLI have a deficit in this program.

It has also been suggested that the children's problems do not reflect deficits in the linguistic representation but are due to problems with processing the linguistic material. The *surface hypothesis* suggested by Leonard (1989, 1998) claims that children with SLI are limited in their auditory processing capacity. They have, for example, difficulties in processing and producing unstressed syllables and morphemes of short duration. Another proposal, which is connected to processing is the one suggested by Bishop (1994). Using Levelt's (1989) model of speech production as a framework, she suggests that children with SLI have problems in processing complex utterances due to their grammatical encoding procedures not being fully automatised.

The above-mentioned explanations of the linguistic problems in children with SLI are, with the exception of Clahsen (1991), based on data from English-speaking children. Since the main problem in English-speaking children with SLI is to produce 3 person singular -*s*, it is this structure that has been focused on. Failure to produce this morpheme has been interpreted either as a problem with the underlying feature person (Gopnik 1990), as an optional infinitive (Rice & Wexler 1996) or as problems with the processing of morphemes of short duration (Leonard 1998). Agreement morphology has been found to be vulnerable both in English-speaking and German-speaking children. In German children a difference has been found between more local inflection, such as participle inflection, which is produced without problems, and inflection on the sentence level, namely subject-verb agreement, which has a lower percentage of correctness (Rothweiler & Clahsen 1994).

Interestingly, in his data from German children with SLI, Clahsen (1991) found that not only agreement morphology but also word order was problematic. He argues that the missing agreement hypothesis is a valid explanation also for the word order problem, since verb-second is tightly connected to agreement morphology in normally developing L1 children.

3.   Processability Theory

According to Processability Theory (Pienemann 1998a, b), language acquisition can be described as the gradual construction of a mental grammar.

> The task of acquiring a language includes the acquisition of the procedural skills needed for the processing of the language. It follows from this that the sequence in which the target language (TL; covers L1 and L2) unfolds in the learner is determined by the sequence in which processing routines develop that are needed to handle the TL's components.   (Pienemann 1998b: 1)

Each stage in the development is built upon the automatisation of the preceding stages. A detailed account of the precise prerequisites needed for the processing of each stage in the development can be found in Pienemann (1998a). In the following, a brief summary of the parts that are relevant for my discussion on L1 and L2 acquisition will be given.

The first step in learning a language is to identify meaningful words and to memorize chunks. The next step is to categorize the lexicon and list the diacritic features of the lexemes in the lexicon in the category procedure. This is when *lexical morphology* emerges. Lexical morphology is a necessary prerequisite for the *phrasal procedure* to work, and make phrasal morphology processable. The processing of phrasal morphology enables the learner to transfer grammatical information between head and modifier within a phrase. It does not, however, allow for grammatical exchange across phrases. For example, the constituents in the verb phrase can influence each other, before the grammatical subject and predicate are recognized. This is the next step and it implies that the pro-

Table 1. Implicational sequence of processing resources (after Pienemann 1998a)

	Time 1	Time 2	Time 3	Time 4	Time 5
Procedures					
Subordinate clause	–	–	–	–	+
S-procedure	–	–	–	+	+
Phrasal procedure	–	–	+	+	+
Category procedure	–	+	+	+	+
Word access	+	+	+	+	+

cedure for inter-phrasal morphology, the *S-procedure*, is processable. When the *S-procedure* is working, the grammatical functions of the words in a clause will be accessible. Thus, the rule that regulates subject-verb inversion in Germanic languages is processable at this level of development. Finally, the hierarchical relation between main and subordinate clauses will be processable and the learner can apply different grammatical rules in *main clauses and subordinate clauses*. Table 1 illustrates the development of processing procedures.

The discussion in this chapter will be focussing on *the phrasal procedure* and the *S-procedure*.

A processing perspective on L1 and L2 acquisition

In Pienemann (1998b) a comparison between the development of German as L1 and as L2 is made. It is claimed that the process of development is basically similar, and that the differences between the rules that L1 and L2 learners use can be explained by their different initial hypotheses. Using the concept of generative entrenchment, Pienemann argues that once a specific structure such as SVO or SOV is used, the range of options to be chosen for the next stage is restricted. The SOV order that German L1 learners start with can easily be developed into verb-second, since the final placement of the main verb is already in place and the learner only needs a slot available in which to place auxiliary verbs. In contrast to this, the SVO order that L2 learners start with demands more intermediate steps before verb-second can be processed. Thus, since SOV demands fewer steps to reach the verb-second stage it is a better option to start with. In Table 2 the relevant developmental steps for L1 and L2 acquisition are summarized.

The middle column in the table illustrates the L2 development of German. L2 learners start with SVO as preferred word order. The next step involves a preposed element, with the order SVO held constant. Before the S-procedure, where subject-verb inversion can be processed, the L2 learner needs the phrasal

Table 2. L1 and L2 development of German morphosyntax (after Pienemann 1998b)

Procedure	L2	L1
5. subordinate clause	comp SOV	comp SOV
4. use of S-procedure for constituents in S	+/– agreement	+ agreement
	X Vf S O Vi	X Vf S O Vi
3. use of phrasal procedure for constituents in VP	X S Aux O V/	–
	X S V O PART	
2. use of saliency principle to relax canonical order	X S V O	–
1. word order constrained into canonical order	SVO	SOV

procedure that ensures that the finite verb is separated from the infinitival verb, or the particle, and the object is placed between them. Otherwise, there would be clauses with the order X Vf S Vi O.[1] When the S-procedure is accessible, subject-verb inversion and subject-verb agreement become processable (although they do not necessarily emerge simultaneously as in L1 acquisition). The last step involves the subordinate clause procedure.

The right column in Table 2 shows the development of German L1 learners. These learners start with a different initial hypothesis, SOV, instead of SVO. They do not use intermediate steps, but proceed directly to the S-procedure, where verb placement and verb morphology is used simultaneously.

4.   A processability perspective on children with SLI

In this section, data from children with SLI will be investigated from a processability perspective, and examples from the area of syntax will be presented. As mentioned above, most earlier SLI research has focused on morphology, and English-speaking children with SLI. However, there is some evidence that word order may be a problem also for English-speaking children. In an experiment with elicited imitation, Menyuk & Looney (1976) found that children with SLI did not repeat sentences with inverted word order such as "When will he come" and "How will he get there", but reformulated them as "When he will come" and "How he will get here" (Mcnyuk & Looney 1976: 274).

As a matter of fact, a closer look at the literature on children with SLI using languages other than English reveals that word order has been pointed out as a major problem for children with verb-second languages, e.g. German (Clahsen 1991; Grimm & Weinert 1990; Lindner 2002), Dutch (de Jong 2000) and Swedish (Håkansson & Nettelbladt 1993, 1996). Just as in the case with

English-speaking children with SLI, it is the subject-verb inversion that causes difficulties.

4.1 German

Processability Theory predicted different developmental paths for L1 learners and L2 learners of German. What about children with SLI? Do they follow the same developmental sequence that other L1 children use? An overview of the literature reveals, interestingly enough, that some of the structures that have been specifically pointed out as problems for German-speaking children with SLI are the same as Pienemann (1998a) discusses as typical in L2 acquisition, namely:

i.   dissociation of verb agreement morphology and verb placement
ii. non-separation of particle and verb
iii. non-inversion after a preposed element

These structures are absent in the production of young L1 children. They use two "key moves", SOV and verb-second with subject-verb agreement, and have no need of the intermediate steps like (ii) and (iii) (Pienemann 1998b).

In contrast to what has been found for young L1 children, studies on children with SLI have found a dissociation between morphology and word order when this relationship has been investigated (Clahsen 1991; Grimm & Weinert 1990; Lindner 2002). Clahsen found this dissociation especially in the child Petra:

> … developmental sequences can arise in dysphasia, which are different from those of normal grammar acquisition. The clearest instance of this is provided by the data from Petra. The investigations in Part I showed that there are close links between the position and inflection of verbs in the utterances of linguistically normal children. As soon as the agreement system has been learned, the position of the verb changes drastically. Within a very short period of time the previously used verb-final patters disappeared and in their place in main clauses we find the verb-second pattern (V2) required for finite verbs. Correlations in development of this kind do not apply to Petra.
>
> (Clahsen 1991:229)

A dissociation between verb morphology and verb placement implies that the child is able to use agreement morphology but not verb-second, as in example (1a), or verb-second but not agreement morphology, as in example (1b).

(1)   a.   *"und jetzt du wieder schreibst"* (Clahsen 1991:178)
             'and now you again write-2p'
      b.   *"ich runtergehen nicht"* (Lindner 2002:20)
             'I down-go not'

Another finding reported in the literature on German-speaking children with SLI is that they have a problem in separating particles from verbs, which involves exchange of grammatical information between the constituents in the verb phrase, and is mentioned as a typical problem also in L2 acquisition. In German the particle is separated from the verb in main clauses. An utterance where the particle is not separated from the verb has been shown to be typical in children with SLI (Grimm & Weinert 1990; Clahsen 1991; Lindner 2002). Lindner (2002) even suggests that this structure has a special diagnostic value in the identification of SLI. It is related to the dissociation of agreement and word order, since children who are unable to relate verb form to verb position, and therefore use finite verbs in final position, are also unable to realize the verb separation pattern. The examples below illustrate the phenomenon.

(2)   a.   *"und hier alle runterrodeln"* (Lindner 2002:24)
             'and here everybody down-slide'
      b.   *"Der Hund den Knochen auffrisst!"* (Grimm & Weinert 1990:225)
             'the dog the bone up-eats'
      c.   *"du dann runterfällt"* (Clahsen 1991:173)
             'you then down-fall'

The third problem mentioned in the literature is the non-inversion after an initial adverb or object. In order to use inversion, the speaker has to be able to process and unify grammatical information between the noun phrase and the verb phrase. This process is found higher in the PT hierarchy than the particle separation. Thus, verb-particle separation is a prerequisite for inversion to be processable. Several studies of German-speaking children with SLI report that the children have problems with the inverted word order (Grimm & Weinert 1990; Clahsen 1991; Lindner 2002). The order XSOV (examples (3a) and (3b)) is particularly interesting, since it has not been reported in L1 data.

(3)   a.   *"jetzt ich eins ehm noch mal"* (Clahsen 1990:317)
             'now I one er another paint'
      b.   *"und dann hier die Baum sich bewegt"* (Lindner 2002:24)
             'and the here the tree itself moves'

Thus, the three structures, (i) dissociation between verb morphology and verb placement, (ii) problems with separating particle and verb, and (iii) use of non-inversion after an initial element, have all been found in L2 acquisition, but not in L1 acquisition.

It is particularly striking that the interlocking of verb morphology and verb placement, which sometimes has been regarded as the critical feature that differentiates L1 acquisition from L2 acquisition, is absent in children with SLI. As mentioned above, normally developing German L1 children show a clear developmental relationship between the emergence of morphological markings of finiteness on verbs and verb-second. In fact, this seems to be the most cited item of evidence for any difference between L1 and L2 acquisition.

The use of SOV together with a preposed adverb, without separating the verb from the particle (XSOVV), is another interesting example from children with SLI. This structure does not occur in Table 2. According to Pienemann (1998b), SOV as an initial hypothesis in L1 children ought to help the learner develop inversion, but this seems not to be the case in children with SLI. Although they have variable order and/or SOV as an initial hypothesis, they do not develop verb-second directly, but use the intermediate steps that are characteristic of L2 learners. Not only do they use XSOV, but also unseparated particle verbs. In L2 acquisition the use of discontinuous particles is acknowledged as a developmental step (Pienemann 1998b). In L1 acquisition this step is superfluous since the SOV order already makes room for a verb in the final position. However, as discussed above, the separation of verb from particle is known to be a problem for children with SLI (Grimm & Weinert 1990; Clahsen 1991; Lindner 2002).

4.2 Swedish

Like German, Swedish is a verb-second language. Unlike German there is no subject-verb agreement, and the verbs are inflected only for tense. Previous research of Swedish as an L2 has shown a development for syntax that is very much in line with what has been found for German as an L2: first canonical SVO order, then adverb in front of SVO, and thereafter subject-verb inversion (Hyltenstam 1978; Bolander 1988). One difference is that there is no verb-particle separation in Swedish and therefore no developmental stage for this structure.

In the project "Variation and deviation in language acquisition" the development of Swedish morphosyntax was investigated longitudinally in three groups of preschool children: L1 children, L2 children and children with SLI

Table 3. The informants: five L1 children, five L2 children and five children with SLI

L1 – children	Age range	L2 – children	Age range	Children with SLI	Age range
L1:1	2;0–3;1	L2:1 (L1 Syrian)	4;0–4;3	SLI:1	4;11–5;11
L1:2	2,2–3;1	L2:2 (L1 Karamanji)	4;6–5;2	SLI:2	5;3–7;0
L1:3	2;3–3;4	L2:3 (L1 Turkish)	4;7–4;10	SLI:3	5;3–7;0
L1:4	2;4–3;1	L2:4 (L1 Arabic)	5;1–5;6	SLI:4	5;7–8;4
L1:5	2;5–3;0	L2:5 (L1 Turkish)	5;5–6;0	SLI:5	5;11–8;3

(Håkansson, Nettelbladt & Hansson 1991; Håkansson & Nettelbladt 1993, 1996; Hansson 1992; Hansson & Nettelbladt 1995). The L1 children were young children in monolingual families. They were recorded monthly from the age of around 2 years. The L2 children came to Sweden at the age of approximately 4 years or later, and they were recorded monthly. They had various mother tongues: Arabic, Karamandji, Syrian and Turkish. Finally, data from five children diagnosed with SLI were analyzed. For each of these children, recordings were made 3 or 4 times with intervals of one year.

The results of the longitudinal study show that word order patterns develop differently in the three groups of children. Already when Swedish-speaking L1 children start using two-word utterances they have a variable word order and use both subject-before-verb and verb-before-subject. The same variability in word order patterns continues in the three-word stage. As soon as the children start preposing elements such as adverbs and objects, they are also able to use the S-procedure, with subject-verb inversion and tense morphology on the verb (XVfSO). The first examples of verb-second are produced around the child's second birthday. Subordinate clauses, with subordinate clause word order (non-inversion and negation in front of the verb) emerge later.

In contrast to L1 children, L2 children and children with SLI develop verb-second slowly and with intermediate steps. They first use a canonical SVO word order. When elements are preposed, SVO word order is still used, with tense markings on the verbs (XSV$_{tense}$[2] O). After that, the children use inversion with the verb in second position directly after the preposed adverb. Thus, the development of verb-second, or subject-verb inversion, involves one extra step for L2 children and children with SLI.

Just as in the case of German-speaking children, there are structures which L2 children and children with SLI have in common, but which are not shared by the L1 children. In Swedish, the structures are:

i.   dissociation of verb morphology and verb placement
ii.   non-inversion after a preposed element (XSV structures)

Table 4. Development of Swedish morphosyntax in L1 children, L2 children and children with SLI (data compiled from Håkansson & Nettelbladt 1993, 1996)

Procedures	L1	L2	SLI
4. subordinate clause	comp S (neg) V_{tense} O	comp S (neg) V_{tense} O	comp S (neg) V_{tense} O
3. S-procedure	X V_{tense} S (neg) O	X V_{tense} S (neg) O	X V_{tense} S (neg) O
2. preposed element		X S V_{tense} O	X S V_{tense} O
1. canonical/ variable order	variable order	S V O	S V O

As mentioned above, Swedish does not have agreement morphology, but finite verbs are morphologically marked for tense only. This may be the reason why the relationship between verb placement and verb morphology is not as clear-cut in the acquisition of Swedish as in the acquisition of German. However, empirical studies of Swedish L1 acquisition have found a tendency for a simultaneous acquisition of verb morphology and verb placement (Platzack 1996; Håkansson 2001).

Logically, a dissociation of verb placement and verb morphology can result both in tensed verbs used in other positions than verb-second, and infinitival/untensed verbs used in verb-second position. In the Swedish data, the first type is the only one that has been attested (examples (4a–d)). Examples (4a) and (4b) come from L2 children and examples (4c) and (4d) from children with SLI.

(4) a. *"nu dom sover"* (Child L2:2, age 4;8)
'now they sleep-PRES'

b. *"nu dom ska vakna"* (Child L2:2, age 4;8)
'now they will-PRES wake'

c. *"sen jag fick en kompis där"* (Child SLI:5, age 5;11)
'then I get-PAST a friend there'

d. *"en gång han äter inte mat"* (Child SLI:4, age 6;7)
'once he eat-PRES not food'

The other phenomenon which L2 children and children with SLI have in common and which differentiates them from L1 children is the non-inversion after a preposed element, or XSV structures. As mentioned earlier, subject-verb inversion after a preposed element is usually acquired by L1 children around the age of two years. In fact, young L1 children use verb-before-subject well before they start using three-word utterances. Håkansson & Nettelbladt (1993, 1996) noted that young L1 children use verb-initial sentences (*kommer bilen* 'comes car-the') in the same contexts that adult speakers of Swedish could have used verb-second sentences (*här kommer bilen* 'here comes car-the').

Both the L2 children and the children with SLI produced XSV structures. Some of the L2 children used XSV during the whole data collection period, i.e. for one year. In contrast, there were no occurrences of XSV in the last recordings from the children with SLI. In their case, the last data collection took place 3 or 4 years after the first one. On this occasion, the children with SLI used only the target structures SVO and XVS (Håkansson & Nettelbladt 1993, 1996).

4.3   Relation between MLU and word order

The previous section gave an overview of the development of word order patterns in L1 children, L2 children and children with SLI. Another way of comparing the three groups is to use the MLU (mean length of utterance) as a starting point and to analyze the syntactic structures in children with a comparable MLU. Table 5 presents cross-sectional data from the L1 children, L2 children and children with SLI. In the table, the children can be found under the headings, L1, L2 and SLI. Within each group, the individual children are ordered from lowest to highest MLU.

As Table 5 shows, L1 children are younger and have shorter MLUs than the other groups. In spite of that, they exhibit more target-like behaviour. They use two types of sentence structure: SVO and XVS (inverted word order). The proportion 64% SVO and 36% XVS already matches before the age of three years the proportion found in adult speech. Approximately 36% of all clauses have inversion.

Only one single case of non-inversion after an initial adverb is found in the data from L1 children. It is child L1:2, who produces a clause with non-target word order.

(5)   "*nu jag gjort den fin*" (Child L1:2, age 3;0)
      'now I done-SUPINE it nice'

Example (5) shows a non-inverted clause with a non-finite verb.[3] This could be interpreted as an omission of an auxiliary verb (cf. Hansson 1997), and it is not as clear a case of XSV as the examples where the verbs are inflected for tense. The L2 children are almost two years older than the L1 children and they have longer MLUs. However, their grammar is less developed. They use the ungrammatical XSV structure and only a few examples with inversion. There are 38 examples with non-inversion after a preposed element. It is striking that all of the L2 children produce the non-target XSV clauses (although some only

Table 5. Data from five L1 children, five L2 children and five children with SLI, with Swedish as the target language

Child	Age	MLU	SV(O)	*XSV(O)	XVS(O)
L1: 1	2;11	2.34	14 (54%)	–	12 (46%)
L1: 2	3;0	2.82	16 (59%)	1 (4%)	10 (38%)
L1: 3	3;1	2.83	56 (66%)	–	29 (34%)
L1: 4	3;1	2.87	33 (70%)	–	14 (30%)
L1: 5	2;7	2.93	14 (58%)	–	10 (42%)
mean:	2;9	2.76	64%	0,5%	36%
L2: 1	4;3	2.83	22 (85%)	4 (15%)	–
L2: 2	4;6	3.53	74 (75%)	20 (20%)	5 (5%)
L2: 3	4;7	3.82	16 (89%)	1 (5%)	1 (5%)
L2: 4	5;1	3.16	74 (82%)	11 (12%)	5 (6%)
L2: 5	5;5	2.43	39 (93%)	2 (5%)	1 (2%)
mean	4;8	3.15	82%	14%	4%
SLI: 1	6;0	2.60	33 (80%)	8 (20%)	–
SLI: 2	5;11	2.64	19 (66%)	8 (28%)	2 (7%)
SLI: 3	6;2	2.98	48 (94%)	–	3 (6%)
SLI: 4	5;11	3.17	41 (63%)	23 (35%)	1 (2%)
SLI: 5	6;7	3.23	34 (81%)	8 (19%)	–
mean	6;1	2.92	77%	21%	3%

have very few). Four of the L2 children have a variable pattern and they produce both the ungrammatical SV and the target verb-second structure after the preposed element. However, when verb-second is used it is restricted to presentational contexts with adverbs and copulas as in example (6) below:

(6) "*där är ambulansbil*" (Child L2:3, age 4;6)
     'there is ambulance-car'

The children with SLI are the oldest informants, with a MLU that is longer than the MLUs of the L1 children but shorter than the MLUs of the L2 children. Similar to the L2 children, the children with SLI produce many examples of the ungrammatical XSV word order. Only one child, SLI:3 keeps to the target structures SVO and XVS. However, this child uses an unproportionally high number of SVO clauses, which might indicate that he avoids preposing an adverb. 47 examples of XSV, 21% of the total amount of clauses, are used by the children with SLI.

5.   Summary

This chapter has shown that Processability Theory is a useful tool in comparing language development in different groups of learners, such as L1 learners, L2 learners and children with SLI. Admittedly, the examples from German are taken from earlier published studies with different research questions and theoretical starting points, and therefore their comparability is unclear. The Swedish data, on the other hand, come from a longitudinal study of the three groups and the data is comparable.

By using longitudinal data, and PT as a theoretical framework, for analysing children with SLI a new picture emerges, in which their language problems can be seen as indicators of language development. The results shed new light on the L1-L2 comparison. Strictly speaking, children with SLI are L1 learners, since they are acquiring their first language. However, some children with SLI do not show the interlocking of morphology and syntax that has been shown to be typical for L1 acquisition. Instead, their acquisition of morphosyntax is characterized by a gradual development over an extended period of time, during which they use the same intermediate steps that are known from L2 acquisition.

Thus, the inclusion of children with SLI in a discussion of L1 and L2 acquisition challenges the traditional distinction of L1 acquisition and L2 acquisition as two different processes. If children with SLI behave like L2 learners, then the dichotomy is not L1-L2. Instead, what we have may be a continuum of several language acquisition types of which L1, L2 and SLI are only three examples.

Notes

* Many thanks to Ulrika Nettelbladt, Manfred Pienemann, Monika Rothweiler and an anonymous reviewer for useful comments on earlier versions of this chapter.

1. Since verb separation is a prerequisite for inversion, this structure should not occur according to Processability Theory. However, Monika Rothweiler (personal communication) reports that it does in fact occur in child L2 German. It needs to be further explored whether this may be a difference between adult and child L2 German.

2. The status of the tense versus finiteness in Swedish can be discussed. The traditional way of treating finiteness in Swedish is to define verbs with tense-marking as finite. Another definition is given in Holmberg & Platzack (1995), where finiteness is defined as V2. To avoid circularity, I will use the concept tense for verbs with tense-marking, and not involve finiteness. For a longer discussion of finiteness in the acquisition of Swedish, see Håkansson (1998).

3. As one referee pointed out, the deletion of the auxiliary *"har"* ('have') is in fact allowed in Swedish subordinate clauses. It is possible that young children overgeneralise the "har-deletion" pattern to main clauses, having heard it in subordinate clauses in their input.

References

Bishop, D. (1994). Grammatical errors in specific language impairment. Competence or performance limitations. *Applied psycholinguistics, 15*, 507–550.

Bolander, M. (1988). Is there any order? On word order in Swedish learner language. *Journal of Multilingual and Multicultural Development, 9*, 97–113.

Clahsen, H. (1991). *Child Language and Developmental Dysphasia.* Amsterdam: John Benjamins.

Clahsen, H. & Muysken, P. (1986). The availability of universal grammar to adult and child learners – a study of the acquisition of German word order. *Second Language Research, 2*(2), 93–119.

Clahsen, H. & Muysken, P. (1989). The UG Paradox in L2 acquisition. *Second Language Research, 5*, 1–29.

Conti-Ramsden, G. (1994). Language interaction with atypical language learners. In C. Gallaway & B. Richards (Eds.), *Input and Interaction in Language Acquisition* (pp. 183–196). Cambridge: Cambridge University Press.

de Jong, J. (2000). Specific Language Impairment in Dutch: Inflectional morphology and argument structure. PhD Dissertation, University of Groningen.

Eubank, L. (1992). Verb movement, agreement, and tense in L2 acquisition. In J. Meisel (Ed.), *The Acquisition of Verb Placement: Functional categories and V2 phenomena in language acquisition* (pp. 225–244). Dordrecht: Kluwer.

Gilger, J. W. (1996). How can behavioural genetic research help us understand language development and disorders? In M. L. Rice (Ed.), *Towards a Genetics of Language* (pp. 77–111). Hillsdale, NJ: Lawrence Erlbaum.

Gopnik, M. (1990). Feature blind grammar and dysphasia. *Nature, 344*, 715.

Gopnik, M. & Crago, M. (1991). Familial aggregation of a developmental language disorder. *Cognition, 39*, 1–50.

Grimm, H. & Weinert, S. (1990). Is the syntax development of dysphasic children deviant and why? New findings to an old question. *Journal of Speech and Hearing Research, 33*, 220–228.

Håkansson, G. (1998). Language impairment and the realization of finiteness. In A. Greenhill, M. Hughes, H. Littlefield, & H. Walsh (Eds.), *Proceedings of the 22nd Annual Boston University Conference on Language Development* (pp. 314–324). Sommerville, MA: Cascadilla Press.

Håkansson, G. (2001). Tense morphology and verb-second in Swedish L1 children, L2 children and children with SLI. *Bilingualism, Language and Cognition, 4*, 85–99.

Håkansson, G. & Nettelbladt, U. (1993). Developmental sequences in L1 (normal and impaired) and L2 acquisition of Swedish. *International Journal of Applied Linguistics, 3*, 131–157.

Håkansson, G. & Nettelbladt, U. (1996). Similarities between SLI and L2 children. Evidence from the acquisition of Swedish word order. In J. Gilbert & C. Johnson (Eds.), *Children's Language*, Vol. 9 (pp. 135–151). Mahwah, NJ: Lawrence Erlbaum.

Håkansson, G., Nettelbladt, U., & Hansson, K. (1991). Variation and deviation in language development: Some hypotheses and preliminary observations. *Lund University Dept of Linguistics Working Papers, 38*, 83–95.

Håkansson, G., Pienemann, M., & Sayehli, S. (2002). Transfer and typological proximity in the context of L2 processing. *Second Language Research, 18*, 250–273.

Hansson, K. (1992). Swedish verb morphology and problems with its acquisition in language impaired children. *Scandinavian journal of Logopedics and Phoniatrics, 17*, 23–29.

Hansson, K. (1997). Patterns of verb usage in Swedish children with SLI: An application of recent theories. *First Language, 17*, 195–217.

Hansson, K. & Nettelbladt, U. (1995). Grammatical characteristics of Swedish children with SLI. *Journal of Speech & Hearing Research, 38*, 589–598.

Harsten, G., Nettelbladt, U., Schalén, L., Kalm, O., & Prellner, K. (1993). Language development in children with recurrent acute otis media during the first three years of life. Follow-up study from birth to seven years of age. *The Journal of Laryngology and Otology, 107*, 407–412.

Holmberg, A. & Platzack, C. (1995). *The Role of Inflection in Scandinavian Syntax.* Oxford: Oxford University Press.

Hyltenstam, K. (1978). Variation in interlanguage syntax. *Lund University Department of Linguistics Working Papers* 18.

Leonard, L. (1989). Language learnability and specific language impairment in children. *Applied Psycholinguistics, 10*, 179–202.

Leonard, L. (1998). *Children with Specific Language Impairment.* Cambridge, MA: The MIT Press.

Levelt, W. (1989). *Speaking. From intention to articulation.* Cambridge, MA: The MIT Press.

Lindner, K. (2002). Finiteness and children with specific language impairment. *Linguistics, 40*, 797–847.

Meisel, J. M. (1991). Principles of Universal Grammar and strategies of language use: On some similarities and differences between first and second language acquisition. In L. Eubank (Ed.), *Point-Counterpoint: Universal Grammar in the Second Language* (pp. 231–276). Amsterdam: John Benjamins.

Meisel, J. M. (1994). Getting FAT. Finiteness, agreement and tense in early grammars. In J. M. Meisel (Ed.), *Bilingual First Language Acquisition. French and German grammatical development.* Amsterdam: John Benjamins.

Meisel, J. M. (1997). The acquisition of the syntax of negation in French and German: Contrasting first and second language development. *Second Language Research, 13*, 227–263.

Menyuk, P. & P. L. Looney. (1976). A problem of language disorder: Length versus structure. In D. Morehead & A. Morehead (Eds.), *Normal and Deficient Child Language* (pp. 259–279). Baltimore: University Park Press.

Pienemann, M. (1981). *Der Zweitspracherwerb ausländischer Arbeiterkinder.* Bonn: Bouvier.

Pienemann, M. (1998a). *Language Processing and Second Language Development: Processability theory.* Amsterdam: John Benjamins.

Pienemann, M. (1998b). Developmental dynamics in L1 and L2 acquisition: Processability theory and generative entrenchment. *Bilingualism, Language and Cognition, 1,* 1–20.

Platzack, C. (1996). The initial hypothesis of syntax. A minimalist perspective on language acquisition and attrition. In H. Clahsen (Ed.), *Generative Perspectives on Language Acquisition* (pp. 369–414). Amsterdam: John Benjamins.

Rice, M. & Wexler, K. (1996). Towards tense as a clinical marker of specific language impairment in English-speaking children. *Journal of Speech and Hearing Research, 39,* 1239–1257.

Rothweiler, M. & Clahsen, H. (1994). Dissociations in SLI children's inflectional systems: A study of participle inflection and subject-verb-agreement. *Scandinavian Journal of Logopedics and Phoniatrics, 18,* 169–179.

Vainikka, A. & Young-Scholten, M. (1994). Direct access to X' theory: Evidence from Korean and Turkish adults learning German. In T. Hoekstra & B. D. Schwartz (Eds.), *Language Acquisition Studies in Generative Grammar* (pp. 265–316). Amsterdam: John Benjamins.

CHAPTER 7

Extending Processability Theory

Manfred Pienemann[*], Bruno Di Biase[**] and
Satomi Kawaguchi[**]
*University of Paderborn and University of Newcastle Upon Tyne
**University of Western Sydney

The original version of PT focused on modelling the transfer of grammatical information within c(onstituent) structure on the basis of feature unification, utilising a simplified version of f(unctional) structure. In this chapter we will explore ways in which linguistic non-linearity can be modelled by including discourse functions and Lexical Mapping Theory (i.e. the mapping of a(rgument) structure onto f-structure) in order to prepare the way for an extended approach that can capture a wider range of linguistic phenomena, including passives, causatives, topicalisation and so-called 'exceptional lexical entries' (such as 'receive'or 'please'). The extension of the scope of PT should be seen as a sketch of a future research programme.

1. Introduction

In Chapter 1 of this volume the original version of PT has been summarised. The reader will recall that PT is based on the notion of transfer of grammatical information which is modelled using feature unification, yielding different degrees of linguistic linearity. Most chapters of this volume utilised this approach and applied it to typologically different languages and different contexts of acquisition, thus demonstrating the typological plausibility of PT.

To highlight the nature of the proposed extension it may be useful to recall that the architecture of LFG is based on three independently motivated parallel structures that have to be mapped onto each other. This is illustrated in Figure 1 which shows the predicator 'see' and its associated argument roles ('experiencer' and 'theme') as an example of an a(rgument)-structure[1] and a rough sketch of the f-structure that this a-structure as well as the corresponding c-structure has to be mapped onto. The arrows in Figure 1 indicate the two kinds of mapping processes mentioned above.

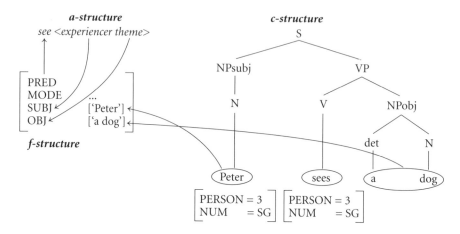

Figure 1. Three parallel structures in LFG

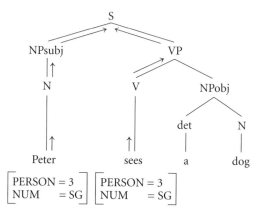

Figure 2. Feature unification in the S-procedure

As mentioned above, the original version of PT focused on c-structure and the transfer of grammatical information within it, using feature unification. The modelling of feature unification, as envisaged in this approach, is illustrated in the example sentence shown in Figure 1 (i.e. 'Peter sees a dog'). In this sentence the insertion of the verbal affix '-s' relies on information contained in the subject-noun phrase, namely the features PERS(ON) and NUM(BER) and their values PERS=3 and NUM=SG. These features are unified in S as shown in Figure 2. In other words, the need to store grammatical information on PERS and NUM during sentence generation illustrates the non-linearity of this morphological process.

In the design of PT, the point of unification is related to a hierarchy of processability that reflects the time course of real time processing as detailed in Levelt (1989). In this way a range of morphological and syntactic processes can be aligned with a universal hierarchy of processability, yielding developmental trajectories for the given target languages as shown in several chapters of this volume.

The basic point of this chapter is to show that there are other aspects of language generation beyond the transfer of grammatical information within c-structure that generate linguistic non-linearity and that these aspects of linguistic non-linearity may be able to be mapped onto the processability hierarchy. In particular, we will show that linguistic non-linearity can be created in the mapping of (i) a-structure onto f-structure and (ii) the mapping of c-structure onto f-structure. Both these components are based on recent innovations in the architecture of LFG, and their inclusion in PT will yield a wider range of phenomena.

Given the psycholinguistic focus of this chapter, it is essential to bear in mind that one cannot assume the relationship between a-structure, f-stucture and c-structure to be linear. If these relationships were linear there would be no leeway for surface structure variation. In other words, semantic predicate-argument relationships could only be expressed by fixed surface word and phrase configurations. However, we know that sentences may vary between active and passive, between affirmative and question forms and that speakers may choose to place constituents in prominent positions by topicalising them or they may choose not to do so. Levelt (1989) demonstrates that in discourse, speakers use various linguistic devices to guide the listener's attention, including topicalisation and passivisation. Many of the structural choices that exist for the native speaker constitute devices of attention-direction and the representation of meaning in the hearer. In other words, attention-direction devices are necessitated by the nature of the comprehension process. However, these choices come at a cost in terms of processing since they require changes to the relationship between either a-structure and f-structure or beween c-structure and f-structure. Changes in these relationships will lead to linguistic non-linearity.

In Chapter 1 the phenomenon of non-linearity was discussed in the context of feature unification. This process is illustrated in Figures 1 and 2 which show that English SV-agreement marking involves a degree of non-linearity by virtue of two sets of lexical features being unified across constituent boundaries.

In the mapping of c-structure onto f-structure, non-linearity is created by the addition of adjuncts to canonical structure and the assignment of discourse functions (FOC and TOP) to elements in c-structure that may not adhere to the canonical pattern. For instance, a canonical (i.e. one-to-one) relationship between c-structure and f-structure can be found in (1) where the first NP is the grammatical subject. In contrast, in (2) this relationship has to be modified.

(1)　He likes Anne.

(2)　Anne, he likes.

The inclusion of this discourse-pragmatic 'dimension' of non-linearity has become possible because of the revised architecture of LFG. Bresnan and Mchombo (1987) and Bresnan (2001) show that some discourse roles (particularly TOPIC and FOCUS) are syntacticised and should therefore be represented in f-stucture. They demonstrate that these functions are subject to syntactic constraints in such cases as English interrogative clauses, cleft constructions, relative clauses etc. These functions have c-structure properties that express their prominence in discourse. In particular, they often precede or c-command other constituents in the clause. The inclusion of the corresponding discourse roles in LFG yields a new dimension of accounting for developing states of interlanguage grammars that allow us to overcome some of the limitations of PT, particularly Kempen's (1998) concern about the absence of the S-procedure in early interlanguage development.

Non-linearity is even more subtle in the mapping of non-canonical argument structure onto f-structure. It is caused by 'exceptional lexical entries' with intrinsic non-canonical a-structure (e.g. 'receive', 'please') and by non-default verb forms (e.g. passives and causative constructions). In both cases, semantic roles are mapped onto non-default grammatical functions. For instance, in the sentence 'the result pleased him' the experiencer is mapped onto the grammatical object, and the theme is mapped onto the subject. These mapping processes go against the default the learner creates earlier and thus add to the non-linearity of the overall production process. Again, this dimension of non-linearity in developing interlanguage grammars can be represented only because in the revised version of LFG the correspondence between argument structure and functional structure is modelled by a formal theory, Lexical Mapping Theory (LMT), which has been incorporated into the LFG formalism.

Apart from our objective of extending the scope of PT by capturing systematically the correspondence between the three parallel levels of representation in a dynamic learner system, there is an additional reason for extending PT, namely to overcome limitations of the original theory.

Some of the limitations of PT were discussed and amended in Chapter 2. One additional limitation was raised by Kempen (1998) who pointed out that in PT, sentences were assumed to be assembled at a point in development before the S-procedure had developed that is needed for the assembly of sentences. Pienemann (1998b) responded that PT was based on the assumption that before the development of the S-procedure, learners produce sentences on the basis of a direct correspondence between argument structure and surface grammatical form. Such direct correspondences (or 'direct mapping') do indeed constitute an alternative and processable route that has been assumed to be accessible to beginning language learners by a number of scholars (e.g. Bever 1970; Slobin 1985a; Pinker 1984, 1989). However, the mere assumption of direct mapping processes does not spell out any formal detail of these processes in the context of an overall theory, nor does it formally interface with the architecture of the proposed theory of language development. It is the objective of this chapter to develop such a formal account of the mapping processes required before the development of the S-procedure and to formally interface this with PT and the overall architecture of LFG.

This chapter is structured as follows. In Section 2 we will highlight the role of LFG as a grammatical formalism in the psycholinguistic framework of Processability Theory. This step is crucial because one needs to bear in mind that even though the objectives of LFG and PT overlap they are not identical. Whereas LFG is a theory of grammar, PT is designed to model the developmental dynamics of interlanguage systems on the basis of the architecture of the syntactic encoding system. In Section 3 we will sketch out two sets of correspondence principles entailed in LFG in order to be in a position to develop our fundamental line of argument. In Section 4 those correspondence principles will be integrated into PT, generating a set of novel predictions for interlanguage development.

2. The psycholinguistic focus of PT and the role of LFG

Given that this chapter aims to explore ways of extending the scope of PT by integrating LFG-style correspondence principles, it may be useful to briefly review the way in which PT handles key psycholinguistic issues and the way in which LFG is used in this endeavour to model the associated processes.

The reader will recall from the overview of PT given in Chaper 1 that PT is a psycholinguistic theory of language development that specifies processable learner grammars in a universal processability hierarchy and that it thus delineates a hypothesis space that constrains developmental trajectories and interlanguage variation. The key psycholinguistic concept underlying PT is the "linearisation problem" in language generation (Levelt 1981, 1989). In PT as well as in Levelt's own work the linearisation problem is modelled using feature unification that permits the exchange of lexical feature information within and across constituents and thus 'solves' the linearisation problem. Above we used English subject-verb agreement marking to illustrate this process. In the example sentence contained in Figures 1 and 2 the insertion of the verbal affix '-s' relies on information contained in the subject-noun phrase, namely the features PERS(ON) and NUM(BER) and their values PERS=3 and NUM=SG. In other words, in (1) the -s-affix constitutes a degree of non-linearity of grammatical information because the feature values PERS=3 and NUM=3 are present in the NP_{subj}, and they need to be utilised again after the verb stem. In sentence generation, such feature values have to be stored in a grammatical memory store. As shown above, the above features are unified in S (cf. Figure 2). In other words, the S-procedure that permits the relevant feature unification acts as a grammatical memory store (cf. Kempen & Hoenkamp 1987).

It was this ability of feature unification to model grammatical memory stores in sentence generation that made LFG attractive as the grammatical theory for PT. Two further characteristics of LFG are also attractive from the perspective of sentence generation, namely (i) the assumption that grammars are lexically driven, and (ii) the separate status of constituency and grammatical functions. The lexically driven nature of sentence generation is an integral part of Levelt's approach and is backed up by extensive empirical evidence. The independent status of constituency and grammatical functions is also supported by a wide range of psycholinguistic empirical evidence including research on slips of the tongue and on-line experiments (cf. Levelt 1989). In other words, we believe LFG to have a high degree of psychological plausibilty. This was demonstrated again recently in experimental work on sentence production by Pickering, Branigan and McLean (2002) which shows that "constituent structure is formulated in one stage"[2] and thus supports the architecture of LFG.

LFG encodes syntactic properties primarily in the lexicon (cf. Schwarze 2002: 148–149). This makes LFG particularly suitable for the study of dynamic linguistic systems such as developing learner grammars, because it affords a formal account of the linguistic dynamics present in developing learner grammars. These dynamics can be expressed in terms of the composition of feature structures of certain lexical items, or in terms of the acquisition of new lexical items that introduce new features into the grammar. Current psycholinguistic research on lexical access is able to model such featural organisation of the lexicon (e.g. Levelt, Roelofs & Meyer 1999).

Pienemann (1998a) showed that every level of the PT hierarchy processing procedures can be captured through feature unification in LFG, which in turn shares key characteristics with Kempen and Hoenkamp's (1987) procedural account of language generation.[3] In other words, an LFG description of the learner language affords an analysis of key aspects of the psycholinguistic process of grammatical information exchange in the developing interlanguage.

This connection between language generation/acquisition and LFG is not coincidental, because the study of language processing and language acquisition is a key issue in the design of LFG, as the following quotation from Kaplan and Bresnan (1982: 177) illustrates:

> [Children] acquire knowledge and skills that enable them to produce and comprehend an infinite number of novel utterances .... The major goal of psycholinguistic research is to devise an explanatory account of the mental operations that underlie these linguistic abilities.

The connection between language generation/ acquisition and LFG is a good reason to use LFG to model learner grammars in PT. A further reason for this choice is linguistic typology and the universal status of the PT hierarchy. If the PT hierarchy is to be universally applicable to language acquisition, then it needs to be interpretable in relation to grammatical structures of individual languages. This can be achieved by interpreting the processability hierarchy through a theory of grammar which is typologically plausible.

Typological plausiblity is a key feature of LFG. For example, well-formedness can be expressed in LFG by testing the fit and compatibility of feature structures of the lexicon. Further, LFG is able to represent abstract grammatical information such as 'SUBJect of' or 'subject PERSon' at the level of f-structure regardless of whether that information is expressed through morphology or syntax. Hence the architecture of LFG does not depend on configurational structure and categories. This lends LFG a high degree of typological power (c.f. Schwarze 2002). Figures 4 and 5 in Section 3.4 illustrate this point in relation to English (a non-prodrop language) and Italian (a prodrop language).

There are two fundamental problems in language acquisition that a theory of language acquisition has to be able to explain, namely (i) the logical and (ii) the developmental problem (cf. Clahsen 1992). The logical problem basically asks for the origin of linguistic knowledge in language learners, whereas the developmental problem asks for an explanation of the universal aspects found in the trajectories of language development. In its original version PT aims at explaining the developmental problem by delineating processable learner grammars. However, in the long run it also needs to be compatible with an approach that aims at explaining the logical problem. Several scholars that work within the LFG framework utilise the interface between LFG and Optimality Theory for that purpose (e.g. Bresnan 2000; Sells 2001). Irrespective of the specific form of the epistemology used for this purpose, Optimality Theory needs to be able to interface with accounts of linguistic representation such as LFG. This requirement is an additional reason for utilising a highly developed, typologically and psychologically plausible theory of grammar as a basis for PT.

Having said all this, one nevertheless needs to bear in mind that the objective of PT is not identical with that of LFG. Whereas LFG is aimed at typological plausibility and the representation of the linguistic knowledge of native speakers, PT is aimed at accounting for developing grammars of non-native speakers, including the dynamics of the developmental process. Therefore accounts of developing linguistic systems may well differ from accounts of the corresponding target language system. For instance, German, Dutch and Swedish are subject to a categorical V2-constraint. In contrast, this constraint does not apply to early learner-German (learner-Dutch or learner-Swedish). Instead, this constraint is acquired by learners of German (and of other Germanic languages) in a non-categorical manner. Therefore, some aspects of the LFG-based PT account of the development of learner-German will be substantially different from standard accounts of native German (e.g. Berman & Frank 1996).

Given the commitment of the LFG approach to language acquisition as evident in the above quotation from Kaplan and Bresnan, such discrepancies between native speaker grammars and developing non-native speaker grammars should be seen as a welcome source of knowledge for an understanding of the processes of acquisition and language generation and their relationship to the representation of the linguistic knowledge that underlies these processes.

3.   Correspondence principles

3.1 Correspondence and linearity

Kaplan and Bresnan (1982: 174) describe the fundamental problem of a theory of syntax in a straightforward manner. The issue is

> ... to characterise the mapping between semantic predicate-argument relationships and surface word and phrase configurations by which they are expressed.

This basic perspective has been maintained in the extended version of LFG (Bresnan 2001) where the mapping of a-structure onto f-structure and the mapping of c-structure onto f-structure is the driving force behind the grammatical formalism.

As mentioned above, the architecture of LFG is based on three independently motivated parallel structures that have to be mapped onto each other. This is illustrated in Figure 1 above. The reader will recall that one cannot assume the relationship between these three parallel levels of representation to be linear.

In Section 2 we discussed the phenomenon of non-linearity in the context of feature unification. This process is illustrated in Figure 2 above, which shows that English SV-agreement marking creates non-linearity because two sets of lexical features need to be unified across constituent boundaries.

One type of linearisation problem is brought about by the fact that there is no one-to-one relationship between the natural order of events and the sequence in which these are represented in the course of language production. For instance, in (3) the word 'after' signals that the natural sequence of events is not preserved.

(3)   He drove off after he jumped into the car.

Levelt shows that this non-linear relationship between conceptual and linguistic structure also applies to concepts that are not based on naturally ordered events but on multidimensional information structure. Levelt (1989: 138ff.) demonstrates in a number of experiments that in discourse speakers use various linguistic devices to guide the listener's attention. One such device is *topicalisation* which allows the speaker to mark as topic the referent that the message is about. As mentioned above, this and other devices of attention direction aid the representation of meaning in the hearer. In other words, attention direction devices are necessitated by the nature of the comprehension process. On the other hand, they create a degree of non-linearity in the language that is produced.

The processing of non-linear relationships between conceptual and grammatical structure or between lexical and syntactic structure has to rely on the temporary storage of the material not being produced at the point when it is activated. In the case of example (3) the proposition 'he jumped into the car' has to be held in a memory store until 'he drove off' has been produced. In a similar manner, the values of the features PERS and NUM have to be held in the S-procedure as a memory store in English subject-verb agreement. In other words, language learners may benefit from non-linearity when it serves to direct their attention to prominent information, but it impedes their ability to process language if it requires the use of procedures which they have not yet acquired.

All languages have such devices for directing attention. However, as has been pointed out repeatedly (e.g. Lambrecht 1994; Van Valin & LaPolla 1997; Sells 2001), languages may differ substantially in their use of the principles that govern the linear precedence relations among the elements of a sentence. In languages with flexible word order (e.g. Italian, Turkish, Japanese) the structural repercussions of focus structure can be massive.[4] For example, in Italian the choice between the sequence NP-V and V-NP depends on the NP being topical or focal (Van Valin & LaPolla 1997:418). Similarly in Japanese, 'scrambling', (i.e. the occurence of a non-subject argument in initial position) is possible only if the scrambled argument has already been established as a discourse topic (Otsu 2000).

In this chapter we argue that in (second) language acquisition the correspondence between the parallel syntactic levels of a-, f- and c-structure develops from a linear default relationship to the more complex non-linear relationships found in mature varieties of the target languages, and that this developmental process is constrained not only by feature unification, the mechanism previously implemented in the PT hierarchy, but also by two types of correspondence relationships, namely (i) the language-specific relationship between c-structure constellations and grammatical functions (Bresnan 2001) and (ii) by the relationship between the thematic hierarchy and grammatical functions (i.e. lexical mapping theory, cf. Bresnan 2001).

To develop this point further it will be useful to review the latter two concepts within the LFG framework before proceeding to explore the development of the relationship between them in the course of language acquisition.

3.2 Mapping c-structure onto f-structure

In LFG the correspondence relationship between c-structure and f-structure is governed by general principles for annotating c-structure with functional schemata (Bresnan 2001:98–108). In the context of this chapter with its focus on language acquisition, it is relevant to note that c-structure configurations are language-specific, whereas f-structure is universal. In addition, a number of principles apply to c-structure. One of the key principles is 'economy of expression' which stipulates that of all the possible phrase structure nodes only those may be used that are required by independent principles.[5]

C-structure can be organised in two different ways that correspond to the typological continuum from configurational to non-configurational. In highly configurational languages c-structure is organised hierarchically following the so-called 'endocentric principle', whereas in non-configurational languages c-structure is organised in a lexocentric manner with flat c-structures where all arguments are sisters of the verb. However, as Bresnan (2001:113) points out,

> … languages may freely mix endocentric and lexocentric modes of categorial organisation. This produces a typology of possible syntaxes much closer to a continuum than to a small, discrete parameterisation.

At an abstract level, language does not contain configurational properties, since functions and arguments of internal structures (e.g. a-structure, f-structure) "are not canonically externalised in phrase structure configurations across languages" (Bresnan 2001:82) since the same kind of functional description can be carried by morphology or by phrasal syntax, or by both. Hence configurational properties are language-specific. Therefore the learner of a (second) language does not know in advance what the relevant canonical mapping of the target language will be, nor what its specific 'mix' of syntactic-morphological realisation of functional and argument structure will entail.[6]

One key component of Bresnan's approach to structure-function mapping is the definition of (grammatical) functions which can briefly be characterised as follows. The list of grammatical functions contains the following: TOP, FOC, SUBJ, OBJ, OBJ_θ, OBL_θ , XCOMP, COMP, ADJUNCTS. These functions can be grouped as follows:

(3)   argument functions

$$\text{TOP, FOC,} \quad \underline{\text{SUBJ, OBJ, OBJ}_\theta\text{, OBL}_\theta\text{, XCOMP, COMP,}} \quad \text{ADJUNCTS}$$

non-a-fns   non-a-fns

According to Bresnan (2001:96)

> [t]he subject and objects are the **core functions** associated with the central participants of the eventuality expressed by the verb. They are formally distinguished from noncore functions … In English, for example, core arguments have canonical c-structure positions which can be occupied only by NPs/DPs; noncore arguments are generally expressed by other c-structure categories (obliques by PPs, other complements by VPs, APs, or CPs, etc.).

Argument functions bind their expressions to an argument role and they are governed by the predicate, whereas non-argument functions bind their expressions to something other than an argument role. Also, argument functions allow only single instances, whereas non-argument functions allow multiple instances.

As mentioned above, Bresnan and Mchombo (1987) and Bresnan (2001) show that some discourse roles (particularly TOPIC and FOCUS) are syntacticised and should therefore be represented in f-stucture. They demonstrate that some of these functions are subject to syntactic constraints in such cases as English interrogative clauses, cleft constructions and relative clauses. For these reasons, discourse functions have been added to the list of grammatical functions in recent developments of LFG. As a result, there is a further dichotomy of syntactic functions along the discourse/ non-discourse divide, as shown in (4).

(4)   non-discourse functions
     TOP, FOC, SUBJ,   OBJ, OBJ_θ, OBL_θ, XCOMP, COMP, ADJUNCTS
     discourse-functions

In other words, the hierarchy of grammatical functions can be divided up following two different dichotomies:

i.   argument functions (AF) versus non-argument functions,
ii. dicourse functions (DF) versus non-discourse functions.

Two connections between (3) and (4) are crucial here: the first is that SUBJ is the only function participating in both sets (DF and AF) and the second is the "universal default that optionally identifies SUBJ and TOP" (Bresnan 2001:117).

As mentioned above, a set of principles governs correspondence relationships between c-structure and f-structure. One such principle stipulates that specifiers of functional projections are grammaticalised discourse markers (i.e. TOP, FOC or SUBJ). The choice of markers (for specifiers of functional projections) varies across languages. The example in (5) and its annotated c-structure may serve to illustrate this point. In the case of English, the specifier of IP is SUBJ. This explains why in (5) DP is annotated for SUBJ.

(5) Yesterday everyone smiled

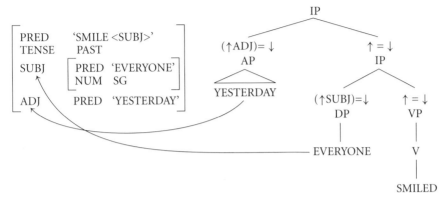

A further principle stipulates that constituents adjoined to XP are one of the non-argument functions TOP, FOC or ADJUNCT. This licences the annotations on the AP in (5). This ensures that the constituent adjoined to XP is ADJ and that the specifier of IP is SUBJ. (5) also serves to illustrate the mapping of c-structure onto f-structure.

The reader will have noticed that in (5) the initial position in c-structure is occupied by a non-subject. This point is relevant to our discussion of linguistic linearity. We will return to this issue in Section 4 after the principles of mapping a-structure onto f-structure (i.e. Lexical Mapping Theory) have been summarised.

(6) What did he buy?

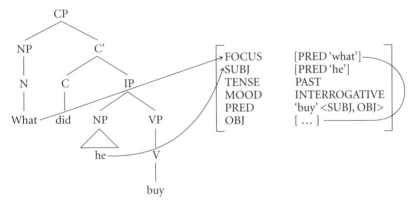

Structure-function mapping can also be illustrated with WH-questions (cf. Dalrymple 2001). (6) shows the simplified c-structure of the question "What did he buy?"', and it illustrates the mapping of c- onto f-structure in this example.

The c-structure shown in (6) is based on the following, again somewhat simplified, rule (cf. Dalrymple 2001: 406):

(7)
$$CP \rightarrow \left(\begin{array}{c} XP \\ (\uparrow FOCUS)=\downarrow \\ (\uparrow FOCUS)= (\uparrow COMP^* \ GF) \end{array} \right) \left(\begin{array}{c} C' \\ \uparrow=\downarrow \end{array} \right)$$

According to the structure-to-function correspondence principle mentioned earlier, only non-argument functions can fill an adjoining XP. In order to se-cure completeness and coherence we must assume that the DF here (i.e. the Wh-Question) is allowed to satisfy the unsatisfied argument (the OBJ) func-tion as illustrated in the f-structure in (6), where the FOC function is linked to the OBJ function. As can be seen in (6), the Wh-question constituent maps onto both, FOCUS and OBJ functions.

In the above section we outlined one additional LFG component that can be integrated into PT, namely the discourse functions TOP and FOC and the ADJ function. In the following section we will outline a further component of LFG that can be integrated into the PT hierarchy, Lexical Mapping Theory.

3.3 Lexical Mapping Theory

Many scholars have pointed out a regularity in the association between gram-matical functions and their characteristic thematic roles. Fillmore's (1968) pioneering work is a prime example. The universality of argument-function mapping relations have been studied in a typological context (e.g. Keenan 1976; Keenan & Comrie 1977; Hopper & Thompson 1980). Within the framework of LFG, Lexical Mapping Theory (LMT) systematically explains this relation-ship, i.e. how conceptual representation of thematic roles is mapped onto the grammatical functions mediated by a-structure.

In LFG, a-structure has two basic aspects, a semantic aspect that specifies the core participants in events, and a syntactic aspect that provides the min-imal information required to identify the dependents of an argument-taking head (Bresnan 2001). Bresnan treats a-structure as an interface between the se-mantics and syntax of predicators. In this perspective, a-structure contains the lexical information about type and number of arguments that allows it to be mapped onto syntactic structure. Bresnan (2001: 306) depicts these relation-ships as in (8).

(8)   lexical semantics

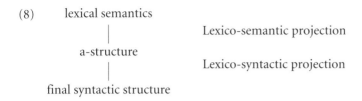

An a-structure consists of a predicator and its argument roles. In Section 1, we discussed the three parallel structures of the sentence *Peter sees a dog* that was illustrated in Figure 1. This example is repeated in (9). The a-structure of (9) is given in (10). In the eventuality described in (9), two participants are involved, i.e. *Peter* and *a dog*. A participant, *Peter*, that is thematically the experiencer, is realised as SUBJ. In contrast, the participant *a dog* that is thematically the theme, is realised as OBJ. However, the same eventuality can be realised as different structural outcomes. For example, if the speaker would like to put more prominence on what is seen by Peter, (11) is the likely structural outcome where *a dog* is promoted to SUBJ and *Peter* is defocused and realised as ADJ. In the case of (11), we need the passive predicator *seen* and the a-structure of (11) is as shown in (12).

(9)   Peter sees a dog.

(10)   see   <experiencer, theme>

               SUBJ   OBJ

(11)   A dog is seen by Peter.

(12)   seen   <experiencer, theme>

               Ø   SUBJ   (ADJ)

The example of the passive illustrates that the same eventuality can be related to c-structure in more than one way[7] due to, for example, the suppression of an argument role or the assignment of prominence/focus to a particular thematic role. LMT systematically explains what type of association is possible between argument roles (such as experiencer, theme, etc.) and grammatical functions (SUBJ, OBJ, etc.). It also sets out principles to govern this association. Intuitively, we can see (9) as being in some sense more basic than (11). LMT shows why this is the case. In (9), the two thematic arguments of the predicator *see*, i.e. 'experiencer' and 'theme' are mapped onto SUBJ (i.e. *Peter*) and OBJ (i.e. *a dog*) respectively. In contrast, in (11) it is the 'theme' that maps onto SUBJ, whereas the 'experiencer' is mapped onto ADJ(unct), or it may be suppressed altogether. In other words, in the active sentence two arguments in a-structure link to their functional correspondents (SUBJ, OBJ) in a default fashion and the canonical sequence of Agent$_{SUBJ}$ and Patient$_{OBJ}$ is maintained in c-structure. In contrast, thematic roles in (12) are mapped onto f-structure in a non-default manner in the passive, and the sequence in c-structure no longer preserves canonicity.

As mentioned above, the same eventuality may correspond to multiple c-structures. However, a- to f-structure mapping is not arbitrary. There are constraints, regularities and a set of governing principles that apply to this mapping process (cf. Darlymple 2001). For instance, examples (13)–(16) show that there are no restrictions for any thematic roles (experiencer, theme, agent, patient, etc.) to be mapped onto SUB.

(13)   Peter patted the dog. (SUBJ = Agent)

(14)   The dog was patted by Peter. (SUBJ = Patient)

(15)   Peter saw a dog. (SUBJ = Experiencer)

(16)   Dogs are nice. (SUBJ = Theme)

In contrast, only some (restricted) argument roles such as locative can be mapped onto the OBL function.

LMT utilises the following four guiding principles that govern argument to f-structure mapping (Bresnan & Kanerva 1989: 22ff.):

i.   hierarchically ordered semantic role structures,
ii.   a classification of syntactic functions along two dimensions,
iii. principles of lexical mapping from semantic roles to (partially specified) functions, and
iv.   well-formedness conditions on lexical forms.

In order to sketch out the 'mechanics' of LMT, it may be useful to briefly summarise each of these principles.

Hierarchically ordered semantic role structures

In agreement with a number of scholars (e.g. Jackendoff 1972; Foley & Van Valin 1984; Givón 1984), a universal hierarchy of thematic roles is assumed in LMT. The ordering of the argument roles in an a-structure follows their markedness (or their relative prominence) from left to right in the thematic hierarchy given in (17). In other words, this hierarchy shows the order of prominence languages attribute to these roles.

(17)   Thematic Hierarchy
agent > beneficiary > experiencer/goal > instrument > patient/theme > locative
       (Bresnan 2001:307)

A classification of syntactic functions

The mapping of a-structure onto f-structure is not entirely free. Instead it is constrained by the classification of syntactic functions based on the features [+/−r] (i.e. whether they are thematically restricted or not) and [+/−o] (that is, 'objective' or 'not objective'). The feature [+r] refers to syntactic functions that express restricted semantic roles. OBJ_θ and OBL_θ have this feature. For instance, OBJ_θ can express only limited thematic roles such as OBJ_{goal} (i.e. *Mary* in *I gave a book to Mary*). Therefore, OBJ_θ is classified as [+r] (thematically restricted). In contrast, SUBJ and OBJ are [−r] (thematically unrestricted) because they can express any semantic role. The unrestricted nature of SUBJ was shown in (13)–(16) above.

The feature [+o] refers to "objectlike functions that appear as arguments of transitive categories of predicates (Verb and Preposition) but not of the intransitive categories Noun and Adjective" (Bresnan & Kanerva 1989:25). OBJ and OBJ_θ possess the feature [+o]. In contrast, [−o] refers to non-objective syntactic functions (i.e. SUBJ and OBL). Bresnan (2001) shows that the four primary (or core) grammatical functions, SUBJ, OBJ, OBJ_θ and OBL_θ can be decomposed into the features [+/−r] and [+/−o], which create four natural classes as shown in (18).

(18)   **Feature Decomposition of Argument Functions** (Bresnan 2001:308)

	−r	+r
−o	SUBJ	OBL_θ
+o	OBJ	OBJ_θ

Lexical mapping principles from semantic roles to syntactic functions

Syntactic functions are specified only partially by thematic roles. LMT postulates three lexical mapping principles to regulate the relationship between the thematic hierarchy and the decomposed features. These principles are: (i) intrinsic role classifications, (ii) morpholexical operations and (iii) default classifications (Bresnan & Kanerva 1989:25–28).

> A constraint on all lexical mapping principles is the preservation of syntactic information: they can only **add** syntactic features, and not delete or change them. This monotonicity is allowed by underspecification.
>
> (Bresnan & Kanerva 1989: 25; emphasis in the original)

According to Bresnan & Kanerva (1989), some thematic roles have intrinsic values, and they apply cross-linguistically:

– Agent has an intrinsic value of [–o]. Agent cannot be encoded as objective function.
– Theme/Patient have an intrinsic value of [–r] realised as SUBJ or OBJ.
– Locative has an intrinsic value of [–o]. Locative expresses only non-objective grammatical functions (i.e. either OBL or SUBJ).

As Bresnan and Kanerva (1989: 26) point out, "[m]orpholexical operations affect lexical argument structures by adding and suppressing thematic roles." For example, ditransitives involve an operation which adds an extra argument to the lexical argument structure. For instance, the ditransitive predicate *cook for* has an extra thematic role (i.e. a beneficiary role). This is apparent in the comparison of (19) and (20).

(19)   Transitive:
       a-structure: cook   < agent patient >
       John cooked pasta

(20)   Ditransitive:
       a-structure: cook-for   < agent patient   beneficiary >
       John cooked pasta for Mary

In contrast, passive is the case where the highest thematic role (i.e. agent) is suppressed as shown in (21).

(21)   Passive (of transitive)
       a-structure: cooked   < agent, patient >

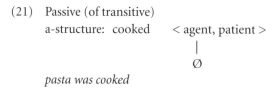

       pasta was cooked

In addition to intrinsic role classification, there is a set of default assignments of features. The default value depends on the thematic hierarchy in (17): the thematic role that is highest in the hierarchy receives the default value of [–r] and other roles receive [+r]. In Bresnan and Kanerva's (1989: 27) words, "[t]he defaults are designed to capture the generalisation that the highest thematic role of a verb will be the subject".

Well-formedness conditions on lexical forms

Finally, two conditions ensure well-formedness.

1. *Function-Argument Bi-uniqueness*: each a-structure role must be associated with a unique function, and conversely.
2. *The subject condition*: every predicator must have a subject.

(Bresnan 2001:311)

These conditions filter out ill-formed structures. In other words, "(i)n every lexical form, every expressed lexical role must have a unique syntactic function, and every syntactic function must have a unique lexical role" (Bresnan & Kanerva 1989:28). Thus, functional-argument bi-uniqueness filters out f-structures that yield, for example, double subjects while, at the same time, every predicator must have a subject. Thus, the subject condition forbids f-structures without SUBJ. These two conditions are illustrated in (25) and (27) below.

Summarizing Bresnan (2001:309–311), the basic syntactic principles for mapping a-structures onto surface grammatical functions operate as follows. Thematic roles are freely mapped onto all compatible grammatical functions subject to a few general constraints: if the given role is the initial argument of the predicator, a most prominent role classified [−o], has to be mapped onto the subject function. – *Note that this rule favours as default an alignment between the three parallel levels of syntactic representation: i.e. the first NP in c-structure aligns with the SUBJect grammatical function and the <agent> semantic role.* – If the given a-structure does not contain such a role, a non-agentive role marked [−r] has to be mapped onto the subject function. All other roles are mapped onto the lowest compatible grammatical function on the following hierarchy of core argument functions:

(22)   SUBJ > OBJ, OBJ$_\theta$ > OBL$_\theta$ (cf. Bresnan 2001:309).

To illustrate the practical operation of the mapping principles it may be useful to exemplify them with the active-passive alternation. Let's take the previous examples of alternate mapping of the predicator *pat, patted* as in (23)–(24).

(23)   Peter patted the dog.

(24)   The dog was patted by Peter.

The mapping of (23) which represents English canonical order SVO, is given in (25):

(25) pat   < agent patient >
      intrinsic   [–o]   [–r]
      default   [–r]
      mapping principle   [+o]
      ───
                                   SUBJ   OBJ
                                   Peter   *the dog*

The English transitive verb *pat* has two thematic roles, i.e. Agent and Patient. Agent and Patient have intrinsic values of [–o] and [–r] respectively. As Agent is the most prominent argument role (i.e. highest in the thematic hierarchy), the general subject default applies and it receives the value [–r]. Therefore, Agent is mapped onto SUBJ (cf. (17) above). Patient, on the other hand, has the intrinsic value [–r]. Logically it can receive either value [+/–o]. But it should receive [+o] linking to OBJ, otherwise Patient would be linked to SUBJ and this would violate Functional-Argument Bi-uniqueness. This is why the resulting mapping shown in (25) can be considered *canonical*. (26) shows more clearly how this alignment of the three parallel structures creates canonical order.

(26) Active: pat   (Agent   Patient)   a-structure

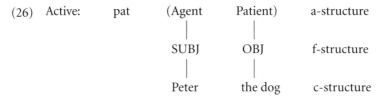

                         SUBJ   OBJ   f-structure

                         Peter   the dog   c-structure

This result is compatible with Optimality treatments of word order (cf. Lee 2001).

Now let us turn to the mapping operations inherent in the Passive alternation in (24). A passive morpholexical operation applies and the highest thematic role is suppressed. Therefore, 'agent' cannot be associated with any core grammatical functions. However, the suppressed 'agent' may appear as ADJ(unct).

The 'patient' role has the intrinsic value of [–r]. In order to fulfill the subject condition it must receive the value [–o]. This mapping mechanism is illustrated in (27a–b). In the context of this chapter it is crucial to note that this mechanism is non-canonical because the most prominent argument ('agent') cannot be linked to SUBJ.

(27) a. Passive (of transitive)

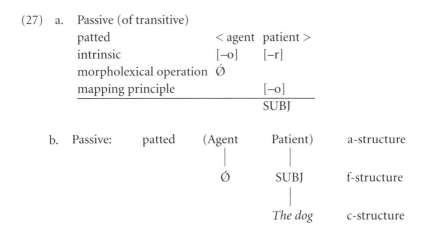

```
        patted                      < agent  patient >
        intrinsic                    [–o]     [–r]
        morpholexical operation  Ø
        mapping principle                     [–o]
                                              ─────
                                              SUBJ
```

b. Passive: patted   (Agent   Patient)   a-structure

```
                            |          |
                            Ø         SUBJ       f-structure
                                       |
                                    The dog      c-structure
```

Note that in terms of c- to f-structure mapping, passives resemble canonical c-structure i.e. SV(X). We will show below that for these structures non-linearity is caused by non-linear a- to f-structure mapping.

In this section we outlined Lexical Mapping Theory, the second of the new LFG components used in PT. Lexical Mapping Theory constitutes a theoretical foundation for further characterizing learners' developmental stages on the basis of lexical feature structure of verbs and their relationship to their nominal arguments. We have shown also that there is a degree of choice in the assignment of prominence to specific arguments through non-canonical mapping onto f-structure. In Section 4 we will show that these choices become available to the learner after canonical a- to f-structure mapping is under control.

3.4 Language-specificity

There are two sources of language-specificity that are crucial to our current discussion: (i) c-structure and (ii) the lexicon. These have been the object of study and experimentation in psycholinguistics as well as linguistics. In this section we will briefly illustrate the language-specific nature of the lexicon and of c-structure.

One set of studies highlights the language-specific nature of the interplay between conceptual-semantic structure and c-structure particularly well. The studies by Bock and Miller (1991) and Bock and Cutting (1992) examine the interplay between these two parallel structures in English by relating conceptual plurals and singulars with verbal agreement marking in sentence completion tasks. As illustrated in (28), informants are to complete sentences referring to multiple tokens (conceptual plural) and to single tokens (conceptual singular), and response differences are measured.

(28)   Sentence completion tasks

(Multiple tokens (conceptual plural):
The label on the bottles ... -> is/are
One token (conceptual singular)
The journey to the islands ... -> is/are

The authors found that errors are equally likely after both preambles. In other words, there was no distributivity effect. The study was initially seen to support a strictly hierarchical model of language production in which conceptual and syntactic processes are entirely independent of each other.

However, a replication of the experiment for Italian (Vigliocco, Butterworth & Semenza 1995) shows that the non-distributivity of the results for English is due to the specific mechanisms involved in English agreement marking which differs significantly from those found in Italian. Vigliocco, Butterworth and Semenza (1995) demonstrated in their study that in Italian agreement errors are more likely after preambles containing a conceptual plural. In other words, they demonstrated a significant distributivity effect for Italian. Further studies (Vigliocco, Butterworth & Garrett, 1996; Vigliocco & Nicol 1998; Franck, Vigliocco & Nicol 2002) demonstrated that features such as number and gender can be retrieved independently from conceptual structures for both number agreement between the subject and the verb and gender agreement between the subject and a predicative adjective.

Taken together, these studies support a model of language production that allows for fundamental differences in processing procedures between languages for verbal agreement marking, including the independent retrieval of features such as plurality from conceptual structure. In contrast, the hierarchical model would be based on the assumption that for all languages the verbal subject marker receives its information from a constituent associated with the subject function by virtue of its configurational properties. Vigliocco's model is mirrored in the architecture of LFG's correspondence mechanisms which permit different mapping procedures for English and Italian with the latter marking SUBJ directly on the verb.[8]

The language-specific nature of the matching of conceptual-semantic structures onto surface c-structure is illustrated by Di Biase and Kawaguchi (2002) who compare the mapping of the predicator 'see' in two different languages, English and Italian. In both languages this predicator requires two arguments, i.e. *experiencer* and *theme*. The *experiencer* and the *theme* map onto

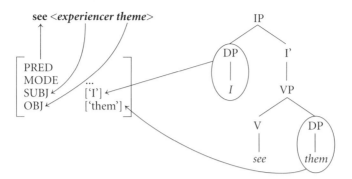

Figure 4. Matching c-structure onto a-structure in English (Di Biase & Kawaguchi 2002: 277)

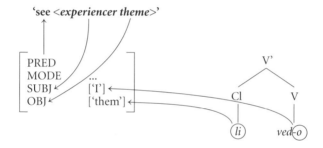

Figure 5. Matching c-structure onto a-structure in Italian (Di Biase & Kawaguchi 2002: 277)

the syntactic functions SUBJect and OBJect, respectively in f-structure for both languages (Figures 4 and 5). Despite the invariance of the f-structure, Di Biase and Kawaguchi show that in English the subject function is marked in DP, whereas in Italian it is marked in V by means of a morphological subject marker (SM), as specified in Bresnan (2001: 150–151).

The differential account of linguistic representation for English and Italian subject marking (illustrated in Figures 4 and 5) deviates significantly from GB and minimalist accounts in which subjecthood is defined through c-structure configurations. The LFG account corresponds to psycholinguistic studies that demonstrate the existence of differential language-specific on-line processes in the matching of conceptual-semantic structures onto surface c-structure.

The second language-specific aspect of linguistic representation and learning is the lexicon. This is also implied in the above experiment: the specific conceptual features (for instance 'gender' or 'number' of the referent) that a language obligatorily encodes is represented in the lexicon. English for instance does not require that the gender of the referent be marked in words such as *friend*, but Italian does require this marking: *amico* refers to 'male friend' while *amica* refers to 'female friend'. This, in turn, has morphosyntactic consequences for Italian where determiners, modifiers or predicators must all be marked for gender (feminine or masculine) as can be seen in (29).

(29) la   mia amica e' australiana
     the F myF friendF is australianF
     'my friend is Australian'

Obviously, the English gloss does not reveal the gender of the referent. This simple example illustrates typological differences in the encoding of conceptual information. In one case gender is encoded morphologically. In the other case it is left unspecified.

A less obvious example of language-specific features that are located in the lexicon is related to the mapping of a-structure onto c-structure. Although there are broad areas of correspondence across languages, the relationship between a-structure and f-structure is by no means universal, and learners of a second language will need to learn which constructions and which verbs are *exceptional*, and how exactly such verbs map which argument to which grammatical function. The Italian verb *piacere* ('to like/to please') may serve as an example of a verb with marked specification. The mapping processes required for this verb constitute a lexically based learning problem for second language learners of Italian as illustrated in (30) which was produced by an intermediate L2 Italian learner.

(30) *tu   piace il   film?
     you.NOM like   the movie?
     'Do you like the movie?'

In (30) the learner canonically connects two participants with the Italian verb *piacere* 'to like'; namely 'experiencer' and 'theme' as in (31). These thematic roles are canonically linked to SUBJ and OBJ in the same manner as in the English verb *like*. However, the Italian verb *piacere* requires a different mapping. With *piacere* 'theme' maps onto SUBJ and 'experiencer' maps onto an oblique function, i.e. OBJ_θ. Comparing the two thematic roles, experiencer and theme, the former is placed higher in the Thematic Hierarchy (see (17) for Thematic Hierarchy). Therefore, default mapping would link experiencer to SUBJ. But the Italian verb 'piacere' requires non-default mapping. This is illustrated in (32).

(31) *Piacere < Experiencer Theme >
                      | |
                    SUBJ   OBJ

(32)   Piacere < Theme Experiencer >
                      | |
                    SUBJ OBJ_θ

In other words, L2 learners have to acquire the specific non-default mapping that is associated with the semantics of the verbs of the target language.

Processability Theory and correspondence principles

3.5 Non-linearity

As we noted above, the original version of PT was based on one specific measure of linguistic linearity in surface structure that was operationalised in terms of feature unification. This was illustrated above in Figure 1 with the non-linearity of English S-V agreement marking. In this section we include two other sources of non-linearity in the PT framework:

i.   The mapping of non-canonical c-structure onto f-structure. Here non-linearity is created by the addition of adjuncts to canonical structure and the assignment of discourse functions (FOC and TOP) to dislocated elements in c-structure.

ii. The mapping of non-canonical argument structure onto f-structure. Here non-linearity is caused by exceptional lexical entries with intrinsic non-canonical a-structure (e.g. 'receive' or 'please') and non-default verb forms (e.g. passive, causative constructions). In the latter case, constituent structure may be canonical while the a- to f- structure mapping is non-canonical.

It may be useful to illustrate how these two mechanisms can produce linguistic non-linearity. We noted in Section 3.3 that if the initial argument of a predicator is non-objective it has to be mapped onto the subject function. For English this implies that the default function of the first argument (which is also the first NP) is SUBJ. The linearity of the default mapping of argument roles onto grammatical functions is exemplified in (33).

(33)   He bought an ice cream.

The predicator of (33) is given in (34). Its first argument role is an agent which is mapped onto SUBJ – according to the default principle. The predicator of (33) also contains the argument role 'theme' which is mapped onto the grammatical function OBJECT.

(34)   buy ____ < *agent*   *theme* >   argument roles
                     | |
            SUBJECT OBJECT   grammatical functions
                     | |
            NP$_{SUBJ}$ NP$_{OBJ}$ c-structure

This results in a one-to-one correspondence of argument roles, grammatical functions and c-structure, yielding an optimal alignment of argument roles with the c-structure default. This correspondence relationship requires no exchange of grammatical information across or within constituents. It therefore ranks low on the processabiliy hierarchy. Lee (2001) derives the same relationship between argument roles, syntactic functions and linear order of constituents from her OT-LFG treatment of word order in Korean and Hindi, based on the notion of 'Harmonic Alignment' (Prince & Smolensky 1993; cited in Sells 2001:7). In other words, one-to-one correspondence as the natural default follows from a processing perspective as well as from an epistemological perspective.

A deviation from the one-to-one correspondence is evident, for instance in WH-questions such as (35).

(35)   What did he buy?

The predicator of (35) is that given in (34) above. As mentioned in Section 3.3, the FOCUS XP is allowed to satisfy the unsatisfied function as indicated in the f-structure illustrated in (36).

(36)   ┌─   ─┐
       │ FOCUS   [PRED 'what']   │
       │ SUBJ   [PRED 'he']   │
       │ TENSE   PAST   │
       │ MOOD   INTERROGATIVE   │
       │ PRED   'buy <(|SUBJ) (|OBJ)>'   │
       │ OBJ   [.....   ]   │
       └─   ─┘

As can be seen in (36), 'what' is mapped onto the FOCUS function which is linked to OBJ. In other words, FOCUS and OBJ are related to the same constituent in c-structure. As shown in (37), this leads to non-canonical mapping due to the appearance of a WH-word in the default position of SUBJ.

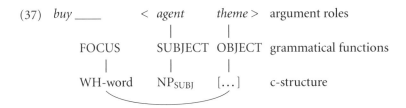

(37)   *buy* ____   < *agent*   *theme* >   argument roles

            FOCUS   SUBJECT OBJECT   grammatical functions

            WH-word   NP_SUBJ   [...]   c-structure

In other words, information about the link between FOCUS and OBJ needs to be exchanged between the two grammatical functions, and this information exchange constitutes the non-linearity that is present in English WH-questions.

In the same way as learners need to develop means for handling non-linearity caused by feature unification, they need to develop means for handling non-linearity created by non-default mapping. Therefore the lack of such means constrains interlanguage grammar, and the acquisition of these means gradually relaxes the above processing-based constraints on the learner's grammar. In the sections below we will describe the constraints that are present at the initial state and how these are relaxed by means of developing additional principles governing the relationship between the three parallel levels of structure.

Although there is a strong relationship between the three levels of syntactic representation (i.e. argument, functional and constituent structure), it is crucial to bear in mind that non-linearity caused by *c-to-f*-structure mapping is quite separate from non-linearity caused by *a-to-f*-structure mapping.

For instance, the mapping processes found in WH-questions and in topicalisation illustrate the choice for any native speaker of establishing a non-linear relationship between c-structure and f-structure by bringing a c-structure element into focus. When this choice is made, a non-linear relationship has to be established between c-structure and f-structure. A new (discourse) function (FOC, TOP) now needs to be mapped onto f-structure in addition to the canonical grammatical functions (SUBJ, OBJ etc.). In interlanguage English this is done without changing in any way the argument structure and its mapping onto f-structure. All the speaker needs to do is ensure that the argument function and the discourse function in f-structure are linked, thus satisfying the extended coherence condition.

3.6 The Unmarked Alignment Hypothesis

The mapping processes found in WH-questions and passives illustrate the speaker's choice of using non-linear relationships between a-structure, f-structure and c-structure. As shown in the previous section, this mapping process is subject to the constraints specified in LFG's correspondence mechanisms. Putting it boldly, adult speakers of English do not always simply map a linear list of argument roles onto a list of grammatical functions and map those onto continuous c-structures as shown in (39).

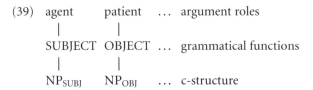

(39)   agent   patient   … argument roles

        SUBJECT OBJECT … grammatical functions

        NP$_{SUBJ}$ NP$_{OBJ}$ … c-structure

However, this is exactly what children aged 4 acquiring English as their first language have been found to do in psycholinguistic experiments. For instance, Bever (1970) studied the accuracy with which informants act out test sentences such as (40 a–e).

(40)   a.   The horse kisses the cow.
        b.   It's the horse that kisses the cow.
        c.   Its the cow the horse kisses.
        d.   The cow is kissed by the horse.
        e.   The dog pats the mother.

Bever found that four-year old children tend to assign the agent role to the first noun in a sentence even in sentences like (40c) and (40d). Strohner and Nelson (1974) confirmed these findings and also included factors such as 'event likelihood' in their analysis which explains why Bever's strategy ('first noun = agent') is unlikely to be applied in (40e). In other words, the children used English canonical order to interpret the events: i.e. the first linear participant was mapped onto subject function and assigned the agentive role – with the exception of (40e), which contradicted children's world knowledge ('event likelihood'). Naturally, neither Bever nor Strohner and Nelson had the benefit of conceptualising these findings in terms of LFG. Instead, they viewed their findings in terms of fixed and direct relationships between semantics and surface grammatical form.

Bloom (1994) reports that knowledge of word order appears to exist even before the two-word stage. A study with 17-month old babies showed that they were sensitive to semantic contrasts expressed by word order (Hirsh-Pasek, Golinkoff, Fletcher, DeGaspe Beaubien, & Cauley 1985). Newport and Meier (1985) show that children acquiring American Sign Language, a free word order language, nevertheless initially use word order to express grammatical relations.

Canonical schemata are also present in adult language processing. Weyerts, Penke, Münte, Heinze and Clahsen (2002) present strong evidence from on-line studies supporting the view that for a configurational language (German) the processor can handle sequences more readily when the subject precedes the object than the other way around, although both sequences do occur in German. The evidence is based on self-paced reading experiments and studies of event-related brain potentials. All studies show a clear subject-first preference and an added processing cost associated with SOV. This research is in line with previous studies by Bates and MacWhinney (e.g. Bates & MacWhinney 1981, 1982, 1987) showing that speakers of English (an SVO language) tend to interpret preverbal NPs as grammatical subjects.

In second language acquisition reliance on canonical word order is even more pronounced than in L1 acquisition, particularly in language production. It is a well-attested finding from a large number of corpus-based studies in most languages that have been studied (including Germanic languages, Italian, Japanese, Chinese and Arabic – for further reference compare the chapters of this volume on the above L2s) that the initial hypothesis of syntax is based on canonical word order.

Sasaki (1998) demonstrated in on-line comprehension studies of L2 processing that the canonical sentence schema is easier to process than non-canonical schemata both for native and non-native speakers. Sasaki demonstrated longer latency and lower accuracy rates in the comprehension of Japanese causative sentences than in canonical (active) double object sentence (see also Kawaguchi's chapter in this volume). He attributed these results to the higher processing cost for sentences requiring non-canonical mapping.

Pinker (1984) reports that in his own re-analysis of Brown's (1973) English L1 data (Eve, Adam and Sara) he found only a handful of verbal passives compared to thousands of active sentences. This corresponds to findings from Bever's (1970) and from de Villiers & de Villiers' (1973) study of L1 learners' comprehension of passive sentences which show that passives cannot be processed reliably before age five or six.

These findings parallel Slobin's[9] (1984) observation that Japanese verbs such as *morau* ('receive') whose recipient argument maps onto the subject (and takes nominative case) is acquired late by Japanese children. In experiments, Marantz (1982) found that three and four year-old children could easily learn made-up verbs whose agent and patient arguments were expressed as sub-

Figure 6. Canonical mapping following Pinker (1984: 298–307)

jects and objects respectively. However, the same informants had difficulties learning verbs with the opposite correspondences.

All of the above studies are compatible with direct canonical mapping. As mentioned above, the notion of direct mapping goes back a long way (e.g. Bever 1970; Slobin 1985; Pinker 1984, 1989). Direct mapping has been discussed in the context of functional as well as rationalist language acquisition research. As Pinker (1984) points out, many linguists have noted a regular relationship between thematic roles and grammatical functions (e.g. Bresnan 1982; Jackendoff 1977; Keenan 1976; Keenan & Comrie 1977; Perlmutter 1980). Pinker (1984: 297ff.) characterises this relationship as follows:

> In a language's 'basic forms' (roughly, simple, active, affirmative, declarative, minimally presuppositional, and pragmatically neutral sentences; see Keenan 1976), agents (if present) are realised as subjects, themes are realised as subjects if there is no agent and as objects otherwise, and sources, locations, and goals are realised as oblique objects if there is an agent or a theme or both, or as objects if there is only a theme.

According to Pinker (1984), canonical mapping occurs when the lexical entry of the verb specifies thematic roles for its arguments that are associated with their grammatical function without crossing the links between the two tiers in Figure 6. Also, there must be exactly one thematic role linked to SUBJ (not necessarily the 'agent').

However, as Pinker (1984) points out, there are also non-basic verb forms, such as passives, and exceptional (intrinsically non-canonical) verbs such as *receive, please* which do not conform to a canonical association between argument structure and grammatical functions. Pinker (p. 307) proposes that canonical mapping is available as an acquisition mechanism and that it requires less knowledge (phrase structure rules and inflectional rules) and less processing of the input (i.e. parsing the string and observing the roles played by the NP referents) than learning non-canonical associations from positive evidence.

Pinker's hypotheses are reminiscent of aspects of LMT, although LMT was created much later than Pinker's hypotheses. In fact, Pinker's work is based on the early version of LFG (Kaplan & Bresnan 1982) and is therefore compatible with our overall approach. However, the mapping processes proposed by Pinker that are sketched out above in Figure 6 focused on cases of canonical mapping and offer no formal LFG account of other cases and their variations across languages or of the development from the initial hypothesis to the mapping processes found in the target language. This was due to the fact that at the time LFG did not contain any general formalism to represent correspondences between argument structure and functional structure across languages. These correspondences can now be represented by LFG's Lexical Mapping Theory. In addition, the correspondence between c-structure and f-structure can be accounted for by the principles outlined in Section 3.2 above.

Lee (2001) treats these correspondence relationships within an OT-LFG framework and on this basis develops a Universal Scale of unmarked mapping such as the following:

> "GF: SUBJ > NonSUBJ
> Case: NOM > OBL
> Position: Initial > Noninitial." (Lee 2001:97)

In other words, Lee's scale implies that the grammatical function SUBJect is less marked than Non-SUBJects, NOMinative case is less marked than OBLique case and that the initial position is less marked than the noninitial position. This approach permits a generic treatment of mapping principles starting from a universal default and covering the full range of typologically possible variations found in interlanguages and target languages.

We can therefore modify the 'direct mapping hypothesis' on the basis of LMT and c-to-f-structure correspondences as in (41).

(41)   *The Unmarked Alignment Hypothesis*[10]
       In second language acquisition learners will initially organise syntax by mapping the most prominent semantic role available onto the subject (i.e. the most prominent grammatical role). The structural expression of the subject, in turn, will occupy the most prominent linear position in c-structure, namely the initial position.

In other words, the Unmarked Alignment Hypothesis predicts that learners will initially organise syntax on the basis of one-to-one correspondences between a-structure and f-structure and between c-structure and f-structure. As we showed above, such one-to-one correspondences will universally result in entirely linear structures that require no internal re-arrangement of linguistic material and no language-specific processors or memory stores. Given this state of L2 linguistic knowledge, the yet immature L2 processor cannot transfer lin-

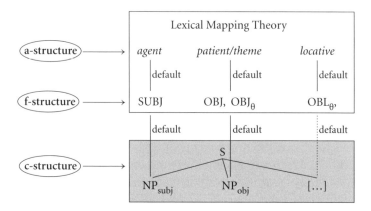

Figure 7. One-to-one correspondences

guistic information as would be required for the unification of lexical features. These one-to-one correspondences, which are illustrated in Figure 7, therefore guarantee the computationally least costly manner of organising L2 syntax and rely entirely on aspects of the syntactic machinery that are not language-specific, including f-structure, the thematic hierarchy and universal aspects of c-structure.

The reader will recall from Section 1 of this chapter that theories of language acquisition have to address two key issues, (i) the logical problem (i.e. the origin of linguistic knowledge) and (ii) the reason(s) for universal patterns in developmental trajectories (i.e. the developmental problem). Both Pinker (1984) and Slobin (1982) tackled both these issues simultaneously in their approaches. In other words, both authors see their approaches as a contribution to explaining the learning mechanisms as well as the developmental schedules involved in language acquisition.

In contrast, PT was designed as a set of psycholinguistic constraints on what learners can process. This set of constraints that was formalised in the processabilty hierarchy serves as an explanation of developmental trajectories. In other words, PT does not contain learning mechanisms. It nevertheless interfaces with LFG, i.e. a theory that can model linguistic knowledge, and PT can therefore be extended to also address the logical problem. The OT-LFG interface offers a powerful epistemological approach that can complement the set of developmental constraints inherent in PT. In the extension of PT that is presented here we have not yet completed this step.

The need for such a complementary relationship of developmental constraints and empistemology is evident in the initial hypothesis of language learners. Pienemann (1998b) discusses the differential initial hypotheses found in German L1 and L2 learners. He shows (following Clahsen 1990) that in L1 learners the initial word order hypothesis is SOV whereas in L2 learners it is SVO and that nevertheless both hypotheses are within the constraints defined by the processability hierarchy. In fact, both word order patterns are canonical. It turns out that this initial hypothesis then sets in motion differential developmental trajectories both of which are in line with the constraints defined by PT and that the L1 trajectory is less error-ridden and more successful.[11] In other words, PT does capture essential aspects of these differential developmental dynamics. However, it is not set up to determine why L1 and L2 learners start out with different initial word orders. This is an issue that can only be resolved by an epistemological approach such as the one present in the OT-LFG interface (cf. Sells 2001).

The Unmarked Alignment Hypothesis implies that L2 learners know the basic architecture of syntax with its three parallel levels of structure. In other words, it implies that L1 knowledge is transferred at an abstract level. This assumption does not in any way contradict the 'developmentally moderated transfer hypothesis' (cf. Pienemann, Di Biase, Kawaguchi & Håkansson this volume), because the latter relates exclusively to language-specific features of grammar, not to its overall design.

Given that many aspects of c-structure are language-specific and the learner can transfer only universal aspects of c-structure to the L2, the 'developmentally moderated transfer hypothesis' predicts that at the initial state c-structure is 'flat' (e.g. without VP) and the S-procedure as well as phrasal procedures are unable to act as linguistic memory stores for grammatical information because such information is language-specific. For instance, as we showed in Pienemann, Di Biase, Kawaguchi and Håkansson, this volume, the entries to the L2 lexicon have not been annotated for any syntactic features. Also, we noted above that c-structure rules and related principles that ensure positional constraints such as the auxiliary in second position in English WH-questions, are highly language-specific and can therefore not be transferred to the L2.

In the original version of PT the initial hypothesis of syntax was described as a state in which no information can be transferred from anywhere in the sentence to any other position in the sentence using lexical unification. The reason for this is that at this point of the developmental process no procedures have been developed that would allow the information transfer to be carried out. Kempen (1998) raised the question of how the learner can form sentences at this point if the S-procedure has not been developed. Pienemann (1998b) assumes that the S-procedure is simplified at this point.

Our present line of argument not only provides an additional motivation for canonical word order at the initial state, but it also allows us to define what is entailed in the learner's simplification of the S-procedure. The Unmarked Alignment Hypothesis implies that a fixed association is established between a-, f- and c-structure when the development of L2 syntax starts. This association relationship specifies how sentences can be formed despite the simple structure of the interlanguage, and it constrains the interlanguage grammar into canonical word order. Viewing SLA from this perspective, the remainder of the acquisition process can be seen as the cumulative adaptation of the interlanguage to the specific linking principles of the L2.

3.7 Non-linearity and discourse functions: The TOPIC hypothesis

The departure from the Unmarked Alignment Hypothesis is marked by the first deviation from the canonical sentence schema. Empirical studies of the second language acquisition of a range of configurational languages such as German or English identified sentence-initial adverbials and WH-words to be the first non-subjects to occur in sentence-initial position in L2 development. In this section we will first consider these post-initial L2 developmental dynamics in English and German, and we will then attempt to represent the underlying mechanisms in more general terms.

In Section 3.2 we described roughly how structures such as sentence-initial adverbials and WH-words can be accounted for. Now it will be useful to see how non-linearity is created in these structures using the correspondence mechanisms sketched out above. The mechanism applying to sentence-initial adverbials was briefly discussed earlier. It stipulates that constituents adjoined to XP be assigned one of the non-argument functions TOP, FOC or AD-JUNCT. This licences sentence-initial arguments adjoined to XP to assume one of these grammatical functions (Bresnan 2001). One principle governing c- to- f-structure mapping stipulates that specifiers of functional projections are grammaticalised discourse markers (i.e. TOP, FOC or SUBJ). Example (42) which repeats (5) illustrates that in the case of English, the specifier of IP is SUBJ and that the constituent adjoined to XP is ADJ.

(42)   Yesterday everyone smiled

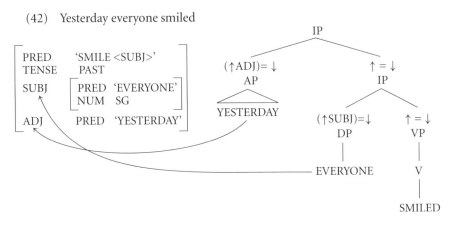

As mentioned above, in (42) the initial position is occupied by a non-subject. This marks a departure from the Unmarked Alignment Hypothesis which assumes that the three parallel levels of syntax are mapped onto each other in a strictly one-to-one manner, thus defining the first sentential position as the default for NP$_{SUBJ}$. The mapping of AP onto ADJUNCT and of DP onto SUBJ is now no longer linear. Instead, assigning the grammatical function ADJ to AP is based on XP-adjunction, and assigning SUBJ to DP now relies on identifying the specifier of functional projections in c-structure. Note that at this point in interlanguage development the rest of the canonical pattern can nevertheless be mapped one-to-one from c-structure onto the hierarchy of grammatical functions.

The assumption that in the presence of XP-adjunction the rest of the canonical pattern can nevertheless be accounted for by one-to-one mapping is supported by the developmental trajectories found in German, Swedish and English interlanguage systems. Note that in native German XP-adjunction constrains the verb into second position (cf. Berman & Frank 1996; Berman 2003). This is similar in Swedish. In English, the XP-adjunction of wh-words that refer to non-subjects constrain an auxiliary into second position (cf. Kaplan & Bresnan 1982). It is a well-attested finding from research on the acquisition of German as a second language (GSL) that learners of GSL always violate this constraint when they first acquire XP-adjunction (cf. Clahsen, Meisel & Pienemann 1983; Pienemann 1981, 1998a). The same is true for Swedish as a second language (cf. Pienemann & Håkansson 1999; Håkansson, Pienemann & Sayehli 2002). In a similar vein, ESL learners initially form WH-questions without the auxiliary in second position (cf. Pienemann 1998a) thus applying canonical

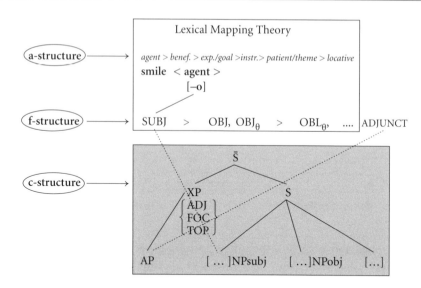

Figure 8. XP-adjunction in *interlanguage*

word order after XP-adjunction. Note that all of these interlanguage rules are obligatory.

Pienemann (1998a) showed that the operations required to produce the verb-second constraint in the above Germanic languages are based on the transfer of grammatical information in the S-procedure, and this is an operation that occurs much later in L2 development than XP-adjunction. Hence, for an extended period in L2 development learners of German, Swedish and English as L2 produce c-structure configurations that violate the verb-second constraint of the target language. Of course, in English the verb-second constraint applies to interrogative sentences with WH-words (referring to non-subjects) in XP only.

The interlanguage violation of the verb-second constraint is exemplified in (43). This example is taken from a longitudinal study of an eight-year old Italian girl acquiring German as L2 – after about one year of contact in a natural setting.

> (43) *auf ein blatt*   *wir schreiben was die sagt*
>   on a sheet (of paper) we   write   what she says
>   'we write on a sheet of paper what she says'
>   (Eva, week 56, Pienemann 1981:58)

Native German would have required the verb to be placed in second position as shown in (44).

(44) *Auf ein Blatt   schreiben wir, was sie sagt.*
      'on a sheet of paper write   we   what she says.'

As this example illustrates, at this stage the c-structure produced by L2 learners can be accounted for by two principles: (i) XP-adjunction and (ii) unmarked alignment.

In this context it is worth noting the following empirical facts that strongly support this assumption of a greatly simplified interlanguage rule system. In their survey of more than one thousand informants Pienemann and Håkansson (1999) found this interlanguage rule to be categorical. The same is true for the extensive longitudinal and cross-sectional studies by Pienemann (1981, 1998a) which did not document even a single instance of a verb-second structure at this point in development. In addition, Håkansson, Pienemann and Sayheli (2002) found that even Swedish learners of German follow this developmental trajectory, although the verb-second constraint is present in *both* languages. Pienemann, Di Biase, Kawaguchi and Håkansson (this volume) explain this on the basis of the 'developmentally moderated transfer hypothesis'. In other words, the interlanguage state described by the above set of two rules is supported by robust data.

It is important to note that the changes to the interlanguage system described above are brought about exclusively by XP-adjunction. In other words, these changes can be described solely in terms of the relationship between c-structure and f-structure. The correspondence between a-structure and f-structure remains unaffected by this.

One aspect of XP-adjunction is somewhat similar to processes found in English and German WH-questions. As mentioned above, the c-structure shown in Figure 8 is based on the following simplified rule (cf. Dalrymple 2001:406):

$$(45) \quad CP \rightarrow \begin{pmatrix} XP \\ (\uparrow FOCUS)=\downarrow \\ (\uparrow FOCUS)=(\uparrow COMP^* \ GF) \end{pmatrix} \begin{pmatrix} C' \\ \uparrow=\downarrow \end{pmatrix}$$

In order to secure completeness and coherence we must assume that the discourse function FOC is allowed to satify the unsatisfied argument function (i.e. OBJ), as illustrated in the f-structure in Figure 9 where the FOC function is linked to the OBJ function. As can be seen in Figure 9, the WH-question constituent maps onto both, FOCUS and OBJ functions.

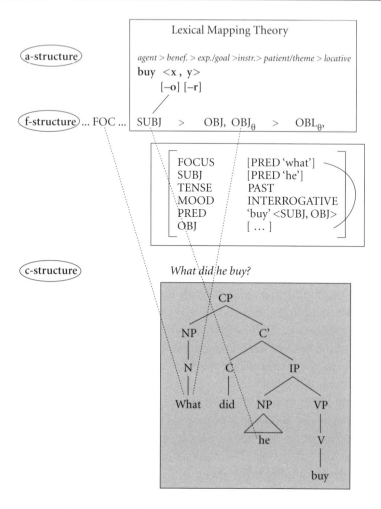

Figure 9. Mapping in WH-questions

In other words, information about the link between FOCUS and OBJ needs to be exchanged between the two grammatical functions, and this information exchange constitutes one aspect of non-linearity that is present in WH-questions. An additional aspect of non-linearity is created by the fact that the assignment of SUBJ to a constituent is no longer canonical and instead relies on identifying c-structure regularities similar to the XP-adjunction of ADJUNCTs that was discussed above.

As we have seen, WH-questions and XP-adjunction have in common that a constituent annotated for a function other than SUBJ appears in initial position. In English, the difference between the two is that XP-adjunction has no further repercussions in c-structure,[12] whereas in English WH-questions the auxiliary is constrained to appear in second position. This can be achieved by tensed auxiliaries appearing in C when inversion is involved and in I when it is not. Dalrymple (2001:64) adds that the auxiliary appears in the proper position on the basis of "[c]onstraints on the functional structure of constructions requiring or forbidding subject-auxiliary inversion ...". Bresnan (1982) and Pinker (1984) specified such constraints on the functional structure in the original version of LFG to account for the position of English auxiliaries.

Pienemann (1998a) showed that the constraints on the functional structure specified by Bresnan (1982) and Pinker (1984) require the type of transfer of grammatical information that is possible only on the basis of information transfer in the S-procedure. However, the presence of a constituent annotated for FOCUS does not require such information transfer. The non-linearity of this structure is limited to a discourse function appearing in the default position of SUBJ. We have shown for XP-adjunction that the remainder of the mapping process may follow a canonical pattern – as illustrated in Figure 7.

In other languages (e.g. in Finnish[13]) WH-question formation has no further repercussions for c-structure, not only if the WH-word is the grammatical subject, but also for other grammatical functions. Therefore these structures can be produced by learners as soon as the WH-word can occupy the first position in the sentence.

Table 1. German L2 development in c-to f-structure mapping and constraints on c-structure

Stage	Structure	Direct mapping	XP	Core argument in XP	V2	Examples from German second language acquisition
4	WH-question	−	+	+	+	Was ißt der Junge? (What eats the boy?)
3	WH-question	+	+	+	−	*Was der Junge ißt? (What the boy eats?)
2	WH-question	+	+	−	−	*Wann der Junge ißt den Apfel? (When the boy eats the apple?)
	ADV	+	+	−	−	*Jetzt der Junge ißt den Apfel. (Now the by eats the apple.)
1	SVO	+	−	−	−	Der Junge ißt den Apfel. (The boy eats the apple.)

The developmental pattern that has emerged so far for German SLA is summarised in Table 1 which lists the structures discussed above in their developmental order together with a number of key features. Table 1 shows that XP-adjunction is acquired as one of the cumulative developmental features of the interlanguage. WH-questions are first formed with non-argument functions in XP position and later with core arguments. Up to this point (i.e. stage 3) interlanguage structures can be produced with XP-adjunction and direct mapping. However, the latter must be abandoned when in WH-questions the verb appears (correctly) in second position based on (target-like) constraints on the functional structure of these constructions because in the resulting c-structure the grammatical function of a core argument in XP position can only be identified correctly if there is a link between its core function and its discourse function in f-structure – as shown in Figure 9. It is this link that creates a degree of linguistic non-linearity that places this structure at the top of the hierarchy in Table 1.

At a more general level, a number of basic principles emerge from the above overview of German L2 development. It starts out with the Unmarked Alignment Hypothesis which is characterised by complete adherence to a linear correspondence relationship in which the first and most prominent position in c-structure is occupied by the most prominent syntactic function (the SUBJECT) representing the most prominent argument available. The appearance of an AP in this position constitutes the first modification of this linear correspondence. At this point, XP-adjunction permits constituents to be marked for discourse functions while the rest of c-structure is mapped canonically onto the universal hierarchy of grammatical core functions. This state of the interlanguage, with XP adjunction and canonical mapping, is attested as the stage following the Unmarked Alignment Hypothesis in the developmental trajectories of a large number of second languages, including Japanese (see Kawaguchi, this volume), Italian (Di Biase & Kawaguchi 2002), Spanish (Taylor 2004) and Turkish (Özdemir 2004).

XP-adjunction triggers the differentiation of the syntacticised discourse functions TOPIC and FOCUS[14] from SUBJECT in the developing interlanguage system. Direct mapping at level 2 does not allow for the differentiation of SUBJECT and TOPIC. Instead, if SUBJ is present it will always occupy the first position. This close connection between SUBJECT and TOPIC is also reflected in Bresnan's typological perspective. She states that it "... comes from the universal default that optionally identifies SUBJ and TOP" (Bresnan 2001: 117). The equilibrium of the direct mapping processes is disturbed once adjuncts or wh-words appear in the default position of the constituent mapped onto

Discourse principle	c- to f- mapping	structural outcomes
Topicalisation of core arguments	TOP = OBJ	The TOP function is assigned to a *core* argument other than SUBJ.
↑	↑	↑
XP adjunction	TOP = ADJ	Initial constituent is a circumstantial adjunct or a FOCUS WH-word. TOPIC is differentiated from SUBJECT
↑	↑	↑
Canonical Order	SUBJ = default TOP	TOPIC and SUBJECT are not differentiated.

Figure 10. The Topic hypothesis

SUBJ. This was shown in Figure 8 above. When the constituent under XP is mapped onto an adjunct or a discourse function (as in WH-questions), TOPIC is differentiated from SUBJECT.

The mapping principles and their structural outcomes are summarised in Figure 10. To account for these dynamics we propose the TOPIC hypothesis in (46).

(46)   *The TOPIC hypothesis.*
   In second language acquisition learners will initially not differentiate be-
   tween SUBJ and TOP. The addition of an XP to a canonical string will trigger
   a differentiation of TOP and SUBJ which first extends to non-arguments and
   successively to non-arguments thus causing further structural consequences.

The TOPIC hypothesis intends to capture the development of syntacticised discourse functions in second language acquisition. The actual position of the adjunct (before or after the canonically mapped structure) is a c-structure issue which the learner may resolve either way, depending on the specific c-structure constraints of the L2. For instance, in Japanese, a verb-last language, only pre-verbal positions are possible (cf. Kawaguchi this volume). However, once core-arguments appear in initial position, linear correspondence is no longer viable. In other words, it is the dynamics of the develomental process starting with the use of non-subjects in focus position that leads to the eventual collapse of the learner's exclusive reliance on purely canonical association.

a- to f- structure mapping	Structural outcomes
Non-default, complex mapping.	Complex predicates e.g. Causative (in Romance languages, Japanese,[15] etc.), raising, light verbs.
↑	↑
Non-default mapping. (single clause)	Passive Exceptional verbs
↑	↑
Default mapping, i.e. Most prominent thematic role is mapped onto SUBJ.	Canonical Order

Figure 11. Lexical Mapping hypothesis

3.8 Non-linearity and Lexical Mapping Theory

In the previous section we focused on deriving predictions for developmental trajectories from the mapping of c-structure onto f-structure. In this section we will focus on the mapping of a-structure onto f-structure (i.e. on Lexical Mapping Theory) and the implications of the mapping process modelled by Lexical Mapping Theory for the processability hierarchy.

In the previous section we discussed the issue of default mapping at the initial state. We have shown that default mapping goes across the three levels of representation in LFG. This is illustrated in Figure 7 above which is based on the Unmarked Alignment Hypothesis. This hypothesis postulates that in second language acquisition learners will initially organise syntax by mapping the most prominent semantic role available onto the subject (i.e. the most prominent grammatical role). In other words, the Unmarked Alignment Hypothesis affects both types of mapping processes, including a- to f-structure mapping and it implies that learners will initially be constrained to follow the default canonical relationship between a-structure and f-structure. Any future deviation from the default has to rely on additional mapping principles or on exceptional lexical entries, both of which create linguistic non-linearity.

It follows from the Unmarked Alignment Hypothesis that L2 learners will not have access L2-specific a-structures for predicates. In other words, in cases where L1 and L2 predicates have different a-structures we can predict that L2 learners will initially have to map arguments canonically onto core grammatical functions following the LMT hierarchy. This is illustrated in (47), an example taken from Kawguchi's L2 Japanese database. In (47) an L2 learner canonically maps the participants in the event, where his lexical learning is incomplete and generates the wrong a-structure for the predicate.

(47) *okaasan-wa kodomo-o ryoorisimasu*
      mother-NOM child-ACC cook-PRES.POL
      Literally: 'Mother cooks the child'
      (Intended. 'Mother cooks [something] for the child')

The Japanese L2 learner attempts to designate two participants in the 'cooking' event: 'agent' and 'beneficiary'. So he creates an a-structure as in (48) where the initial argument is canonically mapped onto SUBJ and the second argument onto OBJ.

(48) *ryoorisuru* 'cook' < agent beneficiary >   [a-structure]
                      | |
                   SUBJ OBJ   [f-structure]
                     | |
                  Okaasan kodomo [c-structure]
                  'mother' 'child'

However, the Japanese verb *ryoorisuru* ('to cook') designates 'agent' and 'patient' (not 'beneficiary'). In fact, the beneficiary role would need to be expressed as OBJ$_\theta$ requiring a dative case marker, and in addition the verb would require a benefactive auxiliary.[16] This construction is acquired much later.

    In a similar way, the Unmarked Alignment Hypothesis also implies a developmental prediction for passives, another area that affects the relationship between a-structure and f-structure. As we pointed out in Section 3.3 above, in the passive the relationship between argument roles and syntactic functions may be altered as can be seen in the suppression of argument roles and altered function-assignment. In Sections 3.3. we described these alterations for passives, and they are illustrated in examples (49)–(52) which are repeated from Section 3.3.

(49) Peter sees a dog.

(50) see   <experiencer, theme>
                | |
          SUBJ   OBJ

(51) A dog is seen by Peter.

(52)   seen   <experiencer, theme>
                      | |
              Ø   SUBJ   (ADJ)

As we pointed out in Section 3.3, sentences (49) and (51) describe the same eventuality involving two participants. The difference between the two is that in (51) the constituent *a dog* that is OBJ in (49) is promoted to SUBJ, and the constituent *Peter* that is SUBJ in (49) is defocused and realised as ADJ.

These alterations of the relationship between argument roles and syntactic functions constitute a deviation from default canonical mapping. Kawaguchi (this volume) argues that in order for non-canonical mapping to be possible, the functional destination of an NP can be established only by assembling information about the constituents and by assembling them at the S-node. "The identification of the phrases' grammatical functions and their functional assignments in passive, causative and benefactive constructions requires the learner to unify information from different sources: the V and the N phrases. This calls for an interphrasal process." (Kawaguchi this volume). In other words, Kawaguchi not only shows that in Japanese the passive is based on a non-canonical relationship between a-structure and f-structure, but that this construction requires the S-procedure. This amounts to an exact location of this construction and its associated LMT processes within the processability hierarchy.

Considering the English passive (and that of related languages) from the perspective of the learner, it is important to note that stative passives ('the fence is painted', 'the city is destroyed' etc.) and predicative adjectives ('he is tall') have two things in common: (1) aspects of their morphology (i.e. they 'look' similar to learners) and (2) the absence of a 'suppressed thematic role' (Bresnan 2001:310). Given that it is the suppression of the agent role that creates non-linear a- to f-structure mapping, the absence of suppression mechanisms allows for canonical mapping in predicative adjectives and stative passives in interlanguage English. This implies that the corresponding syntactic structures conform to the Unmarked Alignment Hypothesis. In other words, these (stative) passive constructions yield canonical order (i.e. SV(X)) at *c-structure level*. This makes them similar to some English adjectival constructions as in (53a–b). Given the canonical mapping process[17] inherent in structures such as (53a–b), the Unmarked Alignment Hypothesis predicts that learners of English as a second language may be able to produce these structures at an early stage. This prediction is borne out by an analysis of our ESL database which shows that passive construction as in (53c) are hardly ever produced by low-stage ESL learners, whereas ill-formed sentences as in (54a–b) do appear early and persist at later stages.

(53)   a.   *I am bored.*
       b.   *I am confused.*
       c.   *Tom was confused by Mary.*

(54)   a.   **I am very confusing* (intended: *I am very confused.*)
       b.   **I always confuse* (intended: *I am always confused.*)

We believe that this observation is due to the lexical learning process required for the target-like lexical entries of the predicates. The lexical entry for the adjectival predicate *confusing*, for instance, requires a single <theme> argument. The learner who produced (54a) intended to express an <experiencer> role. However, in English this feature appears in the lexical entry of the adjectival predicate *confused* as shown in (55a–b).

Hence, there is a mismatch between the argument required by the predicate form and the role assigned to the SUBJ. It is the lexical entry (category and features) of the form which specifies a-structure and its mapping as exemplified in (55a–d).

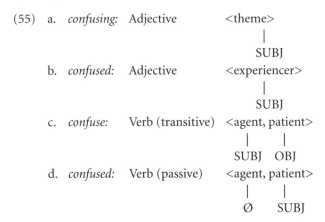

(55)   a.   *confusing:*   Adjective   <theme>
                                                  |
                                                 SUBJ
       b.   *confused:*   Adjective   <experiencer>
                                                  |
                                                 SUBJ
       c.   *confuse:*   Verb (transitive)   <agent, patient>
                                                  | |
                                                 SUBJ   OBJ
       d.   *confused:*   Verb (passive)   <agent, patient>
                                                  | |
                                                  Ø   SUBJ

In other words, developmental errors shown in (54a–b) which are common among English L2 learners, indicate that the learner has not annotated the specific lexical entry appropriately or that he or she fails to match the correct function due to the fact that the S-procedure has not been acquired.

A further area that affects the relationship between a-structure and f-structure are causative constructions. Examples (56) and (57) exemplify intransitive and transitive causatives in Catalan, a Romance language (following Alsina 1997:216)

(56) Intransitive causative
L'elefant   fa   riure les hienes.
the elephant makes laugh the hyenas
'The elephant makes the hyenas laugh'

(57) Transitive causative
Els pagesos fan   escriure un poema al   follet.
the farmers make write   a   poem   to-the elf
'The farmers are making the elf write a poem'

According to Alsina (1996:193), "… causative constructions in Romance have one single complex a-structure in which the causative verb provides the outer a-structure and the infinitive verb provides the embedded a-structure…". In other words, causatives involve an embedded sub-event at a-structure level but this is realised as a single clause in f-structure.

Alsina assumes that "the causative verb and the base verb undergo predicate composition yielding one, single, complex, a-structure" (1996:186). The a-structure and associated syntactic functions of (56) and (57) are illustrated below in (58) and (59).

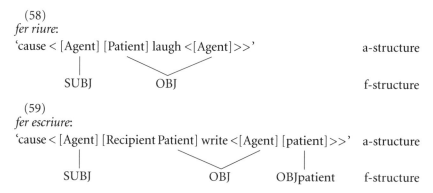

(58)
fer riure:
'cause < [Agent] [Patient] laugh <[Agent] >>'   a-structure

          | \   /
          SUBJ   OBJ   f-structure

(59)
fer escriure:
'cause < [Agent] [Recipient Patient] write <[Agent] [patient] >>'   a-structure

          | \   / |
          SUBJ   OBJ   OBJpatient   f-structure

Thus two thematic roles are fused into one in f-structure. As a result, the causative verb and the base verb act as one single predicate. Hence this mapping process deviates from the default canonical mapping specified in the Unmarked Alignment Hypothesis because two thematic roles are fused in the Event and Subevent. Causatives will therefore appear after canonical mapping due to the fusion of thematic roles.

In summary, the TOP hypothesis and the LMT hypothesis contribute to the characterisation of the higher stages of a learner's development. Structural choices increase hand in hand with a wider and more complex lexical and

functional learning which will ensure greater expressivity and a wider range
of pragmatic choices for the learner.

4. Conclusion

In this chapter we explored principles of processability that extend beyond
the transfer of grammatical information modelled through feature unification.
These new principles contribute to a formal account of levels of processability
utilising aspects of the extended version of LFG. We showed that correspondence mechanisms make predictions for developmental trajectories of aspects
of interlanguage syntax, starting with the Unmarked Alignment Hypothesis.

The Topic Hypothesis constitutes a prediction on how c- to f-structure
mapping develops from rigorously constrained canonical mapping to more
target-like principles that allow for a wider range of syntactic variability and
expressiveness.

The Lexical Mapping Hypothesis is the counterpart to the Topic Hypothesis, and it allows for predictions on how lexical mapping develops from the
constraints of the Unmarked Alignment Hypothesis to more target-like linguistic variability and expressiveness facilitated by the non-canonical mapping
principles of the target language.

We have shown that the two key hypotheses constrain developmental trajectories, and we have identified a number of syntactic structures within this
developmental paradigm, including XP-adjunction in a number of L2s, Ger-

Discourse principle	c- to f- mapping	structural outcomes
Topicalisation of core arguments	TOP = OBJ	The TOP function is assigned to a *core* argument other than SUBJ.
↑	↑	↑
XP adjunction	TOP = ADJ	Initial constituent is a circumstantial adjunct or a FOCUS WH-word. TOPIC is differentiated from SUBJECT
↑	↑	↑
Canonical Order	SUBJ = TOP	TOPIC and SUBJECT are not differentiated.

Figure 10. The Topic hypothesis

a- to f- structure mapping	Structural outcomes
Non-default, complex mapping.	Complex predicates e.g. Causative (in Romance languages,[15] Japanese, etc.), raising, light verbs.
↑	↑
Non-default mapping. (single clause)	Passive Exceptional verbs
↑	↑
Default mapping, ie. Most prominent thematic role is mapped onto SUBJ.	Canonical Order

Figure 11. Lexical Mapping hypothesis

man and English wh-questions, passive constructions, causative constructions and exceptional verbs. We also noted for a number of these structures how they are related to the original PT hierarchy that is based on information transfer. This is evident not only for canonical word order (category procedure) and XP-adjunction (NP-procedure), but also for Japanese passives which Kawaguchi argued require the S-procedure.

The objective of this paper was to sketch out this extended developmental paradigm. It will be the objective of future research to apply it systematically to specific target languages and to relate the resulting developmental trajectories to the original information-based PT hierarchy.

Notes

1. In LFG a-structure represents information about the arguments selected by a predicate. F-structure represents grammatical information that is invariant across languages. In contrast, constituent structure is language-specific.

2. Hence the title of the publication.

3. Franck et al. (2002: 376) characterise IPG (Incremental Procedural Grammar, Kempen & Hoenkamp 1987) and IPF (Incremental Parallel Formulator, De Smedt 1990) as follows:

> [IPG and IPF]... conceive syntactic construction as a process of assembling segments into a tree-like architecture using a single combinatorial operation: unification. In IPF, each segment is composed of two nodes, representing syntactic categories, related by an arc, representing the syntactic function that relates the nodes (e.g., S-subject-HN, HN-head-N). Unification of the different segments would result in the formation of a syntactic structure for the sentence. Unification in this model is conceived as a process that merges features from the different seg-

ments, allowing, therefore, the computation of long-distance dependencies such as agreement ... Hence, and importantly, in a model such as IPF, agreement is the result of assembling the different segments into a hierarchical structure.

4. Refer also to Note 7.

5. In particular 'completeness', 'coherence' and 'semantic expressivity'.

6. A mix of endocentric and lexocentric means within the one language can be illustrated with Figure 1 where functional information regarding the agent (e.g. the fact that *Peter* is the SUBJ) is represented, in English, both in the syntactic pre-verbal position of the subject constituent and in the morphology of the verb *sees* which also represents the singular, third person features of the subject.

7. The following structural outcomes are also possible, e.g.:

   it is Peter who sees a dog.
   it is a dog which is seen by Peter.

8. These correspondence mechanisms explain two further issues, namely (1) how in pro-drop languages such as Italian and Spanish the subject is recovered from the verb (2) how word order alternatives to the pragmatically neutral SVO (e.g. orders with with postverbal subjects) can occur in those languages without assuming feature copying. Both the recovery of the subject and word order alternations can be accounted for by assuming a merging mechanism at the mother node that ensures the compatibility of the feature structure of the dependencies.

9. Slobin's (1985) explanatory approach to direct mapping is data-driven. Slobin collected and analysed large amounts of L1 acquisition data across different languages and found that the majority of his data on early L1 learner language can be accounted for by a 'pro-totypical scene' which is a highly transitive activity that is mapped onto canonical sentence schemata. In this process the agent-role is linked to SUBJ, and the patient-role linked to OBJ. Slobin claims that the child's association of the prototypical scene with the canonical sentence schema is driven by the frequency and saliency of the linguistic input.

10. The term 'Unmarked Alignment Hypothesis' is inspired by OT-LFG research (e.g. Bresnan 2000; Sells 1999, 2001; Lee 2001). This connection between PT and OT-LFG has been pointed out to us by Peter Sells.

11. Some aspects of these developmental dynamics can be modelled by the notion of 'generative entrenchment' (Wimsatt 1986) as shown by Pienemann (1998a).

12. This is not the case in German which requires the inflected verb to appear in second position (cf. Berman & Frank 1996).

13. Cf. Karlson (1987)

14. Bresnan and Mchombo (1987:757–758) adopt three principles relating to the role of TOP and FOC functions in the grammars of natural language. 1. The relativised constituent or relative pronoun in relative clauses universally bears the TOP function. 2. The interrogative pronoun or questioned constituent universally bears the FOC function and 3. The same constituent cannot be both focus and topic of the same level of functional clause structure.

15. The Japanese benefactive construction process is exemplified below:

Okaasan-wa   kodomi-ni   susi-o   ryoorisi-te   agemasu
mother-TOP   child-DAT   sushi-ACC   cook-COMP   BENE-POL
'Mother cook sushi for the child'

16. The existing single argument maps onto SUBJ.

17. See example (56) & (57).

References

Alsina, A. (1996). *The Role of Argument Structure in Grammar.* Stanford, CA: CSLI.

Alsina, A. (1997). Causatives in Bantu and Romance. In A. Alsina, J. Bresnan, & P. Sells (Eds.), *Complex Predicates* (pp. 203–246). Stanford, CA: CSLI.

Bates, E. & MacWhinney, B. (1981). Second-language acquisition from a functionalist perspective: Pragmatic, semantic, and perceptual strategies. In H. Winity (Ed.), *Native Language and Foreign Language Acquisition* [Annals of the New York Academy of Sciences 379] (pp. 190–214). New York, NY: Academy of Sciences.

Bates, E. & MacWhinney, B. (1982). Functionalist approaches to grammar. In E. Wanner & L. R. Gleitman (Eds.), *Language Acquisition: The state of the art* (pp. 173–218). Cambridge: Cambridge University Press.

Bates, E. & MacWhinney, B. (1987). Competition, variation and language learning. In B. MacWhinney (Ed.), *Mechanisms of Language Acquisition* (pp. 157–193). Hillsdale, NJ: Lawrence Erlbaum.

Berman, J. (2003). *Clausal Syntax of German.* Stanford: CSLI.

Berman, J. & Frank, A. (1996). *Deutsche und französische Syntax im Formalismus der LFG.* Tübingen: Niemeyer.

Bever, T. G. (1970). The cognitive basis for linguistic structures. In J. R. Hayes (Ed.), *Cognition and the Development of Language.* New York, NY: Wiley.

Bloom, P. (1994). Recent controversies in the study of language acquisition. In M. A. Gernsbacher (Ed.), *Handbook of Psycholinguistics* (pp. 741–779). San Diego, CA: Academic Press.

Bock, J. K. & Cutting, J. C. (1992). Regulating mental energy: Performance units in language production. *Journal of Memory and Language, 31,* 99–127.

Bock, K. & Miller, C. A. (1991). Broken agreement. *Cognitive Psychology, 23,* 45–93.

Bresnan, J. (2000). Optimal syntax. In J. Dekkers, F. van der Leeuw, & J. van der Weijer (Eds.), *Optimality Theory: Phonology, syntax and acquisition* (pp. 334–385). Oxford: Oxford University Press.

Bresnan, J. (2001). *Lexical-Functional Syntax.* Malden, MA: Blackwell.

Bresnan, J. & Kanerva, J. M. (1989). Locative inversion in Chichewa: A case study of factorization in grammar. *Linguistic Inquiry, 20*(1), 1–50.

Bresnan, J. & Mchombo, S. (1987). Topic, pronoun, and agreement in Chichewa. *Language, 63,* 741–782.

Bresnan, J. (Ed.). (1982). *The Mental Representation of Grammatical Relations.* Cambridge, MA: The MIT Press.

Brown, R. (1973). *A First Language. The early stages.* Cambridge, MA: Harvard University Press.

Clahsen, H. (1990). The comparative study of first and second language development. *Studies in Second Language Acquisition, 12,* 135–153.

Clahsen, H. (1992). Learnability theory and the problem of development in language acquisition. In J. Weissenborn, H. Goodluck, & T. Roeper (Eds.), *Theoretical Issues in Language Acquisition: Continuity and change* (pp. 53–76). Hillsdale, NJ: Lawrence Erlbaum.

Clahsen, H., Meisel, J., & Pienemann, M. (1983). *Deutsch als Zweitsprache. Der Spracherwerb ausländischer Arbeiter.* Tübingen: Narr.

Dalrymple, M. (2001). *Syntax and Semantics. Lexical Functional Grammar.* Vol. 34. San Diego, CA: Academic Press.

De Smedt, K. J. (1990). IPF: An incremental parallel formulator. In R. Dale, C. Mellish, & M. Zock (Eds.), *Current Research in Natural Language Generation* (pp. 167–192). San Diego, CA: Academic Press.

de Villiers, J. G. & de Villiers, P. A. (1973). A cross-sectional study of the acquisition of grammatical morphemes. *Journal of Psycholinguistic Research, 2,* 267–278.

Di Biase, B. & Kawaguchi, S. (2002). Exploring the typological plausibility of Processability Theory: Language development in Italian second language and Japanese second language. *Second Language Research, 18*(3), 272–300.

Fillmore, C. J. (1968). The case for case. In E. Bach & R. T. Harms, *Universals in Linguistic Theory* (pp. 1–210). New York, NY: Holt, Renehart, and Winston.

Foley, W. & Van Valin, R. (1984). *Functional Syntax and Universal Grammar.* Cambridge: CUP.

Franck, J., Vigliocco, G., & Nicol, J. (2002). Subject-verb agreement errors in French and English: The role of syntactic hierarchy. *Language and Cognitive Processes, 17,* 371–404.

Givón, T. (1984). *Syntax: A functional-typological introduction.* Amsterdam: John Benjamins.

Håkansson, G., Pienemann, M., & Sayehli, S. (2002). Transfer and typological proximity in the context of L2 processing. *Second Language Research, 18,* 250–273.

Hirsh-Pasek, K., Golinkoff, R., Fletcher, A., DeGaspe Beaubien, F., & Cauley, K. (1985). In the beginning: One word speakers comprehend word order. Paper presented at *Boston University Conference on Language Development,* Boston.

Hopper, J. P. & Thompson, S. A. (1980). Transitivity in grammar and discourse. *Language, 56,* 251–299.

Jackendoff, R. S. (1972). *Semantic Interpretation in Generative Grammar.* Cambridge, MA: The MIT Press.

Jackendoff, R. S. (1977). *X-bar Syntax: A study of phrase structure.* Cambridge, MA: the MIT Press.

Kaplan, R. & Bresnan, J. (1982). Lexical-functional grammar: A formal system for grammatical representation. In J. Bresnan (Ed.), *The Mental Representation of Grammatical Relations* (pp. 173–281). Cambridge, MA: The MIT Press.

Karlson, F. (1987). *Finnish Grammar.* Helsinki: Söderström.

Keenan, E. O. (1976). Toward a universal definition of 'subject'. In C. Li (Ed.), *Subject and Topic.* San Diego, CA: Academic Press.

Keenan, E. O. & Comrie, B. (1977). Noun phrase accessability and Universal Grammar. *Linguistic Inquiry, 8*, 63–99.

Kempen (1998). Comparing and explaining the trajectories of first and second language acquisition: In search of the right mix of psychological and linguistic factors. *Bilingualism: Language and Cognition, 1*(1), 29–30.

Kempen, G. & Hoenkamp, E. (1987). An incremental procedural grammar for sentence formulation. *Cognitive Science, 11*, 201–258.

Kostic, A. & Katz, L. (1987). Processing differences between nouns, adjectives, and verbs. *Psychological Research, 49*, 229–236.

Lambrecht, K. (1994). *Information Structure and Sentence Form: Topic, focus and the mental representation of discourse referents.* Cambridge: CUP.

Lee, Hanjung (2001). Markedness and word order freezing. In In P. Sells (Ed.), *Formal and Empirical Issues in Optimality Theoretic Syntax* (pp. 63–127). Stanford, CA: CSLI.

Levelt, W. J. M. (1981). The speaker's linearization problem. *Philosophical Transactions* B295, 305–315. London: Royal Society.

Levelt, W. J. M. (1989). *Speaking. From intention to articulation.* Cambridge, MA: The MIT Press.

Levelt, W. J. M, Roelofs, A., & Meyer, A. S. (1999). Lexical access in speech production. *Behavioral and Brain Sciences, 22*, 1–75.

Marantz, A. (1982). On the acquisition of grammatical relations. *Linguistische Berichte: Linguistik als Kognitive Wissenschaft, 80*(82), 32–69.

Newport, E. L. & Meier, R. P. (1985). The acquisition of American Sign Language. In D. I. Slobin (Ed.), *The Crosslinguistic Study of Language Acquisition. The data*, Vol. 1. Hillsdale, NJ: Lawrence Erlbaum.

Otsu, Y. (2000). Scrambling, indirect passive and wanna construction. *Behavior and Brain Sciences, 23*, 45–46.

Özdemir, B. (2004). Language development in Turkish-German bilingual children and implications for English as a third language. MA thesis, University of Paderborn.

Perlmutter, D. (1980). Relational grammar. In E. Moravcsik & J. Wirth (Ed.), *Syntax and Semantics. Current approaches to syntax*, Vol. 13. New York, NY: Academic Press.

Pickering, M. J., Branigan, H. P., & McLean, J. F. (2002). Constituent structure is formulated in one stage. *Journal of Memory and Language, 46*, 586–605.

Pienemann, M. (1981). *Der Zweitspracherwerb ausländischer Arbeiterkinder.* Bonn: Bouvier.

Pienemann, M. (1998a). *Language Processing and Second Language Development. Processability theory.* Amsterdam: John Benjamins.

Pienemann, M. (1998b). Developmental dynamics in L1 and L2 acquisition: Processability theory and generative entrenchment. *Bilingualism: Language and Cognition, 1*, 1–20.

Pienemann, M. & Håkansson, G. (1999). A unified approach towards the development of Swedish as L2: A processability account. *Studies in Second Language Acquisition, 21*, 383–420. Cambridge: CUP.

Pinker, S. (1984). *Language Learnability and Language Development.* Cambridge, MA: Harvard University Press.

Pinker, S. (1989). Language acquisition. In D. N. Osherson & H. Lasnik (Eds.), *An Invitation to Cognitive Science. Language*, Vol. 1. Cambridge, MA: The MIT Press.

Prince, A. S. & Smolensky, P. (1993). *Optimality Theory: Constraint interaction in generative grammar* [Technical Report RuCCS Technical Report #2]. Piscataway, NJ: Center for Cognitive Science, Rutgers University.

Sasaki, Y. (1998). Processing and learning of Japanese double-object active and causative sentences: An error-feedback paradigm. *Journal of Psycholinguistic Research, 27*(4), 453–479.

Schwarze, C. (2002). Representation and variation: On the development of Romance auxiliary syntax. In M. Butt & T. Holloway King (Eds.), *Time over Matter: Diachronic perspectives in morphosyntax.* Stanford, CA: CSLI.

Sells, P. (1999). Constituent ordering as alignment. In S. Kuno et al. (Eds.), *Harvard Studies in Korean Linguistics*, VIII (pp. 546–560). Seoul: Hanshin. Online: http://www-csli.stanford.edu/~sells.

Sells, P. (Ed.) (2001). *Formal and Empirical Issues in Optimality Theoretic Syntax.* Stanford, CA: CSLI Publications.

Slobin, D. I. (1982). Universal and particular in the acquisition of language. In E. Wanner & L. Gleitman (Eds.), *Language Acquisition. The state of the art* (pp. 128–172). Cambridge: Cambridge University Press.

Slobin, D. I. (1985a). Cross-linguistic evidence for the language-making capacity. In D. Slobin (Ed.), *The Cross-linguistic Study of Language Acquisition*, Vol. 2 (pp. 1157–1256). Hillsdale, NJ: Lawrence Erlbaum.

Slobin, D. I. (1985b). *The Crosslinguistic Study of Language Acquisition.* Vols. 1&2. Hillsdale, NJ: Lawrence Erlbaum.

Strohner, H. & Nelson, K. E. (1974). The young child's development of sentence comprehension: Influence of event probability, non-verbal context, syntactic form, and strategies. *Child Development, 45*, 567–576.

Taylor, R. (2004). Spanish L2 from a processability perspective: Two developmental case studies. BA (Honours) Dissertation, University of Western Sydney.

Van Valin, R. D. & LaPolla, R. J. (1997). *Syntax: Structure, meaning and function.* Cambridge: Cambridge University Press.

Vigliocco, G., Butterworth, B., & Semenza, C. (1995). Constructing subject-verb agreement in speech: The role of semantic and morphological factors. *Journal of Memory and Language, 34*, 186–215.

Vigliocco, G., Butterworth, B., & Garrett, M. F. (1996). Subject-verb agreement in Spanish and English: Differences in the role of conceptual constraints. *Cognition, 61*, 261–298.

Vigliocco. G., Hartsuiker, R. J., Jarema, G., & Kolk, H. H. J. (1996). One or more labels on the bottels? Notional concord in Dutch and French. *Language and Cognitive Processes, 11*(4), 407–442.

Vigliocco, G. & Nicol, J. (1998). Separating hierarchical relations and word order in language production: Is proximity concord syntactic or linear? *Cognition, 68*, B13–B29.

Weyerts, H., Penke, M., Münte, T. F., Heinze, H.-J., & Clahsen, H. (2002). Word order in sentence processing: An experimental study of verb placement in German. *Journal of Psycholinguistic Research, 31*(3), 211–268.

Wimsatt, W. C. (1986). Developmental constraints, generative entrenchment and the innate-acquired distinction. In W. Bechtel (Ed.), *Integrating Scientific Disciplines* (pp. 185–208). Dordrecht: Martinus Nijhoff.

CHAPTER 8

Argument structure and syntactic development in Japanese as a second language*

Satomi Kawaguchi

University of Western Sydney

This chapter presents an application of Processability Theory (PT) (Pienemann 1998 and further developments (Pienemann, Di Biase & Kawaguchi, in this volume)) as a theoretical framework to the acquisition of Japanese L2 morphosyntax. A range of Japanese L2 morphosyntactic structures are hypothesised at given PT developmental stages with their grammatical formalisation based on Lexical Functional Grammar (LFG). In order to test the hypothesised PT stages in Japanese, speech data were collected from two concurrent longitudinal studies of English L1 learners of Japanese over periods of two and three years respectively. Then distributional analyses were conducted for the purpose of examining the developmental sequences of syntactic structures. Results were checked against the hypothesised Japanese L2 PT stages. These results suggest that the hypothesised stages are implicational, indicating that the hypothesis is supported.

1. Introduction

This chapter aims to apply Processability Theory (PT) to Japanese and to identify developmental stages of Japanese L2 syntax. The acquisitional stages of Japanese L2 (verbal) morphology have already been developed (Di Biase & Kawaguchi 2002), however the acquisitional stages for Japanese L2 syntax have not been addressed so far. Japanese has an important role to play in PT for testing and further developing its theory because of its typological characteristics. Japanese is a typologically 'head-last' language and typically belongs to SOV languages. PT has been applied and its universal nature tested against various languages, as can be seen in other chapters in this book. However, among these languages, Japanese is the only language which exhibits the typological feature of 'head-last' as well as SOV word order.[1] Therefore, languages such as Japanese offer initial testing ground for the theory.

Establishing a unified account of developmental sequences is important not only in the field of general second language acquisition (SLA) but also in the field of acquisition of Japanese as a second language (JSL). In the last decade, many studies on JSL focused on the issue of developmental sequences (see Yoshioka 1999; and Nagatomo 2002 for reviews of JSL). The nature of these studies is mostly inductive: inducing the developmental sequence of a particular linguistic aspect from detailed analysis and description of the data and providing possible explanations of the perceived acquisitional sequence. For example, Nagatomo (1991) proposed a Systematic Variation Model out of his research on the acquisition of Japanese particles -ga (NOM(inative)) and -wa (Topic). However, it is rare to reach the point of establishing a model from 'inductive' studies (Nagatomo 2002). This is because most 'inductive' studies merely describe the data and can provide plausible explanations for a limited range of acquisitional phenomena; hence, these studies provide evidence supporting a developmental path for acquiring particular syntactic/morphological structures. However, they seem to lack generalisability and predictability, and as a result it is difficult to apply their explanations to other structures or across languages and predict acquisitional sequences of syntactic/morphological phenomena using an 'inductive' approach. Most of the studies focused on the acquisition of a particular grammatical phenomenon, and therefore it is hard to grasp the whole picture of acquisition of JSL, as pointed out by Mine (2002). On the other hand, one of the strong points of PT is its extendability and predictive power. My research, based on PT, attempts to bridge this gap in the acquisition of JSL.

This chapter is organised as follows. In Section 2 I present a short literature review of JSL studies based on Pienemann's theory. Then, there is a brief sketch of Japanese typological characteristics in Section 3. This is followed in Section 4 by the presentation of hypothesised Japanese L2 stages based on PT. In this section I will provide grammatical formalisation within the framework of Lexical Functional Grammar (LFG). After the hypotheses, the empirical studies including its methodological design and results in conjunction with the hypotheses are presented in Section 5. The discussion of the result is presented in Section 6.

2.   Brief review of the application of PT to Japanese L2

The first attempt to apply Pienemann's theory to Japanese L2 was Doi and Yoshioka's (1987, 1990) study. Strictly speaking, Doi and Yoshioka's study was based on PT's predecessor, the Pienemann-Johnston Model (P-J Model henceforth) (Pienemann & Johnston 1987), which was an extension of the processing strategies approach (cf. Clahsen 1984) to morphosyntax. In the development of PT after the P-J Model, the concept of strategies was dismissed and instead a comprehensive speech model of language (cf. Levelt 1989) as well as a psychologically plausible theory of grammar (i.e. LFG) was incorporated.

Doi and Yoshioka looked at three Japanese nominal particles: the topic-marking particle -*wa* and the case-marking particles -*ga* (NOM) and -*o* (ACC). They hypothesised an acquisitional sequence of these particles as follows: the topic-marking particle -*wa* is acquired at Stage 3 (in the P-J Model) while the NOM and ACC case-marking particles -*ga* and -*o* are acquired at Stage 5 (in the P-J Model). The reason for their hypothesis is as follows. As any noun phrase (NP) can be topicalised, the learner does not need to know the grammatical function of the NP which is to be topicalised. This suggests that the topicalisation of NP in Japanese involves neither grammatical knowledge of the lexical category nor internal structure of the clause. NOM and ACC marking, on the other hand, requires an understanding of the grammatical relation between the NP and the predicate in a sentence (Doi & Yoshioka 1987: 23–31).

24 English L1-Japanese L2 students at University of Hawaii, Manoa participated in their study, and the accuracy rates of -*wa* (Topic) (hypothesised at Stage 3), -*o* (OBJ), -*ga* (NOM$_{OBJ}$) and -*ga* (NOM$_{SUBJ}$) (both hypothesised at Stage 5) in the learners' speech were calculated. The result supported their hypothesis: The accuracy rate for -*wa* was higher than for -*o* and -*ga*. The result also suggested that those learners who could use -*wa* correctly could use -*o* and -*ga* correctly as well, but not vice versa. Further, they found that there is an implicational relation within Stage 5: -*o* is acquired before -*ga* and within -*ga*, while -*ga* (NOM$_{OBJ}$) is acquired before -*ga* (NOM$_{SUBJ}$).

Their study contributed to the identification of the processing mechanism of three nominal particles in Japanese and proved the validity of their hypothesised acquisitional sequence empirically. However, there are some shortcomings of this study. First, it looked at the accuracy rate of the usage of three particles. Morpheme studies (Dulay & Burt 1973, 1974; Dulay, Burt & Krashen 1982) were severely criticised because one cannot equate accuracy and acquisition: the rank order of accuracy is the order of difficulty but does not necessarily correspond to the developmental sequences (Pienemann 1998). The same criticism applies to Doi and Yoshioka. Further, this study fails to distinguish the case where NP_{SUBJ} is treated as TOP on one hand, and where the NP of other grammatical functions (i.e. ADJUNCT, OBJ etc.) is topicalised on the other hand. In LFG, SUBJ is universally a default topic, and therefore there may be some differences in acquisition of the structures between TOP functions as SUBJ and as other grammatical functions. I will take up this issue later.

Huter's (1997) three-year longitudinal studies also used the P-J Model (Pienemann & Johnston 1987) and its further development (Pienemann, Johnston & Brindley 1988) as its point of reference. Huter investigated her corpus data and described five university students' developmental sequence of Japanese L2. From the distributional analysis she found several phases which form an implicational relationship in Japanese L2, as follows:

phase 1: Basic sentence structures, basic categories
phase 2: Extension of noun phrase, verb phrase, sentence
phase 3: Change of some category features and thereby establishment of new subcategories (which are filled with new lexical items)
phase 4: Sentence level of clause and syntactic category of lexical items can be changed (depending on syntactic environment and intended meaning) (Huter 1997:11).

Huter concluded that Pienemann's definition of stages can explain the identified acquisitional sequence of sentence structure in Japanese L2, but that "the rules of information processing were not, however, applicable to noun phrases and their development", because "the noun phrase development is dictated by the characteristics inherent to the system of Japanese noun phrases" (Huter 1997:36).

Although Huter's study provides a detailed description of the corpus data, there is an insufficient theoretical base to support her argument. This is mainly because of the unclear status of grammar in her explanation which is crucial for applying it to a new language. In addition, Huter uses a 'strategies approach' where transformation (i.e. movement of elements) is the explanation for the developmental sequences she found in Japanese L2. However, as I previously mentioned, PT dropped the strategies approach, and therefore Huter's explanation is not compatible with PT.

Based on an early application of PT to Japanese by Pienemann (1998:207–214), Kawaguchi (2000) was the first to apply PT formally to Japanese L2. I attempted to establish stages of acquisition of Japanese L2, particularly verbal morphology. I hypothesised that the basic form of verbs (i.e. present-tensed polite form) is acquired as unanalysed formulae at Stage 1. Then verbal ending alternation, such as PAST and NEGATIVE, of the same verbal stem becomes possible at Stage 2 (lexical morphology). At Stage 3, the various combinations of verbal stem-affix(es) become possible since the learner acquires information exchange skills within verb phrases, i.e. the stem and the affix in this case (Phrasal morphology), at this stage. Production of the adverbial clause is possible in Japanese L2 learning at Stage 4 (Inter-phrasal morphology).

Although my hypothesis was upheld in the empirical studies (both longitudinal and cross-sectional), the explanation of the grammatical description at each stage was rather vague and some parts of my explanation were not compatible with LFG, which is a key module in PT. For example, LFG rejects transformational accounts of grammar such as constituent movement because they are psychologically implausible (Bresnan 2001; Sells 1995), but my assumption of agglutinating morphology was based on the successive movement of head in VP (i.e. the verbal auxiliary chose the inflectional category of the stem). Also, I failed to factor in the phonological and morphological processes involved in word formation in learning Japanese L2. The learner will need to acquire these stem-suffix combinations with their morphophonemic variation, eg. where the verb stem is consonantal, however this is an additional learning task. In fact the PT hierarchy is based on information exchange to the exclusion of phonological, derivational or specific morphophonological processes. For instance, the phonology of Japanese verbal affix varies according to whether the stem ends in a consonant or a vowel. These domains lie outside the scope of PT.

These shortcomings were rectified by Di Biase and Kawaguchi (2002), who tested the plausibility of PT with two typologically distant languages, Japanese and Italian. One of the study's contributions is the grammatical formalisation, modelled after LFG, of each stage of morphosyntactic structure in Japanese L2 (and also in Italian L2). Following Bresnan and Mchombo (1995) and Sells (1995, 1999a, b), we assumed that agglutinating morphology is controlled by principles different from syntactic principles, hence we excluded the development of agglutinating morphology from the scope. The acquisition of agglutinating phenomena has to be explained with other modules. The stages we hypothesised in Japanese L2 are:

(Stage 2: Category procedure) verbal inflection and canonical order
(Stage 3: Phrasal procedure) V-*te* V (V-complimentiser V)
(Stage 4: S-procedure) non-canonical argument structure such as passive, causative and benefactive constructions.

Empirical data supported the hypothesis and showed that PT is a typologically plausible SLA theory.

All the studies reviewed above looked at the acquisitional sequence found in adult university-level learners of Japanese L2. However, recent studies connected to PT expand its scope. For example, Itani-Adams's (2003) study on Japanese – English bilingual first language acquisition utilises Pienemann's (1998) as well as Di Biase and Kawaguchi's (2002) studies for Japanese. Also, Iwasaki (2003) looked at how a child learner of JSL (a seven-year-old Australian boy) acquired verbal morphosyntax when he attended a primary school for Japanese children in Perth for nine months. Both researchers compared their findings of the acquisitional sequence with the Japanese L2 stages proposed by Di Biase and Kawaguchi (2002). The results of both studies found similar developmental sequences of acquisition of Japanese L1 and L2 verbal morphosyntax, although there were some differences.

Preston's (2004) study attempts to develop a profiling procedure of adult JSL. In her study, she revisits the issue of data elicitation procedure for collecting specific verbal morphosyntactic structures hypothesised for PT stages in Japanese (Di Biase & Kawaguchi 2002) and for Japanese pre-noun modification morphology.

All the previously mentioned works mainly concentrated on the area of (verbal) morphology. PT has not been applied to the acquisition of Japanese L2 syntax, with the exception of canonical order. In the following, I intend to expand the application of PT to Japanese syntax, especially in relation to Japanese word order and constructions involving TOP(ic).

3.   Typology of Japanese and brief sketch of its grammar

As the present study aims to apply PT to Japanese, a short description of the grammatical structural features and the typology of the language are necessary. Grammatical description of Japanese aims to facilitate formulation of the hypothesis and to analyse the L2 data. Here, syntactic and morphological features related to the later part of the study are touched upon.

Typologically, Japanese is an SOV language and it shares many features with other SOV languages (Shibatani 1990: 257–262; Tsujimura 1996: 160–179). One such feature is head-last characteristic. All kinds of modifiers precede the head. This head-last feature is consistent, and relative and adverbial clauses also precede the main clause. Unlike in English, word order itself does not play a major role in encoding syntactic relations. Instead, Japanese has the same postpositional nominal particle as many other SOV languages. This nominal particle indicates grammatical or semantic relations of the NP to the predicate such as NOM and ACC. Japanese is typologically a NOM-ACC language (Shibatani 1990; Tsujimura 1996) and usually NOM marks both transitive and intransitive SUBJ while ACC marks transitive OBJ as exemplified in (1) below:

(1) *Tamiko-ga   piano-o   hiita*
     Tamiko-NOM piano-ACC play-PAST
     'Tamiko played the piano'

Since Japanese argument structure is indicated by postpositional case particles and grammatical relations do not rely on word order, Japanese allows for a relatively flexible word order (i.e. free scrambling of preverbal constituents), with one important restriction: the verb must be last (Shibatani 1987: 142, 1990: 259). This is also consistent with the head-last characteristic of Japanese (and other SOV languages). Therefore, (1) can have the same meaning when the nominal constituent is scrambled as in (2)[2] thanks to the postpositional case-marking particles.

(2) *Piano-o   Tamiko-ga   hiita*
     piano-ACC Tamiko-NOM play-PAST
     'Tamiko played the piano'

The head-last nature of the Japanese c-structure rule is formally described as below (after Matsumoto 1996: 57):

(R1) a. S → XP*   {V, A}
              ($\uparrow$GF)=$\downarrow$ $\uparrow$=$\downarrow$

Japanese has a phrase structure rule (R1) by which the f-structure of the sentence is headed by either a verb or a predicative adjective (indicated by $\uparrow$=$\downarrow$) appearing in the last position of the sentence, preceded by zero or more XP(s) with a variety of grammatical functions.

   Another important aspect of Japanese grammar is the issue of topic construction. Typological distinctions between topic-prominence and subject-prominence were first introduced by Li and Thompson (1976, 1981) and Thompson (1978). Judging from a number of criteria, Li and Thompson (1976) classify languages into four different types: (1) Subject-prominent languages (SP languages); (2) Topic-Prominent languages (TP languages); (3) SP and TP languages; and (4) Neither SP nor TP Languages (Li & Thompson 1976: 460). According to their classification, Japanese (as well as Korean) belongs to the third type, i.e. they are SP and TP languages since they possess the characteristics of both SP languages and TP languages. These characteristics include the surface coding of the topic (Japanese and Korean have morphological marking for the topic) and "double subject" (Li & Thompson 1976:468) where the topic and the subject co-occur in a topic-comment structure.

In Japanese, the topic marker *-wa* is added after NP plus postpositional particle as in (3).

> (3) *Nakamura-san-ni-wa   moo   tegami-o   dasita*
>   Nakamura-Mr-DAT-TOP   already letter-ACC   send-PAST
>   'To Mr Nakamura, (I) have already sent a letter'

However, NOM and ACC particles are replaced by *-wa* when the SUBJ or OBJ is the TOP. In all other cases the topic marker *-wa* is simply added after NP (i.e., N + postpositional particles). (4) is an example where NP$_{SUBJ}$ is TOP. When the topic equals the subject of the sentence in Japanese as in (4), topic-comment and subj-predicate are identical except for the postpositional particle where the former takes the topic marker *-wa* (as in (4)) and the latter the NOM case-marker *-ga* (as in (5)).

The difference between these two types of sentences lies in the information structure: TOP$_{SUBJ}$ in TOP$_{SUBJ}$OV is the TOP-comment sentence where TOP$_{SUBJ}$ is previously established and the focus is the predicate, whereas the subj-predicate structure in SOV is 'event-reporting' and the focus is both on the subj and the predicate (therefore, omission of SUBJ is possible for the former but not possible for the latter) (Lambrecht 1994:131–146). So (4) as well as (6), where the SUBJ is omitted, can be the answer for the question *Tanaka-san wa nani o sita ka* "what did Mr Tanaka do?" whereas only (5) can be the answer for the question *doo sita ka* "what happened?".

> (4) TOP$_{SUBJ}$ O V
>   *Tanaka-san-wa   kono tegami-o   kaita*
>   Tanaka-Mr-TOP this   letter-ACC write-PAST
>   'Mr Tanaka wrote this letter'
>
> (5) S O V
>   *Tanaka-san-ga   kono tegami-o   kaita*
>   Tanaka-Mr-NOM this   letter-ACC write-PAST
>   'Mr Tanaka wrote this letter'
>
> (6) ø OV
>   *kono tegami-o   kaita*
>   this   letter-ACC write-PAST
>   '(he) wrote this letter'

Not only NP$_{SUBJ}$ but also any emphatic constituent NP in a sentence can be topicalised. The topicalised constituent usually occupies the sentence's initial position. The OBJ in (7) is topicalised. It is also possible that the sentence involves a non-core argument TOP to the clause, such as Adjunct and Oblique locative. In this case, comment itself forms a complete clause (i.e. TOP+SOV) in TOP-comment structure as in (8).

(7)   TOP$_{OBJ}$ S V
    Kono tegami-wa Tanaka-san-ga   kaita
    this   letter-TOP Tanaka-Mr-NOM write-PAST
    'This letter, Mr Tanaka wrote.'

(8)   TOP$_{adjunct}$ S O V
    Kinoo-wa   Tanaka-san-ga   kono tegami-o kaita
    yesterday-TOP Tanaka-Mr-NOM letter-ACC   write-PAST
    'Yesterday, Mr Tanaka wrote this letter.'

It is also possible to have more than one NP marked with -*wa*.[3]

(9)   TOP$_{adjunct}$ FOC$_{SUBJ}$ O V
    Watasi-no e-wa   onnanoko-wa akai doresu-o   ki-te
    I-GEN   picture-TOP girl-FOC   red   dress-ACC wear-COMP
    imasu
    ASP-POL
    'In my picture, it's (a/the) girl who is wearing a red dress'

Another important characteristic of Japanese is the extensive use of ellipsis. In spoken Japanese, redundant constituents tend to be omitted, and all constituents including nominal, postpositional nominal particles as well as verbs can be omitted as long as they are recoverable from the context (Hinds 1982). Therefore, ellipsis is normally used where a pronoun is typically used in English. In fact, the use of pronouns, except the first person singular, is rather rare in Japanese.

In languages such as Spanish and Italian, so-called 'pro-drop' languages, the omitted arguments are realised by inflectional morphology, especially in the agreement system (Taraldsen 1978). Unlike many European languages, Japanese does not have grammatical gender nor morphological plural/singular distinctions as Japanese uses numerals and quantifiers indicating the number. There are no agreement phenomena between subject and verb nor the numeral and the noun, etc. Hence, omitted elements are not recoverable from the verb morphology. Instead, nominal ellipsis is a discourse feature in Japanese (Kuroda 1965) and functions to avoid lexical redundancy and to increase discourse cohesion (Hata 1980). There are two kinds of antecedents found with nominal ellipsis in Japanese: linguistically encoded antecedents (anaphora) and non-linguistically encoded antecedents (deixis), as can be seen in examples (10) and (11) respectively. In the examples below from my learner and NS data, nominal ellipsis is indicated by [ø].

(10)   Linguistically encoded antecedent (anaphora)
(L=Lou, S=Native speaker of Japanese) at T1

   a. L (long pause) *er* (long pause) *tukue-no. migigawa-ni*
                                   desk-GEN   right   side-at

       hito-ga   *imasu*
       person-NOM exist
       'er there is a person at the right side of the desk'

   b. S *mm* [ø] *otokonoko desu ka? onnanoko desu ka?*
          boy   COP Q   girl   COP Q
          'mm is (it) a boy or a girl?'

(11)   Deictic antecedent (non-linguistically encoded)

   J *uhm sorekara um gogo-wa*   [ø] *daigaku-ni ikimasita*
     then   afternoon TOP university-LOC go-POL-PAST
     'then in the afternoon (I) went to the university.'

In (10b), when S answers, *hito* ("a person") is omitted. The retrieval of the reference is assumed to be possible since the antecedent was presented in the preceding turn. On the other hand, in (11) the ellipted reference is pragmatically recoverable although there is no linguistic cue or antecedent for it.

4.   Hypotheses

This section aims to present hypotheses based on PT concerning the developmental stages in Japanese L2 syntax. I will first interpret Japanese (morpho)syntax into PT hierarchy with formal representations based on LFG.

Table 1 presents a summary of the hypothesised stages for the acquisition of Japanese L2 syntax. This hypothesis is based on PT's hierarchy of processing procedures (Pienemann 1998:80). Pienemann (1998), based on Levelt (1989) and Kempen and Hoenkamp (1987), hypothesises that there is a hierarchical relationship for the acquisition of the processing resources by L2 learners. The first column of the table lists the procedural skills the learner needs to build up at each stage. The second column lists the type of grammatical information exchange which is characteristic of each stage. Building up the procedural

Table 1. Processing hierarchy of Japanese structures

	Processing procedures	Exchange of information	Japanese L2 syntax
Stage 4	S-procedure/ WO Rules	Inter-phrasal information	– OBJ topicalisation (i.e. $TOP_{OBJ/IO}$ SV) – Morpholexical operation (PASS, CAUSE, BENE)
Stage 3	phrasal procedure	Phrasal information	– TOP+ SOV (i.e. Adjunct/Locative TOP)
Stage 2	category procedure	None	– Canonical order SOV (i.e. Nominal marking of semantic roles, V-Final) – TOPsubj OV
Stage 1	word or lemma access	None	– single constituents – formulaic expression

skills listed in the first column, the learner becomes able to exchange different types of grammatical information in order to produce L2 morphosyntactic structures.

PT's implicational hierarchy is based on general psychological constraints such as limited working memory capacity, word access, temporal storage of grammatical information, and the linearisation problem. On account of the general nature of these constraints, Pienemann (1998) claims that this hierarchy is universally applicable to L2 learning. However, each language is controlled by different sets of grammatical rules, and therefore it is necessary to find out what type of grammatical information exchange is required in order to produce a particular L2 structure. If the processing hierarchy is implemented into psychologically and typologically plausible formal grammar, it should be possible to predict the structural outcomes at each developmental stage in any language.

Pienemann (1998) chose Lexical Functional Grammar (LFG) (Kaplan & Bresnan 1982; Bresnan 2001) for this purpose. LFG is a well-established formal grammar which is psychologically and typologically plausible (cf. Van Valin 2001:193). LFG utilises a set of key psychological factors involved in language processing for their formalisation and, consequently, it is compatible with psycholinguistic theory: Pinker's (1984) learnability theory and Levelt's (1989) speech model use LFG as their system of grammatical representation. LFG deals with a great variety of typologically different languages, so it strives to be typologically plausible. I will interpret PT stages through LFG and explain my hypotheses on Japanese L2 syntactic structures at each stage, which I list in the last column in Table 1.

Word order issues

i. Single constituents, formulaic expressions
At the first stage in the PT hierarchy no language specific grammatical procedure is developed, and therefore transfer of language specific grammatical information is not a relevant issue. At this pre-syntactic stage, the learners first need to add items to their L2 lexicon. The production of L2 utterances does not depend on any L2 syntactic and/or morphological knowledge/procedure. Therefore, single constituents (not in a sequence) and formulaic expressions represent possible speech production by the learner. This is because the production of single words or formulaic expressions does not require language specific grammatical procedures or information exchange in order to occur.

ii. Canonical Order SOV – Verb final
The Japanese canonical word order SOV is hypothesised at Stage 2. According to PT, at this stage the learners develop category procedures and can recognise major categories such as Verb and Noun in their L2. The learner cannot yet produce L2 sentences where information exchange is required, however the learner can circumvent S-procedure and produce target-like sentences using category procedure at this stage. Such a grammatical structure is a canonical order sentence (Pienemann 1998:84).

In LFG there is only one level of phrase structure representation, c-structure, whose constituents have correspondents in the grammatical function representation, f-structure (Bresnan 2001). Production of canonical word order is achieved at this level by a canonical association of NNV sequences corresponding to [agent-patient-action] because the arguments are morphologically marked and strictly ordered. This is similar to Bever's NVN strategy for Germanic languages (Bever 1970:248). This procedure does not require S-procedure because "it is possible to match semantics directly onto linguistic form without any arbitrariness" (Pienemann 1998:84). The speakers do not have to hold any grammatical information in their short-term memory during this simple canonical construction because the word order [Agent-Patient-Event] corresponds to the sequence of the actual event. Therefore, production of Japanese canonical order is placed at Stage 2. Recent development of PT (Pienemann et al. Chapter 7 in this volume) sees canonical order as the most harmonious linking between a(rgument)-structure, f(unctional)-structure and c(onstituent)-structure. Now this concept is presented as the

"Unmarked Alignment Hypothesis", based on OT-LFG work (Lee 2001; Sells 1999b, 2001). For the test structure of Japanese canonical word order, I propose 'Verb-final' (with at least one nominal element) in the utterance because Japanese allows nominal ellipsis but is consistently verb final (i.e. head-last) as shown in the Japanese phrase structure rule (R1) above.

iii. Marking of semantic role on noun
PT predicts that the marking of semantic roles on the noun occurs also at Stage 2 because this type of marking can be directly activated by the conceptual structure with a strong association of [N-*ga*] with Agent-like participant and [N-*o*] with Patient-like participant. Such morphological marking on nouns is a lexical affix because it involves the identification of the lexical category of the host (in this case N) but it does not require information exchange, or grammatical agreement between the host (i.e. N) and the affix.

Further, Ishikawa (1985) claims that the case-marker is a noun suffixal morpheme rather than an independent free morpheme. Following Simpson's (1983 cited in Ishikawa 1985) representation of case-markers in Walpiri, Ishikawa introduced sublexical rules which show a "word-tree" for Japanese case-marked NP. (R2)[4] is the sublexical rule for nominal constituents for Japanese and the morphological structure of case-marked NP. Suffixation is represented as occurring within a word. Figure 1 shows the tree diagram where up- and down- arrows (i.e. ↑and ↓) indicate information flow. This representation shows that the noun marking morphology occurs below the word level.

(R2) NP → N
                   ↑=↓
        N   → N   Aff
                   (↑GF)=↓ ↑=↓

For Pienemann (1998:84) this kind of noun marking in Japanese is achieved lexically and appears at Stage 2. Thus, PT predicts that acquisition of noun marking in Japanese L2 is achieved at the same stage as the acquisition of canonical word order in English L2. It is interesting to note that the L1 acquisition studies also report that the learning of canonical order in English and the learning of semantic role marking on nouns in Turkish, which is similar to Japanese case-marking, appear around the same time (Slobin 1982). Similar results are also found in Japanese L1. According to Hakuta (1982), Japanese children need to learn a dominant SOV word order as well as inflections and particles in order to understand grammatical roles and meaning within the

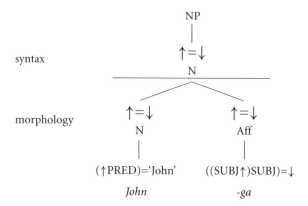

Figure 1.

sentence. He wrote: "In Japanese and Serbo-Croatian, in which there are particles and yet in which there is a dominant canonical order, children hone in on the correlation between particles and their location within the sentence. When this expected correlation is violated, such sentences are difficult for children to comprehend." (Hakuta 1982: 75).

So Japanese L1 children acquire dominant canonical order SOV and the correlation between particles and their location in a sentence at the same period. However, they acquire the interpretation of non-canonical word order OSV much later than SOV (Slobin 1982). The same is predicted with L2 learners. PT hypothesises that both canonical order and the nominal marking of the semantic role will appear at the first Japanese L2 syntactic stage, i.e. Stage 2, because both operations require low demand of information processing (i.e. category procedure).

Then what will happen when the canonical order is disturbed? In that case, appropriate 'case marking' on a noun in conjunction with its host noun as well as its predicate is required, which involves more than lexical procedure. PT claims that the production of non-canonical order sentences requires S-procedure and this is placed at a higher stage of language acquisition. This seems to be true with the sentence comprehension by JSL learners as well as NS of Japanese according to Sasaki's (1998) study where the problem of comprehending Japanese causative and double-object actives in canonical and non-canonical environments is well documented from a psycholinguistic experiment on on-line comprehension. Japanese being a NOM-ACC language, the NP's grammatical function can be reconstructed from the nominal marking. That is the NPs marked with *-ga* (NOM) are SUBJ and NPs marked with

Table 2. Sentence types and stimulus sentences in Sasaki's (1998) study

Sentence type	An example of stimulus sentence
Canonical active	*raion-ga panda-ni tegami-o kaku*
	lion-NOM panda-DAT letter-ACC write
	'The lion writes a letter to the panda'
Non-canonical active	*gorira-ni raion-ga tegami-o kaku*
	gorilla-DAT lion-NOM letter-ACC write
	'The lion writes a letter to the gorilla'
Canonical causative	*raion-ga panda-ni tegami-o kak-aseru*
	lion-NOM panda-DAT letter-ACC write-CAUSE
	'The lion makes the panda write a letter'
Non-canonical causative	*gorira-ni raion-ga tegami-o kak-aseru*
	gorilla-DAT lion-NOM letter-DAT write-CAUSE
	'The lion makes the gorilla write a letter'

-o (ACC) are usually OBJ while NPs marked with *-ni* (DAT) are normally the second or indirect OBJ. However, the semantic role of the noun cannot be reconstructed from the case-marking alone. For instance, the SUBJ may have *agent* or *patient* semantic role. So the interpretation of the semantic role of the NPs relies on both the case-marking and the verb form (i.e. voice). In other words, the semantic role of the NP can be decided at S-node but never locally.

In this study, the subjects are asked to identify the agent of the main lexical verb of four different types of Japanese double-object sentences as soon as they hear the sentence. These sentences are: (i) canonical active (ii) non-canonical active (iii) canonical causative and (iv) non-canonical causative. Table 2 presents examples of stimulus in different sentence types in the study.

The identification of function on NPs is possible only when the listener hears the VP in Japanese. This is because causative morphology is affixed after the verb stem in Japanese. In Sasaki's study the results were analyzed according to four variables: case marking sequence (canonical Vs. non-canonical); voice (active Vs. causative); type of L1 (L1 Japanese Vs. L1 English learning Japanese L2) and; effect of feedback (Pretest Vs. Posttest). In the context of this paper we need to consider the results from Pretest where, as can be expected, native speakers do better than non-native speakers in correctly identifying the agent in canonical sentences. In fact, accuracy was always higher with canonical order compared to non-canonical. Also, there was no significant difference between active and causative sentences in NS's accuracy.

Now, contrasting the canonical/non-canonical alternation, accuracy rates were consistently higher with canonical order compared to non-canonical with both NSs and NNSs regardless of voice (i.e. for both non-canonical active and non-canonical causative). The response-time latency was also significantly longer for non-canonical order. Within canonical order, voice alternation, between active and causative sentences, had a considerable effect on NNSs but there was no significant difference in NS's accuracy. Surprising results obtained by Sasaki were that the NSs made more errors then the learners with the word order-biased sentences: they made numerous errors by imposing the canonical case-marker sequence in reconstructing non-canonical sentences.

Sasaki's psycholinguistic study constitutes an empirical test of our analysis of the word order and the voice (argument structure mapping) and their hypothesised position in the PT hierarchy. The experiment gives an insight into the human processing mechanisms. The logic of the argument runs along the following lines. Both NSs and NNSs showed highest accuracy with canonical active. This is what is expected in PT. Interpretation of such a sentence requires fewer processing resources because of the canonical mapping of the argument structure onto grammatical functions. On the other hand, sentences involving non-canonical case-marking sequences require greater processing resources. The same applies to causative sentences compared to active ones. This is shown by their higher latencies across the board. This suggests that the hearer can identify the NPs' semantic function only when he/she integrates the information of both nominal marking of NP and the VP because the voice marking morphology (causative morphology in this case) is affixed after the verb stem in Japanese. In other words, morphemes expressing voice come at a later processing time, (i.e. they can only go into the syntactic frame AFTER the frame itself is in place.)

On the other hand, voice alternation had no significant effect for NSs but they made a surprisingly large number of errors in correctly identifying the agent in the non-canonical sentences (both active and causative). This fact suggests two important tendencies of NS's sentence processing. Firstly, unlike learners, native speakers' sentence processing is already automatised, therefore they would not need to change their strategy in order to interpret various types of sentences. This is confirmed by the fact that voice alternation did not have significant effect on NSs. Secondly, what did have a large effect on the NS's accuracy was whether or not the sentence displayed canonical order. This suggests that NS has a strong preference for canonical order over noncanonical.

Then the question arises: why did NSs make such large number of errors in interpreting non-canonical sentences? We have to bear in mind that in the experimental setting the sentences were presented out of context, in isolation of discourse e.g. without intonation contours. Non-canonical order is not a purely computational matter but it is influenced by information specified in the message (e.g. which arguments must be mapped to which functions) as well as discourse information (such as prominence, focusing, and so on). Thus, to interpret non-canonical order, the NS would require such information. In its absence the NS will simply apply canonical interpretation.

Sasaki's result provides a piece of robust evidence that the interpretation of a non-canonical order as well as causative voice requires additional processing task in order to decide the functional assignment of NPs. Also, it suggests that discourse and pragmatic information play a crucial role in processing. So, learners will need to acquire, eventually, the different mapping required by differences in argument structure as well as the influence of discourse functions on morphosyntax. In the following, I explain the information processing mechanism involved in producing non-canonical word order sentences.

iv. Morpholexical Operation (Passive, causative and benefactive)
The production of passivisation, causativisation and benefactivisation requires S-procedure because these structures involve non-linearity in the grammatical encoding process. In other words, their production involves non-canonical functional assignment as well as, in Japanese, specific morpholexical operations. The following (12), (13) and (14) are examples of passive, causative and benefactive structures in Japanese respectively.

(12) *Tamiko-wa   sensei-ni   sikar-rare-ta*
      Tamiko-TOP   teacher-DAT   scold-PASS-PAST
      'Tamiko was scolded by the teacher'

(13) *Bosu-wa   mainiti   watasi-ni koohiii-o   tukur-ase-ta*
      boss-TOP   everyday   I-DAT   coffee-ACC   make-CAUSE-PAST
      'My boss got me to make coffee everyday'

(14) *Risa-san-wa   okaasan-ni   keeki-o   tukut-te   morat-ta*
      Lisa-Miss-TOP   mother-DAT   cake-ACC   make-COMP   BENE-PAST
      '(Lit.) Lisa received a favour of making a cake from her mother'
      '= (Lisa's) mother made a cake for Lisa'

In all three sentences above, the grammatical subjects are not the actor/agent of the event described by the base verb. For example, *Tamiko* in (12) is not the person who 'scolds' and *bosu* '(my) boss' in (13) is not the person who 'makes coffee'. Likewise *Risa-san* 'Miss Lisa' in (14) is not the person who 'makes a cake'. Thus the Agent of the base verb is not mapped onto SUBJ in these sentences. All three sentences above can be said to be non-canonical because of the non-canonical association of the semantic role and the grammatical function.

In other words, the insertion of the auxiliary of Passive, Causative and Benefactive instigates a "morpholexical operation" (Bresnan & Kanerva 1989: 26)
which changes the argument structure by adding or suppressing thematic roles.
In order to construct a non-canonical order sentence, the functional destination of NPs is determined by assembling information at the S-node. The identification of the phrases' grammatical functions and their functional assignments
in passive, causative and benefactive constructions requires the learner to unify
information from different sources: the V and the N phrases. This calls for an
interphrasal process. A more detailed explanation of the sort of c- to f-structure
mapping involved in non-canonical construction can be found in Di Biase and
Kawaguchi (2002), who base their work on Bresnan (2001) and Nordlinger's
(1998) "constructive case" model.

Here, I would like to go one step further and explain the mechanism
of a(rgument)-structure mapping onto f-structure by using Lexical Mapping
Theory (LMT) within the framework of LFG (Alsina 1996; Bresnan 2001; Bresnan 1994; Bresnan & Kanerva 1989). In fact, Pienemann et al. (Chapter 7 in this
volume) propose a(rgument)-structure to f-structure mapping as a second set
of principles for PT in addition to the principle of "unification". The inclusion of this new principle expands the range of syntactic structures covered by
the PT hierarchy including Passive, raising and Causative, which were not included in PT hierarchy in Pienemann (1998). Pienemann et al. (ibid.) posit the
"Unmarked Alignment Hypothesis" and state "(i)n second language acquisition learners will initially organise syntax by a direct mapping of a-structure
onto f-structure and by a direct mapping c-structure onto f-structure". Then
the rest of the acquisition is seen as the process of accumulative adaptation
of non-linear mapping by overcoming linearisation problems. Further, the
"Lexical Mapping Hypothesis" in current PT predicts that non-canonical sentences such as passive, causative and benefactive can be produced by the second
language learner when he/she acquires the S-procedure. In other words, the
learner's initial syntax is limited to canonical order due to the restricted a- to
f-structure mapping ability. Later the learner becomes able to produce non-
linear, non-canonical order sentences when he/she acquires S-procedure because now the learner can handle functional assignments involving non-default
mapping between a-and f-structures.

LMT is a theory of the general mapping principle of a-structure onto f-
structure. It explains how non-default mapping structures such as passive and
causative are constructed through the notion of "morpholexical operation".
Utilising LMT, we can see the mechanism of linear and non-linear mapping.
LMT is summarised in Chapter 7 in this volume and interested readers are re-

ferred to Bresnan and Kanerva (1989), Bresnan (2001) and Dalrymple (2001). In the following, I first briefly summarise four components of LMT. Then I explain Japanese passive and causative structures which involve non-canonical a- to f- functional mapping which requires S-procedure.

According to Bresnan and Kanerva (1989: 22), LMT consists of the following four components.

1. A universal hierarchy of thematic roles

This hierarchy shows the prominence of the argument of a predicator: the higher it is, the more prominent.

(15) Thematic hierarchy
AGENT > BENEFICIARY > RECIPIENT/EXPERIENCER > INSTRU-
MENT > THEME/PATIENT > LOCATIVE

2. A classification of syntactic functions

The four primary grammatical functions, SUBJ, OBJ, OBJ_θ and OBL_θ are discomposed into features as below:

(16)

	$-r$	$+r$
$-o$	SUBJ	OBL_θ
$+o$	OBJ	OBJ_θ

$[\pm r] - (un)restricted$ $[\pm o] - (non)objective$
OBJ_θ: secondary object

3. Lexical mapping principles

The specification of which thematic role can map onto which grammatical function depends on the following three lexical mapping principles.

i. intrinsic values
Agent, Theme and Locative have the following intrinsic values respectively:

(17) Agent: $[-o]$
Theme/Patient: $[-r]$
Locative: $[-o]$

ii. Morpholexical operations
"Morpholexical operations affect lexical argument structures by adding and suppressing thematic roles" (Bresnan & Kanerva 1989: 26). For example, the passive suppresses the highest thematic argument (i.e. Agent).

iii.   The default value

The default value depends on the thematic hierarchy in (15) where the thematic role of the predicate that is highest in the thematic hierarchy receives the default value of [–r] and other roles receive [+r]. "The defaults are designed to capture the generalisation that the highest thematic role of a verb will be the subject (as proposed by Givón (1984), Zaenan, Maling & Thráinsson (1985), Kiparsky (1987) and others), and lower roles will be nonsubjects" (Bresnan & Kanerva 1986: 27).

4. Well-formedness conditions

The following two well-formedness conditions ensure the grammaticality of the structure in order to filter out ill-formed structures.

i.   *Function-Argument Bi-uniqueness*: each a-structure role must be associated with a unique function, and conversely.

ii. *The subject condition*: every predicator must have a subject. (Bresnan 2001: 311)

Now we consider the active/passive alternation in Japanese as in (18) and (19) below. (18) is a canonical order sentence where a- structure is mapped onto f-structure in a linear way. Therefore, PT predicts this structure is learnable at Stage 2. On the other hand, Passive is the case where "morpholexical operation" affects the argument structure by suppressing the thematically highest role (Bresnan & Moshi 1990). The mapping principle of the passive blocks the primary thematic role (i.e. Agent) from mapping onto the grammatical SUBJ. This operation requires S-procedure because the successful mapping operation implies that the learner is able to assign grammatical functions in a non-default way.

(18)   Active
       Neko-ga   sakana-o   tabe-ta
       cat-NOM fish-ACC eat-PAST
       'The cat ate the fish'

(19)   Passive
       Sakana-ga neko-ni   tabe-rare-ta
       fish-NOM cat-DAT eat-PASS-PAST
       'The fish was eaten by the cat'

The predicate in the active sentence in (18) has the following a-structure:

(20)   eat <AGENT PATIENT>

The Agent has an intrinsic value of [−o], while PATIENT has a intrinsic value of [−r]. According to Bresnan and Kanerva's (1989) study, in the Thematic hierarchy in (15), Agent receives the default value of [−r] because AGENT is higher in the Thematic hierarchy between two thematic roles of the predicate *eat*, i.e. AGENT and PATIENT. According to (16), the thematic role which has the features [−r] [−o] is mapped onto SUBJ. PATIENT has a intrinsic value of [−r] and it can be linked either to SUBJ or OBJ by receiving the value of [−o] or [+o] respectively. However, PATIENT has to be mapped onto OBJ in accordance with *Function-Argument Bi-uniqueness*. This notion is illustrated in (21):

(21)   eat <Agent   Patient>
         intrinsic value   [−o]   [−r]
         mapping principle [−r](default) *[−o] /[+o]
         ───
                                   SUBJ   *SUBJ/OBJ (*indicates ungrammatical)

Thus if the default value [−r] is given to the highest thematic role of the lexical argument structure, the highest thematic role (i.e. Agent) is realised as SUBJ and consequently canonical order is constructed in accordance with the lexical mapping principle. Figure 2 represents the correspondence between the a-structure, f-structure and c-structure of the sentence (18). The mapping of both a- to f- and c- to f-structure in active sentences is canonical and therefore it is hypothesised to be located at Stage 2.

Now we consider the sentence (19) that is the passive counterpart of the active sentence (18). Bresnan and Moshi (1990) propose that the "passive rule" suppresses the highest argument and overrides the default. Bresnan (2001: 310) wrote:

> The lexical stock of a-structures in a language can be extended by morpholexical means. For example, the a-structure of a passive verb differs from the active in that the most prominent role [i.e. the Agent, n. d. a.] cannot be mapped onto a syntactic argument in the f-structure (though it may be linked to an argument adjunct such as the by-phrase in English). This is called "suppression," and is associated with passive morphology.

Thus in Passive construction, the AGENT that has the most prominent role in the a-structure is suppressed[5] and becomes unavailable for linking. This requires non-linear (non-default) mapping between a- and f-structures. The suppressed argument AGENT may or may not be syntactically expressed. If it is overtly expressed, it is realised as an adjunct.[6] The thematic role PATIENT in Passive, on the other hand, has the intrinsic value [−r] and could be SUBJ or OBJ because these two syntactic functions are both classified as [−r]. However,

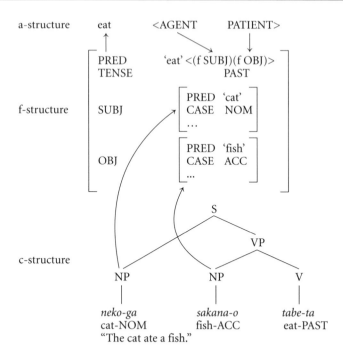

Figure 2. a- structure, f-structure and c-structure correspondence for (active) *neko-ga sakana-o tabe-ta*

PATIENT has to be linked to SUBJ due to the constraint on the mapping called *the subject condition*, which states that "(e)very predicator must have a subject" (Baker 1983 cited in Bresnan 2001: 311). This notion is illustrated in (22) and it clearly shows non-canonical mapping between a- to f-structure. Figure 3 below graphically represents a- and c- structure mapping onto f-structure.

	(22)	eat	<Agent	Patient>
intrinsic			[−o]	[−r]
passive			∅	
mapping principle				[−o]/*[+o]
				SUBJ/*OBJ

Thus, LMT serves as a basis for explaining the linearity/nonlinearity of the mapping of a-structure onto f-structure. In summary, in canonical order sentences, the highest thematic role of the predicate is mapped onto SUBJ. This can be done by the canonical association between thematic roles and grammatical functions. However in passivisation, the initial argument of the predicator, is suppressed. The Agent function is linked to the non-initial argument.

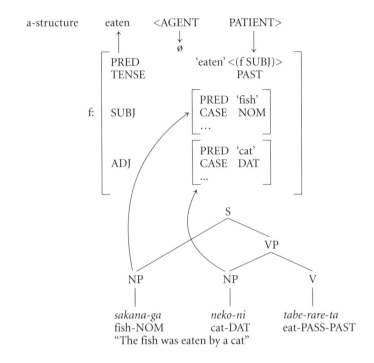

Figure 3. a-structure, f-structure and c-structure correspondence for (passive) *sakana-ga neko-ni tabe-rare-ta*

This triggers the non-linearity of lexical mapping and S-procedure is required for construction of the sentence functional assignment. Therefore, passive in Japanese is hypothesised to be located at Stage 4.

The case marking for the NP argument in Passive involves what Nordlinger (1998: 62) calls inside-out unification. This means that the case morpheme it-self creates the f-structure of the NP to which it belongs and thus contributes to the higher f-structure. The information coming from the f-structure of NP arguments and the information specified by the predicate must be compatible with each other in order to satisfy the well-formedness condition. This requires unification at the S-level.

Causative constructions also involve a morpholexical operation. In Japanese, the same structural frame yields both coercive and permissive interpretation, but here we focus on coercive interpretation. In causative constructions, the morphology associated with the causative adds information to a-structure that has the effect of adding one extra thematic role. In Intransitive causatives in Japanese, the patient is case-marked with either *-o* (ACC) or *-ni* (DAT), whereas in transitive causative it is marked with *-ni* (DAT) due to the so-called "double *O* constraint" rule (i.e. Japanese cannot take more than one *-o* (ACC) in a clause). Examples (23) and (24) below illustrate intransitive and transitive causative respectively.

(23) *Tamiko-ga   musuko-o/ni   hasir-ase-ta*
      Tamiko-NOM   son-ACC/DAT   run-CAUSE-PAST
      'Tamiko made her son run'

(24) *Tamiko-ga   musume-ni   keeki-o   tukur-ase-ta*
      Tamiko-NOM   daughter-DAT   cake-ACC   make-CAUSE-PAST
      'Tamiko made her daughter make a cake'

According to Matsumoto (1996), Japanese coercive causatives involve causer-controlled sub-events where the logical subject of the embedded clause is fused to the patient of the matrix clause. Consequently, Japanese causative involves an embedded sub-event at a-structure level but this is realised as a single clause in f-structure. In (23) above, the logical subject of the base verb is realised as OBJ in the syntactic structure. Alsina (1996:186) assumes that "the causative verb and the base verb undergo predicate composition yielding one, single, complex, a-structure". For example, *musuko* (son) in (23) is the patient of the causative verb and also the agent of the base verb. Likewise, *musume* (daughter) in (24) is the recipient-patient of the causative verb as well as the agent of the base verb. Thus, two thematic roles are fused into one in f-structure. As a result, the causative verb and the base verb behave like one single predicate in the light of case assignment (Alsina 1996).

The a-structure mapping onto f-structure for Japanese causatives is illustrated below following Matsumoto (1996:155). The mapping principle with the intransitive causative is straightforward. The agent and patient have the intrinsic values of [–o] and [–r] respectively. The agent receives the default value of [–r] as it is the most prominent thematic role. The patient can receive either [+o] or [–o]. Functional biuniqueness condition filters out [–o] in order to avoid the double SUBJ in a sentence.

(25) Intransitive Causative

Intransitive Causative

	Cause	< Agent	Patient		<Agent>>
intrinsic		[–o]	[–r]		
Mapping principle		[–r]	[+o]/*[–o]		
		SUBJ	OBJ/*SUBJ		

Therefore, following Alsina (1997), the resulting a- onto f-structure is represented as follows:

(26) 'cause < Agent, Patient, run <Agent>>'   a-structure

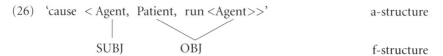

      SUBJ   OBJ   f-structure

A similar explanation applies to transitive causatives in Japanese. According to Matsumoto (1996: 155), the intrinsic value of recipient-patient is [−r] whereas the patient of the subevent can be classified as either [−r] or [+o]. Because of the Functional Biuniqueness Condition, successful mapping occurs only when the patient is classified as [+o] and receives [+r] yielding $OBJ_{patient}$ as illustrated below. (27a) is a valid case where PATIENT of the sub-event receives the value of [+o] while the case (27b) is not valid (invalid mapping is indicated by "*").

(27)   Transitive causative (after Matsumoto 1996: 155)

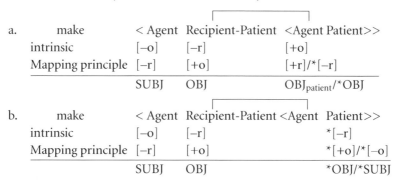

		< Agent	Recipient-Patient	<Agent Patient>>
a.	make			
	intrinsic	[−o]	[−r]	[+o]
	Mapping principle	[−r]	[+o]	[+r]/*[−r]
		SUBJ	OBJ	$OBJ_{patient}$/*OBJ

		< Agent	Recipient-Patient	<Agent	Patient>>
b.	make				
	intrinsic	[−o]	[−r]		*[−r]
	Mapping principle	[−r]	[+o]		*[+o]/*[−o]
		SUBJ	OBJ		*OBJ/*SUBJ

The resulting a- onto f-structure mapping looks like this:

(28) 'cause
      < Agent, Recipient-Patient, make <Agent, Patient>>'   a-structure

      SUBJ   OBJ   OBJpatient   f-structure

As is explained above, a-structure mapping onto f-structure in the causative construction is non-linear due to the fusion of thematic roles in the event and subevent in the a-structure. Similar a- to f- mapping mechanisms are involved in Benefactive construction. Construction of the Causative as well as the Benefactive in Japanese requires appropriate functional assignment. Therefore, both causative and benefactive are hypothesised to emerge at Stage 4 (i.e. S-procedure) in Japanese L2 PT hierarchy.

TOP functions

Doi and Yoshioka (1987) looked at the acquisitional sequence of the three Japanese nominal particles: TOP(ic) -*wa*, NOM(inative) -*ga* and ACC(usative) -*o*. Here, I propose to look at whole sentence structures involving TOP in conjunction with its grammatical function rather than the acquisition of certain nominal morphology. I predict that this is because the differentiation of TOP from SUBJ consists of one of the key issues in acquiring Japanese syntax. In fact, the type of information exchange differs according to the function which links to TOP, i.e. either SUBJ, non-SUBJ argument, or non-argument. I hypothesise that the following three constructions which have different functions of TOP appear at different PT stages based on the "Topic Hypothesis" (Pienemann et al. Chapter 7 in this volume):

i.   TOP and SUBJ are undifferentiated
ii. TOP is assigned to noncore arguments such as ADJUNCT and SUBJ is separated from TOP
iii. TOP is assigned to OBJ (i.e. OBJ topicalisation)

i. TOP equals SUBJ

Bresnan (2001: 98) claims that 'the subject is often identified as the default TOP of the clause'. In fact, according to LFG, SUBJ is unique on the point that it has a grammaticalised discourse function (like TOP and FOCUS) as well as the argument function. Also, Lambrecht (1994) points out that the strong correlation between SUBJ and TOP seems to be a universal feature across the typology of languages. According to him, there is a tendency to "equate grammatical subject-predicate structure with pragmatic topic-comment sentence" (ibid.: 136). Therefore the subject is the unmarked expression of topic.

In some languages such as English, TOP is positionally encoded and appears at the most prominent position (i.e. sentence initial). In Japanese as well as in Korean, TOP also tends to appear at the sentence initial position. However, it is morphosyntactically grammaticised: TOP is indicated by the postnominal particle -*wa*. At the beginning of syntactic acquisition, lemma access and category procedure do not permit the recognition of grammatical functions of NP in a sentence. This implies that the L2 learner lacks resources for linking TOP to another grammatical function (such as SUBJ and OBJ). The learner identifies the agent-like semantic function as a default topic and does not differentiate these two functionally. Therefore, Japanese canonical word order in learners' nominal marking may be realised as:

(29) agent   patient action _____ a-structure
       ↓   ↓   ↓
      N-*ga*/*wa*   N-*o*   V   _____ c-structure
      NOM/TOP   ACC

An example of this sentence structure is found in (4) above and reproduced below as (30).

(30) TOP$_{SUBJ}$ O V
      Tanaka-san-wa   kono tegami-o   kaita
      Tanaka-Mr-TOP this   letter-ACC write-PAST
      'Mr Tanaka wrote this letter'

The structure S → S$_{TOP}$OV is achieved with the phrase structure rule (R1) presented earlier. The noun marked as TOP coincides with SUBJ and the sentence pattern remains SOV which is the canonical word order in Japanese. Hence, it is hypothesised to emerge at Stage 2 (i.e. Categorial procedure).

ii. Noncore argument TOP (S' → TOP + SOV)
This structure is hypothesised to emerge at Stage 3 (i.e. phrasal procedure). An example of 'noncore argument TOP' is shown in (8) and reproduced here as (31) and this structure is represented at c-structure level by (R3).

(31) TOP$_{adjunct}$ S O V
      Kinoo-wa   Tanaka-san-ga   kono tegami-o kaita
      yesterday-TOP Tanaka-Mr-NOM letter-ACC   write-PAST
      'Yesterday, Mr Tanaka wrote this letter.'

(R3) S' → (XP)   S
             (↑TOP)=↓ ↑=↓

Further, Japanese particle *-wa* has the lexical entry listed in (32)[7] which states that 'I mark the topic' and 'I mark some GF'.

(32) *-wa*: ((TOP↑) TOP) =↓
             ((TOP↑(GF)) =↓

The lexical entry of *-wa* in (32) above creates in (33) the f-structure for the sentence in (31) above showing that TOP is linked to ADJ.

(33)

$$
f:\begin{bmatrix} \text{TOP} & \longrightarrow & [\text{``}kinoo \text{ (yesterday)''}] \\ \text{ADJ} & & \\ \text{SUBJ} & & [\text{``}Tanaka\text{-}san \text{ (Mr Tanaka)''}] \\ \text{PRED} & & \text{`}kaku \text{ (write) } <(f\ \text{SUBJ})(f\ \text{OBJ})> \text{'} \\ \text{OBJ} & & [\text{``}kono\ tegami \text{ (this letter)''}] \end{bmatrix}
$$

Bresnan (2001:69) explains that this structure, where the clause initial topic is simultaneously an adjunct, does not involve functional uncertainty. Bearing the double function of adjunct and topic satisfies the completeness and coherence conditions. From the PT perspective, this structure is possible when phrasal procedure is operational because when TOP is ADJUNCT, it has its own PRED and does not refer to argument functions, and therefore it does not involve information exchange with other constituents of S.

iii. OBJ topicalisation (i.e. S → TOP$_{obj}$ SV)

Example (7) reproduced below as (34), represents OBJ topicalisation in Japanese.

(34) TOP$_{OBJ}$ S V
Kono tegami-wa Tanaka-san-ga kaita
'This letter, Mr Tanaka wrote.'

f-structure of this sentence is:

(35)

$$
f:\begin{bmatrix} \text{TOP} & [\text{``}kono\ tegami \text{ (this letter)''}] \\ \text{SUBJ} & [\text{``}Tanaka\text{-}san \text{ (Mr Tanaka)''}] \\ \text{PRED} & \text{`}kaku \text{ (write) } <(f\ \text{SUBJ})\ (f\ \text{OBJ})> \text{'} \\ \text{OBJ} & \end{bmatrix}
$$

The extended coherence condition in LFG states that TOP (as well as FOCUS) needs to bear a grammatical function such as SUBJ or OBJ. In order to bind an argument with TOP, it must be linked either functionally or anaphorically (Darlrymple 2001:185). PRED of OBJ is a gap in the c-structure. However, the f-structure of OBJ is identified with the value of a higher non-argument function DF (discourse function). In the case of (34), DF is TOP. "Without the identification of TOP and OBJ provided by the functional uncertainty equation, the f-structure would be incomplete and incoherent" (Bresnan 2001:68). In order to fulfil both the completeness and coherence conditions, unification at the higher node is required. This operation involves the S-procedure. Therefore, this structure is hypothesised to emerge at Stage 4.

In order to acquire the construction of OBJ topicalisation, the learner needs to relinquish the canonical association of the position of the element in a sentence and its semantic role as well as the nominal morphology and its semantic role. Functional assignment is necessary for OBJ topicalisation.

5.   Empirical study

This section describes the research design and the method of analysis in order to test the hypotheses on developmental stages. I also explain the method of distributional analysis as well as the acquisition criteria for each test structure.

5.1   Research Design

Informants, setting and data collection
Two concurrent longitudinal studies (one three-year longitudinal study and one two-year longitudinal study) were conducted in a formal instructional setting in order to look at the developmental sequence of L2 Japanese syntax in learners' speech production. Both informants, Lou and Jaz,[8] were born in Australia and are native speakers of English. These two learners started a beginners' Japanese class at the University of Western Sydney (UWS henceforth), enrolled in the same Japanese subjects and received six hours of instruction from two different instructors per week for 12 weeks during each academic semester. The academic year consists of two semesters. Therefore, they received approximately 144 hours of formal instruction per year.

Data collection started just after the informants commenced the Japanese beginners' unit. Although oral interviews were carried out monthly during the academic terms, I collected two interviews per semester (one around the middle of the semester and another one towards the end) during the relevant period of time with each informant. The first interview (Time 1) was conducted just four weeks after the commencement of their Japanese course. Data elicitation was dyadic in nature (i.e. the learner and a native speaker of Japanese) and based on both natural conversation and various picture tasks. Interviews were between 20 and 30 minutes long. Each interview was tape-recorded, then transcribed and further transliterated.[9] The transcribing and transliterating were done first by a research assistant (a native speaker of Japanese with a postgraduate degree in applied Japanese linguistics) and then checked by the researcher. There were no major disagreements about the transcription between the research assistant and the researcher.

UWS hosted a number of Japanese overseas students while the informants were studying Japanese. My informants were encouraged to mingle with these overseas students and there were a number of occasions where they interacted together both inside and outside the university. Therefore, input of Japanese came from peer Japanese university students outside the class in addition to formal instruction.

Data analysis

To begin to examine my data, Conc 1.72, one of the Summer Institute of Linguistic software applications for data analysis, is used to generate word concordances and to order linguistic data with an advanced search. Then a distributional analysis is carried out. Implicational scaling (Labov 1972; DeCamp 1973) is adopted for the identification of the variability and systematicity of SLA data. This procedure is also used for testing the hypothesis of the developmental sequence base on PT for other languages (e.g. Mansouri 2002 for Arabic; Di Biase 2002 for Italian; Zhang 2001, 2002 for Chinese).

Naturally the actual distributional analysis needs to be carried out according to language-specific structures. Therefore, prior to the presentation of the results I will explain, structure by structure, the distributional analysis in conjunction with the scoring procedure. Also, I will describe how sufficient evidence of productive use is decided with each hypothesised structure. Unlike morphology, we cannot define the "obligatory" context with syntax: this has to be dealt with pragmatically but this is not of interest in my study. Therefore, in principle, the total number of occurrences of respective structures and the number of valid instances (i.e. positive evidence) are counted. The following explanation clarifies the scoring procedure with individual structures.

i. single constituents

Appearance/non-appearance of L2 Japanese words in the learners' speech production was investigated and represented by '+' or '−'. The plus sign ('+') indicates that Japanese words were observed more than once with a lexical variety in an interview.

ii. V-final

The position of the lexical verb in the sentence was analysed (main clause only). The number of clauses with a verb in sentence final position and the total occurrence of the verb in the main clause were scored and these numbers were entered before and after the slash ('/') respectively in the result table. The following is an example of V-final construction from my data.

(36) (Jaz T1) *and er burakkuboodo erm -ga arimasu*
                 blackboard   -NOM   exist-POL
                 'and there is a blackboard.'

iii. morphological marking of the semantic roles on nouns

As the omission of nominal particles is permitted in colloquial Japanese, I simply looked at the existence/non-existence of morphological markings on nouns in the data. In the results table, the plus sign (i.e. '+') indicates that morphological marking on nouns was observed more than once in the learner's speech. The minus sign (i.e. '–') means that learner did not use this feature. In the examples below, the noun *sandoitti* (sandwich) in (37) is marked by *-o* but *isu* (chair) in (38) does not have a morphological marking. Note that what is relevant here is whether or not the learner marked the semantic role on the noun, and the correctness of the noun morphology is not accounted for.

(37) (Lou T2) *ur.. sandoitti-o tabemasu*
                 sandwich ACC eat-POL
                 'I eat sandwich'

(38) (Jaz T1) *erm. isu um arimasu*
                 chair   exist-POL
                 'There is a chair'

iv. Passive, causative and Benefactive

Passive, Causative and Benefactive constructions involve non-linear mapping of thematic roles onto f-structure and this triggers the S-procedure for the sentence encoding process. Although Japanese allows nominal ellipsis for any predicative arguments, the S-procedure is syntactically visible only when predicative arguments are explicitly encoded. If there is no overt argument at all in a Passive/Causative/Benefactive sentence, the insertion of Passive/Causative/Benefactive morphology to the base verb is simply a lexical operation in Japanese just like verbal inflection. As a result it does not require S-procedure (see Di Biase & Kawaguchi 2002).

For this reason, overt expression of at least one argument is necessary to claim positive evidence for S-procedure. For Passive, either Patient (linked to SUBJ) or Agent (linked to Adjunct) should be overtly expressed in order to count as positive evidence for S-procedure. This is because the linking of both Patient-SUBJ (marked as TOP or NOM) and Agent-Adjunct (marked as DAT) constitute non-canonical mapping in Japanese. Therefore, the inclusion of a syntactic constituent of either Patientive SUBJ or Agentive Adjunct in Passive can show non-linear mapping of a Thematic role to the grammatical function.

Similarly, the positive evidence with Causative constructions in Japanese can be observed only when the Agent/Causer (i.e. SUBJ) or Recipient-Patient/Causee (i.e. OBJ) is overtly encoded with its appropriate nominal marking: SUBJ is marked as TOP/NOM and OBJ is marked as DAT. At least one argument needs to be explicitly encoded with BENE construction in order to count as positive evidence for S-procedure.

When the learner marks NP argument(s) wrongly (for example, if Agent is marked as NOM in Passive), it violates the Well-formedness condition and this represents an "ill-formed" sentence construction. Incorrect marking of the argument in Passive, Causative and Benefactive constructions indicates the inappropriate linking of the role of the argument structure and grammatical functions and shows the learner's inability to handle S-procedure. Hence, the occurrence of ill-formed structures where the NP argument is followed by a wrong morphological marking represents an instance against S-procedure.

In summary, the frequency count of Passive, Causative and Benefactive in L2 Japanese is as follows. It is counted as an instance of valid, positive evidence when:

– either Patientive SUBJ or Agentive Adjunct (or both) is overtly encoded with its appropriate nominal morphology in Passive construction
– either Agentive SUBJ or Recipient-Patientive OBJ (or both) is overtly encoded with its appropriate nominal morphology in Causative construction
– either Agent or Beneficiary (or both) is overtly encoded with its appropriate nominal morphology in Benefactive construction

On the other hand, invalid instances representing S-procedure with Passive, Causative and Benefactive are as follows:

– argument(s) is/are wrongly marked (evidence against acquisition of S-procedure) as in (39)

   (39)   *inu-wa   watasi-ni kam-are-masita*
          dog-TOP I-DAT   bite-PASS-PAST.POL
          (Lit.) 'The dog was bitten by me'
          (Intended) 'I was bitten by the dog'

– no argument is encoded in c-structure (insufficient evidence; the production of this structure involves only lexical procedure) as in (40)

   (40)   *kam-are-masita*
          bite-PASS-PAST.POL
          '(?) was bitten'

In the result table, the frequency count of positive instances is listed before a slash. Then the total occurrence of Passive/Causative/Benefactive is listed after the slash. When both of them are zero, "0" is entered in the cell. The gap between two numbers indicates the frequency count of invalid cases.

v. Topic functions

The sentences which involve TOP are hypothesised to appear at three different stages according to the following three possible functions linked to TOP: (1) SUBJ (Stage 2); (2) noncore argument phrase (such as Adjunct and Locative) (Stage 3); and (3) OBJ (Stage 4). For the distributional analysis, all the NPs marked with -wa were counted according to the grammatical function linked to the -wa marked NP in the (lexical verb) sentence. The examples (41) to (43) given below are taken from my data and they are hypothesised to belong to different stages. When more than one phrase is marked with -wa as seen in (43), each phrase is counted. So in the case of (43), frequency is counted twice: Stage 2 (NP_1-wa = SUBJ) as well as Stage 4 (NP_2-wa = OBJ).

(41)   NP-wa =SUBJ (Stage 2)

   (Lou T3)   *uh* (long pause) *kazoku.. -wa.   er suupaa-e*
                          family-TOP   supermarket-to
                 ikimasita
                 go-POL.PAST
                 'The family went to a supermarket'

(42)   NP-wa = Adjunct (Stage 3)

   (Jaz T4)   *demo er   kayoobi. er   ano to doyoobi-wa*
              but   Tuesday well and   Saturday-TOP
              er hatarakimasu
              work-POL
              'But Tuesday and Saturday, (I) work'

(43) NP_1-wa = SUBJ (Stage 2) & NP_2-wa = OBJ (Stage 4)

   (Lou T11) (long pause) *demo watasi-wa zangyoo-wa*
                        but   I-TOP   overtime-FOC
              sitakunakatta   node   totemo angry desita
              do-DES-NEG-PAST because very   angry COP.PAST
              'But because I did not want to do overtime, I was very angry'

Table 3. Jaz's two-year longitudinal study

Stages / Time	T1	T2	T3	T4	T5	T6	T7	T8
4 S-procedure/ WO Rules								
Causative	0	0	0	0	0	0	0	0
Passive	0	0	0	0	0	0	0	0
Benefactive OBJ	0	0	0	0	0	0	0	0
Topicalisation	0	0	0	0	0	0	0	2^{10}
3 Phrasal procedure Topic + SOV	0	0	0	3	0	1	1	3
2 Lexical procedure TOP$_{SUBJ}$OV	0	4	6	4	19	16	13	13
Verb last	3/3	12/12	17/17	28/28	33/33	22/22	20/20	58/58
Noun marking	+	+	+	+	+	+	+	+
1 Word / Lemma	+	+	+	+	+	+	+	+

5.2 Results

In this section, the results of two longitudinal studies, Jaz and Lou, are presented.

Jaz

The results of the two-year longitudinal study are presented in Table 3. The
first row marks the different points in time in this corpus, and the left-most
column shows the hypothesised syntactic structures based on PT, which are
hierarchically arranged. Inside the table, the number of occurrences or the
existence/non-existence of a given structure (indicated by '+' or '−') is entered
according to the methods of data analysis described above.

At T1, Jaz's speech contained Japanese L2 words and formulaic expressions,
and therefore Stage 1 (lemma access) was achieved. In the same interview, Jaz
produced nominal marking of semantic roles (Stage 2) more than once (as
in example (44)), although there were some cases where Jaz omitted noun
marking (as in the example (45) where 'ø' indicates omission of morphological
marking on noun). So Jaz also had acquired this grammatical feature at T1.

(44)   (Jaz T1, 16) *and er burakkuboodo erm -ga arimasu*
                    blackboard   -NOM exist-POL
                    'There is a blackboard'

(45) (Jaz T1)   *erm. isu-ø*   *um arimasu*
                  chair-ø exist-POL
                  'There is a chair'

In the same interview, Jaz produced three canonical word order sentences with the lexical verb in the sentence final position as shown in (44) and (45). However, these three cases are realised with the same lexical item, i.e. *arimasu* (exist), and the sentence patterns of these cases were exactly the same (i.e. Noun-(*ga*) *arimasu* (Noun-(NOM) exist-POL) 'There is ∼'), so this sentence pattern might have been produced as a formula.

Jaz did not attempt to produce the structure TOP$_{\text{SUBJ}}$OV where SUBJ is marked as TOP with the nominal morphology -*wa*. Therefore, there is no evidence to support Jaz's acquisition of this Stage 2 structure at T1. However, the learner does not have to produce all the hypothesised structures at one time in order to claim the acquisition of a particular stage/procedural skill. We can say that Stage 2 was already acquired by Jaz at T1 because it is evident that at least one syntactic structure predicted at Stage 2 (i.e. Noun marking) had already emerged in his speech production.

At T2, Jaz started to produce the TOP$_{\text{SUBJ}}$OV structure: he produced this structure four times in different syntactic environments. He continued to produce "Noun marking" and "Verb-last" structures, which are both hypothesised to be located at Stage 2. At T2, he did not produce syntactic structures belonging to any higher stages then Stage 2. Jaz expanded the variety of syntactic structures using the same procedural skill (category procedure in this case) while he stayed at the same stage.

The Stage 3 structure 'TOP+SOV' started to appear in Jaz's speech production from T4 onwards. He produced a sentence in which ADJUNCT was marked as TOP as in the example (46). So Jaz's emergence point of Stage 3 is T4. He constantly produced this Stage 3 structure (except in T5) throughout his longitudinal study.

(46) (Jaz T5 104)... *anata-no   er e-wa   inu-ga*
                      your-GEN picture-TOP dog-NOM
                      ton-de imasu ka?
                      fly-COMP ASP-POL.PRES Q
                      'In your picture, is the dog flying?'

Jaz did not seem to develop S-procedure (i.e. Stage 4) until the end of the two-year longitudinal study as he did not produce any syntactic structures from Stage 4. At T12, there were two cases where OBJ nouns were marked by TOP particles, but closer examination revealed that both cases were errors in marking given nouns (i.e. random choice of the particle) rather than attempts at OBJ topicalisation (see Note 10). These instances are considered to be evidence against the acquisition of the S-procedure.

Lou

The results of this three-year longitudinal study are presented below in Table 4, which is laid out in a manner similar to Table 3.

At T1, Lou had already attained Stage 2: she produced single Japanese L2 words and constructed a V-final sentence 10 times. Also, the nouns she produced had morphological markings in a syntactic environment. In this interview, the structure TOP$_{SUBJ}$OV was not observed. This structure emerged from T2 and was consistently produced throughout the longitudinal study.

The Stage 3 structure 'TOP+ SOV' started to appear in Lou's speech production from T3 onwards. In this interview Lou produced this structure twice. As these instances contain a variety of TOP nouns and lexical verbs, it is sufficient to claim that Stage 3 had emerged at T3. However, SUBJ was not overtly expressed with both instances. Lou started producing 'TOP+ SOV' with overt SUBJ marked distinctively from TOP from T4. The sentence (47) below is an example of 'TOP+S(O)V' taken from T6. In this example, Lou first marked the subject noun *isu* (chair) with *-wa* (TOP) but she then self-corrected to *-ga* (NOM). It is evident from this fact that Lou knows that SUBJ can be a topic or non-topic in a sentence and that she is aware of the distinction between TOP and SUBJ in terms of the nominal marking.

(47) (Lou T6)   ... *kuma-no -no kazoku-no uti-wa   mittu*
                  bear-GEN   family-GEN   house-TOP three
                  isu-wa no(English) -ga miemasu
                  chair-TOP -NOM   is seen-POL
                  'In the house of the bear family, three chairs are seen'

Now we look at the acquisition of S-procedure by Lou. Remember that when two numbers are seen before and after slashes (i.e. '/'), the first number signifies the frequency count of positive evidence while the number after the slash indicates the total occurrence of the given structure. The first time Lou produced Stage 4 structure was at T5 where she produced one BENE construction, but in the next two interviews, T6 and T7, she did not produce any instances of BENE or Stage 4 structures. Close examination found that BENE was introduced right before the interview T5 (see Table 5). Therefore, I suspect that BENE construction at T5 was formulaic rather than productive, and I do not conclude that

Table 4. Lou's three-year longitudinal study

Stages / Time	T1	T2	T3	T4	T5	T6	T7	T8	T9	T10	T11	T12
4 S-procedure/ WO Rules												
Causative	0	0	0	0	0	0	0	0	0	4/4	0	0
Passive	0	0	0	0	0	0	0	0	1/1	0/1[11]	2/2	0
Benefactive	0	0	0	0	1/1	0	0	1/1	1/1	1/1	0	4/5[12]
OBJ												
Topicalisation	0	0	0	0	0	0	0	0	0	1	0	2
3 Phrasal procedure												
Topic + SOV	0	0	2	7	0	2	0	4	0	2	3	1
2 Lexical procedure												
TOP$_{SUBJ}$OV	0	1	3	9	14	5	3	9	13	12	9	24
Verb last	10/10	19/19	12/12	27/27	26/26	19/19	10/10	38/38	35/35	27/27	47/47	42/42
Noun marking	+	+	+	+	+	+	+	+	+	+	+	+
1 Word / Lemma	+	+	+	+	+	+	+	+	+	+	+	+

the emergence point of Stage 4 is at T5. Lou started to produce Stage 4 structures from T8, where she produced one BENE construction, and thereafter she produced at least two instances of Stage 4 structures which positively show S-procedure, so the emergence point of Stage 4 is T8. The two sentences below are examples of PASS and CAUSE respectively produced by Lou.

>(48) (Lou T9) *densya-ni notta* *toki doroboo-ni saifu-o*
>train-on ride-PAST time robber-DAT wallet-ACC
>*tor-are-masita*
>stole-PASS-POL.PAST
>'(Lit) When (she) got on the train, (she) was stolen a wallet by the robber'
>'=When (she) got on the train, she had her wallet stolen by the robber'

>(49) (Lou 10) *sosite bosu-wa watasi-ni koohiii-o*
>then boss-TOP I-DAT coffee-ACC
>*tukur-ase-masu*
>make-CAUSE-POL
>'Then my boss makes me make coffee'

6. Discussion

In the result tables of Jaz and Lou above, the stage acquired by each learner is indicated by the dividing line. It can be seen that the acquisition of L2 Japanese syntax by both learners is implicational: Word/lemma > Lexical procedure > Phrasal procedure > S-procedure. The implicational pattern observed in the acquisition of syntactic structure in Japanese L2 is the linguistic manifestation of the acquisition of procedural skills, and the acquisition of the lower level is a prerequisite for the functioning of the higher level (Pienemann 1998). I included Lexical Mapping Theory for explaining S-procedure in PT hierarchy. Lexical Mapping Theory seems to be able to explain linearity/non-linearity of mapping a- onto f-structure. So, the Lexical Mapping Theory Principle can be used to account for the progression from 'canonical order' to 'S-procedure' in the PT hierarchy. The resolution of functional uncertainty requires S-procedure and, therefore, structures involving functional uncertainty are acquired later. My data supported this.

Finally, Table 5 (a & b) summarises the point of introduction of the relevant syntactic structures through formal instruction and their emergence point

Table 5a. Teaching objective and emergence of syntactic structures by the informants (T1–T6)

Syntactic structures		T1	T2	T3	T4	T5	T6
SOV	Null SUBJ	x	L	J			
	V-last	x	L	J			
	N marking	x	L	J			
TOPIC	TOP=SUBJ	x		JL			
	TOP=ADJ		x		JL		
	TOP=OBJ						
Morpho-lexical operation	BENE					x	L
	PASS						
	CAUS						

x = point of time when the structure was introduced as a formal objective
* = point of time when the structure was first included in the textbook but was not taught as a formal objective

Table 5b. Teaching objective and emergence of syntactic structures by the informants (T7–T12)

Syntactic structures		T7	T8	T9	T10	T11	T12
SOV	Null SUBJ						
	V-last						
	N marking						
TOPIC	TOP=SUBJ						
	TOP=ADJ						
	TOP=OBJ	*			L		
Morpho-lexical operation	BENE						
	PASS		x	L			
	CAUS				x	L	

x = point of time when the structure was introduced as a formal objective
* = point of time when the structure was first included in the textbook but was not taught as a formal objective

by the two informants. In the table, the first column lists the syntactic structures hypothesised in my JSL developmental stages. The first row marks the time of interview. The sign "x" indicates the point of introduction of the structure as *a teaching objective* whereas "*" indicates that the structure was not introduced formally as a teaching objective but appeared as part of the text (such as a part of a conversational skit). The students may have been exposed to these structures because they had frequent contact with native speakers of

Japanese studying at the same university. The initials 'J' and 'L' in the table stand for 'Jaz' and 'Lou' respectively and the emergence point of the structure for each learner is marked with their initial. Note that Lou's longitudinal study continued until T12 while Jaz's longitudinal study concluded at T8.

All the structures except OBJ topicalisation emerged only after formal instruction. In the case of OBJ topicalisation, the form was not introduced formally in the class but appears as part of the skit between T6 and T7. Lou first produced the structure once at T10, which is one year after the point of appearance of the structure in the textbook, and then twice at T12. Jaz never produced this structure in this longitudinal study. This structure emerges later than other structures belonging to the same stage, i.e. BENE and PASS; in fact the latter emerged in Lou's data only a couple of weeks after it was taught explicitly. Also, the frequency of production for OBJ topicalisation with the same learner was very low compared to the other two structures. Therefore, the role of formal instruction seems to be important. It also seems that the results support Pienemann's (1984, 1988) Teachability Hypothesis that states that no developmental stage can be skipped by the learner and 'instruction can only promote language acquisition if the interlanguage is close to the point when the structure to be taught is acquired in the natural setting' (Pienemann 1988: 60).

7.   Conclusion

The issue of the application of PT to the developmental stages of Japanese L2 syntax was discussed in this chapter. Various test structures in Japanese L2 were hypothesised for PT stages and the hypothesis was tested empirically. The corpus data from two longitudinal studies showed the implicational pattern and thus the hypothesised stages in Japanese L2 were supported. The study is relevant to current developments in Processability Theory. The original version PT (Pienemann 1998) does not account for the learning of linguistic devices for attention-direction such as Topic and Focus and their influence on linearisation. In this chapter, I included the acquisition of the TOP(ic) function at different stages using the LFG formalism. In second language acquisition learners will initially not differentiate between SUBJ and other discourse functions (e.g. TOP). The addition of an adjunct to a canonical string will trigger a differentiation of TOP and SUBJ which first extends to non arguments and successively to core arguments, thus causing further structural consequences. Discourse functions such as TOP and FOC(us) are currently being included in the PT hierarchy within the "Topic Hypothesis" (Pienemann et al. Chapter

7, this volume). This study supports the inclusion of grammaticised discourse functions in the PT developmental stages.

Also, I included non-canonical order sentences, such as passive and causative, in the Japanese L2 hierarchy. These constructions were also not explicitly included in the original PT hierarchy. Now general mapping principles are more explicitly incorporated into PT through the "Lexical Mapping Hypothesis" (Pienemann et al. Chapter 7 in this volume). This was made possible by recent development in LFG such as the Lexical Mapping Theory (Bresnan & Kanerva 1989; Bresnan 2001; Dalrymple 2001) which formally describes the mapping mechanism between a(rgument)-structure and f(unctional)-structure. The empirical data presented in this study also supports this new hypothesis.

In conclusion, this study has widened the scope of the application of PT to Japanese L2 syntax, which was previously limited to verbal morphology. More importantly, the findings from the empirical study add another piece of evidence for the typological validity of PT's claim that the capacity of speech processing constraints L2 development. However, my study does exhibit some limitations. My study does not offer abundant production data of structures involving TOP. Therefore, experimental studies specially targeted to elicit TOP assignment structures should be conducted to confirm and refine the hypothesis for Japanese and cross-linguistically.

Notes

* I wish to express my special gratitude to Manfred Pienemann for his generous advice in various points of writing this chapter. I also wish to thank Bruno Di Biase for his comments and advice, Stuart Campbell for his proofreading and comments and various people for editing. I also would like to express my sincere appreciation to the anonymous reviewers who gave me invaluable advices to improve my chapter, especially LFG representations. My further gratitude goes to the participants of the symposium at UWS in December 2003, my two informants and students of SLA and Japanese at UWS. Remaining erros are solely my responsibility.

1. Research on acquisitional hierarchy for Turkish morphosyntax is on its way (Özdemir 2004). Turkish also exhibits 'head-last' and SOV characteristics.

2. Otsu (2000) shows that "the use of scrambled sentences is pragmatically accepted only when the scrambled element (e.g. *Piano* in (2) n.d.a.) has already been established as a discourse topic".

3. As one of the reviewers pointed out, when more than one NP is marked with -*wa*, the first NP is assumed to be the TOPic while the non-initial -*wa* marked NP is commonly assumed to be the FOCus in Japanese (also see Kuno 1973: 30f.).

4. I would like to thank one of the reviewers for suggesting me the phrase structure rule (R2) and the annotation in (Figure 1).

5. The notion of 'suppression' which explains Agent in Passive construction was first proposed by Grimshaw (1990).

6. Bresnan (1982) and other earlier work in LFG (e.g. Sells 1985) had a different view of passivisation where changing of grammatical function is triggered by "lexical rules" which are stated in the form of the verb (i.e. "lexical rule for passive is: SUBJ $\rightarrow$ $\varnothing$/OBL$_\theta$, OBJ$\rightarrow$SUBJ"). In this view, the agent of the event in the passive sentence (i.e. "by-phrase in English) is treated as OBL$_\theta$. However, LMT treats it as Adjunct. Even within LMT, some scholars such as Alsina (1996) treat syntactically expressed agents in the Passive as Oblique. The different interpretation of the 'by-phrase' as either Adjunct or Oblique, however, does not cause any conflicting consequences (Bresnan, personal correspondence, 8 July 2004).

7. The annotation of the lexical entry for -*wa* is suggested by one of the reviewers.

8. Informants' names appearing in this chapter are fictitious.

9. The Kunrei-style romanisation system is used here, except for the long vowel sound which I have chosen to transcribe as double vowels (i.e. *aa, ee, ii, oo, uu*) in place of the usual diacritic above the vowel.

10. At T10 Jaz produced OBJ$_{TOP}$ twice (once with and once without SUBJ). In both cases the use of the TOP marker on the object noun was pragmatically incorrect. In one case, Jaz was asked *donna ie o kaitaidesu ka*? (what kind of house do you want to buy?) and he answered *watasi no uti wa kaitaidesu* (I would like to buy my house) where the noun presenting the answer for the question (i.e. new information) was marked with TOP. In Japanese discourse, it is wrong to mark new information with TOP: it has to be marked with -*ga* (NOM). So the choice of -*wa* may have been random rather than topicalisation.

11. This passive sentence has the wrong marking of argument: Agent is marked as TOP and Patient is marked as Adjunct (DAT). (*demo inu-wa (long pause) watasi-ni (long pause) kami-rare-masita?* The literal translation is "but the dog was bitten by me" while the intended meaning is "but I was bitten by the dog")

12. In one case of BENE sentence, there is no argument in the clause. Therefore, this is an instance of an invalid case.

References

Alsina, A. (1996). *The Role of Argument Structure in Grammar*. Stanford, CA: CSLI.

Baker, M. (1983). Objects, themes and lexical rules in Italian. In L. Levin, M. Rappaport, & A. Zaenan (Eds.), *Papers in Lexical-Functional Grammar*. Bloomington: Indiana University Linguistics Club.

Bever, T. G. (1970). The cognitive basis for linguistic structures. In J. Hayes (Ed.), *Cognition and the Development of Language*. New York, NY: Wiley.

Bresnan, J. (Ed.). (1982). *The Mental Representation of Grammatical Relations*. Cambridge, MA: The MIT Press.

Bresnan, J. (2001). *Lexical-Functional Syntax*. Oxford: Blackwell.

Bresnan, J. (1994). Locative inversion and the architecture of Universal Grammar. *Language, 70*(1), 72–131.

Bresnan, J. & Kanerva, J. M. (1989). Locative inversion in Chichewa: A case study of factorization in grammar. *Linguistic Inquiry, 20*(1), 1–50.

Bresnan, J. & Mchombo, S. (1995). The lexical integrity principle: Evidence from Bantu. *Natural Language and Linguistic Theory*, (13), 181–254.

Bresnan, J. & Moshi, L. (1990). Object asymmetries in comparative Bantu syntax. *Linguistic Inquiry, 21*(2), 147–186.

Clahsen, H. (1984). The acquisition of German word order: A test case for cognitive approaches to L2 development. In R. Anderson (Ed.), *Second Language*. Rowley, MA: Newbury House.

Dalrymple, M. (2001). *Syntax and Semantics. Lexical functional grammar*. Vol. 34. San Diego, CA: Academic Press.

DeCamp, D. (1973). Implicational scales and sociolinguistic linearity. *Linguistics, 73*, 30–43.

Di Biase, B. (2002). Focusing strategies in second language development: A classroom-based study of Italian in primary school. In B. Di Biase (Ed.), *Developing a Second language. Acquisition, processing and pedagogy of Arabic, Chinese, English, Italian, Japanese, Swedish* (pp. 95–120). Melbourne: Language Australia.

Di Biase, B. & Kawaguchi, S. (2002). Exploring the typological plausibility of processability theory: Language development in Italian L2 and Japanese L2. *Second Language Research, 18*(3), 274–302.

Doi, Y. & Yoshioka, K. (1987). Which grammatical structure should be taught when? In K. Hijirida & G. Mathias (Eds.), *Proceedings of the 9th HATJ-UH conference on Japanese Linguistics and Language Teaching*.

Doi, Y. & Yoshioka, K. (1990). Jyoshi no shuutoku ni okeru gengo unyoojoo no seiyaku – Pienemann-Johnston moderu no nihongo shuutoku kenkyuu e no ooyoo. (Constraints on the acquisition of (Japanese) particles – application of the Pienemann-Johnston model to acquisition of Japanese). *Proceedings of 1st conference on SLA and Teaching, 1*, 23–33.

Dulay, H. & Burt, M. (1973). Should we teach children syntax? *Language Learning, 23*, 245–258.

Dulay, H. & Burt, M. (1974). Natural sequences in child second language acquisition. *Language Learning, 24*, 37–53.

Dulay, H., Burt, M., & Krashen, S. (1982). *Language Two*. Oxford: Oxford University Press.

Givón, T. (1984). *Syntax: A functional-typological introduction*. Amsterdam: John Benjamins.

Grimshaw, J. (1990). *Argument Structure*. Cambridge, MA: The MIT Press.

Hakuta, K. (1982). Interaction between particles and word order in the comprehension and production of simple sentences in Japanese children. *Developmental Psychology, 18*(1), 62–76.

Hata, H. (1980). Bun to wa nani ka – shugo no shooryaku to sono hataraki. *Nihongo Kyooiku, 41*, 198–208.

Hinds, J. (1982). *Ellipsis in Japanese.* Alberta: Linguistic Research Inc.

Huter, K. I. (1997). Onnanohito wa duressu desu. That's why the lady is a dress: Developmental stages in Japanese second language acquisition. *Australian Studies in Language Acquisition, 6*, 1–39.

Ishikawa, A. (1985). Complex Predicates and Lexical Operations in Japanese. PhD Dissertation. Standford, CA: Stanford University.

Itani-Adams, Y. (2003). From word to phrase in Japanese -English bilingual first language acquisition. Paper presented at The *MARCS seminar*, 15 September 2003, University of Western Sydney.

Iwasaki, J. (2003). The acquisition of verbal morpho-syntax in JSL by a child learner. Paper presented at *13th Biennial Conference of the JSAA*, 2–4 July 2003, Brisbane.

Kaplan, R. & Bresnan, J. (1982). Lexical-functional grammar: A formal system for grammatical representation. In J. Bresnan (Ed.), *The Mental Representation of Grammatical Relations* (pp. 173–281). Cambridge, MA: The MIT Press.

Kawaguchi, S. (2000). Acquisition of Japanese verbal morphology: Applying processability theory to Japanese. *Studia Linguistica, 54*(2), 238–248.

Kempen, G. & Hoenkamp, E. (1987). An incremental procedural grammar for sentence formulation. *Cognitive Science, 11*, 201–259.

Kiparsky, P. (1987). Morphology and grammatical relations. Ms., Stanford University.

Kuno, S. (1973). *The Structure of the Japanese Language.* Cambridge, MA: MIT Press.

Kuroda, S. (1965). Generative Grammatical Studies in the Japanese Language. PhD Dissertation, MIT.

Labov, E. (1972). *Language in the Inner City.* Philadelphia, PA: University of Pennsylvania Press.

Lambrecht, K. (1994). *Information Structure and Sentence Form: Topic, focus, and the mental representation of discourse referents.* Cambridge: CPU.

Lee, Hanjung. (2001). Markedness and word order freezing. In P. Sells (Ed.), *Formal and Empirical Issues in Optimality Theoretical Syntax* (pp. 63–127). Stanford, CA: CSLI.

Levelt, W. J. M. (1989). *Speaking. From intention to articulation.* Cambridge, MA: The MIT Press.

Li, C. & Thompson, S. (1976). Subject and topic: A new typology. In C. Li (Ed.), *Subject and Topic* (pp. 457–489). San Diego, CA: Academic Press.

Li, C. & Thompson, S. (1981). *Mandarin Chinese: A functional reference grammar.* Berkeley, CA: University of California Press.

Mansouri, F. (2002). Exploring the interface between syntax and morphology in second language development. In B. Di Biase (Ed.), *Developing a Second Language. Acquisition, processing and pedagogy of Arabic, Chinese, English, Italian, Japanese, Swedish.* Melbourne: Language Australia.

Matsumoto, Y. (1996). *Complex predicates in Japanese: A syntactic and semantic study of the notion of "word."* Stanford, CA/Tokyo: CSLI and Kurosio.

Mine, F. (2002). Processability theory and the acquisition of Japanese as a second language. In The Society for Research on Japanese language and Culture (Ed.), *The State of the Art in Second Language Acquisition and Instruction Research. A guidepost to Japanese language education for the new century* (pp. 28–44). Tokyo: Bonjinsha.

Nagatomo, K. (1991). Danwa ni okeru 'ga' 'wa' to sono shuutoku ni tsuite [Systematic Variation Model]. *Gengo riron to Nihongo kyooiku no soogo kasseika. Tsuda Nihongo Kyooiku Sentaa*, 10–24.

Nagatomo, K. (2002). My quest for the development of JSL acquisition research: An autobiographical research review. In The Society for Research on Japanese language and Culture (Ed.), *The State of the Art in Second Language Acquisition and Instruction Research. A guidepost to Japanese language education for the new century* (pp. 2–8). Tokyo: Bobjinsha.

Nordlinger, R. (1998). *Constructive Case: Evidence from Australian languages*. Stanford, CA: CSLI.

Otsu, Y. (2000). Scrambling, indirect passive and wanna contraction. *Behavioral and Brain Sciences, 23*, 45–46.

Özdemir, B. (2004). Language Development in Turkish-German Bilingual Children and the Implications for English as a Third Language. MA thesis, University of Paderborn.

Pienemann, M. (1984). Psychological constraints on the teachability of languages. *Studies in Second Language Acquisition, 6*(2), 186–214.

Pienemann, M. (1988). Is language teachable? Psycholinguistic experiments and hypotheses. *Applied Linguistics, 10*(1), 52–79.

Pienemann, M. (1998). *Language Processing and Second Language Development: Processability theory*. Amsterdam: John Benjamins.

Pienemann, M. & Johnston, M. (1987). Factors influencing the development of language proficiency. In D. Nunan (Ed.), *Applying Second Language Acquisition Research* (pp. 45–141). Adelaide: National Curriculum Resource Centre, Adult Migrant Education Program Australia.

Pienemann, M., Johnston, M., & Brindley, G. (1988). Constructing an acquisition-based procedure for second language assessment. *Studies in Second Language Acquisition, 10*, 217–224.

Pinker, S. (1984). *Language Learnability and language development*. Cambridge, MA: Harvard University Press.

Preston, J. (2004). Developing a profiling procedure for Japanese second language acquisition. Paper presented at *4th International Symposium on Processability, Second Language Acquisition and Bilingualism*, 13–16 April 2004, at the University of Sassari, Italy.

Sasaki, Y. (1998). Processing and learning of Japanese double-object active and causative sentences: An error-feedback paradigm. *Journal of Psycholinguistics Research, 27*(4), 453–479.

Sells, P. (1985). *Lectures on Contemporary Syntactic Theories*. Stanford, CA: CSLI.

Sells, P. (1995). Korean and Japanese morphology from a lexical perspective. *Linguistic Inquiry, 26*, 277–325.

Sells, P. (1999a). Constituent Ordering as Alignment. In S. Kuno et al. (Eds.), *Harvard Studies in Korean Linguistics* VIII (pp. 546–560). Seoul: Hanshin. Online: http://www-csli.stanford.edu/~sells.

Sells, P. (1999b). Japanese postposing involves no movement. Paper presented at *AILA* 1999. Online, Stanford University: http://www-csli.stanford.edu/~sells/.

Sells, P. (Ed.). (2001). *Formal and Empirical Issues in Optimality Theoretic Syntax*. Stanford, CA: CSLI.

Shibatani, M. (1987). Japanese. In B. Comrie (Ed.), *The Major Language of East and South-East Asia* (pp. 127–152). London: Routledge.

Shibatani, M. (1990). *The Languages of Japan*. Cambridge: Cambridge University Press.

Simpson, J. (1983). Aspect of Warlpiri Morphology and Syntax. PhD Dissertation, MIT.

Slobin, D. I. (1982). Universal and particular in the acquisition of language. In E. Wanner & L. R. Glaitman (Eds.), *Language Acquisition: State of the art* (pp. 128–170). Cambridge: Cambridge University Press.

Taraldsen, T. (1978). *On the NIC. Vacuous application and the that-trace filter*. Bloomington, IN: Indiana University Linguistic Club.

Thompson, S. (1978). Modern English from a typological point of view: Some implications of the function of word order. *Linguistische Berichte, 54*, 19–35.

Tsujimura, N. (1996). *An Introduction to Japanese Linguistics*. Cambridge, MA: Blackwell.

Van Valin Jr., R. D. (2001). *An Introduction to Syntax*. Cambridge: Cambridge University Press.

Yoshioka, K. (1999). Research in Japanese as a second language: some current issues. *Nihongo Kyoiku [Journal of Japanese Language Teaching] 100*, 19–32.

Zhang, Y. (2001). Second Language Acquisition of Chinese Grammatical Morphemes: A processability perspective. PhD Dissertation, The Australian National University.

Zhang, Y. (2002). A processing approach to the L2 acquisition of Chinese grammatical morpheme. In B. Di Biase (Ed.), *Developing a Second Language. Acquisition, processing and pedagogy of Arabic, Chinese, English, Italian, Japanese, Swedish*. Melbourne: Language Australia.

Zaenen, A., Maling, J., & Thráinsson, H. (1985). Case and grammatical functions: The Icelandic passive. *Natural Language and Linguistic Theory, 3*, 483.

Subject index

In the series *Studies in Bilingualism* (SiBil) the following titles have been published thus far or are scheduled for publication:

30 PIENEMANN, Manfred (ed.): Cross-Linguistic Aspects of Processability Theory. 2005. xiii, 303 pp.

29 AYOUN, Dalila and M. Rafael SALABERRY (eds.): Tense and Aspect in Romance Languages. Theoretical and applied perspectives. 2005. x, 318 pp.

28 SCHMID, Monika S., Barbara KÖPKE, Merel KEIJZER and Lina WEILEMAR (eds.): First Language Attrition. Interdisciplinary perspectives on methodological issues. 2004. x, 378 pp.

27 CALLAHAN, Laura: Spanish/English Codeswitching in a Written Corpus. 2004. viii, 183 pp.

26 DIMROTH, Christine and Marianne STARREN (eds.): Information Structure and the Dynamics of Language Acquisition. 2003. vi, 361 pp.

25 PILLER, Ingrid: Bilingual Couples Talk. The discursive construction of hybridity. 2002. xii, 315 pp.

24 SCHMID, Monika S.: First Language Attrition, Use and Maintenance. The case of German Jews in anglophone countries. 2002. xiv, 259 pp. (incl. CD-rom).

23 VERHOEVEN, Ludo and Sven STRÖMQVIST (eds.): Narrative Development in a Multilingual Context. 2001. viii, 431 pp.

22 SALABERRY, M. Rafael: The Development of Past Tense Morphology in L2 Spanish. 2001. xii, 211 pp.

21 DÖPKE, Susanne (ed.): Cross-Linguistic Structures in Simultaneous Bilingualism. 2001. x, 258 pp.

20 POULISSE, Nanda: Slips of the Tongue. Speech errors in first and second language production. 1999. xvi, 257 pp.

19 AMARA, Muhammad Hasan: Politics and Sociolinguistic Reflexes. Palestinian border villages. 1999. xx, 261 pp.

18 PARADIS, Michel: A Neurolinguistic Theory of Bilingualism. 2004. viii, 299 pp.

17 ELLIS, Rod: Learning a Second Language through Interaction. 1999. x, 285 pp.

16 HUEBNER, Thom and Kathryn A. DAVIS (eds.): Sociopolitical Perspectives on Language Policy and Planning in the USA. With the assistance of Joseph Lo Bianco. 1999. xvi, 365 pp.

15 PIENEMANN, Manfred: Language Processing and Second Language Development. Processability theory. 1998. xviii, 367 pp.

14 YOUNG, Richard and Agnes Weiyun HE (eds.): Talking and Testing. Discourse approaches to the assessment of oral proficiency. 1998. x, 395 pp.

13 HOLLOWAY, Charles E.: Dialect Death. The case of Brule Spanish. 1997. x, 220 pp.

12 HALMARI, Helena: Government and Codeswitching. Explaining American Finnish. 1997. xvi, 276 pp.

11 BECKER, Angelika and Mary CARROLL: The Acquisition of Spatial Relations in a Second Language. In co-operation with Jorge Giacobbe, Clive Perdue & Rémi Porquier. 1997. xii, 212 pp.

10 BAYLEY, Robert and Dennis R. PRESTON (eds.): Second Language Acquisition and Linguistic Variation. 1996. xix, 317 pp.

9   FREED, Barbara F. (ed.): Second Language Acquisition in a Study Abroad Context. 1995. xiv, 345 pp.

8   DAVIS, Kathryn A.: Language Planning in Multilingual Contexts. Policies, communities, and schools in Luxembourg. 1994. xix, 220 pp.

7   DIETRICH, Rainer, Wolfgang KLEIN and Colette NOYAU: The Acquisition of Temporality in a Second Language. In cooperation with Josée Coenen, Beatriz Dorriots, Korrie van Helvert, Henriette Hendriks, Et-Tayeb Houdaïfa, Clive Perdue, Sören Sjöström, Marie-Thérèse Vasseur and Kaarlo Voionmaa. 1995. xii, 288 pp.

6   SCHREUDER, Robert and Bert WELTENS (eds.): The Bilingual Lexicon. 1993. viii, 307 pp.

5   KLEIN, Wolfgang and Clive PERDUE: Utterance Structure. Developing grammars again. In cooperation with Mary Carroll, Josée Coenen, José Deulofeu, Thom Huebner and Anne Trévise. 1992. xvi, 354 pp.

4   PAULSTON, Christina Bratt: Linguistic Minorities in Multilingual Settings. Implications for language policies. 1994. xi, 136 pp.

3   DÖPKE, Susanne: One Parent – One Language. An interactional approach. 1992. xviii, 213 pp.

2   BOT, Kees de, Ralph B. GINSBERG and Claire KRAMSCH (eds.): Foreign Language Research in Cross-Cultural Perspective. 1991. xii, 275 pp.

1   FASE, Willem, Koen JASPAERT and Sjaak KROON (eds.): Maintenance and Loss of Minority Languages. 1992. xii, 403 pp.